AMERICAN HISTORY FIRSTHAND

Working with Primary Sources

Peter J. Frederick
Wabash College

Julie Roy Jeffrey
Goucher College

With research assistance from:

Alan Berolzheimer, Vermont Historical Society (PhD, University of Virginia)
Susanne DeBerry Cole, Maryland Historical Society (PhD, Miami University, Ohio)
Martha King, The Papers of James Madison, University of Virginia (PhD, College of William and Mary)
Leslie Lindenauer, Connecticut Women's Hall of Fame at Hartford College for Women, University of Hartford (PhD, New York University)
Charles Pennacchio, Delaware Valley College (PhD, University of Colorado)
Sarah Vosmeier, Hanover College (PhD, Indiana University, Bloomington)
Shane Blackman (ABD, Indiana University, Bloomington)
Michael Johnston Grant (PhD, University of Kansas)
Geoffrey Hunt, Community College of Aurora (Colorado) (PhD, University of Colorado-Boulder)

New York San Francisco Boston
London Toronto Sydney Tokyo Singapore Madrid
Mexico City Munich Paris Cape Town Hong Kong Montreal

"History is a means of access to ourselves."

–Lynn White Jr.

Executive Editor: Michael Boezi
Executive Marketing Manager: Sue Westmoreland
Supplements Editor: Brian Belardi
Media Supplements Editor: Melissa Edwards
Production Manager: Stacey Kulig
Project Coordination, Text Design, and Electronic Page Makeup: Nesbitt Graphics, Inc.
Cover Design Manager: Wendy Ann Fredericks
Cover Designer: Kay Petronio
Photo Researcher: Jody Potter
Senior Manufacturing Buyer: Alfred C. Dorsey

Volume One Cover Photos: The Granger Collection; Rhode Island Historical Society; Library of Congress; American Antiquarian Society, Worchester, Massachusetts; and iStockphoto

Volume Two Cover Photos: Library of Congress; Samuel Milton Jones Papers, Toledo-Lucas County Public Library; and iStockphoto

Please visit us at www.ablongman.com

ISBN 13: 978-0-205-55992-3 (Volume One)
ISBN 10: 0-205-55992-1 (Volume One)

ISBN 13: 978-0-205-55993-0 (Volume Two)
ISBN 10: 0-205-55993-x (Volume Two)

14 2023

Contents

Volume One

Volume Two

Introduction and Overview: A Guide to the Sources for Both Students and Instructors

Why Study History? Historians have suggested many reasons. These include: (1) studying the past in order to better understand the present; (2) preserving the past in order to remember the record of the human struggle for freedom and dignity; and (3) self-knowledge: understanding who we are by learning about those like—and unlike—us from the past. In each of these ways historical study helps us to acquire the skills to gain "access to ourselves" and to our own time. The student of history is always exploring the connections between past and present and between distant historical actors and oneself. The key elements in these interactions are the **primary sources** that provide clues, or **windows into the past.** In analyzing these original sources, you are actually **"doing history firsthand,"** the basic work of all students of history.

For example: Imagine that some future historian, say, 200 years from now, is writing an article about the social history of college students early in the 21st century. He or she finds a dozen or more items from a dormitory room or an off-campus apartment. In the room are some letters from "Mom," several photographs of a happy young couple, a diary or journal entry filled with intimate thoughts and feelings, a copy of the student newspaper with articles on a proposed tuition raise to fund the new athletic building and an environmental group's opposition to the new facility because it would cut into the arboretum, empty Coke and beer cans, a parking ticket, a Derek Jeter poster, a Mariah Carey CD, an iPod, a T-shirt from a U2 concert, jogging shoes, a campus map with notations and numbers on it, and a history paper on Ben Franklin. In the off-campus apartment of an older student, our historian finds similar items but also a paycheck stub from Wendy's, a Spanish-English dictionary, a copy of the U.S. Constitution, a second grader's report card, a Catholic church bulletin, a grocery list, a framed photograph of smiling grandparents looking proud, and a painting of a Mexican village.

What questions would our historian ask of each of those documents? Are there any themes represented by these items? What further steps should he or she take in pursuing the topic? The historian would want to find items from several dormitory rooms and university apartments, in different parts of the country, and from different kinds of institutions, in order to base conclusions about the lives of college students on a wider sample than one or two rooms. Then, and only then, he or she might see some **patterns,** or **recurring themes,** and from them **develop an interpretive point of view** about university students in the early years of the 21st century. Another historian, looking at the same sources, and others, might come up with different themes and an alternative interpretation. That is how history is written. It is impossible to recover the full history of early 21st century students, yet through the use of primary sources historians peer through windows into the past and begin to understand how people lived and what they felt and thought.

American History Through Primary Sources

Primary sources are created in the time period under study. They are the basic records and artifacts, the building blocks with which historians and history students recover and reconstruct the past. Primary sources are found everywhere, including your grandmother's attic, your uncle's basement, and your parents' photograph albums. But mostly they are collected in libraries, local historical societies, and of course, the National Archives. *American History Firsthand* is an archival-like collection of primary sources organized around topics, questions, and problems found in the typical American history textbook (compare the table of contents here to your textbook's). We have divided the topics into "Archives," or collections of sources. As you work through them, imagine yourself in the archives of an historical society or large library (or grandpa's attic) discovering a treasure of old, original documents.

Most primary sources are firsthand, immediate accounts, written (or told, sung, photographed, painted, or made) by eyewitnesses to the events at the time they happened, while others may be created later. Primary sources fall into four categories: (1) oral traditions and stories; (2) written and printed documents; (3) visual sources; and (4) physical objects, or artifacts. The written and printed sources can be subdivided into private, perhaps even handwritten, items (such as a letter, diary, or grocery list), and public printed documents (a newspaper article, parking ticket, church bulletin, or the U.S. Constitution). The visual materials (photographs, maps, posters, and paintings) and physical objects (Coke and beer cans, jogging shoes, T-shirt, iPod, and CD) are all windows into the past, in this case into the lives of college students in the early 21st century.

Oral Traditions and Stories

Oral stories (such as a people's origin tales, legends and folktales, family stories) are part of our everyday life, and are an important window into the past. We listen to such stories with respect and even reverence, and we pass them on as accurately as we can. The oral traditions that historians use often are preserved in written form, perhaps changed from the original as in the "telephone game" many of us have played. It is important to remember the long, often sacred history of a story being passed on through the ages, for such stories tell us who we are as families, towns, tribal or religious communities, colleges and other institutions, and as nations.

Written and Printed Documents

When studying oral stories, and **written or printed primary sources,** read carefully, underlining or circling what seem to be key words, phrases, and sentences, even if you are not yet certain what they mean or how they come together. Consider what kind of source it is, who the author is, and the audience and purpose. If it is not clear who the author is, or when and where the source was written, or for what purpose, look for internal clues in the document by which you can infer author, date, place, and purpose. Consider whether the source was created immediate to the event, or later. It helps to work with other students. If the document is short, read it out loud and listen—as a group—to what is going on and what the key points and basic message seem to be. Explore different interpretations and the evidence the source provides for each interpretation, for this is exactly what historians do. Thus, you are **doing history firsthand!**

As you work with the document, pay attention to emotional tone as well as to content and ideas, for the underlying feelings and attitudes might lead you more clearly to the intended audience and purpose. Also examine stated (and assumed) social norms and beliefs, for these two shape how people write, what they write about (or leave out), and how they think about themselves and their world. Imagine some future historian looking at the written and printed sources in the dorm room and apartment. What would he or she learn about the lives of college students in say, 2008?

Examples of oral, written, and printed primary sources in this collection include: Indian origin stories and speeches; personal narratives and oral histories; public and private letters, journals and diaries; church and court records; Congressional acts, laws and speeches, presidential addresses, treaties, and other government documents; work contracts and business reports; petitions and protest documents; newspapers and popular magazines; and poems, songs, and sheet music.

Visual Sources

With **visual sources** (photographs, paintings, etc.) begin by asking two questions: what do you see? And what does it mean? (why is it significant?) Examine visuals just like you read a book: Start at the upper left corner and run your eye back and forth across the paper from left to right, noting each detail. Describe each image in each part of the visual before you begin to analyze it. What appear to be small details may turn out to have an important message that shapes the larger meaning of the picture. Imagine why earlier Americans would have selected a photograph or painting for their house or scrapbook. What purposes do they have? Would different people prefer different kinds of visuals? What visuals are on the walls and tables of your living quarters?

Both technology and aesthetic style influence the appearance of a visual. Early photographs look stiff and staged because subjects had to pose for several minutes until technical improvements reduced photographic exposure time. Therefore, the fact of "staging" a photo should raise questions. As in the present, photographs reflect the intent of a photographer to capture a certain image for some purpose, just as an author decides to address a particular subject in a document for a purpose. Again, interpreting visuals in small groups is helpful because you will generate many different interpretations. Ask yourselves why a photograph or painting was created, and what clues in it help your interpretation. Remember: With visual sources first describe what you see and then analyze what you think is the meaning and intent of the artist. What would some future historian infer from the photographs and visuals in your college dorm room or apartment?

Examples of visual primary sources in this collection include: maps, paintings, engravings, political cartoons, propaganda and film posters, photographs, advertisements, and movie and TV scripts.

Physical Objects

When working with **material culture (artifacts),** you will ask similar questions as with visuals and printed materials. Although here you only have visual copies of an object, imagine touching it: What does it feel like? What is the texture (hard, soft, hot, cold, etc.)? What elements is the object made of (wood, cloth, metal, a mixture, etc.)? What does it look like (plain, decorated, etc.)? Who do you think made it? What is the object's use? Would it be used primarily by men or by women? Why do you think so? Is it for commercial or private use? Is it an object widely available to ordinary people, or only to those with significant resources?

Material culture artifacts, like paintings and printed items, reflect the culture of how a people lived and thought. Sometimes material culture can reveal aspects of life that people do not bother to write about. Think now about the Coke and beer cans, T-shirt, jogging shoes, iPod, dictionary, and other objects in your rooms. What might an historian in the future learn about contemporary student life from such material objects?

Examples of material culture in this collection include: buildings, clothing, family artifacts and household implements, sheet music, and political buttons.

Pedagogical Suggestions (for Students and Instructors)

As the opening imaginary dorm room and apartment scenario suggests, we believe that most students will be more motivated to learn about history if they understand its importance and can connect to it personally. In *Cultivating Humanity* (1997), Martha Nussbaum wrote, "education must be very personal. It must be concerned with the actual situation . . . [and] current state of the [student's] knowledge and beliefs." We have therefore sought to *ask questions and provide introductions and contexts about these primary sources that invite students to connect the sources to situations, concerns, and issues in their own lives.* Although a large part of studying the past is to realize the wide gulf that exists between how we live now and how people lived in earlier centuries and places ("the past is a foreign country"), we want you to identify with as many of these sources as possible. In this way, as you look through windows into the past we hope you will not only develop the basic skills of *doing history firsthand,* but also will confront enduring questions about the human condition, and therefore yourself.

The Recurring Format

To help you use these sources, we have divided the sources in each volume into 12 "Archives," or collections, each corresponding to an important question or problem in American history. We strongly suggest that you read carefully the appropriate chapter in your textbook before working with the pertinent collection of sources. Each archive follows the same format:

- An **Overview** states the primary focus or problem, a suggested task, and a broad question or two to organize your work with the primary sources in that section.
- A **Timeline,** occasionally a **Map,** and a **Placing the Sources in Content** provide the minimal chronological, geographical, and contextual historical information you will need to work with the sources.
- **About the Sources** describes a little background on the types of sources in that archive and how to use them.
- The **List of Sources** is numbered for easy reference, citing the bibliographical source references for each source as a guide to your proper citation for class assignments and essays; the number on each document corresponds with the numbers on the source list.
- **Questions to Consider** will help you read, interpret, and use the sources. These generally begin with basic questions intended to tease out as much information as possible from each source and then, in the last two or three questions, to ask larger, more complex questions about the primary task or problem of the archive and deeper themes and values.

Core Questions for Primary Sources

Throughout *American History Firsthand* you will find questions specifically aimed at helping you interpret each source. There are, however, *four basic, core questions to ask of any source.*

1. What kind of source is it? Public? Private? Political? Cultural? Social?
2. What is the subject, or topic, of the source? What is happening? What events or situations are revealed and discussed? Is there a story? How complete is it? What is missing?
3. Who is the author, or artist, and what viewpoint is being shown? How is that perspective shaped in the source? How reliable does the source seem to be?
4. Who is the intended audience and what purpose does the source seem to have?

Although you will find it helpful to look at the specific "questions to consider" for each source in each archive, it may be helpful to remember these four basic questions. For those sources where the answers to the questions are unclear, you will need to make inferences about what sort of person you think the author or artist is, and what you think the intended audience or purpose of the document is. This is how historians actually work. If different students come up with different inferences and therefore different interpretations about the source, who wrote it and what it means, you are, again, acting like professional historians and, in fact, are *doing history firsthand.*

A Suggested Source Analysis Paper Assignment

Writing source analyses throughout the term will give students—either individually or in groups—valuable practice in doing the work of an historian. Perhaps do three or four per term? The following four sets of questions, expanding on the list of four questions above, could be asked of any historical primary source.

1. The basics: what kind of a source is it (written, private, public, oral, visual, religious, political, etc.)? Who wrote, spoke, or drew it, about where, and about when? So, first describe **who, what, where,** and **when**? This essentially summarizes most of the four core questions.
2. Go to a deeper level and ask: **What does the source mean? Why is it significant? Why important?** What does it tell us about how the people of that culture and time period thought and lived? What values, beliefs and cultural ideas and experiences are revealed?
3. **Compare and contrast the source** with a different time period, or another culture or, perhaps, compare two or three sources from different archives with one another. How are they similar? How different?
4. In a concluding paragraph, indicate **how you connect personally with or relate to the source, if at all.** In what ways are the issues in it still relevant to your and others' lives today?

Classroom Exercises Using the Sources (for Students and Teachers)

1. *Practice Interpreting Sources in Pairs or Trios in Large "Lecture" Class Settings.* First, bring the pertinent archive of documents to class each day. Second, no matter the size of a class, an instructor can enrich the lecture/discussion of the day by asking students to pair off (or get in threes) and decide on their two or three favorite sources on a topic, and why. Identify particular quotations, passages, or images that help understand the message, meaning, and importance of the sources selected in terms of the basic question or problem of the archive. Third, get a show of hands from the whole class on which sources they picked and why. A lively discussion, revealing different interpretations and tastes, will follow. It is helpful to have either a slide or overhead transparency of many of the sources (the likely favorites, or the teacher's favorites!) to focus the whole class's attention for the large group discussion.
2. *An Exercise Combining Work Outside of Class and In.* First, the class studies the Archive Overview of a particular archive in preparation for the next class. In that next class students brainstorm (listing on the board or a transparency) all the issues, images, and insights they discovered in the set of sources. Also, list problems, questions, and confusions. Next, the class divides into groups of three or four and each group decides first on a one- to two-sentence thesis statement responding to the question or problem posed in that archive. The groups then list three to four sources they would use in a paper to make an argument supporting their thesis. After the groups have finished their work, each could present their thesis statements in a general discussion. At the end, a written paper assignment would be created for the following week.
3. *Choosing the Most Significant Source on a Topic or Problem.* The class considers an archive full of sources on a particular problem or question, and either individually or in groups, decides which *one* source best captures the essence of the problem of that archive, and why. Lively discussion and multiple interpretations guaranteed.
4. *Working in Groups Out of Class.* There are two basic ways of working with the sources in groups of three to five outside of class. One is to divide the work equally among group members. Each person is responsible for interpreting two to three sources on a topic. When the group comes together, each person contributes his or her analysis of the sources, and then the whole group develops a response to the larger questions of that archive. A second approach is for each member of the group to analyze each source, and then come together to compare the work, noting differing interpretations, learning from them, and then answering the archive's problem. The first approach has the virtue of efficiency and asks less of students; the second provides a richer interpretive and cooperative experience, and generally yields better insights.

In working together, it is helpful to assign different members to different responsibilities. Thus, one person can arrange times and places to meet and lead the meeting. Another student can take notes on group discussions, differences, and conclusions, and perhaps write up the first draft of the group's work. A third student monitors the group's process, keeping track of how and how well the group worked. What sorts of things facilitated the group's work? What got in the way? How did the group handle and resolve differences? To ask and answer process questions like these is important in becoming a reflective learner. When, say, a group of three or four works together again, rotate these responsibilities so that each person gets an opportunity to learn the leadership skills of each role. To be able to work together well in small groups is an extremely important skill to learn, not only for doing work in the history class but also for life.

Summary of Goals of *American History Firsthand*

We wish you well working with these historical sources. It is our hope that, as students of American history, you will have fun as you learn how to

1. become practiced in the essential skills of *doing history firsthand*
2. analyze primary sources and evaluate their significance and reliability
3. distinguish between different kinds of primary sources
4. experience the process by which historians come up with differing interpretations
5. develop your *own* interpretations and judgments about the past
6. understand how looking through windows into the past can also help you look into yourself and your own times

Peter J. Frederick
Julie Roy Jeffrey

ARCHIVE 12

Reconstruction: Clashing Dreams and Realities, 1865–1868

Archive Overview

THE end of the Civil War initiated a conflict between revised goals for the defeated southern Confederates dedicated to the old slave South and fresh dreams of freedom for the newly freed black men and women. This archive focuses on the political and economic machinations and the powerful emotions involved in these divergent goals and dreams during the period immediately following the end of the Civil War. White and black Americans sought to reconstruct their lives in a climate of resentment and hatred. This climate inevitably followed the enormous physical and human costs of a civil war that had lasted four long years, killed over 600,000 men, thrown the nation into a constitutional crisis, disrupted the southern way of life, and resulted in the emancipation of four million slaves. The sources here focus on contested issues of land, work, and race relations.

The problem presented by these sources is in fact the major problem of Reconstruction itself: how could both groups achieve their goals, their dreams? How did the emotional mood of the years 1865–1868 manifest itself? What attitudes and resources bolstered southern whites in their efforts to restore old economic and social relationships as they adjusted to the realities of postwar life as a defeated confederacy? What attitudes and resources supported the freedmen's dreams, and what barriers lay in the way of achieving their goals? In short, what were the contrasting goals and dreams of the two groups, and what happened to them?

Placing the Sources in Context

THE American people faced many questions in the aftermath of Appomattox, and the most challenging was whether new race relationships could replace the prejudice, hatred, and hurts of the past. Although some white southerners reached out to freedmen and women, the rise of diehard groups like the Ku Klux Klan and the growth of northern indifference made problematic any possibility that the New South would be much different from the Old South. Slavery had ended, yet southern life—socially, economically, and politically—remained permeated with the culture of slavery and slaveholding. Creating a new basis of race relationships between whites and blacks and fulfilling the dreams of both groups would be difficult.

The usual story of Reconstruction focuses on events in Washington and the battles between the plans of presidents Lincoln and Andrew Johnson and those of Congress for the readmission to the Union of the former Confederate states. But a more compelling human story was unfolding throughout the South—and the North—as Confederate and Union soldiers returned home to their families and sought to renew their lives.

TIMELINE

1863	Emancipation Proclamation
1865	Lincoln's Second Inaugural Address; Freedmen's Bureau established; General Lee surrenders at Appomattox; Lincoln assassinated; President Johnson issues Proclamation of General Amnesty, restoring lands; Thirteenth Amendment (freeing the slaves) passed by Congress and ratified by the states; Black Codes passed; work contracts implemented
1866	Ku Klux Klan formed
1867	Freedmen's Bureau ends; Reconstruction Acts divide the South into military districts
1868	Fourteenth Amendment (citizenship and equal protection of the laws) ratified
1870	Fifteenth Amendment (black male suffrage) ratified
1875	Civil Rights Act passed (declared unconstitutional in 1883)
1877	All former Confederate states have reestablished conservative white Democratic control
1880s	Disfranchisement and segregation of southern blacks intensifies

Whites and blacks warily reassessed their relationship with each other. Freed slaves dreamed of an education and the rights freedom might bring; they picked new names and looked for missing family members and work. White landowners sought ways of finding a labor force to put their ruined cotton and rice fields back in cultivation. This human story unfolded within a context of political actions in the nation's capital and in the states.

In the Gettysburg Address and in his Second Inaugural Address (Archive 11), Abraham Lincoln showed his genius and ability to read the mood and psychological needs of the devastated, divided nation by expressing in eloquent, deeply religious language the higher purposes and meaning of the Civil War. The Second Inaugural shows that Lincoln understood the relationship between the brutalities of slavery and the horrors of killing and loss during the war. He also hoped "to bind up the nation's wounds."

Lincoln was more than the brooding idealist that some have portrayed; he was also a stern realist and a cagey politician. Although he consistently showed his "great heart," it is difficult to reconcile Lincoln as both the Great Emancipator and the man who would welcome the former Confederate states back into the Union "with malice toward none." He knew the process of freeing the slaves (accomplished not by his Proclamation but by the Thirteenth Amendment) would make more difficult the return of unrepentant southerners to the Union. Yet he was determined to do both, and he was in the process of setting forth rather mild terms for the southern states to reenter the Union when he was assassinated.

The Republican Congress had different ideas about reconstructing the nation. Congress was composed of a mixture of far-seeing "radicals," who dreamed of a new basis for race relations and a South made over in the image of the industrial North, and moderates, who sought more harmonious, economically based ways of reconnecting the Old South with the Union. These Republicans battled Lincoln's successor, Andrew Johnson, a Democrat and ex-slaveholder from Tennessee, to define a Reconstruction policy for the nation. In one of his first acts after succeeding Lincoln, Johnson inflamed many Republicans by issuing a Proclamation of General Amnesty, which pardoned most ex-Confederates and restored most confiscated lands to the original southern white owners, including some lands that had been given to the freedmen.

The battle was joined. Congress passed the Freedmen's Bureau and Civil Rights bills to smooth the freedmen's path to liberty with schools, work, and guaranteed civil rights. Johnson vetoed the bills, and Congress passed them over his veto. However, Congress responded inconsistently to southern intransigence, even in the early years after the war. It underfunded and understaffed the Freedmen's Bureau, and in 1883 the Supreme Court declared the Civil Rights Act unconstitutional. A land bill giving the freedmen "forty acres and a mule" never got out of committee for a vote on the floor of Congress.

Things got worse. In 1866 Congress proposed to the states (which ratified it in 1868) the pivotal Fourteenth Amendment defining black males as citizens and assuring them of equal protection of the laws. Yet Congress failed to back up the amendment forcefully. In 1867 Congress passed Reconstruction Acts that put token U.S. troops, including black soldiers, on duty in the South, then withdrew them all by 1877, leaving the freedmen at the mercy of southern whites. This situation remained largely unchanged until the intervention of federal troops in the Civil Rights movement of the 1960s. Thus, Washington played its own cruel game of lifting expectations only to dash them later.

Meanwhile, die-hard southerners had taken matters into their own hands in the first months after Appomattox. Southern state legislatures passed comprehensive Black Codes, seriously restricting the freedom and rights of the freedmen and women and forcing them back into plantation cotton fields by using various kinds of work contracts (see source 12.5a) that looked much like the restoration of slavery. Among the cruelest of the Black Codes were apprenticeship laws by which young orphaned black children were hired out as field workers, often by falsifying their age (source 12.5b). In 1866, a former Confederate general, Nathan Bedford Forrest, founded the Ku Klux Klan. The Klan and many other secret white groups like it intimidated and sometimes killed blacks who failed to show proper deference to whites, who tried to pursue an independent economic livelihood, or who participated actively as citizens, a right guaranteed them by the Fourteenth Amendment.

The freedmen did indeed dream of land of their own, economic independence, and political and civil rights. They also called for and went to the new Freedmen's Bureau schools that were founded throughout the South (many of which were burned down by whites). Black leaders, despite Klan opposition and their conspicuous absence from national politics, entered state and local politics for a brief time, where they supported public education and other moderate means of becoming full U.S. citizens.

The toughest battles for independence were fought over land. Freedmen wanted their own land to work, free from the restrictions of white landlords. Unfortunately, few freedmen secured possession of their own land, and most were forced to turn, first, to contracts that put them in the fields as hired hands under strict control and, later, to various forms of tenant farming. As tenant sharecroppers, blacks borrowed seed and credit on land owned by often absent white landlords. Thus began a cycle of credit and debt that tied black families to whites in relationships some called "debt slavery." No tenant could leave until the debt was paid, and no debt could be paid without having to get more credit in hopes that in the next growing season their share of the crop would yield a profit. Blacks caught in this cycle often ended up in a convict labor camp—a far cry from their emancipation dream of "forty acres and a mule."

About the Sources

The sources in this archive reveal how the national political conflict affected the human drama of whites and blacks struggling to put their lives back together and work out new meanings of race relations. Note, however, that all the sources come from the early years of Reconstruction. These materials include a song, a painting, a property restoration document, a cartoon, a labor contract, examples of the Mississippi Black Codes, an affidavit (or sworn testimony) on black child labor, and several letters. The letters reflect the Reconstruction experiences of a white from Louisiana, two African-Americans, one of them a Union soldier, and a northern white soldier on duty in Virginia with an outsider's perspective on southern race relations.

The oil painting *The Armed Slave* (12.1), created around 1865 by William Spang, a little-known white Philadelphia artist, raises many questions to explore as you determine what his intended message was. The painting contains mixed images. An African-American man with an exotic look (earring, braided beard, and side lock) sits at his ease reading a book, while a rifle with bayonet fixed backward (usually a sign of peace) leans against the wall nearby. Analyze the painting as you have analyzed other visuals in *American History Firsthand* by looking at each image in the picture.

The original authorship of the angry song "I'm a Good Old Rebel" (12.2) is in some dispute, but most historians of the music of the Civil War era attribute it to R. Bishop Buckley of Buckley's Minstrels. Minstrels were popular shows in which whites in blackface sang silly little songs and put on skits that mocked and demeaned African-Americans to the delight of white, mostly working-class audiences. This version of "I'm a Good Old Rebel" was first printed in New Orleans in 1866 and has survived largely in the oral tradition. Study the attitudes expressed in the song, which we are sure you will find extremely strong even by disappointed, ex-Confederate standards. Try reading it aloud.

The "restoration of confiscated property" document (12.3) is typical of many such legal restorations in the Sea Islands area off the Carolina and Georgia coast following President Johnson's Amnesty Proclamation restoring southern lands to former white owners. The problem, as you will see in the document, is that freedmen had been given these lands during the war by Union generals, and they thought the Freedmen's Bureau was holding them on their behalf. After Johnson's proclamation, southern whites applied for the return of their lands, and this document tells what happened to the freedmen. Note the full name of the bureau.

The Black Codes (12.4), labor contract (12.5a), and affidavit (12.5b) bear careful study, for they describe in chilling detail the methods white southerners used in achieving their goals, and the harsh realities freedmen and women faced in trying to achieve theirs. The codes are excerpts only, not the full set of laws, which were extensive, covering the restrictions on the rights of the freedmen in nearly all aspects of social, economic, and legal life. These three documents also reveal, by implication, the fears of both whites and blacks in the South.

The affidavit (12.5b) also suggests the role of the Freedmen's Bureau in the postwar years. The illustration from *Frank Leslie's Illustrated Newspaper* (12. 5c) highlights some of the educational efforts for former slaves while the political broadside (12.5d) points to some northerners' dislike of the Bureau and its work. The broadside was created during the 1866 governor's campaign in Pennsylvania. Hiester Clymer, whom the broadside supports, adopted a platform that included white supremacy. He backed President Andrew Johnson.

The letter by Payne (12.6) provides a white view of the early years of Reconstruction. The letter by Calvin Holly (12.7) to General O. O. Howard, Commissioner of the Freedmen's Bureau, and the Hawkins Wilson letter (12.8) reveal much of the typical experiences of freedmen and women in the first years after "emancipation."

The cartoon "This Is a White Man's Government" (12.9), by Thomas Nast, is from *Harper's Weekly*, a modestly reformist magazine published in the late 19th century and aimed at middle class northeasterners. The best way to "read" the cartoon is to begin by describing everything you see in it, including details of the four men and the scenes in the background. See if you can figure or find out the significance of "5 Points" on the cap of the figure to the left, the "NBF," "Fort Pillow," and "CSA" references on the figure in the middle, and "votes" in the hand of the well-dressed person to the right. Don't forget the fourth person in the cartoon, and note the date and caption quoted below it. The irony of the cartoon provided a fitting summary of the tragedy of Reconstruction and, unfortunately, heralded future race relations.

List of Sources

12.1 **Painting, *The Armed Slave*,** by William Spang, about 1865, in Harold Holzer and Mark Neely, Jr., *Mine Eyes Have Seen the Glory* (New York, 1993), p. 251. The Civil War Library and Museum.

12.2 **Confederate song, "I'm a Good Old Rebel,"** by R. B. Buckley, 1866, from *Songs of the Civil War: First Recordings from Original Editions* (New York: New World Records, 1976).

12.3 **Legal form for the restoration of confiscated property held by the Freedmen's Bureau,** South Carolina Freedmen's Bureau records, Box 483; in Martin Abbott, *Freedmen's Bureau in South Carolina, 1865–1872* (Chapel Hill, NC, 1967), pp. 137–138.

12.4 **Black Codes [Laws] of Mississippi, 1865,** in Henry Steele Commager, ed., *Documents of American History*, 7th ed. (New York: Appleton, 1963), pp. 452–455.

12.5a **Legal contract between Alonzo T. Mial and 27 freed laborers,** 1866, in Roger Ransom and Richard Sutch, *One Kind of Freedom: The Economic Consequences of Emancipation* (Cambridge: Cambridge U. Press, 1977), pp. 58–59. Original in the Alonzo T. Mial and Millard Mial Papers, Courtesy of the North Carolina Division of Archives and History.

12.5b **Affidavit of ex-slave Enoch Braston,** enclosed in letter from Chaplain L. S. Livermore to Lt. Col. R. S. Donaldson, January 10, 1866. Records of the Bureau of Refugees, Freedmen, and Abandoned Lands, National Archives, Washington, DC.

12.5c **Freedmen's School,** 1866, appearing in *Frank Leslie's Illustrated Newspaper*, September 22, 1866. Library of Congress, LC-US262-33264(5-5).

12.5d **Broadside, The Freedman's Bureau,** 1866. Broadside Collection, portfolio 159, no. 9a-c, rare book collection, Library of Congress.

12.6 **Letter from James A. Payne to stepdaughter Katherine F. Sterrett,** September 1, 1867. Barnhart Mss. Collection, Lilly Library, Indiana University, Bloomington.

12.7 **Letter from a Mississippi black soldier, Calvin Holly, to Major General O. O. Howard,** December 16, 1865. in Joseph P. Reidy and Leslie S. Rowland, eds., *Freedom Series II: The Black Military Experience* (Cambridge: Cambridge U. Press, 1982), pp. 754–756. Records of the Bureau of Refugees, Freedmen, and Abandoned Lands, National Archives.

12.8 **Letter from ex-slave Hawkins Wilson to Jane Wilson,** May 11, 1867, in Ira Berlin and Leslie S. Rowland, eds., *Families and Freedom* (New York: New Press, 1997), pp. 18–20.

12.9 **Cartoon, "This Is a White Man's Government,"** by Thomas Nast, *Harper's Weekly*, vol. 12, September 5, 1868, p. 568.

Questions to Consider

1. What is your "reading" of the painting *The Armed Slave*? What do you think each element of the image means: his body posture, the look on his face, the earring, braided beard and side lock, the book, the cigar, the rifle and bayonet? What is the attitude of this man? What do you think Spang's message was in doing this painting?

2. What attitudes are expressed in the song "I'm a Good Old Rebel" (source 12.2)? It is pretty obvious how the writer feels about Yankees. But what about the freedmen—can you infer his attitude about them? How would he regard *The Armed Slave*?

3. Read carefully the document restoring confiscated lands, the Mississippi Black Codes, the labor contract, and the affidavit (12.3–12.5), noting how they all work together to put freedmen back on lands owned by whites in a state of semi-slavery. What are the legal, contractual terms outlined in the restoration document (12.3), and who benefits? What seems to be the role of the "Bureau of Refugees, Freedmen and Abandoned Lands"? What fate (positive and negative) awaits the freedmen?

4. What rights do the freedmen have and not have according to the Black Codes (12.4)? Examine each section, especially those on apprenticeship and vagrancy, to see the relationship between the codes and the work contract (12.5a) and the affidavit (12.5b). What is it? What civil rights do the freedmen have? What white fears are implied in these sources?

5. In the labor contract (12.5a), what contractual rights does the owner Mial agree to? What contractual obligations do the "freed laborers" agree to? How fair was the contract? Would you have signed it? What other options do you think you might have had? What do you make of the list of names and specific terms at the bottom of the contract? What is Enoch Braston complaining about in his affidavit? Do you think he was justified? Were the apprenticeship provisions of the Black Codes a help or a hindrance to his case? What do you suppose Chaplain Livermore's feelings were?

6. What positive insights do we get of the operations of the Freedmen's Bureau in the affidavit (12.5b) and newspaper picture (12.5c)? What kind of instruction are the black women receiving? Why might they need such instruction for their lives in freedom? How are the women depicted? Is this a favorable view of them or not? What does the broadside (12.5d) suggest about why some northerners opposed the Bureau? Try and read as much of the text in the picture as you can.

7. What attitudes toward the freedmen does Payne, the southerner, reveal in his letter (12.6)? What emotions does he show? Although the Payne letter has a transcription, try reading it in the original handwritten version to get a feeling for what it is like to do original research in real manuscript collections that are filled with handwritten letters. Can you read it without the transcription? What do you learn about daily life in the 1860s from this letter?

8. What experiences and emotions are expressed in the letters by Calvin Holly and Hawkins Wilson (12.7 and 12.8)? What picture of the freedmen's condition and rights do you get from these letters? How do you interpret the fact that in the Wilson letter life seems not to be as difficult for blacks as in the others? What role does religion play in these letters?

9. What is your interpretation of the meaning of Nast's cartoon (12.9)? Look at the background as well as at the four figures. How would you characterize each of the four men in the cartoon? What does each represent? What do you think "5 Points," "NBF," and the other labels mean? What role does symbolism play in this cartoon? To what extent are the figures stereotypes? What larger statement about Reconstruction do you think Nast is making in the cartoon, and in what ways is his cartoon an apt summary of the Reconstruction era and its lasting legacy?

10. In summary, what were the contrasting goals and dreams of southern whites and black freedmen and women in the first three years after Appomatox, and what happened to them? What attitudes and resources did each group have as they sought to fulfill their goals and dreams? What barriers were in the way? What role did the North play as whites and blacks struggled to redefine race relations?

11. Whose goals and dreams, according to these sources, were best being fulfilled in the 1860s? Which one or two sources best capture for you the strong emotional feelings of this era of American history? Which captures best the feelings and experience of the South? the feelings and experience of the freedmen?

To review, as you look at the sources in this and other archives throughout *American History Firsthand,* Volume Two, pay close attention to:

- **What kind of source is it? Public? Private? Political? Cultural? Social?**
- **What is the subject or topic of the source? What is happening? What events or situations are revealed and discussed? How complete is it? What is missing?**
- **Who is the author or artist, and what viewpoint is being shown? Is he or she shaping the content of the source? How reliable does the source seem to be?**
- **Who is the intended audience and what purpose does the source seem to have?**
- **What emotions, attitudes, values, and cultural perspectives are revealed in the source?**

Note: It might be helpful to detach or copy this list of basic questions and keep it near you as you work with other archives in *American History Firsthand.*

THE STRUGGLES OF RECONSTRUCTION

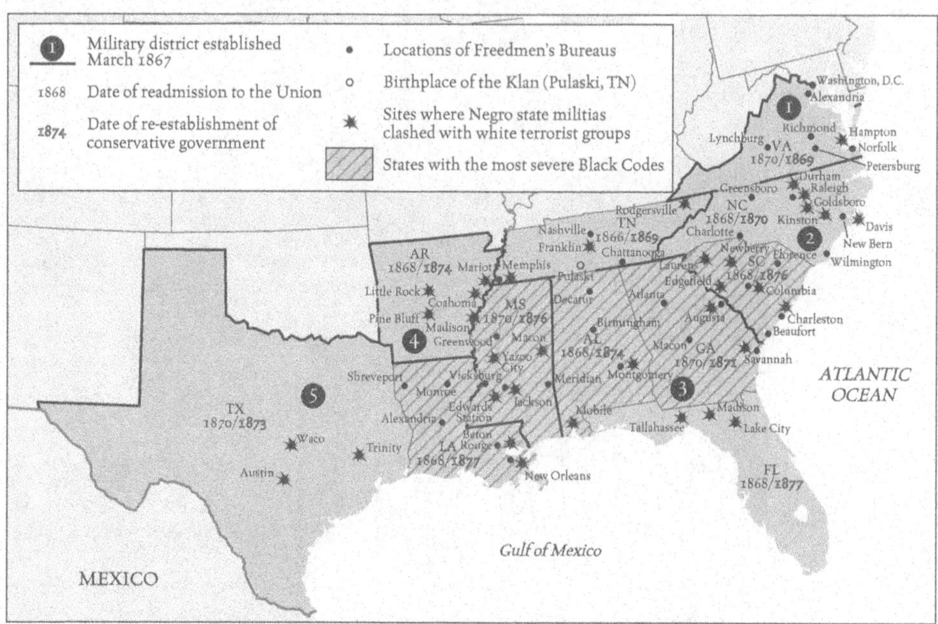

✧ DOCUMENT 12.1 ✧

Painting, *The Armed Slave*, by William Spang, about 1865, in Harold Holzer and Mark Neely, Jr., *Mine Eyes Have Seen the Glory* (New York, 1993), p. 251. The Civil War Library and Museum.

→ DOCUMENT 12.2 ←

Confederate song, "I'm a Good Old Rebel," by R. B. Buckley, 1866, from *Songs of the Civil War: First Recordings from Original Editions* (New York: New World Records, 1976).

O I'm a good old Rebel,
Now that's just what I am,
For this "Fair Land of Freedom"
I do not care AT ALL;
I'm glad I fit against it,
I only wish we'd won,
And I don't want no pardon
For anything I done.

I hates the Constitution,
This great Republic too,
I hates the Freedman's Buro,
In uniforms of blue;
I hates the nasty Eagle,
With all his braggs and fuss,
The lyin', thievin' Yankees,
I hates 'em wuss and wuss.

I hates the Yankee nation
And everything they do,
I hates the Declaration
Of Independence, too;
I hates the glorious Union—
'Tis dripping with our blood—
I hates their striped banner,
I fit it all I could.

I followed old mas' Robert
For four year near about,
Got wounded in three places
And starved at Pint Lookout.
I cotch the roomatism
A campin' in the snow,
But I killed a chance o' Yankees,
I'd like to kill some mo'.

Three hundred thousand Yankees
Is still in Southern dust;
We got three hundred thousand
Before they conquered us;
They died of Southern fever
And Southern steel and shot,
I wish they was three million
Instead of what we got.

I can't take up my musket
And fight 'em now no more,
But I ain't going to love 'em,
Now that is sarten sure;
And I don't want no pardon
For what I was and am,
I won't be reconstructed
And I don't care a dam.

→ DOCUMENT 12.3 ←

Legal form for the restoration of confiscated property held by the Freedmen's Bureau, South Carolina Freedmen's Bureau records, Box 483; in Martin Abbott, *Freedmen's Bureau in South Carolina, 1865–1872* (Chapel Hill, NC, 1967), pp. 137–138.

Richard H. Jenkins, an applicant for the restoration of his plantation on Wadmalaw Island, S. C., called "Rackett Hall," the same having been unoccupied during the past year and up to the 1st of Jan. 1866, except by one freedman who planted no crop, and being held by the Bureau of Refugees, Freedmen and Abandoned Lands, having conformed to the requirements of Circular No. 15 of said Bureau, dated Washington, D. C., Sept. 12, 1865, the aforesaid property is hereby restored to his possession.

The above instrument to be considered null and void unless the obligation herewith attached and subscribed to by said Richard H. Jenkins be faithfully and fully complied with.

All differences arising under this instrument and obligation are to be adjusted by the Board of Supervisors constituted by order of the Commissioner of the Bureau of Refugees, Freedmen and Abandoned Lands, dated Charleston, November 14, 1865.

. . . . . .

The Undersigned, Richard H. Jenkins, does hereby solemnly promise and engage, that he will secure to the Refugees and Freedmen now resident on his Wadmalaw Island Estate, the crops of the past year, harvested or unharvested; also, that the said Refugees and Freedmen shall be allowed to remain at their present houses or other homes on the island, so long as the responsible Refugees and Freedmen (embracing parents, guardians, and other natural protectors) shall enter into contracts, by leases or for wages, in terms satisfactory to the Supervising Board.

Also, that the undersigned will take the proper steps to enter into contracts with the above described responsible Refugees and Freedmen, the latter being required on their part to enter into said contracts on or before the 15th day of February, 1866, or surrender their right to remain on the said estate, it being understood that if they are unwilling to contract after the expiration of said period, the Supervising Board is to aid in getting them homes and employment elsewhere.

Also, that the undersigned will take the proper steps to enter to schools sanctioned by the Supervising Board, or by the Bureau of Refugees, Freedmen and Abandoned Lands.

But nothing in this instrument shall be so construed as to relieve the above mentioned persons from the ordinary judicial consequences of crime and misdemeanor.

Neither the land owners nor the Refugees and Freedmen will be obligated by this instrument beyond one year from this date unless the instrument is renewed.

✧ DOCUMENT 12.4 ✧

Black Codes [Laws] of Mississippi, 1865, in Henry Steele Commager, ed., *Documents of American History*, 7th ed. (New York: Appleton, 1963), pp. 452–455.

1. Civil Rights of Freedmen in Mississippi
(Laws of Mississippi, 1865, p. 82 ff.)

Sec.1. *Be it enacted,* . . . That all freedmen, free negroes, and mulattoes may sue and be sued, implead and be impleaded, in all the courts of law and equity of this State, and may acquire personal property, and choses in action, by descent or purchase, and may dispose of the same in the same manner and to the same extent that white persons may: *Provided,* That the provisions of this section shall not be so construed as to allow any freedman, free negro, or mulatto to rent or lease any lands or tenements except in incorporated cities or towns, in which places the corporate authorities shall control the same. . . .

Sec. 3. . . . All freedmen, free negroes, or mulattoes who do now and have here before lived and cohabited together as husband and wife shall be taken and held in law as legally married, and the issue shall be taken and held as legitimate for all purposes; that it shall not be lawful for any freedman, free negro, or mulatto to intermarry with any white person; nor for any white person to intermarry with any freedman, free negro, or mulatto; and any person who shall so intermarry, shall be deemed guilty of felony, and on conviction thereof shall be confined in the State penitentiary for life; and those shall be deemed freedmen, free negroes, and mulattoes who are of pure negro blood, and those descended from a negro to the third generation, inclusive, though one ancestor in each generation may have been a white person.

Sec. 4. . . . In addition to cases in which freedmen, free negroes, and mulattoes are now by law competent witnesses, freedmen, free negroes, or mulattoes shall be competent in civil cases, when a party or parties to the suit, either plaintiff or plaintiffs, defendant or defendants, and a white person or white persons, is or are the opposing party or parties, plaintiff or plaintiffs, defendant or defendants. They shall also be competent witnesses in all criminal prosecutions where the crime charged is alleged to have been committed by a white person upon or against the person or property of a freedman, free negro, or mulatto: *Provided,* that in all cases said witnesses shall be examined in open court, on the stand; except, however, they may be examined before the grand jury, and shall in all cases be subject to the rules and tests of the common law as to competency and credibility. . . .

Sec. 6. . . . All contracts for labor made with freedmen, free negroes, and mulattoes for a longer period than one month shall be in writing, and in duplicate, attested and read to said freedman, free negro, or mulatto by a beat, city or county officer, or two disinterested white persons of the county in which the labor is to be performed, of which each party shall have one; and said contracts shall be taken and held as entire contracts, and if the laborer shall quit the service of the employer before the expiration of his term of service, without good cause, he shall forfeit his wages for that year up to the time of quitting.

Sec. 7. . . . Every civil officer shall, and every person may, arrest and carry back to his or her legal employer any freedman, free negro, or mulatto who shall have quit the service of his or her employer before the expiration of his or her term of service without good cause; and said officer and person shall be entitled to receive for arresting and carrying back every deserting employe aforesaid the sum of five dollars, and ten cents per mile from the place of arrest to the place of delivery; and the same shall be paid by the employer, and held as a set-off for so much against the wages of said deserting employe: *Provided,* that said arrested party, after being so returned, may appeal to the justice of the peace or member of the board of police of the county, who, on notice to the alleged employer, shall try summarily whether said appellant is legally employed by the alleged employer, and has good cause to quit said employer; either party shall have the right of appeal to the county court, pending which the alleged deserter shall be remanded to the alleged employer or otherwise disposed of, as shall be right and just; and the decision of the county court shall be final. . . .

Sec. 9. . . . If any person shall persuade or attempt to persuade, entice, or cause any freedman, free negro, or mulatto to desert from the legal employment of any person before the expiration of his or her term of service, or shall knowingly employ any such deserting freedman, free negro, or mulatto, or shall knowingly give or sell to any such deserting freedman, free negro, or mulatto, any food, raiment, or other thing, he or she shall be guilty of a misdemeanor, and, upon conviction, shall be fined not less than twenty-five dollars and not more than two hundred dollars and the costs; and if said fine and costs shall not be immediately paid, the court shall sentence said convict to not exceeding two months' imprisonment in the county jail, and he or she shall moreover be liable to the party injured in damages: *Provided,* if any person shall, or shall attempt to, persuade, entice, or cause any freedman, free negro, or mulatto to desert from any legal employment of any person, with the view to employ said freedman, free negro, or mulatto without the limits of this State, such person, on conviction, shall be fined not less than fifty dollars, and not more than five hundred dollars and costs; and if said fine and costs shall not be immediately paid, the court shall sentence said convict to not exceeding six months imprisonment in the county jail. . . .

2. Mississippi Apprentice Law
(Laws of Mississippi, 1865, p. 86)

Sec. 1. . . . It shall be the duty of all sheriffs, justices of the peace, and other civil officers of the several counties in this State, to report to the probate courts of their respective counties semi-annually, at the January and July terms of said courts, all freedmen, free negroes, and mulattoes, under the age of eighteen, in their respective counties, beats or districts, who are orphans, or whose parent or parents have not the means or who refuse to provide for and support said minors; and thereupon it shall be the duty of said probate court to order the clerk of said court to apprentice said minors to some competent and suitable person, on such terms as the court may direct, having a particular care to the interest of said minor: *Provided,* that the former owner of said minors shall have the preference when, in the opinion of the court, he or she shall be a suitable person for that purpose.

Sec. 2. . . . The said court shall be fully satisfied that the person or persons to whom said minor shall be apprenticed shall be a suitable person to have the charge and care of said minor, and fully to protect the interest of said minor. The said court shall require the said master or mistress to execute bond and security, payable to the State of Mississippi, conditioned that he or she shall furnish said minor with sufficient food and clothing; to treat said minor humanely; furnish medical attention in case of sickness; teach, or cause to be taught, him or her to read and write, if under fifteen years old, and will conform to any law that may be hereafter passed for the regulation of the duties and relation of master and apprentice. . . .

Sec. 3. . . . In the management and control of said apprentice, said master or mistress shall have the power to inflict such moderate corporal chastisement as a father or guardian is allowed to inflict on his or her child or ward at common law: *Provided,* that in no case shall cruel or inhuman punishment be inflicted.

Sec. 4. . . . If any apprentice shall leave the employment of his or her master or mistress, without his or her consent, said master or mistress may pursue and recapture said apprentice, and bring him or her before any justice of the peace of the county, whose duty it shall be to remand said apprentice to the service of his or her master or mistress; and in the event of a refusal on the part of said apprentice so to return, then said justice shall commit said apprentice to the jail of said county, on failure to give bond, to the next term of the county court; and it shall be the duty of said court at the first term thereafter to investigate said case, and if the court shall be of opinion that said apprentice left the employment of his or her master or mistress without good cause, to order him or her to be punished, as provided for the punishment of hired freedmen, as may be from time to time provided for by law for desertion, until he or she shall agree to return to the service of his or her master or mistress: . . . if the court shall believe that said apprentice had good cause to quit his said master or mistress, the court shall discharge said apprentice from said indenture, and also enter a judgment against the master or mistress for not more than one hundred dollars, for the use and benefit of said apprentice. . . .

3. Mississippi Vagrant Law
(Laws of Mississippi, 1865, p. 90)

Sec. 1. *Be it enacted,* etc., . . . That all rogues and vagabonds, idle and dissipated persons, beggars, jugglers, or persons practicing unlawful games or plays, runaways, common drunkards, common night-walkers, pilferers, lewd, wanton, or lascivious persons, in speech or behavior, common railers and brawlers, persons who neglect their calling or employment, misspend what they earn, or do not provide for the support of themselves or their families, or dependents, and all other idle and disorderly persons, including all who neglect all lawful business, habitually misspend their time by frequenting houses of ill-fame, gaming-houses, or tippling shops, shall be deemed and considered vagrants, under the provisions of this act, and upon conviction thereof shall be fined not exceeding one hundred dollars, with all accruing costs, and be imprisoned at the discretion of the court, not exceeding ten days.

Sec. 2. . . . All freedmen, free negroes and mulattoes in this State, over the age of eighteen years, found on the second Monday in January, 1866, or thereafter, with no lawful employment or business, or found unlawfully assembling themselves together, either in the day or night time, and all white persons so assembling themselves with freedmen, free negroes or mulattoes, or usually associating with freedmen, free negroes or mulattoes, on terms of equality, or living in adultery or fornication with a freed woman, free negro or mulatto, shall be deemed vagrants, and on conviction thereof shall be fined in a sum not exceeding, in the case of a freedman, free negro or mulatto, fifty dollars, and a white man two hundred dollars, and imprisoned at the discretion of the court, the free negro not exceeding ten days, and the white man not exceeding six months. . . .

Sec. 7. . . . If any freedman, free negro, or mulatto shall fail or refuse to pay any tax levied according to the provisions of the sixth section of this act, it shall be *prima facie* evidence of vagrancy, and it shall be the duty of the sheriff to arrest such freedman, free negro, or mulatto or such person refusing or neglecting to pay such tax, and proceed at once to hire for the shortest time such delinquent tax-payer to any one who will pay the said tax, with accruing costs, giving preference to the employer, if there be one. . . .

4. Penal Laws of Mississippi
(Laws of Mississippi, 1865, p. 165.)

Sec. 1. *Be it enacted,* . . . That no freedman, free negro or mulatto, not in the military service of the United States government, and not licensed so to do by the board of police of his or her county, shall keep or carry fire-arms of any kind, or any ammunition, dirk or bowie knife, and on conviction thereof in the county court shall be punished by fine, not exceeding ten dollars, and pay the costs of such proceedings, and all such arms or ammunition shall be forfeited to the informer; and it shall be the duty of every civil and military officer to arrest any freedman, free negro, or mulatto found with any such arms or ammunition, and cause him or her to be committed to trial in default of bail.

2. . . . Any freedman, free negro, or mulatto committing riots, routs, affrays, trespasses, malicious mischief, cruel treatment to animals, seditious speeches, insulting gestures, language, or acts, or assaults on any person, disturbance of the peace, exercising the function of a minister of the Gospel without a license from some regularly organized church, vending spirituous or intoxicating liquors, or committing any other misdemeanor, the punishment of which is not specifically provided for by law, shall, upon conviction thereof in the county court, be fined not less than ten dollars, and not more than one hundred dollars, and may be imprisoned at the discretion of the court, not exceeding thirty days.

Sec. 3. . . . If any white person shall sell, lend, or give to any freedman, free negro, or mulatto any fire-arms, dirk or bowie knife, or ammunition, or any spirituous or intoxicating liquors, such person or persons so offending, upon conviction thereof in the county court of his or her county, shall be fined not exceeding fifty dollars, and may be imprisoned, at the discretion of the court, not exceeding thirty days. . . .

Sec. 5. . . . If any freedman, free negro, or mulatto, convicted of any of the misdemeanors provided against in this act, shall fail or refuse for the space of five days, after conviction, to pay the fine and costs imposed, such person shall be hired out by the sheriff or other officer, at public outcry, to any white person who will pay said fine and all costs, and take said convict for the shortest time.

DOCUMENT 12.5a

Legal contract between Alonzo T. Mial and 27 freed laborers, 1866, in Roger Ransom and Richard Sutch, *One Kind of Freedom: The Economic Consequences of Emancipation* (Cambridge: Cambridge U. Press, 1977), pp. 58–59. Original in the Alonzo T. Mial and Millard Mial Papers, Courtesy of the North Carolina Division of Archives and History.

"We Alonzo T. Mial of the County of Wake State of North Carolina of the One part, and the undersigned freed laborers of the other part have entered into the following Contract herein & after mentioned Witnesseth. That the Said laborers have agreed to work on the plantation of the Said Mial in the County of Wake & State aforesaid, from the date which Stands opposite their respective names to the 31st day of December 1866, That we will rise at day brake & attend to all duties preparatory to getting to work by Sun rise, and work till Sun Set, and when ever necessary, even after Sun Set to Secure the Crop from frost, or taking up fodder or housing Cotton in picking Season after the days work is over, or any other Small jobs liable to loss by not being attended to the night before. Stoping in the ~~Spring~~ & Summer Months for dinner One hour and a half, at 12 Oc, & in the Fall and Winter, Spring Months one hour, That we will do our work faithfully and in good order, and will ~~to~~ be respectful in our deportment to the Said Mial & family or Superintendent, That we will work under the directions and managment of the Said Mial or any Superintendent whose Services he may employ. That we will attend to all duties necessary to the plantation on Sundays, and will be responsible for the loss or damage from neglect or carelessness of all Tools placed in our possession, the ordinary wear and tare of the Same excepted. And we further agree that time lost by idleness or absence without leave shall not be paid for, but for all time So lost we agree to pay double the amount of our wages that all loss of time from Sickness or absence with leave will not be paid for, Also That we will pay for our rations advanced during all lost time. And we further agree that one half of our monthley wages Shall be retained by The Said Mial till the end of the year, and the amount So retained Shall be forfeited by a violation of this Contract on our part.

The Said Mial has agreed on his part in Consideration of the faithful performance of the above obligations of the undersigned freed laborers to pay the Said laborers the amount of money pr, month which stands apposite their respective names, or in no event payment to be delayed longer than three months. reserving one half however of the above amount till the end of the year which amount shall then be paid if not forfeited by a violation of this Contract by the Said freed laborers. I also agree to furnish the first day of evry Month free of Charge to evry full hand fifteen lbs of Bacon and one Bushel of Meal pr, month or as pr, amount which

Stands opposite their respective names. I also agree to sell to them for their family support not in my employ provisions such as I may have to spare at the retail shop price in the City of Raleigh. I also agree to give them half of every other Saturday between the 1st day of March and the 1st day of August, and will furnish them land for a small crop, also will furnish the teams and tools for the cultivation of the same provided the teams & tools are not abused by them. To all of which we do this day mutually agree, this the 29th day of January A.D. 1866.

Witness

Malachi Hinton

No.	Names of Freedlabourers	Age	Pay pr Mo.	Pr month Amount of Rations.	Date of Commencement
1	John his X mark Miles	29	$10.00	15 lbs Bacon 1 Bush Meal	8th Jan, 1866
2	Lewis his X mark Miles	63	$10.00	15 lbs Bacon 1 Bus Meal	22d Jan, 1866
3	Dick his X mark Miles	68	$10.00	15 lbs Bacon 1 Bush Meal	1st Jan, 1866
4	Allen his X mark Miles	39	$10.00	15 lbs Bacon 1 Bush Meal	1 Jan, 1866
5	Joseph his X mark Rhodes	21	$10.00	15 lbs Bacon 1 Bush Meal	1 Jan, 1866
6	Deaton his X mark Hinton	18	$10.00	15 lbs Bacon 1 Bush Meal	30th Jan 1866
7	Scott his X mark Miles	37	$10.00	15 lbs Bacon 1 Bush Meal	1st Jan, 1866
8	Short his X mark Alston	63	$10.00	15 lbs Bacon 1 Bush Meal	1 Jan, 1866
9	Frances her X mark Alston	20	$6.00	12 lbs Bacon 1 Bush Meal	1 Jan, 1866
10	Elizabeth her X mark Alston	18	$5.00	12 lbs Bacon 1 Bush Meal	1 Jan, 1866
11	Stella her X mark Alston	15	$4.00	12 lbs Bacon 1 Bush Meal	1 Jan 1866
12	Weston his X mark Miles	47	$10.00	15 lbs Bacon 1 Bush Meal	10th Jan, 1866

List of Freed mens Names Continued

No	Names	Age	Pay pr. Mo.	Pr Month Amount of Rations	Date of Commen
13	George his X mark Miles —	16	$6.	12 lbs Bacon 1 Bush Meal	10th Jan, 1866
14	Chapman his X mark Miles —	14	$6.	12 lbs Bacon 1 Bush Meal	10th Jan, 1866
15	Joseph his X mark Miles	51	$10.00	15 lbs Bacon 1 Bush Meal	1 Jan 1866
16	Robert his X mark Miles	20	$10.00	15 lbs Bacon 1 Bush Meal	8th Jan, 1866
17	Burnet his X mark Miles	17	$6.00	12 lbs Bacon 1 Bush Meal	8th Jan 1866
18	Rheubin his X mark Miles	15	$6.00	12 lbs Bacon 1 Bush Meal	8th Jan 1866
19	Rebecca his X mark Miles	11	$3.	10 lbs Bacon 1 Bush Meal	8th Jan 1866
20	John his X mark Miles	9	$2	10 lbs Bacon 1 Bush Meal	8th Jan, 1866
21	Calvin his X mark Miles	48	$10.00	15 lbs Bacon 1 Bush Meal	1 Jan 1866
22	Alex Miles	12	$2.00	10 lbs Bacon 1 Bush Meal	1 Jan, 1866
23	Isaac High	21	$10.00	15 lbs Bacon 1 Bush Meal	5th Feb, 1866
24	Haywood Whitley	25	$10.00	15 lbs Bacon 1 Bush Meal	24th Feb/66
25	Amanda Whitley	22	$5.00	12 lbs Bacon 1 Bush Meal	19th Mar/66
26	Mary Whitley	38	$5.00	furnished from Table =	5th Mar/66
27	Henry Whitley	21	$	12 lbs Bacon 1 Bush Meal	2nd Apr/66

We Alonzo T. Mial of the County of Wake State of North Carolina of the one part, and the undersigned freed laborers of the other part have entered into the following Contract here in and after mentioned.

Witnesseth. That the Said laborers have agreed to work on the plantation of the Said Mial in the County of Wake and State aforesaid, from the date which Stands opposite their respective names to the 31st day of December 1866. That we will rise at day brake and attend to all duties preparatory to getting to work by Sun rise, and work till Sun Set, and when ever necessary even after Sun Set to Secure the Crop from frost, or taking up fodder or housing Cotton in picking Season after the days work is over, or any other Small jobs liable to loss by not being attended to the night before. Stoping in the Spring and Summer months for dinner one hour and a half, at 12 O'C, and in the Fall and Winter [and] Spring months one hour.

That we will do our work faithfully and in good order, and will be respectful in our deportment to the Said Mial and family or Superintendent. That we will work under the directions and management of the Said Mial or any Superintendent whoes Services he may employ. That we will attend to all duties necessary to the plantation on Sundays, and will be responsible for the loss or damage from neglect or carelessness of all tools placed in our possession. The ordinary ware and tare of the Same excepted. And we further agree that time lost by idleness or absence without leave shall not be paid for, but for all time So lost we agree to pay double the amount of our wages and that all loss of time from Sickness or absence with leave will not be paid for. Also That we will pay for our rations advanced during all lost time. And we further agree That one half of our monthly wages Shall be retained by The Said Mial till the end of the year, and the amount So retained Shall be forfeited by a violation of this Contract on our part.

The Said Mial has agreed on his part in Consideration of the faithful performance of the above obligations of the undersigned freed laborers to pay the Said laborers the amount of money pr. month which stands opposite their respective names, or in no event payment to be delayed longer than three months, reserving one half however of the above amount till the end of the year which amount shall then be paid if not forfeited by a violation of this Contract by the Said freed laborers. I also agree to furnish the first day of every month free of charge to every full hand fifteen lbs of Bacon and one Bushel of meal pr. month or as pr. amount which Stands opposite their respective names. I also agree to Sell to them for their family Support not in my employ provisions Such as I may have to Spare at the retail Shop price in the City of Raleigh. I also agree to give them half of every other Saturday between the 1st day of March and the 1st day of August, and will furnish them land for a Small Crop. Also will furnish the teams and tools for the cultivation of the Same provided the teams and tools are not abused by Them. To all of which we do this day mutually agree. This the 29th day of January A. D. 1866.

Witness

Malcolm Hinton [signed] *A. T. Mial* [signed]

No.	Names of Freed Laborers	Age	Pay pr. Mo.	Amount of Rations pr. Mo.	Date of Commencement
1	*John his* X *mark Miles*	29	$10.00	15lbs Bacon 1 Bush Meal	8th Jan. 1866
2	*Lewis his* X *mark Miles*	63	$10.00	15lbs Bacon 1 Bush Meal	22nd Jan. 1866
3	*Dick his* X *mark Miles*	68	$10.00	15lbs Bacon 1 Bush Meal	1st Jan. 1866
4	*Allen his* X *mark Miles*	39	$10.00	15lbs Bacon 1 Bush Meal	1 Jan. 1866
5	*Joseph his* X *mark Rhodes*	21	$10.00	15lbs Bacon 1 Bush Meal	1 Jan. 1866
6	*Seaton his* X *mark Hinton*	18	$10.00	15lbs Bacon 1 Bush Meal	30th Jan. 1866
7	*Scott his* X *mark Miles*	37	$10.00	15lbs Bacon 1 Bush Meal	1st Jan. 1866
8	*Short his* X *mark Alston*	63	$10.00	15lbs Bacon 1 Bush Meal	1 Jan. 1866
9	*Frances her* X *mark Alston*	20	$6.00	12lbs Bacon 1 Bush Meal	1 Jan. 1866
10	*Elizabeth her* X *mark Alston*	18	$5.00	12lbs Bacon 1 Bush Meal	1 Jan. 1866
11	*Stetler his* X *mark Alston*	15	$4.00	12lbs Bacon 1 Bush Meal	1 Jan. 1866
12	*Wiston his* X *mark Miles*	47	$10.00	15lbs Bacon 1 Bush Meal	10th Jan. 1866
13	*George his* X *mark Miles*	16	$6.	12lbs Bacon 1 Bush Meal	10th Jan. 1866
14	*Chapman his* X *mark Miles*	14	$6.	12lbs Bacon 1 Bush Meal	10th Jan. 1866
15	*Joseph his* X *mark Miles*	51	$10.00	15lbs Bacon 1 Bush Meal	1 Jan. 1866
16	*Robert his* X *mark Miles*	20	$10.00	15lbs Bacon 1 Bush Meal	8th Jan. 1866
17	*Barnet his* X *mark Miles*	17	$6.00	12lbs Bacon 1 Bush Meal	8th Jan. 1866
18	*Rheubin his* X *mark Miles*	15	$6.00	12lbs Bacon 1 Bush Meal	8th Jan. 1866
19	*Rebecca her* X *mark Miles*	11	$3.	10lbs Bacon 1 Bush Meal	8th Jan. 1866
20	*John his* X *mark Miles*	9	$2.	10lbs Bacon 1 Bush Meal	8th Jan. 1866
21	*Calvin his* X *mark Miles*	48	$10.00	15lbs Bacon 1 Bush Meal	1 Jan. 1866
22	*Alex Miles*	12	$2.00	10lbs Bacon 1 Bush Meal	1 Jan. 1866
23	*Isaac High*	21	$10.00	15lbs Bacon 1 Bush Meal	5th Feb. 1866
24	*Haywood Whitley*	25	$10.00	15lbs Bacon 1 Bush Meal	27th Feb/66
25	*Amanda Whitley*	22	$5.00	12lbs Bacon 1 Bush Meal	19th Mar/66
26	*Mary Whitley*	38	$5.00	furnished from table	5th Mar/66
27	*Henry Whitley*	21	$	12lbs Bacon 1 Bush Meal	2nd Ap/66

✧ DOCUMENT 12.5b ✧

Affidavit of ex-slave Enoch Braston, enclosed in letter from Chaplain L. S. Livermore to Lt. Col. R. S. Donaldson, January 10, 1866. Records of the Bureau of Refugees, Freedmen, and Abandoned Lands, National Archives, Washington, DC.

Grenada [*Miss.*] Jan 109 1866

Col. I have the honor to report the inclosed affidavits of freedmen, as examples of general cases. My office is & has been crowded from "early morn to dewey eve" with complaints similar to these. There is "none to plead the cause of the poor." I am yet to know the first case where a Negro has carried his cause to the civil officers & a suit in his behalf commenced, & much less justice done him by way of council or getting a settlement.

I state what from my observation seems the fact "there is no law for one darkie, that a white man is bound to respect." I have written quires of paper & sent scores of Tho's Circular No 9 & it amounts to just about as one of the darkis said when he came back, "Now Probo Maser [*provost marshal*], yus wans to git us justice, but your writins to dese peles, help us jus as much as ifs you say to us up on house top, you's got wings & yo can fly. Wese trys it & wese come *flat down!!*

And it is just so! I could send you hundreds of affidavits but such has been the crowd around the office, this cold morning is the first opportunity I could command to write. Children are almost invariably bound out from two to 12 years younger than they are. Bosworth, the white man that hired Braston & released him, told me he saw the papers over Sam who is 18 years old & sam is bound out 6 years & six moths old!

I have hired out to othe partis many young persons from 12 years old to 19 who have been apprenticed as paupers, & where a white ma[*n'*]s interest comes in & will stand up for the darkie, none try the strength of their missconstrued apprentice law!!

The avaricious Slaveholder of former days, in this apprentice law, sees a chance to effectively apply it in case of young bright & active children, & stay not for the law to be carried out by proper officers, but run before they are sent, snatching all irrespective of "orphanage, willingness or ability of parents or relatives to take care of their children. In many cases the aged parent & gradnd parents last dependance for support is taken away from them an in no instance has the negroes consent been willingly obtained, but in several instances they have said "I consented for I was afraid of my life if I did not.

. . .

L. S. Livermore

[*Enclosure*] Grenada [*Miss.*] Jan. 109 1866

Affidvit of Enoch Braston (colored)

I was the slave of John Heath for twelve years. I staid with him until about the 20 of July [*1865*]. The crops were made & I had got half of the fodder pulled of which we all (fellow servnts were to have a third. This was all he had offered us in any of the crops.

My child had the flux, & I told him I had better go to Grenada, to get medicine for it, of the Yankie doctor. John Heath said I was getting mighty high up, & if I wanted to shew my freedom, I must get out of that yard, I could shew it there. Said never to put another track in that yard, if I did he would put a ball through me. I then left.

I went back at Christmas for my wife & famely. I had hired out, to John Bosworth & family for one third of the cotton raised & half of every thing else. I was to furnish myself—he to furnish all working utensils. Befor Christmas while I was at work with Whitticar, I went to Heaths & he offered me half I would make this year. But I told him no. I never could please him, so I thought we had better be apart. He said he could not make a bargain with me somebody had been talking with me.

I raised 13 1/2 bushels potatoes. He sold them for six bits pr bushel & refuses to let me have any of it.

Heath refuses to pay me a dime & says he will not.

He has given a shoat to others but will not let Enoch have his pig.

At christmas day I went after my family at Heaths to begin my years worth Bosworth.

Heath said I could have Enoch 12 years old Mary 8. Silas 14 month & Peter six years old—

Graves a citizen as far as I know, was then making out the papers to bind Sam 18 years old Bob, 15 years, Hayword 13, Enoch 12 years old and Delia 10 leaving me all the youngest. Heath said the Buzzard would pick me. I made no reply.

I got my wife and four children. Sam the oldest ran awy from Heaths, while Heath was at Carolton to get his papers approved and Sam is now with me. After we went to Bosworths to begin our years work, Heath & Dr Bartlet came to Bosworths (6 miles) & Said Sam must be sent home that night, and if he did not come it would be wors for him for he would get officers & come after him.

Bosworth advised me to leave him for Heath would bushwhack me sometime. I did so & brought a note to Chaplain Livermore from Bosworth. I then hired out to Mr Towne for $225. & all the family clear of all expense. My Bedding for the children and their clothing, & Bob, 15, Haywood 13, Delia 10 are all at Heaths & I dare not go after them, for when Heath (at christmas) said buzzards would pick my bones, Fanny Guy his stepdaughter had a doubled barrelled gun & said she would shoot me if I came in the yard.

→ DOCUMENT 12.5c ←

Freedmen's School, 1866, appearing in *Frank Leslie's iIllustrated Newspaper*, September 22, 1866. Library of Congress, LC-US 262-33264 (5.5).

DOCUMENT 12.5d

Broadside, The Freedman's Bureau, 1866. Broadside Collection, portfolio 159, no. 9a–c, rare book collection, Library of Congress.

THE FREEDMAN'S BUREAU!

AN AGENCY TO KEEP THE **NEGRO** IN IDLENESS AT THE **EXPENSE** OF THE WHITE MAN.

TWICE VETOED BY THE **PRESIDENT,** AND MADE A LAW BY **CONGRESS.**

SUPPORT CONGRESS & YOU SUPPORT THE NEGRO. SUSTAIN THE PRESIDENT & YOU PROTECT THE WHITE MAN

For 1864 and 1865, the **FREEDMAN'S BUREAU** cost the Tax-payers of the Nation, at le TWENTY-FIVE MILLIONS OF DOLLARS. For 1866, THE SHARE of the Tax-payers of Pennsylvania will be about ON ION OF DOLLARS. **GEAR** is FOR the Freedman's Bureau. **CLYMER** is OPPOSED to it.

→ DOCUMENT 12.6 ←

Letter from James A. Payne to stepdaughter Katherine F. Sterrett, September 1, 1867. Barnhart Mss. Collection, Lilly Library, Indiana University, Bloomington.

Baton Rouge Sept 1/67

Dear Kate

Your last letter I think was mailed from point Pleasant yet I am not certain and I cant Just put my hands upon it you must not think it is indifference that I dont write you all oftener but when Grace and the little boys ~~with~~ were with me my mind felt reconciled and I become careless and neglectfull (but I am again alone)

Perhaps all of you may think it strange that I should break up housekeeping so soon after getting there but this country

is changing so rapidly That
it is Impossible to point out
The future My predijudices
against Negroe equality can
Never be got over it is coming
about here That equality is so
far forced upon you That you
May protest as Much as you
please but your Childrens
Associates will be the Negroes
The Schools are equal The
Negroe have the ascendency
and can out vote The Whites
upon every Thing Then it
has always been My intention
to put The Boys to boarding
School Just as soon as They
were old enough I would like
to have Kept Them with Jesse
one More year she was carrying
Them along well Making Them
Little Gentlemen

but I became satisfied we were Going to have Yellow fever And I did not feel willing to Keep the Children here and risk their lives when there was nothing particular to be gained

The one at School at or near frankfort Kentucky I received a letter from Frank since he was there he is well pleased and wrote me a very good letter I think for him I will send you a copy of his words

There is no yellow fever in Town yet but it is getting pretty Bad in New Orleans and we look for it evry day

I am in Good health

Respects to all &

Love to yourself J.M. Bryan

Baton Rouge Sept 1/67

Dear Kate

Your Last letter I think was mailed from Point Pleasant yet I am not certain and I cant just put my hands upon it   you must not think it is indifferince [sic] that I dont write you all oftener but when Grace and the little boys were with me my mind felt reconsiled and I became Careless and Neglectfull (but I am again alone)

perhaps all of you may think it strange that I should break up Housekeeping so soon after getting them here but this country is changing so rapidly that it is Impossible to point out the future. My predjudices against Negroe equality can never be got over it is coming about here that equality is so far forced upon you that you may protest as much as you please but your Childrens Associates will be the Negroes   The schooles are equal.   the Negroe have the ascendency, and can out vote the whites upon every thing   Then it has always been my intention to put the Boys to boarding School Just as soon as they were old enough   I would like to have kept them with Grace one more year. she was carrying them along well making them Little Gentlemen.

but I became satisfied we were going to have yellow fever and I did not feel willing to keep the children here and risk their lives when there was nothing particular to be gained.

The [sic] are at school at or near Frankfort Kentucky. I received a letter from Frank since he was there   he is well pleased and wrote me a very good letter I think, for him   I will send you a copy of his words.

There is no yellow fever in Town yet but it is getting pretty bad in New Orleans and we look for it every day

I am in good health

Respects to all &

Love to yourself

J.A. Payne

DOCUMENT 12.7

Letter from a Misssissippi black soldier, Calvin Holly, to Major General O. O. Howard, December 16, 1865 in Joseph P. Reidy and Leslie S. Rowland, eds., *Freedom Series II, The Black Military Experience* (Cambridge: Cambridge U. Press, 1982), pp. 774–756. Records of the Bureau of Refugees, Freedmen, and Abandoned Lands, National Archives.

Vicksburg. Miss. Dec 16th 1865.

Sir

Major, General, O. O. Howard, Suffer me to address you a few lines in reguard to the Colered people in this State, from all I can learn and see, I think the Colered people are in a great many ways being outraged beyound humanity, houses have been torn-down from over the heades of women and Children-- and the old Negroes after they have worked them till they are 70 or 80 yers of age drive them off in the cold to frieze and starve to death, - - - - - -

One Woman come to Col, Thomas, the coldest day that has been this winter and said that she and her eight children lay out last night, and come near friezing after She had paid Some went on the house Some are being knocked down for saying they are free, while a great many are being worked Just as they use to be when Slaves, without any compensation, Report Came in town this morning that two Colered women was found dead side the Jackson road with their throats cut lying side by side, I see an account in the Vicksburg Journal where the Col, people was having a party where they formily had ~~had~~ one. and got into a fuss and a gun was fired and passed into a house,

ARCHIVE 12

they was forbidden not to have any more but did not heed. the result was the house was fired and a guard placed at the door one man attempted to come out but was shot and throwed back and burned five was Consumed in the flames, while the balance saught refuge in a church and it was fired and burned. The Rebbles are going a bout in many places through the State and robbing the Colored people of arms ~~and~~ money and all they have and in many places killing.— — So, General, to make short of a long story I think the Safety of this Country depones upon giving the Colored man all the rights ~~that~~ of a white man, ~~but~~ and especialy the Rebs. and let him know that their is power enough in the arm of the Government to give Justice, to all her loyal citizens— — —

They talk of taking the armes a way from Col. people and arresting them and put them on farmes next month and if they go at that I think there will be trouble and in all probbility a great many lives lost. They have been accusing the Colored people of an insurection which is a lie, in order that they might get arms to carrie out their wicked designs — — —

for to my own knowledge I have seen them buying arms and Amunitions ever since the lins have been opened and carring them to the Country, In view of these things I would sugjust to you if it is not incompatible with the public interest

to pass some laws that will give protection to
the colored man and meet out Justice to traters
in arms.— — — — — — —
For you have whiped them and tried them
and founded out that they will not do to be
depended upon, now if you have any true harted
men send them down here to carrie out your
wishes through the Bureau in reguarde to the freedmen
if not get Congress to stick in a few competent
colored men as they did in the army and the thing
will all go right, a trouble now with the colored
peaple on account of Rebs. after they have rendered
the Government such great survice through the
rebellion would spoil the whole thing—
and it is what the Rebles would like to bring
a bout, and they are doing all they can to prevent
free labor, and reastablish a kind of secondary
slavery Now believe me as a colored man that is a friend
to law and order, I blive without the intervention of
of the General government in the protection of the col,
peaple that there will be trouble in Miss before spring
please excuse this for I could not have said less
and done the subject Justice. infact I could say
more, but a hint to the wise is soficient. If you wish
to drop me a line Direct Calvin Holly. Vick Miss Box 2[illegible]
yours Most Respectfully,
Calvin Holly. colored Privt. on det. at Col. Thom..

Vicksburg. Miss. De' 16th 1865.

Sir

Major General, O. O. Howard, Suffer me to address you a few lines in reguard to the colered people in this State, from all I can learn and see, I think the colered people are in a great many ways being outraged beyound humanity, houses have been tourn down from over the heades of women and Children—and the old Negroes after they have worked there till they are 70 or 80 yers of age drive them off in the cold to frieze and starve to death.

One Woman come to (Col) Thomas, the coldest day that has been this winter and said that she and her eight children lay out last night, and come near friezing after She had paid some wrent on the house Some are being knocked down for saying they are free, while a great many are being worked just as they ust to be when Slaves, without any compensation. Report came in town this morning that two colered women was found dead side the Jackson road with their throats cot lying side by side, I see an account in the Vickshurg. Journal where the (col) peple was having a party where they formily had one, and got into a fuss and a gun was fired and passed into a house, they was forbidden not to have any more but did not heed. The result was the house was fired and a guard placed at the door one man attemped to come out but was shot and throed back and burned five was consumed in the flames, while the balance saught refuge in a church and it was fired and burned. The Rebbles are going a bout in many places through the State and robbing the colered peple of arms money and all they have and in many places killing.

So, General, to make short of a long story I think the safety of this country depenes upon giving the Colered man all the rights of a white man, and especialy the Rebs. and let him know that their is power enough in the arm of the Govenment to give Justice, to all her loyal citizens—

They talk of taking the armes a way from (col) people and arresting them and put them on farmes next month and if they go at that I think there will be trouble and in all probability a great many lives lost. They have been accusing the colered peple of an insorection which is a lie, in order that they might get arms to carrie out their wicked designs—

for to my own knowledge I have seen them buying arms and munitions ever since the lins have been opened and carring them to the country. In view of these things I would suggust to you if it is not incompatible with the public interest to pass some laws that will give protection to the colered men and meet out Justice to traters in arms.

For you have whiped them and tried them and found out that they will not do to be depended upon, now if you have any true harted men send them down here to carrie out your wishes through the Bureau in reguarde to the freedmen, if not get Congress to stick in a few competent colered men as they did in the army and the thing will all go right. A trouble now with the colered peple on account of Rebs. after they have rendered the Government such great survice through the rebellion would spoil the whole thing—and it is what the Rebles would like to bring a bout, and they are doing all they can to prevent free labor, and reasstablish a kind of secondary slavery Now believe me as a colered man that is a friend to law and order, I blive without the intervention of the General governmt in the protection of the (col) popble that there will be trouble in *Miss.* before spring please excuse this for I could not have said less and done the subject Justice. infact I could say more, but a hint to the wise is soficient If you wish to drop me a line Direct Calvin. Holly, *Vick* Miss Box 2^{d} yours Most Respectfully.

Calvin. Holly., colered Privt.

→ DOCUMENT 12.8 ←

Letter from ex-slave Hawkins Wilson to Jane Wilson, May 11, 1867, in Ira Berlin and Leslie S. Rowland, eds., *Families and Freedom* (New York: New Press, 1997), pp. 18–20.

[*Enclosure*] [*Galveston, Tex. May 11, 1867*]

Dear Sister Jane, Your little brother Hawkins is trying to find out where you are and where his poor old mother is—Let me know and I will come to see you—I shall never forget the bag of buiscuits you made for me the last night I spent with you—Your advice to me to meet you in Heaven has never passed from my mind and I have endeavored to live as near to my God, that if He saw fit not to suffer us to meet on earth, we might indeed meet in Heaven—I was married in this city on the 10th March 1867 by Rev. Samuel Osborn to Mrs. Martha White, a very intelligent and lady-like woman—You may readily suppose that I was not fool enough to marry a Texas girl—My wife was from Georgia and was raised in that state and will make me very happy—I have learned to read, and write a little—I teach Sunday School and have a very interesting class—If you do not mind, when I come, I will astonish you in religious affairs—I am sexton of the Methodist Episcopal Church colored—I hope you and all my brothers and sisters in Virginia will stand up to this church; for I expect to live and die in the same—When I meet you, I shall be as much overjoyed as Joseph was when he and his father met after they had been separated so long—Please write me all the news about you all—I am writing tonight all about myself and I want you to do likewise about your and my relations in the state of Virginia—Please send me some of Julia's hair whom I left a baby in the cradle when I was torn away from you—I know that she is a young lady now, but I hope she will not deny her affectionate uncle this request, seeing she was an infant in the cradle when he saw her last—Tell Mr. Jackson Talley how-do-ye and give my love to all his family, Lucy, Ellen and Sarah—Also to my old playmate Henry Fitz who used to play with me and also to all the colored boys who, I know, have forgotten me, but I have not forgotten them—I am writing to you tonight, my dear sister, with my Bible in my hand praying Almighty God to bless you and preserve you and me to meet again—Thank God that now we are not sold and torn away from each other as we used to be—we can meet if we see fit and part if we like—Think of this and praise God and the Lamb forever—I will now present you a little prayer which you will say every night before you go to sleep—Our father who art in heaven &c, you will know what the rest is—Dear sister, I have had a rugged road to travel, since I parted with you, but thank God, I am happy now, for King Jesus is my Captain and God is my friend. He goes before me as a pillar of fire by night and a cloud by day to lead me to the New Jerusalem where all is joy, and happiness and peace—Remember that we have got to meet before that great triune God—My reputation is good before white and black. I am chief of all the turnouts of the colored people of Galveston—Last July 1866, I had the chief command of four thousand colored people of Galveston—So you may know that I am much better off, than I used to be when I was a little shaver in Caroline, running about in my shirt tail picking up chips—Now, if you were to see me in my fine suit of broadcloth, white kid gloves and long red sash, you would suppose it was Gen. Schofield marching in parade uniform into Richmond—The 1st day of May, 1867, I had 500 colored people, big and little, again under my command—We had a complete success and were complimented by Gen. Griffin and Mr. Wheelock the superintendent of the colored schools of Texas—We expect to have a picnic for the Sunday School soon—I am now a grown man weighing one hundred and sixty odd pounds—

I am wide awake and full of fun, but I never forget my duty to my God—I get eighteen dollars a month for my services as sexton and eighteen dollars a week outside—I am working in a furniture shop and will fix up all your old furniture for you, when I come to Virginia if you have any—I work hard all the week—On Sunday I am the first one in the church and the last to leave at night; being all day long engaged in serving the Lord; teaching Sunday School and helping to worship God—Kind sister, as paper is getting short and the night is growing old and I feel very weak in the eyes and I have a great deal to do before I turn in to bed and tomorrow I shall have to rise early to attend Sunday School, I must come to a conclusion—Best love to yourself and inquiring friends—Write as quickly as you can and direct to Hawkins Wilson care of Methodist Episcopal church, colored, Galveston, Texas—Give me your P. Office and I will write again—I shall drop in upon you some day like a thief in the night.—I bid you a pleasant night's rest with a good appetite for your breakfast and no breakfast to eat—Your loving and affectionate brother—

HAWKINS WILSON

✧ DOCUMENT 12.9 ✧

Cartoon, "This Is a White Man's Government," by Thomas Nast, *Harper's Weekly*, vol. 12, September 5, 1868, p. 568.

"THIS IS A WHITE MAN'S GOVERNMENT."

"We regard the Reconstruction Acts (so called) of Congress as usurpations, and unconstitutional, revolutionary, and void."—*Democratic Platform.*

→ARCHIVE 13←

Conflict on the Plains: Assaults on Indian Lands and Cultures

Archive Overview

THE sources in this archive reveal the gradual deterioration of the lands and the threats to the cultures of the Plains Indians from the 1860s to the 1890s. Military, diplomatic, political, and cultural differences and conflicts were all involved in the struggle over who would control the Great Plains. The sources here (ranging from a treaty and an act of Congress to Indian autobiographies and pictographs) represent these areas of struggle and the different modes of expression between the "first" Americans and those from Europe. The Plains Indians included many diverse groups, from the Arapaho, Cheyenne, and Kiowa to the Crow, Omaha, and Pawnee. The sources here, however, focus primarily on the largest and strongest of the Plains nations, the Dakota, Lakota, and Yanktonai Sioux, whose lands spread from Minnesota across the Dakotas to Wyoming.

The problems to examine in working with these sources are, first, the nature of the policies white Americans used to take control of the Plains Indians' lands and to destroy native cultures and, second, the ways in which Indians responded to these policies. Note throughout the archive the clash of cultural values in the various attitudes toward treaty-making, land, education, and culture. What kinds of policies did whites use to assault Indian lands and culture, and how effective did they seem to be? How successful was the Indian response? In what ways did the Plains Indians attempt to preserve their dignity and culture against these assaults, and to what extent did they accommodate white life and culture?

Placing the Sources in Context

IN the period before the Civil War, white emigrants moving west passed over the Great Plains, their wagons headed for Oregon and Utah and the California and Colorado mine districts. After the war, however, farmers moved in increasing numbers into Kansas, Minnesota, Colorado, Wyoming, and the Dakotas,

TIMELINE

1851	Treaty of Fort Laramie setting Plains Indian tribal boundaries and guaranteeing secure westward trails for overland white travelers
1864	Sand Creek (Colorado) massacre of the Cheyenne
1865–1867	Red Cloud's war over the Bozeman Trail in Wyoming
1868	Fort Laramie Treaty ending the war, closing the Bozeman Trail, and establishing the Great Sioux (Lakota) reservation in South Dakota (including the Black Hills)
1868–1872	Black Hills gold rush
1869	Transcontinental railroad completed in Utah
1870s	Settlers continue to move into Kansas and the Great Plains; destruction of southern plains buffalo herds and defeat of southern Plains Indians (Kiowa, southern Cheyenne, and others)
1876	Battle of Little Bighorn (Greasy Grass to the Lakota) in southern Montana
1877	Killing of Crazy Horse; Black Hills cession
1879	Founding of Carlisle Indian School; Standing Bear arrives at Carlisle
1880s	Destruction of northern plains buffalo herds
1884	Zitkala-Sa arrives at boarding school in Indiana
1887	General Allotment (Dawes) Act
1889	Act reducing further the size of the Great Sioux reservation
1889–1890	Ghost Dance movement; Sitting Bull killed
1890	Wounded Knee massacre of Big Foot's band of Lakota Sioux

helped by the nation's expanding railroad network. These settlers came into contact and conflict with Cheyenne, Shoshone, Ute, Arapaho, Pawnee, Comanche, Kiowa, and other Indian peoples of the Great Plains. But the largest clash was between these settlers, supported by the United States government, and the several bands (tribal communities) of the Dakota and Lakota Sioux nation: Brule, Yanktonai, Minniconjou, Hunkpapa, and the mighty Oglala of Red Cloud, Crazy Horse, and Sitting Bull.

The determination of whites to possess lands belonging to these western nations and to move Indians onto reservations led to Indian resistance and full-scale war in the 1860s. Whites persisted in their efforts, using strategies that ranged from war, treaties, and the destruction of buffalo herds to the encouragement of Indian agriculture and boarding schools. Underlying both white military aggression and the attempts of progressive reformers at cultural assimilation was the conviction that Indians would have to give up most of their lands and adapt to whites' values and life style or die out. Either way was an assault on Indian land, life, and cultural values.

The timeline and your textbook provide the details of the growing conflict between the Plains Indian nations and the expanding United States in the years following the Treaty of Fort Laramie in 1851, the first effort to establish peace in the plains. In the 1860s the massacre at Sand Creek in Colorado was followed by Red Cloud's successful war against United States soldiers for control of the Bozeman Trail in present-day Wyoming. The war was concluded with the Fort Laramie Treaty of 1868, which guaranteed peace, protection, hunting rights, and Indian control over their sacred Black Hills. However, the treaty also contained clauses that encouraged Indians to settle on reservations and learn white ways through schooling and by pursuing agriculture rather than continuing the nomadic hunting of buffalo.

No sooner had the treaty been signed than gold was discovered in the Black Hills. The U.S. government sent General George Custer to set up camp in the shadow of the Black Hills as protection for the expected invasion of gold-seeking prospectors lured west by the Union Pacific railroad. Meanwhile, in the southern plains, Kiowa, southern Cheyenne, and other native peoples were succumbing to the military pressure of the 1860s, which was marked by General George Custer's massacre of the Cheyenne at Washita in Oklahoma in 1868 and the virtual destruction of their buffalo-based livelihood. Captured Indians from these wars, including a young Kiowa warrior named Wo-Haw, were taken as prisoners to the federal bastion of Fort Marion in St. Augustine, Florida, far from their ancestral homelands.

In the northern plains, sporadic warfare continued; Cheyenne Dog Soldiers, one of six military societies among the Cheyenne, were especially effective against the Americans, as were Crazy Horse, Sitting Bull, and other Oglala Sioux warriors. The defeat and massacre of Custer and his troops in 1876 at the battle of the Little Bighorn River (Greasy Grass to the Lakota) was, however, only a momentary success for the Indians, for it served to stiffen white determination to remove entirely the Indian military threat on the plains. Within a year, the legendary warrior Crazy Horse had been killed and the Sioux were forced to cede the Black Hills, diminishing the size of their reservation. The slaughter of the northern buffalo herds, further reductions of Sioux lands, and the murder of Sitting Bull and the massacre of Big Foot's cold and sickly band of Miniconjou Sioux at Wounded Knee in December 1890 all combined to end Indian resistance to the loss of their lands.

Not all white Americans sought to kill the Plains Indians and take their lands. Reformers, influenced by Helen Hunt Jackson's *A Century of Dishonor* in 1881, an attack on government Indian policies, sincerely believed that the only way to save the Indians was by helping them assimilate white ways. Well-intentioned efforts by "friends" of the Indians took two main forms, both potentially devastating to Indian identity and culture. The first was the establishment of Indian boarding schools, which sought to eradicate all expressions of Indian culture and language. The second was the passage by Congress in 1887 of the General Allotment Act, or Dawes Act, which instituted a policy of dividing reservation lands into square land plots allotted provisionally to Indian heads of family. Although final official ownership was delayed for several years, it brought with it United States citizenship. But this was rare: not surprisingly, two-thirds of all allotted lands eventually passed to speculators and other whites.

About the Sources

IN reading the Fort Laramie Treaty of 1868 (source 13.1), it is important to know that whites and Indians had very different approaches to making treaties. Indians came to a treaty council primarily for communication with neighboring peoples, for the rituals of talking, smoking the pipe, and gift-giving. White Americans, by contrast, were primarily interested in concluding legal contractual agreements, in getting Indian representatives, who did not represent all their people in the same way as whites do theirs, to agree to the "touching the pen" to a formal treaty. The omitted articles mostly describe reservation boundaries, the details of selecting and applying for land on the reservation, and the government's commitment to construct mills, schoolhouses, warehouses, and buildings for tradesmen. Look carefully at the "three-fourths" clause in article 12 and note the names at the bottom of the treaty (which go on for a full two more pages than what is included here). You might ask who these Indians were who put their "x mark" on the paper; you will also look in vain for the names of Red Cloud and Crazy Horse, whose military victories had forced the council to meet. Consider why they chose not to attend.

The advertisement (13.2) would have been posted on buildings and in eastern newspapers and magazines after the discovery of gold in the Black Hills right after the Fort Laramie Treaty in 1868. The influx of gold seekers undermined the promises made in that treaty.

The third set of sources shows the Plains Indian pictograph tradition of recording significant historical events. Here are a sketch of war exploits on a tanned buffalo hide (13.3a), a Yanktonai Sioux winter count (13.3b), named for the time of year when tribal historians usually recorded the major events of the year, and one of Sioux chief Red Horse's many pictographic descriptions of the Battle of the Little Bighorn (13.3c). The winter count depicts the winter of 1890–1891, when Sitting Bull was killed and disease and starvation were rampant among the Sioux people. In studying pictographs, as with any visual source, it is best first to describe each item in the picture and then to interpret what they mean. Decide what you think is the overall meaning.

The General Allotment Act (13.4b), like many of the articles in the Fort Laramie Treaty, was designed to turn Indians into farmers by allotting to them, by an elaborate and difficult process, individually held plots of poorly arable land on increasingly smaller reservations. (A section is 640 acres.) The act contained, as you can see, highly complex ownership provisions, which permitted non-Indians to purchase unassigned or unimproved lands. It was administered by government agents located at the reservation agency town. Source 13.4c is a map showing a typical distribution of allotted (and unassigned) lands on the Rosebud reservation in south-central South Dakota. Source 13.4d is an actual allotment form for an Arapaho man and his son. Notice their names.

Alice Fletcher, who worked for the Bureau of Indian Affairs, was one of those responsible for implementing the allotment policy in the 1880s. At the beginning of the decade, she traveled to Dakota Territory to document the Sioux way of life. Her 1861 journals give insights into the perspective of white reformers as well as a picture of the Native Americans she encountered. She was a staunch supporter of the Carlisle Indian School in Pennsylvania.

As Captain Richard Henry Pratt, founder of that school, put it in a comment meant to be friendly, the purpose of the Indian boarding schools was to "kill the Indian and save the man." Indian youths from the Great Plains would arrive at Carlisle, or some other boarding school, where their long hair would be cut off and where speaking in their native language and practicing native religious rituals and games were strictly forbidden. School life was rigidly regimented as officials thwarted all challenges to their authority. For some students (13.5 and 13.6), like Luther Standing Bear, an Oglala Lakota Sioux from western South Dakota near the Black Hills, and Zitkala-Sa (aka Gertrude Bonin), a Yanktonai Sioux from eastern South Dakota, their boarding school experience led to a successful assimilation into white society. As you read their stories, however, note the extent to which they also managed to retain their Indian cultural values. Others, however, who never wrote an autobiography, were devastated by the forced transition from the Dakotas to Carlisle or other nearby boarding schools; many suffered depression and died of infectious diseases and even suicide.

Pratt and other reformers focused on what was positive about the boarding schools. One of their favorite approaches to show how well the schools were working was to show before-and-after photographs (13.7a and b). Back on the Rosebud (Brule Sioux) reservation in South Dakota, a photographer in 1906 arranged to have the Brule leader, Two Strike, who was born in 1819 and fought at both Little Bighorn and Wounded Knee, to pose with his son, grandson, and great-grandson (13.7c). Notice the various symbols in the picture, including the dress and the banners on the tent in the back.

Captain Pratt experimented with efforts to assimilate Indians into white culture while he was a young officer at Fort Marion; his first "students" were imprisoned warriors from the southern plains. A young Kiowa man, Wo-Haw, encouraged by Pratt, expressed himself in a remarkable series of pictographs, four of which are included here. Wo-Haw used the pictograph to recapture aspects of Indian life before and after his imprisonment. Two drawings show Kiowa life before the intrusion of whites (13.8a and b), and two show the challenges presented by white culture and its pressures to assimilate (13.8c and d). Examine each figure or image in his drawings, describe what you see, and then ask yourself what you think Wo-Haw meant by his drawing. There are many possible meanings, especially of the *Classroom at Fort Marion* and *Self-Portrait*. It also helps to know the symbols (falling stars as ominous signs, for example) and artistic conventions (straight lines for mouths, neither smiling nor sad) of a pictographic drawing.

List of Sources

13.1 **Treaty of Fort Laramie between the United States and the Sioux (Lakota),** 1868, in Charles J. Kappler, ed., *Indian Treaties, 1778–1883* (New York, 1972), pp. 998–1005.

13.2 **Railroad advertisement, "To the Gold Fields of the Black Hills,"** 1870s, in Charles Hall, ed., *Documents of Wyoming Heritage* (Cheyenne, 1976). The Newberry Library.

13.3a **Indian pictograph of heroic exploits, on buffalo hide,** northern Plains, probably Cheyenne; the British Museum, Ethnography 917, in J. C. H. King, *First Peoples First Contacts: Native Peoples of North America* (Cambridge, MA, 1999), p. 266. ©The British Museum.

13.3b **Yanktonai Sioux pictograph, *Winter Count*,** 1890–1891, Ethnography 1942, in J. C. H. King, *First Peoples First Contacts*, p. 266. ©The British Museum.

13.3c **Pictographic account of the Battle of Little Bighorn by the Miniconjou Lakota Sioux Chief Red Horse,** June 25–26, 1876. National Anthropological Archives, Smithsonian Institution.

13.4a **Camping with the Sioux, Fieldwork Diary of Alice Cunningham Fletcher,** September 24, and October 5, 1881. Records of the National Anthropological Archives, Washington, DC.

13.4b **Act of Congress, the General Allotment Act (Dawes Act),** 1887, in Francis Paul Prucha, ed., *Documents of United States Indian Policy* (Lincoln, NE, 1975), pp. 171–174.

13.4c **Map platting, Indian Allotments on the Rosebud Reservation,** 1903, Records of the Bureau of Indian Affairs, National Archives, Washington; in Henry W. Hamilton and Jean Tyree Hamilton, *The Sioux of the Rosebud: A History in Pictures* (Norman: U. of Oklahoma Press, 1971), pp. 120–121.

13.4d **Legal allotment certificate for William Shakespeare (War Bonnet),** Shoshone Agency, 1904, in Charles "Pat" Hall, ed., *Documents of Wyoming Heritage* (Cheyenne: Wyoming Bicentennial Commission, 1976), p. 6.

13.5a **Autobiographical narrative by Luther Standing Bear on his first days at the Carlisle (Pennsylvania) Indian School,** in Luther Standing Bear, *Land of the Spotted Eagle* (Lincoln: U. of Nebraska Press, 1978), pp. 230–235. Reprinted from LAND OF THE SPOTTED EAGLE by Luther Standing Bear by permission of the University of Nebraska Press. Copyright, 1933, by Luther Standing Bear. Renewal copyright, 1960, by May Jones.

13.5b **Photograph of Chief Standing Bear the elder visiting his son at Carlisle,** in Luther Standing Bear, *Land of the Spotted Eagle*, p. 234. Reproduced from LAND OF THE SPOTTED EAGLE by Luther Standing Bear by permission of the University of Nebraska Press. Copyright, 1933, by Luther Standing Bear. Renewal copyright, 1960, by May Jones.

13.6 **Autobiographical narrative by Zitkala-Sa on her first days at boarding school in Indiana,** in Zitkala-Sa [Gertrude Bonin], *American Indian Stories* (Lincoln: U. of Nebraska Press, 1985), pp. 49–56. Originally published in *The Atlantic Monthly* in 1900.

13.7a **Photograph of young Sioux at Carlisle boarding school,** 1879, in Robert Utley, *The Indian Frontier of the American West, 1846–1890* (Albuquerque, NM, 1984), p. 222. J.N. Choate/Denver Public Libary, Western History Department.

13.7b **Photograph of the first graduating class at Carlisle boarding school,** 1889, in Robert Utley, *The Indian Frontier of the American West, 1846–1890* (Albuquerque, NM, 1984), p. 223. J. N. Choate/Denver Public Library, Western History Department.

13.7c **Photograph of four generations of the Two Strike family,** by John A. Anderson, about 1906, in *The Sioux of the Rosebud: A History in Pictures* (Norman, OK, 1971), plate 204, p. 277. Nebraska State Historical Society, John A. Anderson Collection.

13.8a **Indian pictograph by Wo-Haw, *The Buffalo Who Wouldn't Die*,** in Moira Harris, *Between Two Cultures: Kiowa Art from Fort Marion* (Pogo Press, 1989). Missouri Historical Society, St. Louis.

13.8b **Indian pictograph by Wo-Haw, *Skinning a Buffalo*,** in Moira Harris, *Between Two Cultures: Kiowa Art from Fort Marion* (Pogo Press, 1989). Missouri Historical Society, St. Louis.

13.8c **Indian pictograph by Wo-Haw, *Classroom at Fort Marion*,** in Moira Harris, *Between Two Cultures: Kiowa Art from Fort Marion* (Pogo Press, 1989). Missouri Historical Society, St. Louis.

THE PLAINS INDIANS WARS AND LOST LANDS

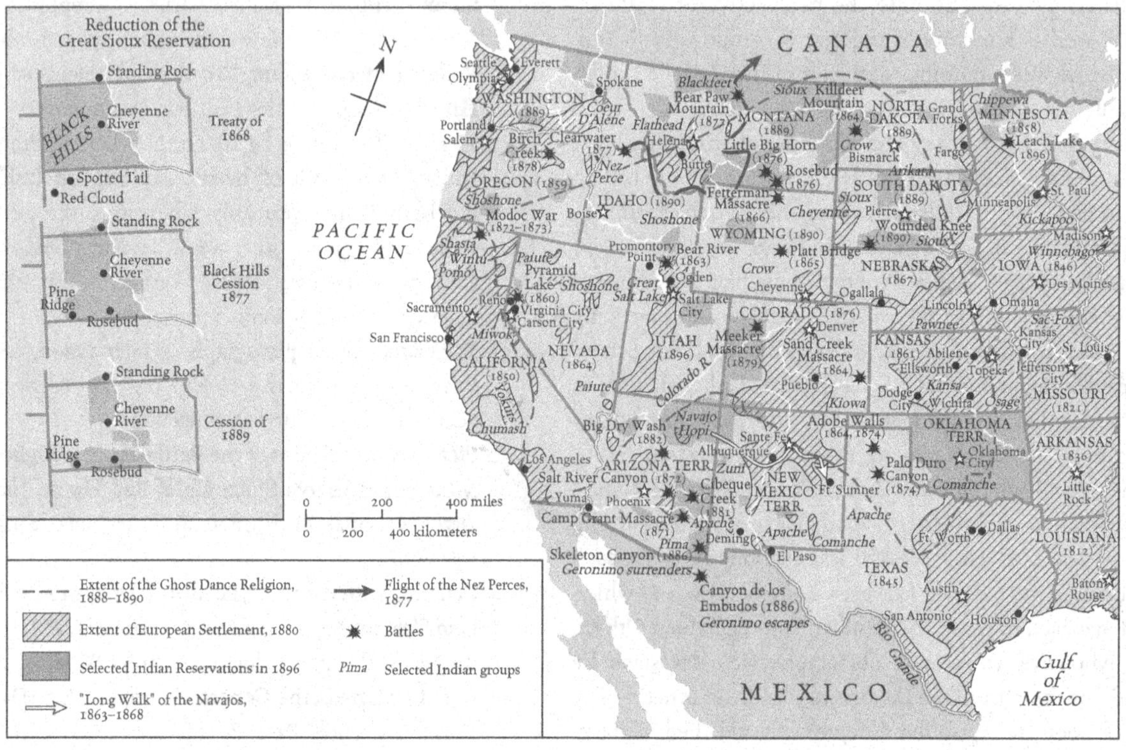

13.8d **Indian pictograph by Wo-Haw, "Self-Portrait" or "Between Two Cultures,"** Missouri Historical Society, St. Louis; in Moira Harris, *Between Two Cultures: Kiowa Art from Fort Marion* (Pogo Press, 1989). Missouri Historical Society, St. Louis.

Questions to Consider

1. Note the specific terms of the Treaty of Fort Laramie (source 13.1): What are the major areas covered by the treaty? What does each side "get"? What does each lose? Look especially at articles 13.10 and 13.11. Why do you think much of the treaty (articles 13.3–13.10, some of which has been excerpted) focuses on such things as farming, agents, the payment of annuities, and education? What would be the danger to Plains Indians of farming and the annuity system as described in article 10? Note the $10 and $20 differential: what is its purpose?

2. Using the articles in the treaty, how might you explain that the Lakota Sioux do or do not still have a legitimate claim to the Black Hills? See especially sources 13.12 and 13.16.

3. What do you read in the Black Hills Union Pacific advertisement (13.2)? What is offered? What dangers are mentioned or implied? What reassurances are people given?

4. What do you see in the three pictograph records of three kinds of historical events (13.3)? How are they similar? How are they different? How do they show change over time, from the pre-1868 images to Red Horse's depiction of Little Bighorn in 1876 to the Yanktonai winter count describing the winter of 1890–1891? What has happened to the Plains Indians over this time? How have their values changed? Or have they?

5. What does Fletcher mean when she says Wajapa wears "citizen's dress"? What does the term suggest about her values? What terms does she use to describe Buffalo-chip and Wajapa in her October 5 entry? What are her views of the Native Americans in these entries? What do they need? Is she sympathetic to Indians? Why or why not?

6. Describe the terms of the General Allotment (Dawes) Act (13.4b). To what extent does it continue the policies of the Fort Laramie Treaty of 1868? How is it different? What do you see on the map of the allotments on the Rosebud reservation (13.4c)? What do you notice about the names? How well do you think the allotment system worked? Did it fit or not fit with Plains Indians values? What were the main differences? What do you make of the names on the Arapaho allotment form (13.4d)?

7. The autobiographical recollections of Luther Standing Bear and Zitkala-Sa make powerful reading (13.5 and 13.6). What was life like for the Indians educated at Carlisle and other boarding schools? What options did they have? What did they find positive and negative about their education? What differences exist in the accounts by Standing Bear and Zitkala-Sa? To what extent do they preserve their cultural values and to what extent are they made into white Americans? How are father and son different (13.5b)?

8. What obvious differences do you see in the before-and-after photographs of the first class of young Indian people at Carlisle (13.7a and b)? How do you react to these pictures? Look at their faces. How do you respond to the photograph of Two Strike's family (13.7c)? How many symbols of nationhood do you find in the photo? To what extent are the members of this family "Indian" and to what extent "white"?

9. Study each of Wo-Haw's pictographs. What do you see? What do you learn about male warrior culture for the Kiowa? What do you learn about the division of roles between men and women? (There are two men and two women in *Skinning a Buffalo*.) What is Wo-Haw's message in the *Classroom* drawing? What is the significance of the figure to the right? Is he disappearing or not going away? What is his message in *Self-Portrait*? Remember that breath has special spiritual significance for Plains Indians; is the figure in the middle welcoming or warding off the animal to his left? There are many valid interpretations here, and no clear answers.

10. What do you conclude about the effectiveness of white policies in assaulting the Plains Indians' lands and cultures? Which policies do you think worked best? Which worked least well? What evidences do you see of the clash of values between the two cultures?

11. To what extent did the Indians accommodate to white culture and values, and to what extent were they successful in preserving their own?

→ DOCUMENT 13.1 ←

Treaty of Fort Laramie between the United States and the Sioux (Lakota), 1868, in Charles J. Kappler, ed., *Indian Treaties, 1778–1883* (New York, 1972), pp. 998–1005.

Treaty with the Sioux—Brulé, Oglala, Miniconjou, Yanktonai, Hunkpapa, Blackfeet, Cuthead, Two Kettle, Sans Arcs, and Santee—and Arapaho, 1868.

Apr. 29, 1868.
15 Stats., 635.
Ratified. Feb. 16, 1869.
Proclaimed, Feb. 24, 1869.

Articles of a treaty made and concluded by and between Lieutenant-General William T. Sherman, General William S. Harney, General Alfred H. Terry, General C. C. Augur, J. B. Henderson, Nathaniel G. Taylor, John B. Sanborn, and Samuel F. Tappan, duly appointed commissioners on the part of the United States, and the different bands of the Sioux Nation of Indians, by their chiefs and head-men, whose names are hereto subscribed, they being duly authorized to act in the premises.

War to cease and peace to be kept.

ARTICLE 1. From this day forward all war between the parties to this agreement shall forever cease. The Government of the United States desires peace, and its honor is hereby pledged to keep it. The Indians desire peace, and they now pledge their honor to maintain it.

Offenders against the Indians to be arrested, etc.

If bad men among the whites, or among other people subject to the authority of the United States, shall commit any wrong upon the person or property of the Indians, the United States will, upon proof made to the agent and forwarded to the Commissioner of Indian Affairs at Washington City, proceed at once to cause the offender to be arrested and punished according to the laws of the United States, and also re-imburse the injured person for the loss sustained.

Wrongdoers against the whites to be punished.

If bad men among the Indians shall commit a wrong or depredation upon the person or property of any one, white, black, or Indian, subject to the authority of the United States, and at peace therewith, the Indians herein named solemnly agree that they will, upon proof made to their agent and notice by him, deliver up the wrong-doer to the United States, to be tried and punished according to its laws; and in case they wilfully refuse so to do, the person injured shall be re-imbursed for his loss from the annuities or other moneys due or to become due to them under this or other treaties made with the United States. And the President, on advising with the Commissioner of Indian Affairs, shall prescribe such rules and regulations for ascertaining damages under the provisions of this article as in his judgment may be proper. But no one sustaining loss while violating the provisions of this treaty or the laws of the United States shall be re-imbursed therefor.

Damages.

Reservation boundaries.

ARTICLE 2. The United States agrees that the following district of country, to wit, viz: commencing on the east bank of the Missouri River where the forty-sixth parallel of north latitude crosses the same, thence along low-water mark down said east bank to a point opposite where the northern line of the State of Nebraska strikes the river, thence west across said river, and along the northern line of Nebraska to the one hundred and fourth degree of longitude west from Greenwich, thence north on said meridian to a point where the forty-sixth parallel of north latitude intercepts the same, thence due east along said parallel to the place of beginning; and in addition thereto, all existing reservations on the east bank of said river shall be, and the same is, set apart for the absolute and undisturbed use and occupation of the Indians herein named, and for such other friendly tribes or individual Indians as from time to time they may be willing, with the consent of the United States, to admit amongst them; and the United States now solemnly agrees that no persons except those herein designated and authorized so to do, and except such officers, agents, and employés of the Government as may be authorized to enter upon Indian reservations in discharge of duties enjoined by law, shall ever be permitted to pass over, settle upon, or reside in the territory described in this article, or in such territory as may be added to this reservation for the use of said Indians, and henceforth they will and do hereby relinquish all claims or right in and to any portion of the United States or Territories, except such as is embraced within the limits aforesaid, and except as hereinafter provided.

Certain persons not to enter or reside thereon.

Additional arable land to be added, if, etc.

ARTICLE 3. If it should appear from actual survey or other satisfactory examination of said tract of land that it contains less than one hundred and sixty acres of tillable land for each person who, at the time, may be authorized to reside on it under the provisions of this treaty, and a very considerable number of such persons shall be disposed to commence cultivating the soil as farmers, the United States agrees to set apart, for the use of said Indians, as herein provided, such additional quantity of arable land, adjoining to said reservation, or as near to the same as it can be obtained, as may be required to provide the necessary amount. . . .

Agent's residence, office, and duties.

ARTICLE 5. The United States agrees that the agent for said Indians shall in the future make his home at the agency-building; that he shall reside among them, and keep an office open at all times for the purpose of prompt and diligent inquiry into such matters of complaint by and against the Indians as may be presented for investigation under the provisions of their treaty stipulations, as also for the faithful discharge of other duties enjoined on him by law. In all cases of depredation on person or property he shall cause the evidence to be taken in writing and forwarded, together with his findings, to the Commissioner of Indian Affairs, whose decision, subject to the revision of the Secretary of the Interior, shall be binding on the parties to this treaty.

Heads of families may select lands for farming.

ARTICLE 6. If any individual belonging to said tribes of Indians, or legally incorporated with them, being the head of a family, shall desire to commence farming, he shall have the privilege to select, in the presence and with the assistance of the agent then in charge, a tract of land within said reservation, not exceeding three hundred and twenty acres in extent, which tract, when so selected, certified, and recorded in the "land-book," as herein directed, shall cease to be held in common, but the same may be occupied and held in the exclusive possession of the person selecting it, and of his family, so long as he or they may continue to cultivate it.

Others may select land for cultivation.

Any person over eighteen years of age, not being the head of a family, may in like manner select and cause to be certified to him or her, for purposes of cultivation, a quantity of land not exceeding eighty acres in extent, and thereupon be entitled to the exclusive possession of the same as above directed.

Certificates.

For each tract of land so selected a certificate, containing a description thereof and the name of the person selecting it, with a certificate endorsed thereon that the same has been recorded, shall be delivered to the party entitled to it, by the agent, after the same shall have been recorded by him in a book to be kept in his office, subject to inspection, which said book shall be known as the "Sioux Land-Book." . . .

Education.

ARTICLE 7. In order to insure the civilization of the Indians entering into this treaty, the necessity of education is admitted, especially of such of them as are or may be settled on said agricultural reservations, and they therefore pledge themselves to compel their children, male and female, between the ages of six and sixteen years, to attend school; and it is hereby made the duty of the agent for said Indians to see that this stipulation is strictly complied with; and the United States agrees that for every thirty children between said ages who can be induced or compelled to attend school, a house shall be provided and a teacher competent to teach the elementary branches of an English education shall be furnished, who will reside among said Indians, and faithfully discharge his or her duties as a teacher. The provisions of this article to continue for not less than twenty years.

Children to attend school.

Schoolhouses and teachers.

Seeds and agricultural implements.

ARTICLE 8. When the head of a family or lodge shall have selected lands and received his certificate as above directed, and the agent shall be satisfied that he intends in good faith to commence cultivating the soil for a living, he shall be entitled to receive seeds and agricultural implements for the first year, not exceeding in value one hundred dollars, and for each succeeding year he shall continue to farm, for a period of three years more, he shall be entitled to receive seeds and implements as aforesaid, not exceeding in value twenty-five dollars.

Instructions in farming.

And it is further stipulated that such persons as commence farming shall receive instruction from the farmer herein provided for, and whenever more than one hundred persons shall enter upon the cultivation of the soil, a second blacksmith shall be provided, with such iron, steel, and other material as may be needed.

Second blacksmith.

Physician, farmer, etc., may be withdrawn.

ARTICLE 9. At any time after ten years from the making of this treaty, the United States shall have the privilege of withdrawing the physician, farmer, blacksmith, carpenter, engineer, and miller herein provided for, but in case of such withdrawal, an additional sum thereafter of ten thousand dollars per annum shall be devoted to the education of said Indians, and the Commissioner of Indian Affairs shall, upon careful inquiry into their condition, make such rules and regulations for the expenditure of said sum as will best promote the educational and moral improvement of said tribes.

Additional appropriation in such cases.

Delivery of goods in lieu of money or other annuities.

ARTICLE 10. In lieu of all sums of money or other annuities provided to be paid to the Indians herein named, under any treaty or treaties heretofore made, the United States agrees to deliver at the agency-house on the reservation herein named, on or before the first day of August of each year, for thirty years, the following articles, to wit:

Clothing.

For each male person over fourteen years of age, a suit of good substantial woolen clothing, consisting of coat, pantaloons, flannel shirt, hat, and a pair of home-made socks.

For each female over twelve years of age, a flannel skirt, or the goods necessary to make it, a pair of woolen hose, twelve yards of calico, and twelve yards of cotton domestics.

For the boys and girls under the ages named, such flannel and cotton goods as may be needed to make each a suit as aforesaid, together with a pair of woolen hose for each.

Census.

And in order that the Commissioner of Indian Affairs may be able to estimate properly for the articles herein named, it shall be the duty of the agent each year to forward to him a full and exact census of the Indians, on which the estimate from year to year can be based.

Other necessary articles.

And in addition to the clothing herein named, the sum of ten dollars for each person entitled to the beneficial effects of this treaty shall be annually appropriated for a period of thirty years, while such persons roam and hunt, and twenty dollars for each person who engages in farming, to be used by the Secretary of the Interior in the purchase of such articles as from time to time the condition and necessities of the Indians may indicate to be proper. And if within the thirty years, at any time, it shall appear that the amount of money needed for clothing under this article can be appropriated to better uses for the Indians named herein, Congress may, by law, change the appropriation to other purposes; but in no event shall the amount of this appropriation be withdrawn or discontinued for the period named. And the President shall annually detail an officer of the Army to be present and attest the delivery of all the goods herein named to the Indians, and he shall inspect and report on the quantity and quality of the goods and the manner of their delivery. And it is hereby expressly stipulated that each Indian over the age of four years, who shall have removed to and settled permanently upon said reservation and complied with the stipulations of this treaty, shall be entitled to receive from the United States, for the period of four years after he shall have settled upon said reservation, one pound of meat and one pound of flour per day, provided the Indians cannot furnish their own subsistence at an earlier date. And it is further stipulated that the United States will furnish and deliver to each lodge of Indians or family of persons legally incorporated with them, who shall remove to the reservation herein described and commence farming, one good American cow, and one good well-broken pair of American oxen within sixty days after such lodge or family shall have so settled upon said reservation.

Appropriation to continue for thirty years.

Army officer to attend the delivery.

Meat and flour.

Cows and oxen.

Right to occupy territory outside of the reservation surrendered.

ARTICLE 11. In consideration of the advantages and benefits conferred by this treaty, and the many pledges of friendship by the United States, the tribes who are parties to this agreement hereby stipulate that they will relinquish all right to occupy permanently the territory outside their reservation as herein defined, but yet reserve the right to hunt on any lands north of North Platte, and on the Republican Fork of the Smoky Hill River, so long as the buffalo may range thereon in such numbers as to justify the chase. And they, the said Indians, further expressly agree:

Right to hunt reserved.

Agreements as to railroads.

1st. That they will withdraw all opposition to the construction of the railroads now being built on the plains.

2d. That they will permit the peaceful construction of any railroad not passing over their reservation as herein defined.

Emigrants, etc.

3d. That they will not attack any persons at home, or travelling, nor molest or disturb any wagon-trains, coaches, mules, or cattle belonging to the people of the United States, or to persons friendly therewith.

Women and children.

4th. They will never capture, or carry off from the settlements, white women or children.

5th. They will never kill or scalp white men, nor attempt to do them harm.

Pacific Railroad, wagon roads, etc.

6th. They withdraw all pretence of opposition to the construction of the railroad now being built along the Platte River and westward to the Pacific Ocean, and they will not in future object to the construction of railroads, wagon-roads, mail-stations, or other works of utility or necessity, which may be ordered or permitted by the laws of the United States. But should such roads or other works be constructed on the lands of their reservation, the Government will pay the tribe whatever amount of damage may be assessed by three disinterested commissioners to be appointed by the President for that purpose, one of said commissioners to be a chief or head-man of the tribe.

Damages for crossing their reservation.

Military posts and roads.

7th. They agree to withdraw all opposition to the military posts or roads now established south of the North Platte River, or that may be established, not in violation of treaties heretofore made or hereafter to be made with any of the Indian tribes.

No treaty for cession of reservation to be valid unless, etc.

ARTICLE 12. No treaty for the cession of any portion or part of the reservation herein described which may be held in common shall be of any validity or force as against the said Indians, unless executed and signed by at least three-fourths of all the adult male Indians, occupying or interested in the same; and no cession by the tribe shall be understood or construed in such manner as to deprive, without his consent, any individual member of the tribe of his rights to any tract of land selected by him, as provided in article 6 of this treaty.

United States to furnish physician, teachers, etc.

ARTICLE 13. The United States hereby agrees to furnish annually to the Indians the physician, teachers, carpenter, miller, engineer, farmer, and blacksmiths as herein contemplated, and that such appropriations shall be made from time to time, on the estimates of the Secretary of the Interior, as will be sufficient to employ such persons.

Presents for crops.

ARTICLE 14. It is agreed that the sum of five hundred dollars annually, for three years from date, shall be expended in presents to the ten persons of said tribe who in the judgment of the agent may grow the most valuable crops for the respective year.

Reservation to be permanent home of tribes.

ARTICLE 15. The Indians herein named agree that when the agency-house or other buildings shall be constructed on the reservation named, they will regard said reservation their permanent home, and they will make no permanent settlement elsewhere; but they shall have the right, subject to the conditions and modifications of this treaty, to hunt, as stipulated in Article 11 hereof.

Unceded Indian territory.

ARTICLE 16. The United States hereby agrees and stipulates that the country north of the North Platte River and east of the summits of the Big Horn Mountains shall be held and considered to be unceded Indian territory, and also stipulates and agrees that no white person or persons shall be permitted to settle upon or occupy any portion of the same; or without the consent of the Indians first had and obtained, to pass through the same; and it is further agreed by the United States that within ninety days after the conclusion of peace with all the bands of the Sioux Nation, the military posts now established in the territory in this article named shall be abandoned, and that the road leading to them and by them to the settlements in the Territory of Montana shall be closed.

Not to be occupied by whites, etc.

Effect of this treaty upon former treaties.

ARTICLE 17. It is hereby expressly understood and agreed by and between the respective parties to this treaty that the execution of this treaty and its ratification by the United States Senate shall have the effect, and shall be construed as abrogating and annulling all treaties and agreements heretofore entered into between the respective parties hereto, so far as such treaties and agreements obligate the United States to furnish and provide money, clothing, or other articles of property to such Indians and bands of Indians as become parties to this treaty, but no further.

In testimony of all which, we, the said commissioners, and we, the chiefs and headmen of the Brulé band of the Sioux nation, have hereunto set our hands and seals at Fort Laramie, Dakota Territory, this twenty-ninth day of April, in the year one thousand eight hundred and sixty-eight.

N. G. Taylor, [SEAL.]
W. T. Sherman, [SEAL.]
Lieutenant-General.
Wm. S. Harney, [SEAL.]
Brevet Major-General U. S. Army.
John B. Sanborn, [SEAL.]
S. F. Tappan, [SEAL.]
C. C. Augur, [SEAL.]
Brevet Major-General.
Alfred H. Terry, [SEAL.]
Brevet Major-General U. S. Army.

Attest:
A. S. H. White. Secretary.

Executed on the part of the Brulé band of Sioux by the chiefs and headmen whose names are hereto annexed, they being thereunto duly authorized, at Fort Laramie, D. T., the twenty-ninth day of April, in the year A. D. 1868.

Ma-za-pon-kaska, his x mark, Iron Shell. [SEAL.]
Wah-pat-shah, his x mark, Red Leaf. [SEAL.]
Hah-sah-pah, his x mark, Black Horn. [SEAL.]
Zin-tah-gah-lat-skah, his x mark, Spotted Tail. [SEAL.]
Zin-tah-skah, his x mark, White Tail. [SEAL.]
Me-wah-tah-ne-ho-skah, his x mark, Tall Mandas. [SEAL.]
She-cha-chat-kah, his x mark, Bad Left Hand. [SEAL.]
No-mah-no-pah, his x mark, Two and Two. [SEAL.]
Tah-tonka-skah, his x mark, White Bull. [SEAL.]
Con-ra-washta, his x mark, Pretty Coon. [SEAL.]
Ha-cah-cah-she-chah, his x mark, Bad Elk. [SEAL.]
Wa-ha-ka-zah-ish-tah, his x mark, Eye Lance. [SEAL.]
Ma-to-ha-ke-tah, his x mark, Bear that looks behind. [SEAL.]
Bella-tonka-tonka, his x mark, Big Partisan. [SEAL.]
Mah-to-ho-honka, his x mark, Swift Bear. [SEAL.]
To-wis-ne, his x mark, Cold Place. [SEAL.]
Ish-tah-skah, his x mark, White Eyes. [SEAL.]
Ma-ta-loo-zah, his x mark, Fast Bear. [SEAL.]
As-hah-kah-nah-zhe, his x mark, Standing Elk. [SEAL.]
Can-te-te-ki-ya, his x mark, The Brave Heart. [SEAL.]
Shunka-shaton, his x mark, Day Hawk. [SEAL.]
Tatanka-wakon, his x mark, Sacred Bull. [SEAL.]
Mapia shaton, his x mark, Hawk Cloud. [SEAL.]
Ma-sha-a-ow, his x mark, Stands and Comes. [SEAL.]
Shon-ka-ton-ka, his x mark, Big Dog. [SEAL.]

Attest:

Ashton S. H. White, secretary of commission.
George B. Withs, phonographer to commission.
Geo. H. Holtzman.
John D. Howland.
James C. O'Connor.
Chas. E. Guern, interpreter.
Leon F. Pallardy, interpreter.
Nicholas Janis, interpreter.

Execution by the Ogallalah band.

Executed on the part of the Ogallalah band of Sioux by the chiefs and headmen whose names are hereto subscribed, they being thereunto duly authorized, at Fort Laramie, the twenty-fifth day of May, in the year A. D. 1868.

Tah-shun-ka-co-qui-pah, his x mark, Man-afraid-of-his-horses. [SEAL.]
Sha-ton-skah, his x mark, White Hawk. [SEAL.]
Oh-wah-she-cha, his x mark, Bad Wound. [SEAL.]
Pah-gee, his x mark, Grass. [SEAL.]
Wah-non-reh-che-geh, his x mark, Ghost Heart. [SEAL.]
Con-reeh, his x mark, Crow. [SEAL.]
Oh-he-te-kah, his x mark, The Brave. [SEAL.]
Tah-ton-kah-he-yo-ta-kah, his x mark, Sitting Bull. [SEAL.]
Shon-ka-oh-wah-mon-ye, his x mark, Whirlwind Dog. [SEAL.]
Ha-hah-kah-tah-miech, his x mark, Poor Elk. [SEAL.]
Wam-bu-lee-wah-kon, his x mark, Medicine Eagle. [SEAL.]
Chon-gah-ma-he-to-hans-ka, his x mark, High Wolf. [SEAL.]
Wah-se-chun-ta-shun-kah, his x mark,American Horse. [SEAL.]
Mah-hah-mah-ha-mak-near, his x mark,Man that walks under the ground. [SEAL.]
Mah-to-tow-pah, his x mark, Four Bears. [SEAL.]
Ma-to-wee-sha-kta, his x mark, One that kills the bear. [SEAL.]
Oh-tah-kee-toka-wee-chakta, his x mark, One that kills in a hard place. [SEAL.]
Tah-ton-kah-ta-miech, his x mark, The poor Bull. [SEAL.]
Oh-huns-ee-ga-non-sken, his x mark, Mad Shade. [SEAL.]
Shah-ton-oh-nah-om-minne-ne-oh-minne, his x mark, Whirling Hawk. [SEAL.]
Sha-ton-sapah, his x mark, Black Hawk. [SEAL.]
E-ga-mon-ton-ka-sapah, his x mark, Black Tiger. [SEAL.]
Mah-to-chun-ka-oh, his x mark, Bear's Back. [SEAL.]
Che-ton-wee-koh, his x mark, Fool Hawk. [SEAL.]
Wah-hoh-ke-za-ah-hah, his x mark, One that has the lance. [SEAL.]
Shon-gah-manni-toh-tan-ka-seh, his x mark, Big Wolf Foot. [SEAL.]
Eh-ton-kah, his x mark, Big Mouth. [SEAL.]
Ma-pah-che-tah, his x mark, Bad Hand. [SEAL.]
Wah-ke-yun-shah, his x mark, Red Thunder. [SEAL.]
Wak-sah, his x mark, One that Cuts Off. [SEAL.]
Cham-nom-qui-yah, his x mark, One that Presents the Pipe. [SEAL.]
Wah-ke-ke-yan-puh-tah, his x mark, Fire Thunder. [SEAL.]
Mah-to-nonk-pah-ze, his x mark, Bear with Yellow Ears. [SEAL.]
Con-ree-teh-ka, his x mark, The Little Crow. [SEAL.]
He-hup-pah-toh. his x mark, The Blue War Club. [SEAL.]
Shon-kee-toh, his x mark, The Blue Horse. [SEAL.]
Wam-Balla-oh-con-quo, his x mark, Quick Eagle. [SEAL.]
Ta-tonka-suppa, his x mark, Black Bull. [SEAL.]
Moh-to-ha-she-na, his x mark, The Bear Hide. [SEAL.]

Attest:
S. E. Ward.
Jas. C. O'Connor.
J. M. Sherwood.
W. C. Slicer.
Sam Deon.
H. M. Matthews.
Joseph Bissonette, interpreter.
Nicholas Janis, interpreter.
Lefroy Jott, interpreter.
Antoine Janis, interpreter.

Execution by the Minneconjon band.

Executed on the part of the Minneconjon band of Sioux by the chiefs and headmen whose names are hereto subscribed, they being thereunto duly authorized.

At Fort Laramie, D. T., May 26, '68, 13 names.

Heh-won-ge-chat, [SEAL.]
his x mark, One Horn.

Oh-pon-ah-tah-e-manne, [SEAL.]
his x mark, The Elk that bellows Walking.

At Fort Laramie, D. T., May 25, '68, 2 names.

Heh-ho-lah-reh-cha-skah, [SEAL.]
his x mark, Young White Bull.

Wah-chah-chum-kah-coh-kee-pah, his x mark, One that is afraid of Shield. [SEAL.]
He-hon-ne-shakta, his x mark, The Old Owl. [SEAL.]
Moc-pe-a-toh, his x mark, Blue Cloud. [SEAL.]
Oh-pong-ge-le-skah, his x mark, Spotted Elk. [SEAL.]
Tah-tonk-ka-hon-ke-schne, his x mark, Slow Bull. [SEAL.]
Shonk-a-nee-shah-shah-a-tah-pe, his x mark, The Dog Chief. [SEAL.]
Ma-to-tah-ta-tonk-ka, his x mark, Bull Bear. [SEAL.]
Wom-beh-le-ton-kah, his x mark, The Big Eagle. [SEAL.]
Ma-toh-eh-schne-lah, his x mark, The Lone Bear. [SEAL.]
Mah-toh-ke-su-yah, his x mark, The One who Remembers the Bear. [SEAL.]
Ma-toh-oh-he-to-keh, his x mark, The Brave Bear. [SEAL.]
Eh-che-ma-heh, his x mark, The Runner. [SEAL.]
Ti-ki-ya, his x mark, The Hard. [SEAL.]
He-ma-za, his x mark, Iron Horn. [SEAL.]

Attest:

Jas. C. O'Connor.
Wm. H. Brown.
Nicholas Janis, interpreter.
Antoine Janis, interpreter.

Execution by the Yanctonans band.

Executed on the part of the Yanctonais band of Sioux by the chiefs and headmen whose names are hereto subscribed, they being thereunto duly authorized.

Mah-to-non-pah, his x mark, Two Bears. [SEAL.]
Ma-to-hna-skin-ya, his x mark, Mad Bear. [SEAL.]
He-o-pu-za, his x mark, Louzy. [SEAL.]
Ah-ke-che-tah-che-ca-dan, his x mark, Little Soldier. [SEAL.]
Mah-to-e-tan-chan, his x mark, Chief Bear. [SEAL.]
Cu-wi-h-win, his x mark, Rotten Stomach. [SEAL.]
Skun-ka-we-tko, his x mark, Fool Dog. [SEAL.]
Ish-ta-sap-pah, his x mark, Black Eye. [SEAL.]
Ih-tan-chan, his x mark, The Chief. [SEAL.]
I-a-wi-ca-ka, his x mark, The one who Tells the Truth. [SEAL.]
Ah-ke-che-tah, his x mark, The Soldier. [SEAL.]

Ta-shi-na-gi, his x mark, Yellow Robe. [SEAL.]
Nah-pe-ton-ka, his x mark, Big Hand. [SEAL.]
Chan-tee-we-kto, his x mark, Fool Heart. [SEAL.]
Hoh-gan-sah-pa, his x mark, Black Catfish. [SEAL.]
Mah-to-wah-kan, his x mark, Medicine Bear. [SEAL.]
Shun-ka-kan-sha, his x mark, Red Horse. [SEAL.]
Wan-rode, his x mark, The Eagle. [SEAL.]
Can-hpi-sa-pa, his x mark, Black Tomahawk. [SEAL.]
Tall Bear, his x mark. [SEAL.]
Top Man, his x mark. [SEAL.]
Neva, his x mark. [SEAL.]
The Wounded Bear, his x mark. [SEAL.]
Thirlwind, his x mark. [SEAL.]
The Fox, his x mark. [SEAL.]
The Dog Big Mouth, his x mark. [SEAL.]
Spotted Wolf, his x mark. [SEAL.]
Sorrel Horse, his x mark. [SEAL.]
Black Coal, his x mark. [SEAL.]
Big Wolf, his x mark. [SEAL.]
Knock-knee, his x mark. [SEAL.]
Black Crow, his x mark. [SEAL.]
The Lone Old Man, his x mark. [SEAL.]

War-he-le-re, his x mark, Yellow Eagle. [SEAL.]
Cha-ton-che-ca, his x mark, Small Hawk, or Long Fare. [SEAL.]
Shu-ger-mon-e-too-ha-ska, his x mark, Tall Wolf. [SEAL.]
Ma-to-u-tah-kah, his x mark, Sitting Bear. [SEAL.]
Hi-ha-cah-ge-na-skene, his x mark, Mad Elk. [SEAL.]
Arapahoes:
Little Chief, his x mark. [SEAL.]
Paul, his x mark. [SEAL.]
Black Bull, his x mark. [SEAL.]
Big Track, his x mark. [SEAL.]
The Foot, his x mark. [SEAL.]
Black White, his x mark. [SEAL.]
Yellow Hair, his x mark. [SEAL.]
Little Shield, his x mark. [SEAL.]
Black Bear, his x mark. [SEAL.]
Wolf Mocassin, his x mark. [SEAL.]
Big Robe, his x mark. [SEAL.]
Wolf Chief, his x mark. [SEAL.]

Witnesses:

Robt. P. McKibbin, captain, Fourth Infantry, brevet lieutenant-colonel, U. S. Army, commanding Fort Laramie.
Wm. H. Powell, brevet major, captain, Fourth Infantry.
Henry W. Patterson, captain, Fourth Infantry.
Theo. E. True, second lieutenant, Fourth Infantry.
W. G. Bullock.
Chas. E. Guern, special Indian interpreter for the peace commission.

Oh-wah-she-cha, his x mark, Bad Wound. [SEAL.]
Pah-gee, his x mark, Grass. [SEAL.]
Wah-non-reh-che-geh, his x mark, Ghost Heart. [SEAL.]
Con-reeh, his x mark, Crow. [SEAL.]
Oh-he-te-kah, his x mark, The Brave. [SEAL.]
Tah-ton-kah-he-yo-ta-kah, his x mark, Sitting Bull. [SEAL.]
Shon-ka-oh-wah-mon-ye, his x mark, Whirlwind Dog. [SEAL.]
Ha-hah-kah-tah-miech, his x mark, Poor Elk. [SEAL.]
Wam-bu-lee-wah-kon, his x mark, Medicine Eagle. [SEAL.]
Chon-gah-ma-he-to-hans-ka, his x mark, High Wolf. [SEAL.]
Wah-se-chun-ta-shun-kah, his x mark, American Horse. [SEAL.]
Mah-hah-mah-ha-mak-near, his x mark, Man that walks under the ground. [SEAL.]
Mah-to-tow-pah, his x mark, Four Bears. [SEAL.]
Ma-to-wee-sha-kta, his x mark, One that kills the bear. [SEAL.]
Oh-tah-kee-toka-wee-chakta, his x mark, One that kills in a hard place. [SEAL.]
Tah-ton-kah-ta-miech, his x mark, The poor Bull. [SEAL.]

→ DOCUMENT 13.2 ←

Railroad advertisement, "To the Gold Fields of the Black Hills," 1870s, in Charles Hall, ed., *Documents of Wyoming Heritage* (Cheyenne, 1976). The Newberry Library.

TO THE GOLD FIELDS
—OF THE—
BLACK HILLS!
VIA
OMAHA & SIDNEY, or CHEYENNE.

THE
UNION PACIFIC R. R.
OFFERS THE QUICKEST, SAFEST AND MOST RELIABLE ROUTE
TO THE NEW ELDORADO!

By it you avoid the SNOWS of the FAR NORTH, the BAD LANDS of Eastern and Northern Dakota, and the dangers and delays of Missouri River navigation. By it you secure all rail transportation to Sidney or Cheyenne, from which points fast Stage Lines convey you to the Hills over good Government roads and under the protection of the military stationed along the route.

These are the ONLY LINES running STAGES into the Hills. These are the routes by which nine-tenths of the people now in the Hills have gone there. These routes are used EXCLUSIVELY by business men and others from the Hills returning to the States for the purchase of goods, etc. These are the only routes along which Telegraph Lines to the Hills have been constructed. The only routes over which Government mails are carried. The only routes open the whole year. The only routes having Stage Stations, Supply Depots, Wood, Water and Grass, along their whole length.

ALL THE GOLD

(amounting to millions), which has been shipped from the Hills has come by these routes, they being the only ones by which it could be SAFELY transported. These are the only routes that offer First Class Transportation through to the Hills. With good roads and weather, the Stage trip can be made in

48 HOURS!

These routes are the QUICKEST, SAFEST, BEST, and taking into account, Speed, Comfort and Safety, they are

BY FAR THE CHEAPEST!

The Cheyenne Line is now running Daily Stages and has ample equipment for a double daily service when needed. The Sidney Line will run Daily Stages after April 15th, and will increase its facilities as rapidly as may be required. The wagon transportation from these points is sufficient for any number of third class passengers that may offer.

These are the ONLY routes which it has been possible to operate during the winter. The short season during which other routes can be kept open will prevent the investment there of the large amounts of capital in Stages, Stations, Supply Depots, Bridges, &c., necessary to enable parties going to the Hills to make the trip without hardship.

DO NOT BE DECEIVED!

By circulars of other routes offering lower rates or equal accommodations. Stage transportation, first and second class, with rates named for each, was advertised throughout the country, during the whole of last year, and is still advertised, *by two routes on which not a single Stage has ever been run.* IT IS NOT POSSIBLE to give on routes open only during the summer months equal accommodations for the same money with those furnished by lines in operation the entire year.

Through Tickets and the Reduced Through Rates, via either Sidney or Cheyenne, can ONLY BE SECURED by buying tickets via OMAHA and the

UNION PACIFIC RAILROAD!

Parties not ticketed via Omaha must pay local Stage Fare from Sidney or Cheyenne, as the Stage Companies have refused to accept any through tickets not sold over the Union Pacific Railroad, and have also declined to grant the reduced through rates to any person, except purchasers of through tickets over the U. P. R. R.

For further information, call on or address

I. S. HODSDON, General Agent, 60 Clark Street, Chicago.

F. KNOWLAND, General Agent, 287 Broadway, New York.

W. P. COOLEY, Traveling Agent, Chicago.

F. L. GRAMMER, Traveling Agent, New York.

Or, **THOS. L. KIMBALL,**
Gen'l Passenger and Ticket Agent, Omaha, Neb.

Omaha Republican Steam Print.

✧ DOCUMENT 13.3a ✧

Indian pictograph of heroic exploits, on buffalo hide, northern Plains, probably Cheyenne; the British Museum, Ethnography 917, in J. C. H. King, *First Peoples First Contacts: Native Peoples of North America* (Cambridge, MA, 1999), p. 266. ©The British Museum.

→ DOCUMENT 13.3b ←

Yanktonai Sioux pictograph, *Winter Count,* 1890–1891, Ethnography 1942, in J. C. H. King, *First Peoples First Contacts*, p. 266. © The British Museum.

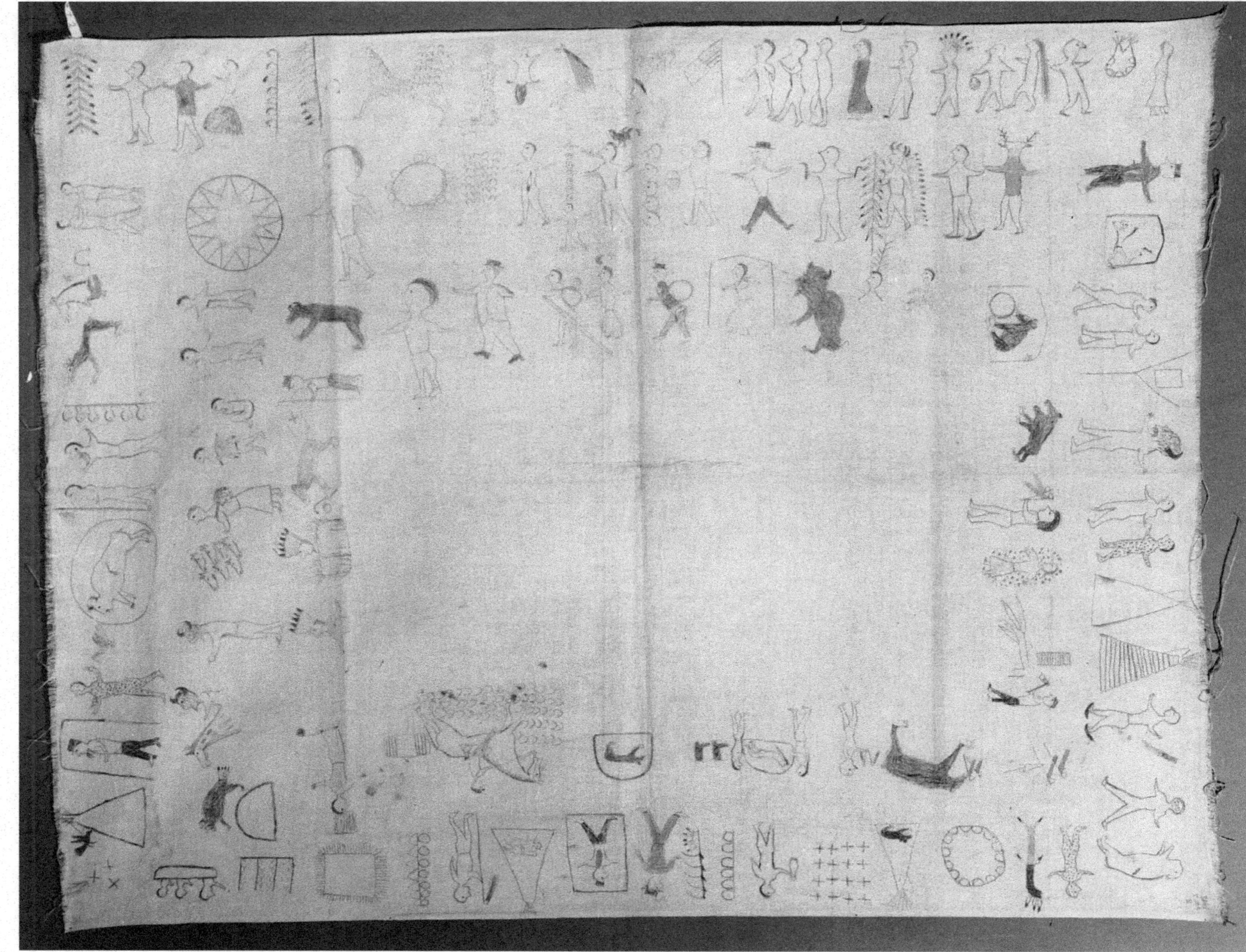

→ DOCUMENT 13.3c ←

Pictographic account of the Battle of Little Bighorn by the Miniconjou Lakota Sioux Chief Red Horse, June 25–26, 1876. National Anthropological Archives, Smithsonian Institution.

→ DOCUMENT 13.4a ←

Camping with the Sioux, Fieldwork Diary of Alice Cunningham Fletcher, September 24, and October 5, 1881. Records of the National Anthropological Archives, Washington, DC.

September 24, 1881

. . . The talk about the camp fire was serious. The future struggles of the Indians.

Wajapa—Grandfather a chief, father, leader of band. S.'s father succeeded. Five years ago the Omahas lived in a village, mud lodges. Now he has a fine farm. Two years since changed to citizen's dress, has sent daughter east to Miss Read's school. Indians think him hard hearted to send away a little girl. He says "No, I look to the future, I shall sleep easy when I die if my children are prepared to meet the struggle that is coming when they must—cope with the white settlers". His mind is alert and of a statesman like character, tho he is rather restless, made so by the uncertainty of Indian tenure of land. Indians love their land as no white man realizes, and will not part from it for any cause if possible to prevent it. Wajapa rides ahead, when the road is good he will sometimes make short cuts. When a distance off he will sing in the expressive Indian fashion. At every high hill he gallops to the top and then stands, he and his horse silhouetted against the clear blue sky. He picks out the way for us. The trails lie over the boundless, billowy prairie, like the marks of two fingers a little apart, drawn side by side. Often the ruts are deep and the gutter nearly perpendicular. It is a desolate wilderness, yet it is not without charm. On some of the high lands, for we are up and down all the time, we could see nearly one hundred miles, off into Dakota. Log houses, dirt roofs, clay walls, Dug out. Snakes made their way in. Mr. T. lying in bed once in a dugout saw a great snake crawl along the center beam.

We made our beds early before the dew began to fall and went to bed by 8.30 or earlier. My first night under the stars. I waken about midnight for the ground makes me ache very badly. The stars were wonderfully fine. The dew on my waterproof was in puddles. I had put my hat over my head for the cold was great. Orion was just coming up over the horizon. By turning over and taking a fresh side I fell asleep but pain wakened me again. Then I tried all sorts of ways and at last slept once more, when I wakened again I was thankful for the sight of the morning star. I watched and waited for the first grey light when I rose and began to dress. It was wet and cold but clear.

October 5, 1881

Wednesday A.M. Rainy again and we cant get on. Buffalo-chip is a Medicine man, has little positive humor, rather sober and dignified. A queer childish consciousness. He wears the scalp lock. This morning he took a stick and with queer mumblings, he raised it to and fro. This was to gain better weather. It is a strange thing to sit opposite and witness veritable, heathen performances. One realizes the power and gift of spiritual life by the blessed Lord. I needed to see all this to realize the verity of "I am the way, the truth and the life". The darkness and paucity of their mental life is pitiful. Buffalo-chip is far behind Wajapa who is free and blithe in comparison.

This A.M. I have been teaching Wajapa more arithmetic, addition by object lessons in plums, trying to make the figures a verity to him. One feels so sorry for them, so longs to broaden and deepen and brighten their life.

Deer are reported ahead. We are promised deer to eat, and I have asked for the antlers. By Indian rule the skin belongs to the owner of the gun. As Buffalo-chip owns the gun they will be his. The antlers are thrown away, so I may get mine.

Spotted Tail was made by the government, Head Chief. He was only a subordinate chief. This angered the people and also that he had a salary from Government, and was sustained by it against the Indians. Government aims to turn the soldier lodge into a police and it pays them a salary.

Spotted Tail received all the money from Government.

I sketched Wajapa's profile. When I said I was going to, he sprang up and said in his hearty, impulsive loud voice, "I will go and wash my face". I laughed, thinking it a joke, but it was not, he returned and his face glossy, his hair combed and shining and sat down by me. That was queer to experience. We had more arithmetic, while Buffalo-chip's wife went out and gathered Kinikinick and Buffalo-chip made a sort of screen to dry it on the sticks which had been stripped of the inner bark, and weaving in and out of the three prongs (Sketch)—split partly down the stick. Buffalo-chip says, that Rabbit says, "We use too much salt over the fire". In earnest, he said, "The Rabbit says, after".

→ DOCUMENT 13.4b ←

Act of Congress, the General Allotment Act (Dawes Act), 1887, in Francis Paul Prucha, ed., *Document of United States Indian Policy* (Lincoln, NE, 1975), pp. 171–174.

An act to provide for the allotment of lands in severalty to Indians on the various reservations, and to extend the protection of the laws of the United States and the Territories over the Indians, and for other purposes.

Be it enacted . . . , That in all cases where any tribe or band of Indians has been, or shall hereafter be, located upon any reservation created for their use,' either by treaty stipulation or by virtue of an act of Congress or executive order setting apart the same for their use, the President of the United States be, and he hereby is, authorized, whenever in his opinion any reservation or any part thereof of such Indians is advantageous for agricultural and grazing purposes, to cause said reservation, or any part thereof, to be surveyed, or resurveyed if necessary, and to allot the lands in said reservation in severalty to any Indian located thereon in quantities as follows:

To each head of a family, one-quarter of a section;

To each single person over eighteen years of age, one-eighth of a section;

To each orphan child under eighteen years of age, one-eighth of a section; and

To each other single person under eighteen years now living, or who may be born prior to the date of the order of the President directing an allotment of the lands embraced in any reservation, one-sixteenth of a section: *Provided,* That in case there is not sufficient land in any of said reservations to allot lands to each individual of the classes above named in quantities as above provided, the lands embraced in such reservation or reservations shall be allotted to each individual of each of said classes pro rata in accordance with the provisions of this act: *And provided further,* That where the treaty or act of Congress setting apart such reservation provides for the allotment of lands in severalty in quantities in excess of those herein provided, the President, in making allotments upon such reservation, shall allot the lands to each individual Indian belonging thereon in quantity as specified in such treaty or act: *And provided further,* That when the lands allotted are only valuable for grazing purposes, an additional allotment of such grazing lands, in quantities as above provided, shall be made to each individual.

SEC. 2. That all allotments set apart under the provisions of this act shall be selected by the Indians, heads of families selecting for their minor children, and the agents shall select for each orphan child, and in such manner as to embrace the improvements of the Indians making the selection. Where the improvements of two or more Indians have been made on the same legal subdivision of land, unless they shall otherwise agree, a provisional line may be run dividing said lands between them, and the amount to which each is entitled shall be equalized in the assignment of the remainder of the land to which they are entitled under this act: *Provided,* That if any one entitled to an allotment shall fail to make a selection within four years after the President shall direct that allotments may be made on a particular reservation, the Secretary of the Interior may direct the agent of such tribe or band, if such there be, and if there be no agent, then a special agent appointed for that purpose, to make a selection for such Indian, which selection shall be allotted as in cases where selections are made by the Indians, and patents shall issue in like manner.

SEC. 3. That the allotments provided for in this act shall be made by special agents appointed by the President for such purpose, and the agents in charge of the respective reservations on which the allotments are directed to be made, under such rules and regulations as the Secretary of the Interior may from time to time prescribe, and shall be certified by such agents to the Commissioner of Indian Affairs, in duplicate, one copy to be retained in the Indian Office and the other to be transmitted to the Secretary of the Interior for his action, and to be deposited in the General Land Office.

SEC. 4. That where any Indian not residing upon a reservation, or for whose tribe no reservation has been provided by treaty, act of Congress, or executive order, shall make settlement upon any surveyed or unsurveyed lands of the United States not otherwise appropriated, he or she shall be entitled, upon application to the local land-office for the district in which the lands are located, to have the same allotted to him or her, and to his or her children, in quantities and manner as provided in this act for Indians residing upon reservations; and when such settlement is made upon unsurveyed lands, the grant to such Indians shall be adjusted upon the survey of the lands so as to conform thereto; and patents shall be issued to them for such lands in the manner and with the restrictions as herein provided. And the fees to which the officers of such local land-office would have been entitled had such lands been entered under the general laws for the disposition of the public lands shall be paid to them, from any moneys in the Treasury of the United States not otherwise appropriated, upon a statement of an account in their behalf for such fees by the Commissioner of the General Land Office, and a certification of such account to the Secretary of the Treasury by the Secretary of the Interior.

SEC. 5. That upon the approval of the allotments provided for in this act by the Secretary of the Interior, he shall cause patents to issue therefor in the name of the allottees, which patents shall be of the legal effect, and declare that the United States does and will hold the land thus allotted, for the period of twenty-five years, in trust for the sole use and benefit of the Indian to whom such allotment shall have been made, or, in case of his decease, of his heirs according to the laws of the State or Territory where such land is located, and that at the expiration of said period the United States will convey the same by patent to said Indian, or his heirs as aforesaid, in fee, discharged of said trust and free of all charge or incumbrance whatsoever: *Provided,* That the President of the United States may in any case in his discretion extend the period. And if any conveyance shall be made of the lands set apart and allotted as herein provided, or any contract made touching the same, before the expiration of the time above mentioned, such conveyance or contract shall be absolutely null and void. . . . *And provided further,* That at any time after lands have been allotted to all the Indians of any tribe as herein provided, or sooner if in the opinion of the President it shall be for the best interests of said tribe, it shall be lawful for the Secretary of the Interior to negotiate with such Indian tribe for the purchase and release by said tribe, in conformity with the treaty or statute under which such reservation is held, of such portions of its reservation not allotted as such tribe shall, from time to time, consent to sell, on such terms and conditions as shall be considered just and equitable between the United States and said tribe of Indians, which purchase shall not be complete until ratified by Congress, and the form and manner of executing such release shall also be prescribed by Congress: *Provided however,* That all lands adapted to agriculture, with or without irrigation so sold or released to the United States by any Indian tribe shall be held by the United States for the sole purpose of securing homes to actual settlers and shall be disposed of by the United States to actual and bona fide settlers only in tracts not exceeding one hundred and sixty acres to any one person, on such terms as Congress shall prescribe, subject to grants which Congress may make in aid of education: *And provided further,* That no patents shall issue therefor except to the person so taking the same as and for a homestead, or his heirs, and after the expiration of five years occupancy thereof as such homestead; and any conveyance of said lands so taken as a homestead, or any contract touching the same, or lien thereon, created prior to the date of such patent, shall be null and void. And the sums agreed to be paid by the United States as purchase money for any portion of any such reservation shall be held in the Treasury of the United States for the sole use of the tribe or tribes of Indians; to whom such reservations belonged; and the same, with interest thereon at three per cent per annum, shall be at all times subject to appropriation by Congress for the education and civilization of such tribe or tribes of Indians or the members thereof. The patents aforesaid shall be recorded in the General Land Office, and afterward delivered, free of charge, to the allottee entitled thereto. And if any religious society or other organization is now occupying any of the public lands to which this act is applicable, for religious or educational work among the Indians, the Secretary of the Interior is hereby authorized to confirm such occupation to such society or organization, in quantity not exceeding one hundred and sixty acres in any one tract, so long as the same shall be so occupied, on such terms as he shall deem just; but nothing herein contained shall change or alter any claim of such society for religious or educational purposes heretofore granted by law. And hereafter in the employment of Indian police, or any other employes in the public service among any of the Indian tribes or bands affected by this act, and where Indians can perform the duties required, those Indians who have availed themselves of the provisions of this act and become citizens of the United States shall be preferred.

SEC. 6. That upon the completion of said allotments and the patenting of the lands to said allottees, each and every member of the respective bands or tribes of Indians to whom allotments have been made shall have the benefit of and be subject to the laws, both civil and criminal, of the State or Territory in which they may reside; and no Territory shall pass or enforce any law denying any such Indian within its jurisdiction the equal protection of the law. And every Indian born within the territorial limits of the United States to whom allotments shall have been made under the provisions of this act, or under any law or treaty, and every Indian born within the territorial limits of the United States who has voluntarily taken up, within said limits, his residence separate and apart from any tribe of Indians therein, and has adopted the habits of civilized life, is hereby declared to be a citizen of the United States, and is entitled to all the rights, privileges, and immunities of such citizens, whether said Indian has been or not, by birth or otherwise, a member of any tribe of Indians within the territorial limits of the United States without in any manner impairing or otherwise affecting the right of any such Indian to tribal or other property. . . .

→ DOCUMENT 13.4c ←

Map platting, Indian Allotments on the Rosebud Reservation, 1903, Records of the Bureau of Indian Affairs, National Archives, Washington; in Henry W. Hamilton and Jean Tyree Hamilton, *The Sioux of the Rosebud: A History in Pictures* (Norman: U. of Oklahoma Press, 1971), pp. 120–121

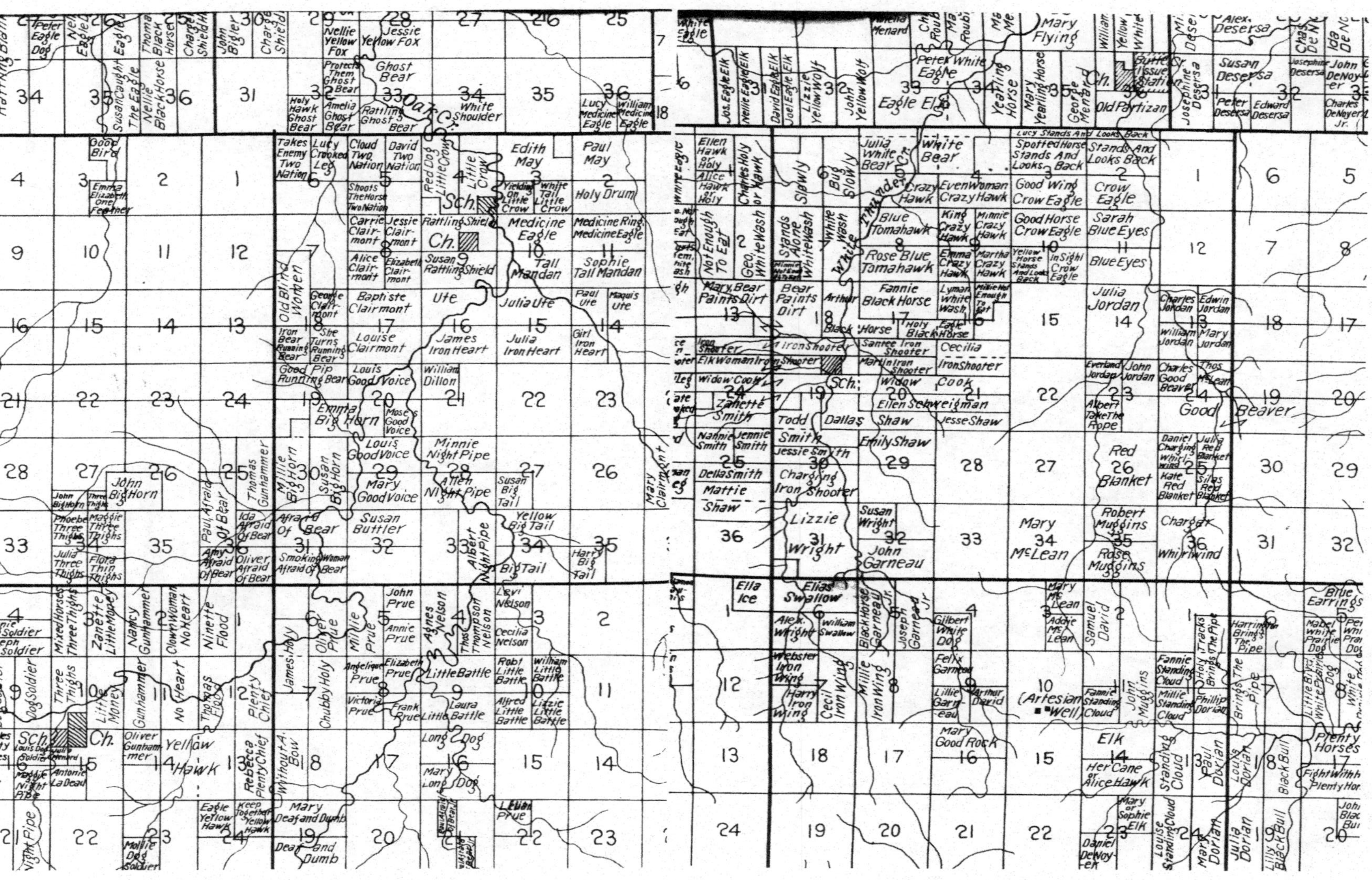

→ DOCUMENT 13.4d ←

Legal allotment certificate for William Shakespeare (War Bonnet), Shoshone Agency, 1904, in Charles "Pat" Hall, ed., *Documents of Wyoming Heritage* (Cheyenne: Wyoming Bicentennial Commission, 1976), p. 6.

Township Range 2 E W R M
Fremont County

NORTH

6	5	4	3	2	1
7	8	9	10	11	12
18	17	16	15	14	13
19	20	21	22	23	24
30	29	28	27	26	25
31	32	33	34	35	36

SOUTH

(5–149 b.)

No. 212

SHOSHONE AGENCY, WYO. Agency,

OCT 14 1904, 18

I hereby certify that William Shakespeare (War Bonnet), a member of the Arapaho tribe of Indians, has selected as his allotment of land for his minor child Thomas Shakespeare (White Shirt) under the provisions of the act of Congress approved February 8, 1887, the E½ SW¼ of Section 11

of Township 1 S., Range 2 E W.R.M. containing 80. ag acres subject to the approval of the Secretary of the Interior.

Selection No. 212, dated OCT 14 1904, 18

H. G. Nickerson
U. S. Special Agent to allot Lands to Indians.

16959 b—10 m

⇾ DOCUMENT 13.5a ⇽

Autobiographical narrative by Luther Standing Bear on his first days at the Carlisle (Pennsylvania) Indian School, in Luther Standing Bear, *Land of the Spotted Eagle* (Lincoln: U. of Nebraska Press, 1978), pp. 230–235. Reprinted from LAND OF THE SPOTTED EAGLE by Luther Standing Bear by permission of the University of Nebraska Press.

At the age of eleven years, ancestral life for me and my people was most abruptly ended without regard for our wishes, comforts, or rights in the matter. At once I was thrust into an alien world, into an environment as different from the one into which I had been born as it is possible to imagine, to remake myself, if I could, into the likeness of the invader.

By 1879, my people were no longer free, but were subjects confined on reservations under the rule of agents. One day there came to the agency a party of white people from the East. Their presence aroused considerable excitement when it became known that these people were school teachers who wanted some Indian boys and girls to take away with them to train as were white boys and girls.

Now, father was a 'blanket Indian,' but he was wise. He listened to the white strangers, their offers and promises that if they took his son they would care well for him, teach him how to read and write, and how to wear white man's clothes. But to father all this was just 'sweet talk,' and I know that it was with great misgivings that he left the decision to me and asked if I cared to go with these people. I, of course, shared with the rest of my tribe a distrust of the white people, so I know that for all my dear father's anxiety he was proud to hear me say 'Yes.' That meant that I was brave.

I could think of no reason why white people wanted Indian boys and girls except to kill them, and not having the remotest idea of what a school was, I thought we were going East to die. But so well had courage and bravery been trained into us that it became a part of our unconscious thinking and acting, and personal life was nothing when it came time to do something for the tribe. Even in our play and games we voluntarily put ourselves to various tests in the effort to grow brave and fearless, for it was most discrediting to be called *can'l wanka,* or a coward. Accordingly there were few cowards, most Lakota men preferring to die in the performance of some act of bravery than to die of old age. Thus, in giving myself up to go East I was proving to my father that he was honored with a brave son. In my decision to go, I gave up many things dear to the heart of a little Indian boy, and one of the things over which my child mind grieved was the thought of saying good-bye to my pony. I rode him as far as I could on the journey, which was to the Missouri River, where we took the boat. There we parted from our parents, and it was a heart-breaking scene, women and children weeping. Some of the children changed their minds and were unable to go on the boat, but for many who did go it was a final parting.

On our way to school we saw many white people, more than we ever dreamed existed, and the manner in which they acted when they saw us quite indicated their opinion of us. It was only about three years after the Custer battle, and the general opinion was that the Plains people merely infested the earth as nuisances, and our being there simply evidenced misjudgment on the part of Wakan Tanka. Whenever our train stopped at the railway stations, it was met by great numbers of white people who came to gaze upon the little Indian 'savages.' The shy little ones sat quietly at the car windows looking at the people who swarmed on the platform. Some of the children wrapped themselves in their blankets, covering all but their eyes. At one place we were taken off the train and marched a distance down the street to a restaurant. We walked down the street between two rows of uniformed men whom we called soldiers, though I suppose they were policemen. This must have been done to protect us, for it was surely known that we boys and girls could do no harm. Back of the rows of uniformed men stood the white people craning their necks, talking, laughing, and making a great noise. They yelled and tried to mimic us by giving what they thought were war-whoops. We did not like this, and some of the children were naturally very much frightened. I remember how I tried to crowd into the protecting midst of the jostling boys and girls. But we were all trying to be brave, yet going to what we thought would end in death at the hands of the white people whom we knew had no love for us. Back on the train the older boys sang brave songs in an effort to keep up their spirits and ours too. In my mind I often recall that scene—eighty-odd blanketed boys and girls marching down the street surrounded by a jeering, unsympathetic people whose only emotions were those of hate and fear; the conquerors looking upon the conquered. And no more understanding us than if we had suddenly been dropped from the moon.

At last at Carlisle the transforming, the 'civilizing' process began. It began with clothes. Never, no matter what our philosophy or spiritual quality, could we be civilized while wearing the moccasin and blanket. The task before us was not only that of accepting new ideas and adopting new manners, but actual physical changes and discomfort has to be borne uncomplainingly until the body adjusted itself to new tastes and habits. Our accustomed dress was taken and replaced with clothing that felt cumbersome and awkward. Against trousers and handkerchiefs we had a distinct feeling—they were unsanitary and the trousers kept us from breathing well. High collars, stiff-bosomed shirts, and suspenders fully three inches in width were uncomfortable, while leather boots caused actual suffering. We longed to go barefoot, but were told that the dew on the grass would give us colds. That was a new warning for us, for our mothers had never told us to beware of colds, and I remember as a child coming into the tipi with moccasins full of snow. Unconcernedly I would take them off my feet, pour out the snow, and put them on my feet again without any thought of sickness, for in that time colds, catarrh, bronchitis, and *la grippe* were unknown. But we were soon to know them. Then, red flannel undergarments were given us for winter wear, and for me, at least, discomfort grew into actual torture. I used to endure it as long as possible, then run upstairs and quickly take off the flannel garments and hide them. When inspection time came, I ran and put them on again, for I knew that if I were found disobeying the orders of the school I should be punished. My niece once asked me what it was that I disliked the most during those first bewildering days, and I said, 'red flannel.' Not knowing what I meant, she laughed, but I still remember those horrid, sticky garments which we had to wear next to the skin, and I still squirm and itch when I think of them. Of course, our hair was cut, and then there was much disapproval. But that was part of the transformation process and in some mysterious way long hair stood in the path of our development. For all the grumbling among the bigger boys, we soon had our heads shaven. How strange I felt! Involuntarily, time and time again, my hands went to my head, and that night it was a long time before I went to sleep. If we did not learn much at first, it will not be wondered at, I think. Everything was queer, and it took a few months to get adjusted to the new surroundings.

Almost immediately our names were changed to those in common use in the English language. Instead of translating our names into English and calling Zinkcaziwin, Yellow Bird, and Wanbli K'leska, Spotted Eagle, which in itself would have been educational, we were just John, Henry, or Maggie, as the case might be. I was told to take a pointer and select a name for myself from the list written on the blackboard. I did, and since one was just as good as another, and as I could not distinguish any difference in them, I placed the pointer on the name Luther. I then learned to call myself by that name and got used to hearing others call me by it, too. By that time we had been forbidden to speak our mother tongue, which is the rule in all boarding-schools. This rule is uncalled for, and today is not only robbing the Indian, but America of a rich heritage. The language of a people is part of their history. Today we should be perpetuating history instead of destroying it, and this can only be effectively done by allowing and encouraging the young to keep it alive. A language, unused, embalmed, and reposing only in a book, is a dead language. Only the people themselves, and never the scholars, can nourish it into life.

Of all the changes we were forced to make, that of diet was doubtless the most injurious, for it was immediate and drastic. White bread we had for the first meal and thereafter, as well as coffee and sugar. Had we been allowed our own simple diet of meat, either boiled with soup or dried, and fruit, with perhaps a few vegetables, we should have thrived. But the change in clothing, housing, food, and confinement combined with lonesomeness was too much, and in three years nearly one half of the children from the Plains were dead and through with all earthly schools. In the graveyard at Carlisle most of the graves are those of little ones.

I am now going to confess that I had been at Carlisle a full year before I decided to learn all I could of the white man's ways, and then the inspiration was furnished by my father, the man who has been the greatest influence in all my life. When I had been in school a year, father made his first trip to see me. After I had received permission to speak to him, he told me that on his journey he had seen that the land was full of 'Long Knives.' 'They greatly outnumber us and are here to stay,' he said, and advised me, 'Son, learn all you can of the white man's ways and try to be like him.' From that day on I tried. Those few words of my father I remember as if we talked but yesterday, and in the maturity of my mind I have thought of what he said. He did not say that he thought the white man's ways better than our own; neither did he say that I could be like a white man. He said, 'Son, try to be like a white man.' So, in two more years I had been 'made over.' I was Luther Standing Bear wearing the blue uniform of the school, shorn of my hair, and trying hard to walk naturally and easily in stiff-soled cowhide boots. I was now 'civilized' enough to go to work in John Wanamaker's fine store in Philadelphia.

I returned from the East at about the age of sixteen, after five years' contact with the white people, to resume life upon the reservation. But I returned, to spend some thirty years before again leaving, just as I had gone—a Lakota.

Outwardly I lived the life of the white man, yet all the while I kept in direct contact with tribal life. While I had learned all that I could of the white man's culture, I never forgot that of my people. I kept the language, tribal manners and usages, sang the songs and danced the dances. I still listened to and respected the advice of the older people of the tribe. I did not come home so 'progressive' that I could not speak the language of my father and mother. I did not learn the vices of chewing tobacco, smoking, drinking, and swearing, and for all this I am grateful. I have never, in fact, 'progressed' that far.

→ DOCUMENT 13.5b ←

Photograph of Chief Standing Bear the elder visiting his son at Carlisle, in Luther Standing Bear, *Land of the Spotted Eagle*, p. 234. Reproduced from LAND OF THE SPOTTED EAGLE by Luther Standing Bear by permission of the University of Nebraska Press. Copyright, 1933, by Luther Standing Bear. Renewal copyright, 1960, by May Jones.

→ DOCUMENT 13.6 ←

Autobiographical narrative by Zitkala-Sa on her first days at boarding school in Indiana, in Zitkala-Sa [Gertrude Bonin], *American Indian Stories* (Lincoln: U. of Nebraska Press, 1985), pp. 49–56. Originally published in *The Atlantic Monthly* in 1900.

It was night when we reached the school grounds. The lights from the windows of the large buildings fell upon some of the icicled trees that stood beneath them. We were led toward an open door, where the brightness of the lights within flooded out over the heads of the excited palefaces who blocked our way. My body trembled more from fear than from the snow I trod upon.

Entering the house, I stood close against the wall. The strong glaring light in the large whitewashed room dazzled my eyes. The noisy hurrying of hard shoes upon a bare wooden floor increased the whirring in my ears. My only safety seemed to be in keeping next to the wall. As I was wondering in which direction to escape from all this confusion, two warm hands grasped me firmly, and in the same moment I was tossed high in midair. A rosy-cheeked paleface woman caught me in her arms. I was both frightened and insulted by such trifling. I stared into her eyes, wishing her to let me stand on my own feet, but she jumped me up and down with increasing enthusiasm. My mother had never made a plaything of her wee daughter. Remembering this I began to cry aloud.

They misunderstood the cause of my tears, and placed me at a white table loaded with food. There our party were united again. As I did not hush my crying, one of the older ones whispered to me, "Wait until you are alone in the night."

It was very little I could swallow besides my sobs, that evening.

"Oh, I want my mother and my brother Dawée! I want to go to my aunt!" I pleaded; but the ears of the palefaces could not hear me.

From the table we were taken along an upward incline of wooden boxes, which I learned afterward to call a stairway. At the top was a quiet hall, dimly lighted. Many narrow beds were in one straight line down the entire length of the wall. In them lay sleeping brown faces, which peeped just out of the coverings. I was tucked into bed with one of the tall girls, because she talked to me in my mother tongue and seemed to soothe me.

I had arrived in the wonderful land of rosy skies, but I was not happy, as I had thought I should be. My long travel and the bewildering sights had exhausted me. I fell asleep, heaving deep, tired sobs. My tears were left to dry themselves in streaks, because neither my aunt nor my mother was near to wipe them away.

II. The Cutting of my Long Hair.

The first day in the land of apples was a bitter-cold one; for the snow still covered the ground, and the trees were bare. A large bell rang for breakfast, its loud metallic voice crashing through the belfry overhead and into our sensitive ears. The annoying clatter of shoes on bare floors gave us no peace. The constant clash of harsh noises, with an under-current of many voices murmuring an unknown tongue, made a bedlam within which I was securely tied. And though my spirit tore itself in struggling for its lost freedom, all was useless.

A paleface woman, with white hair, came up after us. We were placed in a line of girls who were marching into the dining room. These were Indian girls, in stiff shoes and closely clinging dresses. The small girls wore sleeved aprons and shingled hair. As I walked noiselessly in my soft moccasins, I felt like sinking to the floor, for my blanket had been stripped from my shoulders. I looked hard at the Indian girls, who seemed not to care that they were even more immodestly dressed than I, in their tightly fitting clothes. While we marched in, the boys entered at an opposite door. I watched for the three young braves who came in our party. I spied them in the rear ranks, looking as uncomfortable as I felt.

A small bell was tapped, and each of the pupils drew a chair from under the table. Supposing this act meant they were to be seated, I pulled out mine and at once slipped into it from one side. But when I turned my head, I saw that I was the only one seated, and all the rest at our table remained standing. Just as I began to rise, looking shyly around to see how chairs were to be used, a second bell was sounded. All were seated at last, and I had to crawl back into my chair again. I heard a man's voice at one end of the hall, and I looked around to see him. But all the others hung their heads over their plates. As I glanced at the long chain of tables, I caught the eyes of a paleface woman upon me. Immediately I dropped my eyes, wondering why I was so keenly watched by the strange woman. The man ceased his mutterings, and then a third bell was tapped. Every one picked up his knife and fork and began eating. I began crying instead, for by this time I was afraid to venture anything more.

But this eating by formula was not the hardest trial in that first day. Late in the morning, my friend Judéwin gave me a terrible warning. Judéwin knew a few words of English; and she had overheard the paleface woman talk about cutting our long, heavy hair. Our mothers had taught us that only unskilled warriors who were captured had their hair shingled by the enemy. Among our people, short hair was worn by mourners, and shingled hair by cowards!

We discussed our fate some moments, and when Judéwin said, "We have to submit, because they are strong," I rebelled.

"No, I will not submit! I will struggle first!" I answered.

I watched my chance, and when no one noticed I disappeared. I crept up the stairs as quietly as I could in my squeaking shoes,—my moccasins had been exchanged for shoes. Along the hall I passed, without knowing whither I was going. Turning aside to an open door, I found a large room with three white beds in it. The windows were covered with dark green curtains, which made the room very dim. Thankful that no one was there, I directed my steps toward the corner farthest from the door. On my hands and knees I crawled under the bed, and cuddled myself in the dark corner.

From my hiding place I peered out, shuddering with fear whenever I heard footsteps near by. Though in the hall loud voices were calling my name, and I knew that even Judéwin was searching for me, I did not open my mouth to answer. Then the steps were quickened and the voices became excited. The sounds came nearer and nearer. Women and girls entered the room. I held my breath and watched them open closet doors and peep behind large trunks. Some one threw up the curtains, and the room was filled with sudden light. What caused them to stoop and look under the bed I do not know. I remember being dragged out, though I resisted by kicking and scratching wildly. In spite of myself, I was carried downstairs and tied fast in a chair.

I cried aloud, shaking my head all the while until I felt the cold blades of the scissors against my neck, and heard them gnaw off one of my thick braids. Then I lost my spirit. Since the day I was taken from my mother I had suffered extreme indignites. People had stared at me. I had been tossed about in the air like a wooden puppet. And now my long hair was shingled like a coward's! In my anguish I moaned for my mother, but no one came to comfort me. Not a soul reasoned quietly with me, as my own mother used to do; for now I was only one of many little animals driven by a herder.

DOCUMENT 13.7a

Photograph of young Sioux at Carlisle boarding school, 1879, in Robert Utley, *The Indian Frontier of the American West, 1846–1890* (Albuquerque, NM, 1984), p. 222. J. N. Choate/Denver Public Library, Western History Department.

→ DOCUMENT 13.7b ←

Photograph of the first graduating class at Carlisle boarding school, 1889, in Robert Utley, *The Indian Frontier of the American West, 1846–1890* (Albuquerque, NM, 1984), p. 223. J. N. Choate/Denver Public Library, Western History Department.

DOCUMENT 13.7c

Photograph of four generations of the Two Strike family, by John A. Anderson, about 1906, in *The Sioux of the Rosebud: A History in Pictures* (Norman, OK, 1971), plate 204, p. 277. Nebraska State Historical Society, John A. Anderson Collection.

DOCUMENT 13.8a

Indian pictograph by Wo-Haw, *The Buffalo Who Wouldn't Die,* in Moira Harris, *Between Two Cultures: Kiowa Art from Fort Marion* (Pogo Press, 1989). Missouri Historical Society, St. Louis.

→ DOCUMENT 13.8b ←

Indian pictograph by Wo-Haw, *Skinning a Buffalo*, in Moira Harris, *Between Two Cultures: Kiowa Art from Fort Marion* (Pogo Press, 1989). Missouri Historical Society, St. Louis.

→ DOCUMENT 13.8c ←

Indian pictograph by Wo-Haw, *Classroom at Fort Marion,* in Moira Harris, *Between Two Cultures: Kiowa Art from Fort Marion* (Pogo Press, 1989). Missouri Historical Society, St. Louis.

DOCUMENT 13.8d

Indian pictograph by Wo-Haw, *Self-Portrait or Between Two Cultures,* in Moira Harris, *Between Two Cultures: Kiowa Art from Fort Marion* (Pogo Press, 1989). Missouri Historical Society, St. Louis.

ARCHIVE 14
American Imperialism: War with the Philippines

Archive Overview

THE Philippine–American War, 1899–1902, provides a rich set of sources for exploring American imperialism as the United States changed the nature of its relationship with the larger world beyond the Western Hemisphere. The Philippine War at the turn of the 20th century was the forceful beginning of the American military, moral, political, and economic presence throughout the world that we see clearly realized at the dawn of the 21st century. This archive considers the mixed blessing of being an international power: the difficulties a strong nation faces in trying to be both powerful and good, both responsible and loved. As the sources here demonstrate, it is difficult to be both.

Not all Americans shared the missionary, moral, and monetary zeal that drove the decision to go to war with the Filipinos in 1899. Many wondered why, in the midst of a war to liberate the Cuban people from Spanish imperial rule, the United States decided to fight the Filipinos and then to annex the Philippine Islands, thus establishing American imperial rule in that distant land. Your task is to decide, on the basis of these sources, first, why Americans engaged in war and annexed the Philippines and, second, how well that behavior squared with American values and ideals. Finally, in an era when European nations were assuming the "burden" of imperial control of peoples in Africa and Asia, to what extent do you think the American role in the Philippines was morally right? The answer is not as simple as it might first seem.

Placing the Sources in Context

THE American people's belief that they had a sacred obligation to spread their institutions and way of life ("manifest destiny") shaped the westward expansion in the 1840s into Texas and the southwest, Utah and the Great Basin, and California, Oregon, and the Pacific northwest. The process of empire-building resumed soon after the Civil War. In 1867, Secretary of State William Seward acquired Alaska from Russia for $7.2 million, and, in the early 1870s, the United States debated the annexation of the island of Santo Domingo in the Caribbean. Although the Senate refused to ratify the Santo Domingo treaty, American activity overseas continued with economic interventions in Latin America and with growing interest in gaining islands in the Pacific and a share of the Asian market. Washington negotiated a treaty in 1878 to gain a naval station in Samoa. In July 1898, Congress approved the annexation of Hawaii, and in 1899 Secretary of State John Hay's first Open Door note attempted to lay claim to trading rights in China equal to those enjoyed by occupying imperial powers already there.

No step in American empire-building was as significant as Washington's war with Spain in 1898 and the resulting global territorial expansion involving Cuba, Puerto (Porto) Rico, Guam, Hawaii, and the islands of the Philippine archipelago. America's war with Spain occurred within a larger wave of European and Japanese global expansion sometimes called the "new imperialism." What became a rush for territorial acquisition sprang from

TIMELINE

1895	Renewal of the Cuban revolution for independence from Spain
1898	Explosion of the battleship *Maine* in Havana Harbor
1898	Spanish–American War; Battle of Manila Harbor; annexation of Hawaii, Puerto Rico, and Guam
1898–1899	Senate debates annexation of the Philippines
1899	Outbreak of war with Filipinos; Senate annexes the Philippines; Open Door notes
1900	Boxer Rebellion in China; McKinley reelected president
1901	McKinley assassinated; Theodore Roosevelt becomes president
1902	Philippine–American War ends

many different motivations ranging from economic, missionary, and moral imperatives to a policy of pure "realpolitik"—a raw, competitive drive for national power and prestige. Basic to the missionary rhetoric of European and U.S. imperialism was the assumption that white, Anglo-Saxon, western nations were superior to the "inferior" peoples of the world and therefore had the right to spread their principles, institutions, and religion around the globe. Many considered this a God-given responsibility (and a "burden") to advance the progress of the world.

For the United States, this Great Power race for empire coincided with the Spanish mismanagement of colonial Cuba, an island only 90 miles from American shores. News reports of Spanish atrocities created American sympathy for the Cubans. When the Cuban insurrection escalated early in 1898, President William McKinley sent the battleship U.S.S. *Maine* into Havana Harbor, ostensibly to protect U.S. citizens. In an atmosphere of heightened tension, the *Maine* mysteriously blew up and American newspapers fanned the angry reaction at home, accusing Spain of treachery. Domestic pressure contributed to McKinley's declaration of war on Spain in April. After only four months, an American victory left the United States in control of the former Spanish colonies of Cuba and Puerto Rico in the Caribbean, and Guam in the Pacific.

The war over Cuba in the Caribbean soon involved the United States with Spain's colonial possessions in East Asia. The entanglement with the Philippine Islands was largely due to the actions of McKinley's Assistant Secretary of the Navy, Theodore Roosevelt. Roosevelt ordered Admiral George Dewey to move the American fleet from Hong Kong to Manila to keep the Spanish navy from leaving the Philippines for Cuba. The Americans easily won a battle in Manila Harbor on May 1, 1898. Filipino nationalists were ecstatic. Led by the young General Emilio Aguinaldo, they had long been fighting for their independence, and they hoped that they would be given the honor of liberating Manila. However, American officials and troops shunted Filipino soldiers off to the outskirts of Manila, liberated the capital city themselves, and declared American military rule throughout the islands.

Undeterred by American actions, the Filipinos approved a constitution in January 1899 based on the republican representative principles of the United States Constitution. Also that January, the United States Senate debated whether to ratify (a two-thirds vote was needed) the Treaty of Paris concluding the Spanish–American War. An incident on February 4, 1899, led to fighting between Filipino and American soldiers. Two days later, the Senate ratified the Treaty of Paris by a vote of 57 to 27, thus formally annexing all of the Philippines.

As a result of the Senate action, advocated by President McKinley, the U.S. Army fought Aguinaldo's Filipino nationalist insurgents for four years, from 1898 to 1902, a war that lasted ten times longer than the war with Spain over Cuba. The war caused the deaths of over 4,000 Americans (there had been only 385 combat deaths in Cuba) and at least 50,000 Filipinos, many of them civilians relocated to internment villages by American policies. Many of the American soldiers in the Philippines were veterans of the Plains Indians wars who carried their negative attitudes toward peoples of color with them. The Philippines would not gain complete independence from the United States until July 4, 1946, following World War II. The liberation date suggests the final irony of the war forty-six years earlier.

About the Sources

THE American war in the Philippines gave rise to strong sentiments for and against the conflict. The sources here are intended to give you a range of views on the war, both from soldiers serving in that far-off land and from supporters and opponents in the United States. The assumptions that were the basis of the imperial policy (sources 14.4–14.6 especially) may seem offensively racist to us today, but they were, at least for these important politicians, sincerely and deeply felt to be good, Christian, morally progressive values. Be careful not to judge too harshly, but rather to consider the prevailing moral climate and attitudes of the period.

The Colorado soldier's verses praising his Filipina girlfriend (14.1a) raise the danger of making light of the contact between Americans and Filipinos. The war was destructive and brutal. American forces tortured and slaughtered thousands of Filipino soldiers, displaced large portions of the civilian population, and intentionally destroyed crops and other food supplies. Carl Larsen's amazingly revealing letter (14.2) not only describes the war and his attitudes toward it but also his feelings toward his "friend" and the life he is missing back home. As you read John Bass's brief dispatch from the Philippines (14.3), try to establish whether the attitudes he expresses toward "the Filipino" are literal or satirical.

There is no confusing the attitudes of Theodore Roosevelt, who gave his "strenuous life" speech (14.4) in Chicago in April 1899. He began with the importance of the strenuous life for individuals and then extended the idea to the nation. President McKinley delivered his remarks (14.6) to a group of Methodist missionaries in 1900. They offer a fascinating insight into the process of presidential decision making, just as Indiana Senator Albert Beveridge's speech in the U.S. Senate (14.5), his first, reflects the majority attitude of most United States senators. Massachusetts Senator George Hoar (14.5 and 14.8b), founder of the Anti-Imperialist League in New England, responded to Beveridge. Citing the principles of consent of the governed from the Declaration of Independence throughout his many speeches, Hoar passionately opposed the treaty annexing the Philippines.

You will be reading portions of two selections (14.5 and 14.8b) from the *Congressional Record*, an official government publication that claims to include every word spoken in Congress. Senator Orville Platt of Connecticut was an ardent advocate of expansionism. He was opposed by Hoar and by Senator George Vest of Missouri, who introduced, in vain, a resolution banning Congress from acquiring any overseas territories and making them into colonies. General Elwell S. Otis was commander of American forces in the Philippines.

Rudyard Kipling, a prominent English writer, supported British imperialism around the globe. His poem "The White Man's Burden" (14.7a), which the American Ernest Howard Crosby bitingly satirized (14.7b), shows the Anglo-Saxon western nations' understanding of the values (and the "burden") of imperialism. Crosby, a wealthy New Yorker and a judge, had—ironically—replaced Theodore Roosevelt in the New York State Assembly in 1887 before the influence of Leo Tolstoy, the great Russian novelist and pacifist, turned him into a leading anti-imperialist activist and full-time poet. Other writers, like Mark Twain (14.10), joined the Anti-Imperialist League (14.8a) and were often bitter in their intense opposition to American imperial policies. The debate these sources will open up for you reflects the real one that occurred in the Senate and in the nation a little over one hundred years ago.

Look closely in each source for the attitudes toward race, religion, destiny, duty, and American responsibility in the world. Note also the variety and kinds of sources represented here: letters, poems, speeches by political leaders, journalists' reports and essays, manifestoes and cartoons. In interpreting the cartoons (14.9), you want to "read" back and forth across the picture, looking at each image and each detail, to describe what you see, and then to interpret what you think the cartoonist's message was and how effective he was in making it.

List of Sources

14.1a **Poem by 1st Colorado volunteer soldier praising his Filipina girlfriend, "Colorado Soldier's DELF,"** *Denver Post*, undated, author unknown. Subject Collections/Military Affairs/Spanish-American War/Letters, Colorado Historical Society.

14.1b **Description of warfare by 1st Colorado Infantry Regiment volunteer Guy Sims,** TMs, Wauneta, Nebraska, 1941; Collection No. 1898–142, United States Army Military History Research Collection, Carlisle Barracks, Carlisle, Pennsylvania, pp. 15–16.

14.2 **Letter from Private Carl Larsen, 1st Colorado volunteer, to "Dear Friend,"** February 25, 1899. Subject Collections/Military Affairs/Spanish-American War/Letters, Colorado Historical Society.

14.3 **Magazine dispatch filed August 30, 1898, by John Bass,** in *Harper's Weekly*, vol. 42 (October 15, 1898), p. 1008.

14.4 **Speech/essay by Theodore Roosevelt, "The Strenuous Life,"** in *The Strenuous Life: Essays and Addresses* (New York: Century, 1900), pp. 115–121.

14.5 **Congressional speeches on imperialism, by Senator Albert Beveridge (Indiana) and Senator George Hoar (Massachusetts),** United States Senate, January 9, 1900, in *Congressional Record*, 56th Congress, 1st session, pp. 704, 708, 711–712.

14.6 **Speech by President William McKinley,** in Charles S. Olcott, *The Life of William McKinley*, 2 vols. (Boston, 1916), vol. 2, pp. 110–111.

14.7a **Poem by Rudyard Kipling, "The White Man's Burden,"** 1899, in *McClure's Magazine*, 21 (February 1899), p. 291.

14.7b **Poem by Ernest Howard Crosby, "The Real 'White Man's Burden',"** 1899, in Ernest Howard Crosby, *Swords and Plowshares* (New York: Funk and Wagnalls, 1902), pp. 33–34. Originally appeared in *New York Times* (February 15, 1899).

14.8a **Platform of the American Anti-Imperialist League,** October 18, 1899. Papers of the Anti-Imperialist League, Michigan Historical Collection, University of Michigan, Ann Arbor.

14.8b **Speech on imperialism by Senator George F. Hoar (Massachusetts),** United States Senate, January 9, 1899, in *Congressional Record*, 55th Congress, 3rd session, pp. 501–503.

14.9a **Cartoon in magazine, "The Spanish Brute Adds Mutilation to Murder,"** by Grant Hamilton, in *Judge*, July 9, 1898. Culver Pictures.

14.9b **Cartoon in magazine, "Is He to Be a Despot?"** artist unknown, in *The Verdict*, 1899.

14.10 **Essay by Mark Twain, "To the Person Sitting in Darkness,"** in *North American Review*, February 1901, pp. 461–473.

Questions to Consider

1. What attitudes toward the Filipino people can you discern in the Colorado soldiers' accounts of fights with Filipino soldiers and romances with the Filipina girlfriend (sources 14.1a and b)? What does Guy Sims's account say about American and Filipino concepts of honor? What kind of honor does the soldier's poetry express? Who do you think is the audience for this poetry?

2. What view of the war and its purpose does Carl Larsen's letter (14.2) reveal? Notice the design (a stamp?) on page 9 of his stationery: Why is it there? Can you tell whether Carl Larsen's "friend" is male or female? Does it matter? What do you learn about the nature of courtship one hundred years ago?

3. Do you think John Bass's attitudes (14.3) are genuine, or is he being sarcastic? In what ways does his report indirectly reflect Filipino attitudes toward Americans?

4. Identify the assumptions and arguments in the speeches by Roosevelt, Beveridge, and McKinley (sources 14.4–14.6). Are the arguments persuasive? Who do you think might

have responded positively to them? To what extent are these speeches moral, economic, political, religious, and strategic? Are you able to put aside today's values about race, religion, and nationality in order to appreciate the attitudes and beliefs of these late 19th century American leaders?

5. What view of imperialism does Kipling express in his poem (14.7a)? For whom is imperialism good, and why? Compare Kipling's poem to Roosevelt's speech. Are there similarities? Differences? What is your response to the poem? What values does Ernest Crosby reveal in his satire of Kipling's poem (14.7b) and Mark Twain (14.10) in his satirical ridicule of prevailing American values? How effective do you think they were? Do the two writers succeed in undermining imperialist ideas?

6. What kinds of points does the platform of the Anti-Imperialist League make (14.8a)? To what traditional American ideas and values does the platform appeal? How persuasive is it? Is it more or less persuasive than the McKinley and Beveridge speeches? Contrast the Senate speeches of Albert Beveridge (14.5) and George Hoar (14.5 and 14.8b). Which do you think is most convincing? Why do you think McKinley was reelected president in 1900, in a campaign shaped by the debate over imperialism?

7. What point does each political cartoon make (14.9)? How would you compare the two? What images appear in both cartoons? How do the cartoonists manipulate the images to make their points? How do you respond to them?

8. Taking all the sources into account, why did the United States fight the Filipino people, and why did they annex the Philippine Islands? Did the war and annexation reflect a departure from American traditions or a continuation? Was it morally right? Was it politically right? Which sources did you find most persuasive? If you had been living in 1899, which do you think you would have found most persuasive?

9. What is the current American attitude toward the rest of the world? How has it changed from those attitudes expressed a century ago? What remains similar? To what extent is the United States still having difficulty being both powerful and good?

AMERICAN EXPANSIONISM TO THE PHILIPPINES

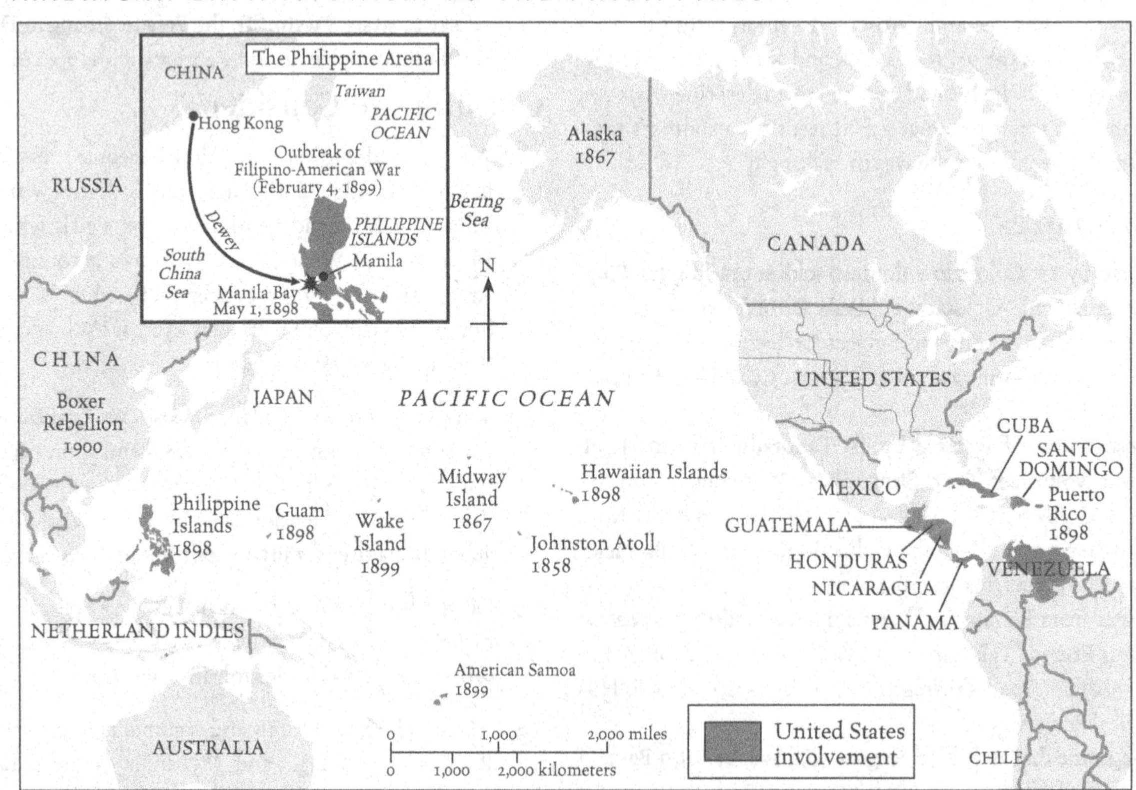

→ DOCUMENT 14.1a ←

Poem by 1st Colorado volunteer soldier praising his Filipina girlfriend, "Colorado Soldier's DELF," *Denver Post*, undated, author unknown. Subject Collections/Military Affairs/Spanish-American War/Letters, Colorado Historical Society.

COLORADO SOLDIER'S DELF.

I would like to write a sonnet and put loving trimmin's on it
To the pretty little girl I left behind me.
But she's got another feller, and I simplz want to tell her
That her loss with bitter tears will never blind me.
Here in beautiful Manila, far across the bounding billow,
I have found another sugar plum. God bless her!
And although she is the color of a fried New England cruller,
It will never drain my pocketbook to dress her.

Hers a figure like a Juno, doesn't try to hide it, you kno .
With the finery our Yankee girls so covet;
And her mouth is a creation built for blissful osculation,
With the very cutest nose on earth, above it.
And her smile! O! holy Moses! What a vision it discloses
Of a rosy portal gemmed with grinders pearly.
O! there are no flies upon her., and I fear I am a goner
To the wiles of this sweet Filipino girlie.

So the girl I left behind me isn't very apt to find me
Shedding tears of disappointment should I lose her.
For I'm really quite enraptured with the native belle I've captured,
And she's gone upon her Colorado snoozer.
So exultantly I tell her, that her once best steady feller,
Whom she thinks she's downed forever in the soup,
Has been happily re-lovered, has quite easily discovered
That she's not the only chicken in the coop.
—Denver Post.

→ DOCUMENT 14.1b ←

Description of warfare by 1st Colorado Infantry Regiment volunteer Guy Sims, TMs, Wauneta, Nebraska, 1941; Collection No. 1898-142, United States Army Military History Research Collection, Carlisle Barracks, Carlisle, Pennsylvania, pp. 15–16.

Before stepping out on the bare hillside I looked back. The plum thicket (containing an *insurrecto* outpost) was about 400 yards away, and it didn't seem reasonable that the natives would let our fellows walk up and down that hill-side in plain sight, and not do something about it. But I didn't know any other route, so I took a long breath and stepped out and right now rifles began to spatter behind me and bullets to snap and whine overhead. Within a few seconds not only the outpost but also a long sector of their mainline was firing at me. Of course my first impulse was to see just how quick I could streak it up the hill, but I had never made a home run so far (that was before Mariquina) and hated to spoil my record. I noticed, too, that the bullets were all far above my head, none were close down, so I maintained the regulation military cadence—120 per minute—but gosh, how I stretched the stride! As I neared the shelter of the hedgerow at the top of the hill, I noticed that it was literally snowing green leaves that the bullets were cutting from the bamboo. When I was within 20 feet of the hedge the firing ceased like turning off the switch, and the Little Brown Brothers gave me a rousing cheer. They hadn't been able to either drop me or make me run. Very few lone soldiers have ever received a cheer from the enemy and fewer still have lived to tell about it. I have regretted ever since that I didn't think to turn and wave to them before stepping out of sight, but I was so intent on getting out of sight I never thought of it till too late.

→ DOCUMENT 14.2 ←

Letter from Private Carl Larsen, 1st Colorado volunteer, to "Dear Friend," February 25, 1899. Subject Collections/Military Affairs/Spanish-American War/Letters, Colorado Historical Society.

Manila Fb 25.

Dear friend.

I received your letter yesterday. and as my correspondance is very limited. I will pay prompt attention to what I have. or else I suppose. I will not get any letters at all.

The situation is rather interesting here at present. fighthing more or less every day, on our firing line around town. and the last 3 or 4 days there has been an awfull lot of fires here in town, a big part of this City is in ashes now. and at the same time big riots. we have not lost many men in the Street fights. but a ~~t~~ lot of natives has been killed, and a whole lot of innocent people to.

The situation here is awfull. and what seems to me to be the worst ting. is, that it is to a great extent our own doings. If U.S. intended to do the right ting to these people — give them their Independence ~~ting~~ and told them so, they would, instead of being our enemies, been our best friends and if we are going to hold these Islands, the Insurgents ought to been disarmed at the time we took Manila, as it could been done very easy at that time. I do not criticize our Government, but there certainly has been made some terrible blunders here.

what will cost the life of thousands of Soldiers, but I dont know who is to blame.
Of course, now we have to kill all the Insurgents we can: but as far as I am concerned, and I know it is the same way with many others. I fight these people with an very difference feeling from what I had toward the Spaniards. Than we was fighting for a good cause, and now? the fact is, I dont know what we are fighting for now.
I suppose you know all about the trouble here. through the papers. any how, I will try to give you a short description

of the trouble so far.
It started on saturday Febr. 4. in the evening. Time and again the Nebraska outposts had dis agreements with the Insurgents about the line, and position of outposts, and that night our outpost fired on the Insur: gents and they returned the fire, and in about an hour the firing was general all along the line. the firing was kept up all night, but no advancement was atemp ted before morning. The Insur: gents had a very strong position in Blockhouses & trences all along. about sunrise sunday morning we advanced on their intrence ments. I was with General Hale that night and all day

Sunday. we was with Colo Regim. when they made the first charge at Blo-ckhouse N.5. we went over the ground afterwards and counted 25 dead and 11 wounded Insurgents, on a space of ground about 2 or 3 acres. As we rode along the line that day, I saw over a hundred dead Insurgents, and some terrible wounded. I saw one with his whole face shot ~~shot~~ away, from his forehead to his chin was nothing but a terrible gap with splinters of bone sticking out. he was still alive and had been laying out in the sun from early morning til 4 in the afternoon.

Now I am getting used to such sights. In that first days fight our loss was a little over 50 dead and some 200 or 225 wounded. we burried about 800 Insurgents that first day. Not a day since than have passed, with out more or less fighting, some where on the line, but we have not had a general engagement, and everyday we have some dead and wounded. Our men is getting prettey well tired out as they are kept on duty nearly all the time, day and night. and it's getting fearfull hot now. As far as I am concerned I got a snap. I am at City Headquarters most of the time, and only when there is some trouble in our Brigade, do I

have to go to the front.
Some time ago Gen Hale with
about 500 men went out to
a town called Maraquina
several miles ahead of our
line, there was noone in
town. there was a house what
had been used as an Insur:
gent headquarter. from there
the officers took a lot of truk
as I had to bring back for them
I got a few trinkets myself.
I got a desswaist, as the ladies
use them here. if you are a
relic fiend I will kepp it
for you. if I ever get back
to gods country again. a
thing what is very uncertain
under present cercumstances.
I dont think I will tell any
more war storys this time.

I will preserve them til I get back. in your letter you said something about coming home. I dont believe people as a rule, know how to apreciate anything until they are about to loose it. I am sure you realise more in 3 weeks what your home is to you, when you are away from it, than you do in so many years when you are there. And I will promiss you the soldiers as well as their folks will be happy whenever we get back. I have no home to go to, but it will seems the next thing to it, when I get back to Minn again.

Reinforcements is beginning to come in now. the 20. Inf. came yesterday. and 5000 more

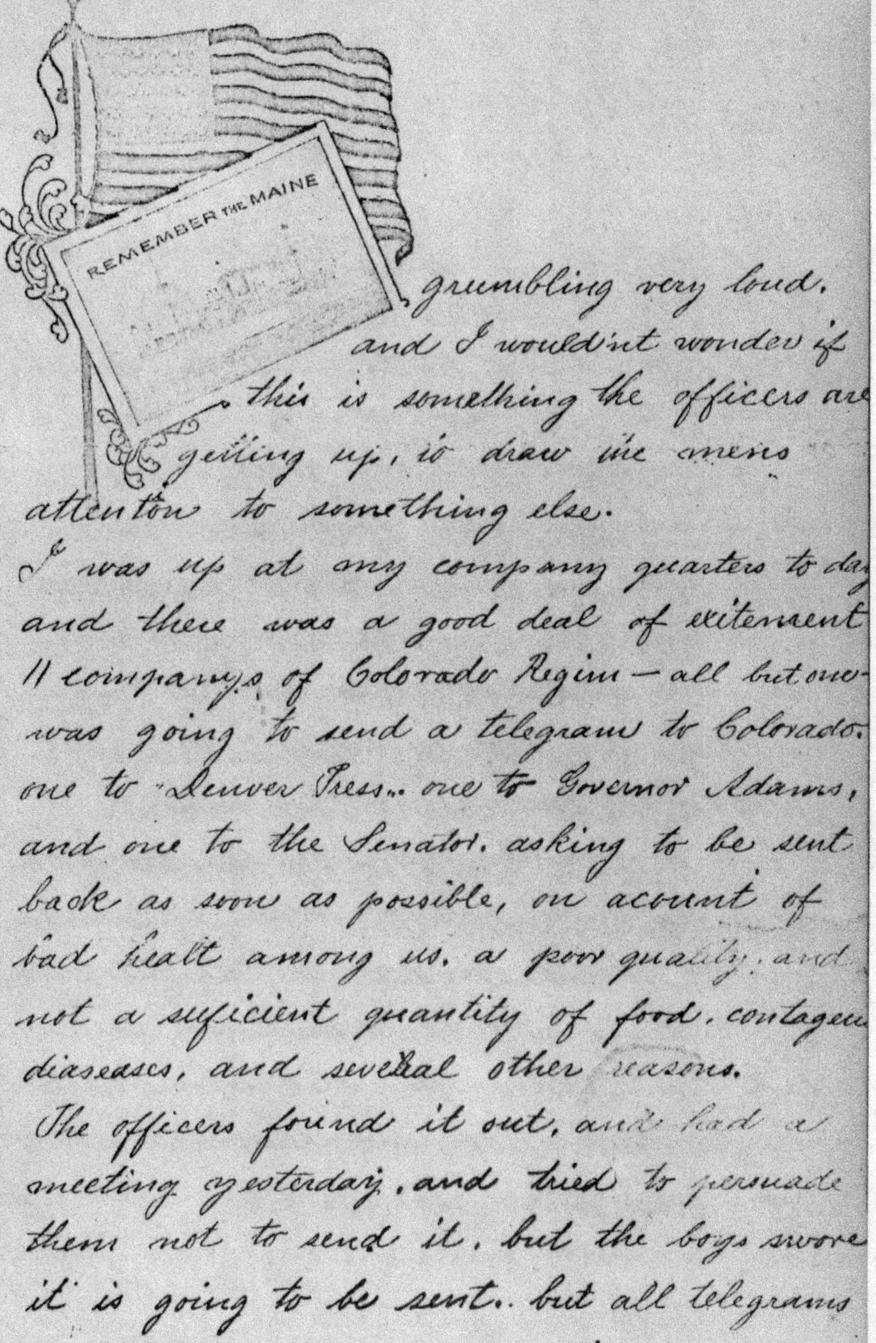

grumbling very loud.
and I wouldn't wonder if
this is something the officers are
getting up, to draw the mens
attention to something else.
I was up at my company quarters to day
and there was a good deal of excitement
11 companys of Colorado Regim—all but one—
was going to send a telegram to Colorado.
one to Denver Press.. one to Governor Adams,
and one to the Senator. asking to be sent
back as soon as possible, on acount of
bad healt among us. a poor quality. and
not a suficient quantity of food. contageus
diaseases, and several other reasons.
The officers found it out. and had a
meeting yesterday. and tried to persuade
them not to send it. but the boys swore
it is going to be sent.. but all telegrams

leaving here, have to be aproved by General Otis, and likely he will stop it.
When we went over here, there was several tousand Dollars worth of caned fruit and several other thing, on board Ship, donated to us, by the red cross society, it has not ween given to us, yet the goods has disapeare and is not accounted for, but we all know where it went to, it was sold to us on board ship, coming over, and after we got here in camp, we was starved so we had to buy something, they sold us the red cross goods. but who got the money?.

Just as I write this they are coming along the street with 4 more canons, may be, there is going to be trouble after all. Lewis and I have bought a Kodak, and have taken quite lot of pictures. we had one roll developed, but half of them are spoiled, the fillms are to old, and we can't get any here, but we will have some good ones.

You said I ought to be back to help husk corn, you bet. I only wish I was there, I would a good deal rather be husking corn there, than do nothing here. I believe I will learn at least one thing in this war, and that is to be satisfied when I got a good place.

I dont know about that hundred Dollars my hair is turning gray—it is no joke—and of course I know I will have to remaine single, and I cant loose the money.

I suppose it will be close to your birthday, when you get this letter, and I send you my congratulation, wishing you will be happy and contended, and dont get married til I come back, because I expect an invitation.

If I should not return from this Country, I send you this card to remember one by. The House below Merrits picture is situated in the center of our trences.

and I dont believe, there is two square inches in that house, where there is not one or more bullet holes, I went trugh that house several times, the Fort & powder magazine was captured by Colorado Aug 13. we went acros the bridge, you se on there and raised the flag, a wonder nobody got killed there, the bullets came pretty thick.

Now, please write soon, I depend on you, for news, you are doing me a greater favor than you think, by writing. I feel like it was my home there, whenever any one ask me where I am from, I generaly say Minnesota, without thinking, that I have no right to call any particular place in the U.S. my home. My best wishes for you & all of you. I am, ever your friend Carl.

Carl Larsen

Comp. C. 1st Colo
U.S. Vols.
Manila. P.I.

If I am not mistaken your birthday is 30 of Nov. and I hope you will have a surprise party again this year.

→ DOCUMENT 14.3 ←

Magazine dispatch filed August 30, 1898, by John Bass, in *Harper's Weekly*, vol. 42 (October 15, 1898), p. 1008.

The Filipino is the true child of the East. His moral fibre is as the web of the pineapple gauze of which the women make their dresses. He will cheat, steal, and lie beyond the orthodox limit of the Anglo-Saxon. His unreliability and the persistence with which he disobeys orders are irritating beyond description; besides this, his small stature and color invite abuse. There can be no doubt our soldiers are spoiling for a fight. They hate and despise the native for the manner he has lied to and cheated them, and on the whole they are inclined to treat the Filipino the way a burly policeman treats a ragged street urchin. The native is like a child, unreasonable, and easily affected by small things. Unable to appreciate the benefits of a good government, he fiercely resents the rough manner in which the soldier jostles him out of the way.

→ DOCUMENT 14.4 ←

Speech/essay by Theodore Roosevelt, "The Strenuous Life," in *The Strenuous Life: Essays and Addresses* (New York: Century, 1900), pp. 115–121.

. . . The army and the navy are the sword and the shield which this nation must carry if she is to do her duty among the nations of the earth—if she is not to stand merely as the China of the western hemisphere. Our proper conduct toward the tropic islands we have wrested from Spain is merely the form which our duty has taken at the moment. Of course we are bound to handle the affairs of our own household well. We must see that there is civic honesty, civic cleanliness, civic good sense in our home administration of city, State, and nation. We must strive for honesty in office, for honesty toward the creditors of the nation and of the individual; for the widest freedom of individual initiative where possible, and for the wisest control of individual initiative where it is hostile to the welfare of the many. But because we set our own household in order we are not thereby excused from playing our part in the great affairs of the world. A man's first duty is to his own home, but he is not thereby excused from doing his duty to the State; for if he fails in this second duty it is under the penalty of ceasing to be a free-man. In the same way, while a nation's first duty is within its own borders, it is not thereby absolved from facing its duties in the world as a whole; and if it refuses to do so, it merely forfeits its right to struggle for a place among the peoples that shape the destiny of mankind.

In the West Indies and the Philippines alike we are confronted by most difficult problems. It is cowardly to shrink from solving them in the proper way; for solved they must be, if not by us, then by some stronger and more manful race. If we are too weak, too selfish, or too foolish to solve them, some bolder and abler people must undertake the solution. Personally, I am far too firm a believer in the greatness of my country and the power of my countrymen to admit for one moment that we shall ever be driven to the ignoble alternative.

The problems are different for the different islands. Porto Rico is not large enough to stand alone. We must govern it wisely and well, primarily in the interest of its own people. Cuba is, in my judgment, entitled ultimately to settle for itself whether it shall be an independent state or an integral portion of the mightiest of republics. But until order and stable liberty are secured, we must remain in the island to insure them, and infinite tact, judgment, moderation, and courage must be shown by our military and civil representatives in keeping the island pacified, in relentlessly stamping out brigandage, in protecting all alike, and yet in showing proper recognition to the men who have fought for Cuban liberty. The Philippines offer a yet graver problem. Their population includes half-caste and native Christians, warlike Moslems, and wild pagans. Many of their people are utterly unfit for self-government, and show no signs of becoming fit. Others may in time become fit but at present can only take part in self-government under a wise supervision, at once firm and beneficent. We have driven Spanish tyranny from the islands. If we now let it be replaced by savage anarchy, our work has been for harm and not for good. I have scant patience with those who fear to undertake the task of governing the Philippines, and who openly avow that they do fear to undertake it, or that they shrink from it because of the expense and trouble; but I have even scanter patience with those who make a pretense of humanitarianism to hide and cover their timidity, and who cant about "liberty" and the "consent of the governed," in order to excuse themselves for their unwillingness to play the part of men. Their doctrines, if carried out, would make it incumbent upon us to leave the Apaches of Arizona to work out their own salvation, and to decline to interfere in a single Indian reservation. Their doctrines condemn your forefathers and mine for ever having settled in these United States.

England's rule in India and Egypt has been of great benefit to England, for it has trained up generations of men accustomed to look at the larger and loftier side of public life. It has been of even greater benefit to India and Egypt. And finally, and most of all, it has advanced the cause of civilization. So, if we do our duty aright in the Philippines, we will add to that national renown which is the highest and finest part of national life, will greatly benefit the people of the Philippine Islands, and, above all, we will play our part well in the great work of uplifting mankind. But to do this work, keep ever in mind that we must show in a very high degree the qualities of courage, of honesty, and of good judgment. Resistance must be stamped out. The first and all-important work to be done is to establish the supremacy of our flag. We must put down armed resistance before we can accomplish anything else, and there should be no parleying, no faltering, in dealing with our foe. As for those in our own country who encourage the foe, we can afford contemptuously to disregard them; but it must be remembered that their utterances are not saved from being treasonable merely by the fact that they are despicable.

When once we have put down armed resistance, when once our rule is acknowledged, then an even more difficult task will begin, for then we must see to it that the islands are administered with absolute honesty and with good judgment. If we let the public service of the islands be turned into the prey of the spoils politician, we shall have begun to tread the path which Spain trod to her own destruction. We must send out there only good and able men, chosen for their fitness, and not because of their partizan service, and these men must not only administer impartial justice to the natives and serve their own government with honesty and fidelity, but must show the utmost tact and firmness, remembering that, with such people as those with whom we are to deal, weakness is the greatest of crimes, and that next to weakness comes lack of consideration for their principles and prejudices.

I preach to you, then, my countrymen, that our country calls not for the life of ease but for the life of strenuous endeavor. The twentieth century looms before us big with the fate of many nations. If we stand idly by, if we seek merely swollen, slothful ease and ignoble peace, if we shrink from the hard contests where men must win at hazard of their lives and at the risk of all they hold dear, then the bolder and stronger peoples will pass us by, and will win for themselves the domination of the world. Let us therefore boldly face the life of strife, resolute to do our duty well and manfully; resolute to uphold righteousness by deed and by word; resolute to be both honest and brave, to serve high ideals, yet to use practical methods. Above all, let us shrink from no strife, moral or physical, within or without the nation, provided we are certain that the strife is justified, for it is only through strife, through hard and dangerous endeavor, that we shall ultimately win the goal of true national greatness.

✧ DOCUMENT 14.5 ✧

Congressional speeches on imperialism by Senator Albert Beveridge (Indiana) and Senator George Hoar (Massachusetts), United States Senate, January 9, 1900, in *Congressional Record*, 56th Congress, 1st session, pp. 704, 708, 711–712.

Policy Regarding the Philippines.

Mr. BEVERIDGE. I ask for the reading of the joint resolution introduced by me on Thursday last.

The PRESIDENT pro tempore. The Chair lays before the Senate the joint resolution introduced by the Senator from Indiana, which was laid on the table subject to his call. The joint resolution will be read.

The Secretary read the joint resolution (S. R. 53) defining the policy of the United States relative to the Philippine Islands, as follows:

Be it resolved by the Senate and House of Representatives of the United States of America in Congress assembled, That the Philippine Islands are territory belonging to the United States; that it is the intention of the United States to retain them as such and to establish and maintain such governmental control throughout the archipelago as the situation may demand.

Mr. BEVERIDGE. Mr. President, I address the Senate at this time because Senators and Members of the House on both sides have asked that I give to Congress and the country my observations in the Philippines and the far East, and the conclusions which those observations compel; and because of hurtful resolutions introduced and utterances made in the Senate, every word of which will cost and is costing the lives of American soldiers.

Mr. President, the times call for candor. The Philippines are ours forever, "territory belonging to the United States," as the Constitution calls them. And just beyond the Philippines are China's illimitable markets. We will not retreat from either. We will not repudiate our duty in the archipelago. We will not abandon our opportunity in the Orient. We will not renounce our part in the mission of our race, trustee, under God, of the civilization of the world. And we will move forward to our work, not howling out regrets like slaves whipped to their burdens, but with gratitude for a task worthy of our strength, and thanksgiving to Almighty God that He has marked us as His chosen people, henceforth to lead in the regeneration of the world.

Philippines Command the Pacific.

This island empire is the last land left in all the oceans. If it should prove a mistake to abandon it, the blunder once made would be irretrievable. If it proves a mistake to hold it, the error can be corrected when we will. Every other progressive nation stands ready to relieve us.

But to hold it will be no mistake. Our largest trade henceforth must be with Asia. The Pacific is our ocean. More and more Europe will manufacture the most it needs, secure from its colonies the most it consumes. Where shall we turn for consumers of our surplus? Geography answers the question. China is our natural customer. She is nearer to us than to England, Germany, or Russia, the commercial powers of the present and the future. They have moved nearer to China by securing permanent bases on her borders. The Philippines give us a base at the door of all the East.

Lines of navigation from our ports to the Orient and Australia; from the Isthmian Canal to Asia: from all Oriental ports to Australia, converge at and separate from the Philippines. They are a self-supporting, dividend-paying fleet, permanently anchored at a spot selected by the strategy of Providence, commanding the Pacific. And the Pacific is the ocean of the commerce of the future. Most future wars will be conflicts for commerce. The power that rules the Pacific, therefore, is the power that rules the world. And, with the Philippines, that power is and will forever be the American Republic. . . .

"The Blood of Our Soldiers."

Mr. President, reluctantly and only from a sense of duty am I forced to say that American opposition to the war has been the chief factor in prolonging it. Had Aguinaldo not understood that in America, even in the American Congress, even here in the Senate, he and his cause were supported; had he not known that it was proclaimed on the stump and in the press of a faction in the United States that every shot his misguided followers fired into the breasts of American soldiers was like the volleys fired by Washington's men against the soldiers of King George his insurrection would have dissolved before it entirely crystallized.

The utterances of American opponents of the war are read to the ignorant soldiers of Aguinaldo and repeated in exaggerated form among the common people. Attempts have been made by wretches claiming American citizenship to ship arms and ammunition from Asiatic ports to the Filipinos, and these acts of infamy were coupled by the Malays with American assaults on our Government at home. The Filipinos do not understand free speech, and therefore our tolerance of American assaults on the American President and the American Government means to them that our President is in the minority or he would not permit what appears to them such treasonable criticism. It is believed and stated in Luzon, Panay, and Cebu that the Filipinos have only to fight, harass, retreat, break up into small parties, if necessary, as they are doing now, but by any means hold out until the next Presidential election, and our forces will be withdrawn.

All this has aided the enemy more than climate, arms, and battle. Senators, I have heard these reports myself; I have talked with the people; I have seen our mangled boys in the hospital and field; I have stood on the firing line and beheld our dead soldiers, their faces turned to the pitiless southern sky, and in sorrow rather than anger I say to those whose voices in America have cheered those misguided natives on to shoot our soldiers down, that the blood of those dead and wounded boys of ours is on their hands, and the flood of all the years can never wash that stain away. In sorrow rather than anger I say these words, for I earnestly believe that our brothers knew not what they did.

The Filipinos Are Children, Utterly Incapable of Self-Government.

But, Senators, it would be better to abandon this combined garden and Gibraltar of the Pacific, and count our blood and treasure already spent a profitable loss, than to apply any academic arrangement of self-government to these children. They are not capable of self-government. How could they be? They are not of a self-governing race. They are Orientals, Malays, instructed by Spaniards in the latter's worst estate.

They know nothing of practical government except as they have witnessed the weak, corrupt, cruel, and capricious rule of Spain. What magic will anyone employ to dissolve in their minds and characters those impressions of governors and governed which three centuries of misrule has created? What alchemy will change the oriental quality of their blood and set the self-governing currents of the American pouring through their Malay veins. How shall they, in the twinkling of an eye, be exalted to the heights of self-governing peoples which required a thousand years for us to reach, Anglo-Saxon though we are? . . .

The Whole Question Elemental.

Mr. President, this question is deeper than any question of party politics; deeper than any question of the isolated policy of our country even; deeper even than any question of constitutional power. It is elemental. It is racial. God has not been preparing the English-speaking and Teutonic peoples for a thousand years for nothing but vain and idle self-contemplation and self-admiration. No! He has made us the master organizers of the world to establish system where chaos reigns. He has given us the spirit of progress to overwhelm the forces of reaction throughout the earth. He has made us adepts in government that we may administer government among savage and senile peoples. Were it not for such a force as this the world would relapse into barbarism and night. And of all our race He has marked the American people as His chosen nation to finally lead in the regeneration of the world. This is the divine mission of America, and it holds for us all the profit, all the glory, all the happiness possible to man. We are trustees of the world's progress, guardians of its righteous peace. The judgment of the Master is upon us: "Ye have been faithful over a few things; I will make you ruler over many things."

What shall history say of us? Shall it say that we renounced that holy trust, left the savage to his base condition, the wilderness to the reign of waste, deserted duty, abandoned glory, forget our sordid profit even, because we feared our strength and read the charter of our powers with the doubter's eye and the quibbler's mind? Shall it say that, called by events to captain and command the proudest, ablest, purest race of history in history's noblest work, we declined that great commission? Our fathers would not have had it so. No! They founded no paralytic government, incapable of the simplest acts of administration. They planted no sluggard people, passive while the world's work calls them. They established no reactionary nation. They unfurled no retreating flag.

God's Hand in All.

That flag has never paused in its onward march. Who dares halt it now—now, when history's largest events are carrying it forward; now, when we are at last one people, strong enough for any task, great enough for any glory destiny can bestow? How comes it that our first century closes with the process of consolidating the American people into a unit just accomplished, and quick upon the stroke of that great hour presses upon us our world opportunity, world duty, and world glory, which none but a people welded into an indivisible nation can achieve or perform?

Blind indeed is he who sees not the hand of God in events so vast, so harmonious, so benign. Reactionary indeed is the mind that perceives not that this vital people is the strongest of the saving forces of the world: that our place, therefore, is at the head of the constructing and redeeming nations of the earth; and that to stand aside while events march on is a surrender of our interests, a betrayal of our duty as blind as it is base. Craven indeed is the heart that fears to perform a work so golden and so noble: that dares not win a glory so immortal.

Do you tell me that it will cost us money? When did Americans ever measure duty by financial standards? Do you tell me of the tremendous toil required to overcome the vast difficulties of our task? What mighty work for the world, for humanity, even for ourselves, has ever been done with ease? Even our bread must we eat by the sweat of our faces. Why are we charged with power such as no people ever knew, if we are not to use it in a work such as no people ever wrought? Who will dispute the divine meaning of the fable of the talents?

Do you remind me of the precious blood that must be shed, the lives that must be given, the broken hearts of loved ones for their slain? And this is indeed a heavier price than all combined. And yet as a nation every historic duty we have done, every achievement we have accomplished, has been by the sacrifice of our noblest sons. Every holy memory that glorifies the flag is of those heroes who have died that its onward march might not be stayed. It is the nation's dearest lives yielded for the flag that makes it dear to us: it is the nation's most precious blood poured out for it that makes it precious to us. That flag is woven of heroism and grief, of the bravery of men and women's tears, of righteousness and battle, of sacrifice and anguish, of triumph and of glory. It is these which make our flag a holy thing. Who would tear from that sacred banner the glorious legends of a single battle where it has waved on land or sea? What son of a soldier of the flag whose father fell beneath it on any field would surrender that proud record for the heraldry of a king? In the cause of civilization, in the service of the Republic anywhere on earth, Americans consider wounds the noblest decorations man can win, and count the giving of their lives a glad and precious duty.

Pray God that spirit never fails. Pray God the time may never come when Mammon and the love of ease shall so debase our blood that we will fear to shed it for the flag and its imperial destiny. Pray God the time may never come when American heroism is but a legend like the story of the Cid, American faith in our mission and our might a dream dissolved, and the glory of our mighty race departed.

And that time will never come. We will renew our youth at the fountain of new and glorious deeds. We will exalt our reverence for the flag by carrying it to a noble future as well as by remembering its ineffable past. Its immortality will not pass, because everywhere and always we will acknowledge and discharge the solemn responsibilities our sacred flag, in its deepest meaning, puts upon us. And so, Senators, with reverent hearts, where dwells the fear of God, the American people move forward to the future of their hope and the doing of His work.

Mr. President and Senators, adopt the resolution offered, that peace may quickly come and that we may begin our saving, regenerating, and uplifting work. Adopt it, and this bloodshed will cease when these deluded children of our islands learn that this is the final word of the representatives of the American people in Congress assembled. Reject it, and the world, history, and the American people will know where to forever fix the awful responsibility for the consequences that will surely follow such failure to do our manifest duty. How dare we delay when our soldiers' blood is flowing? [Applause in the galleries.]

The PRESIDENT pro tempore. Applause is not permitted in the United States Senate.

Mr. HOAR. Mr. President—

The PRESIDENT pro tempore. The Senator from Massachusetts will suspend for one moment. The Chair lays before the Senate the unfinished business, the title of which will be stated.

The SECRETARY. A bill (H. R. 1) to define and fix the standard of value, to maintain the parity of all forms of money issued or coined by the United States, and for other purposes.

Mr. HOAR. Mr. President, I ask that the unfinished business be informally laid aside, as I understand no Senator wishes to speak upon it this afternoon, and I desire to make a very few observations on the pending resolution.

The PRESIDENT pro tempore. The Senator from Massachusetts asks that the unfinished business may be temporarily laid aside. Is there objection? The Chair hears none, and the Senator from Massachusetts will proceed.

Mr. HOAR. Mr. President, I have listened, delighted, as have, I suppose, all the members of the Senate, to the eloquence of my honorable friend from Indiana [Mr. BEVERIDGE]. I am glad to welcome to the public service his enthusiasm, his patriotism, his silver speech, and the earnestness and the courage with which he has devoted himself to a discharge of his duty to the Republic as he conceives it. Yet, Mr. President, as I heard his eloquent description of wealth and glory and commerce and trade, I listened in vain for those words which the American people have been wont to take upon their lips in every solemn crisis of their history. I heard much calculated to excite the imagination of the youth seeking wealth or the youth charmed by the dream of empire. But the words Right, Justice, Duty, Freedom were absent, my friend must permit me to say, from that eloquent speech. I could think as this brave young Republic of ours listened to what he had to say of but one occurrence:

> Then the devil taketh Him up into an exceeding high mountain and sheweth Him all the kingdoms of the world and the glory of them.
>
> And the devil said unto Him. "All these things will I give Thee if Thou wilt fall down and worship me."
>
> Then saith Jesus unto him, "Get thee behind me, Satan."

Mr. President, the Senator himself and the evidence coming from our two commanders, General Otis and Admiral Dewey, and witnesses for whom they vouch, refute every one of the propositions of fact on which my honorable friend has built his glittering temple of glass. He describes the impotence and ineffectual attempt of Spain for three hundred years to reduce that people to subjection: tells us that she had failed. He counsels us to avoid the errors and the mistakes and the sins she has committed. If that be true, Mr. President, where did Spain get the right to sell the people of the Philippine Islands to us? They had risen against that effete and impotent and ineffectual effort of Spain; they had driven her from the entire soil of their island, save a single city; they hemmed in her troops in that single city of Manila by a cordon of their troops stretching from water to water; and Spain surrendered to us only because her soldiers could not get out of reach of the American guns without being compelled to surrender to the Filipinos.

I think you will have to enlarge the doctrines of the American Declaration of Independence. I think you will have to build anew a Constitution which, he says, is only an instrument and not a rule of duty, before you can find your right to buy and sell that people like sheep.

My honorable friend, I am sure, when he reflects upon it, will never advise the people of the United States to do a base thing for all this wealth, for all this glory, for all this empire. I say if it be true that that was a people that desired independence and were fit for independence, then it would be a base thing for this young giant in its might to strike down that infant republic.

DOCUMENT 14.6

Speech by President William McKinley, in Charles S. Olcott, *The Life of William McKinley*, 2 vols. (Boston, 1916), vol. 2, pp. 110–111.

Before you go I would like to say just a word about the Philippine business. I have been criticized a good deal about the Philippines, but don't deserve it. The truth is I didn't want the Philippines, and when they came to us, as a gift from the gods, I did not know what to do with them. When the Spanish War broke out, Dewey was at Hong-kong, and I ordered him to go to Manila and to capture or destroy the Spanish fleet, and he had to; because, if defeated, he had no place to refit on that side of the globe, and if the Dons were victorious, they would likely cross the Pacific and ravage our Oregon and California coasts. And so he had to destroy the Spanish fleet, and did it! But that was as far as I thought then.

"When next I realized that the Philippines had dropped into our laps I confess I did not know what to do with them. I sought counsel from all sides—Democrats as well as Republicans—but got little help. I thought first we would take only Manila; then Luzon; then other islands, perhaps, also. I walked the floor of the White House night after night until midnight; and I am not ashamed to tell you, gentlemen, that I went down on my knees and prayed Almighty God for light and guidance more than one night. And one night late it came to me this way—I don't know how it was, but it came: (1) That we could not give them back to Spain—that would be cowardly and dishonorable; (2) that we could not turn them over to France or Germany—our commercial rivals in the Orient—that would be bad business and discreditable; (3) that we could not leave them to themselves—they were unfit for self-government—and they would soon have anarchy and misrule over there worse than Spain's was; and (4) that there was nothing left for us to do but to take them all, and to educate the Filipinos, and uplift and civilize and Christianize them, and by God's grace do the very best we could by them, as our fellow-men for whom Christ also died. And then I went to bed, and went to sleep, and slept soundly, and the next morning I sent for the chief engineer of the War Department (our map-maker), and I told him to put the Philippines on the map of the United States [pointing to a large map on the wall of his office], and there they are, and there they will stay while I am President!"

➔ DOCUMENT 14.7a ➔

Poem by Rudyard Kipling, "The White Man's Burden," 1899, in *McClure's Magazine*, 21 (February 1899), p. 291.

THE WHITE MAN'S BURDEN

(The United States and the Philippine Islands)

Take up the White Man's burden—
Send forth the best ye breed—
Go bind your sons to exile
To serve your captives' need;
To wait in heavy harness
On fluttered folk and wild—
Your new-caught, sullen peoples,
Half devil and half child.

Take up the White Man's burden—
In patience to abide,
To veil the threat of terror
And check the show of pride;
By open speech and simple,
An hundred times made plain,
To seek another's profit,
And work another's gain.

Take up the White Man's burden—
The savage wars of peace—
Fill full the mouth of Famine
And bid the sickness cease;
And when your goal is nearest
The end for others sought,
Watch Sloth and heathen Folly
Bring all your hope to nought.

Take up the White Man's burden—
No tawdry rule of kings,
But toil of serf and sweeper—
The tale of common things.
The ports ye shall not enter,
The roads ye shall not tread,
Go make them with your living,
And mark them with your dead!

Take up the White Man's burden—
And reap his old reward:
The blame of those ye better,
The hate of those ye guard—
The cry of hosts ye humour
(Ah, slowly) toward the light:—
'Why brought ye us from bondage,
'Our loved Egyptian night?'

Take up the White Man's burden—
Ye dare not stoop to less—
Nor call too loud on Freedom
To cloak your weariness;

By all ye cry or whisper,
   By all ye leave or do,
The silent, sullen peoples
   Shall weigh your Gods and you.

Take up the White Man's burden—
   Have done with childish days—
The lightly proffered laurel,
   The easy, ungrudged praise.
Comes now, to search your manhood
   Through all the thankless years,
Cold-edged with dear-bought wisdom.
   The judgment of your peers!

1899

✧ DOCUMENT 14.7b ✧

Poem by Ernest Howard Crosby, "The Real 'White Man's Burden'," 1899, in Ernest Howard Crosby, *Swords and Plowshares* (New York: Funk and Wagnalls, 1902), pp. 33–34. Poem originally appeared in *New York Times* (February 15, 1899).

THE REAL "WHITE MAN'S BURDEN"

by Ernest Howard Crosby

Take up the White Man's burden.
Send forth your sturdy kin,
And load them down with Bibles
And cannon-balls and gin.
Throw in a few diseases
To spread the tropic climes
For there the healthy niggers
Are quite behind the times.

And don't forget the factories
On those benighted shores
They have no cheerful iron mills
Nor eke department stores.
They never work twelve hours a day,
And live in strange content
Altho' they never have to pay
A single sou of rent.

Take up the White Man's Burden,
And teach the Phillippines
What interest and taxes are
And what a mortgage means.
Give them electrocution chairs,
And prisons, too, galore,
And if they seem inclined to kick
Then spill their heathen gore.

They need our labor question, too,
And politics and fraud—
We've made a pretty mess at home,
Let's make a mess abroad.
And let us ever humbly pray
The Lord of Hosts may deign
To stir our feeble memories
Lest we forget—the *Maine*.

→ DOCUMENT 14.8a ←

Platform of the American Anti-Imperialist League, October 18, 1899. Papers of the Anti-Imperialist League, Michigan Historical Collection, University of Michigan, Ann Arbor.

We hold that the policy known as imperialism is hostile to liberty and tends toward militarism, an evil from which it has been our glory to be free. We regret that it has become necessary in the land of Washington and Lincoln to reaffirm that all men, of whatever race or color, are entitled to life, liberty, and the pursuit of happiness. We maintain that governments derive their just powers from the consent of the governed. We insist that the subjugation of any people is "criminal aggression" and open disloyalty to the distinctive principles of our Government.

We earnestly condemn the policy of the present National Administration in the Philippines. It seeks to extinguish the spirit of 1776 in those islands. We deplore the sacrifice of our soldiers and sailors, whose bravery deserves admiration even in an unjust war. We denounce the slaughter of the Filipinos as a needless horror. We protest against the extension of American sovereignty by Spanish methods.

We demand the immediate cessation of the war against liberty, begun by Spain and continued by us. We urge that Congress be promptly convened to announce to the Filipinos our purpose to concede to them the independence for which they have so long fought and which of right is theirs.

The United States have always protested against the doctrine of international law which permits the subjugation of the weak by the strong. A self-governing state cannot accept sovereignty over an unwilling people. The United States cannot act upon the ancient heresy that might makes right.

Imperialists assume that with the destruction of self-government in the Philippines by American hands, all opposition here will cease. This is a grievous error. Much as we abhor the war of "criminal aggression" in the Philippines, greatly as we regret that the blood of the Filipinos is on American hands, we more deeply resent the betrayal of American institutions at home. The real firing line is not in the suburbs of Manila. The foe is of our own household. The attempt of 1861 was to divide the country. That of 1899 is to destroy its fundamental principles and noblest ideals.

Whether the ruthless slaughter of the Filipinos shall end next month or next year is but an incident in a contest that must go on until the Declaration of Independence and the Constitution of the United States are rescued from the hands of their betrayers. Those who dispute about standards of value while the Republic is undermined will be listened to as little as those who would wrangle about the small economies of the household while the house is on fire. The training of a great people for a century, the aspiration for liberty of a vast immigration are forces that will hurl aside those who in the delirium of conquest seek to destroy the character of our institutions.

We deny that the obligation of all citizens to support their Government in times of grave National peril applies to the present situation. If an Administration may with impunity ignore the issues upon which it was chosen, deliberately create a condition of war anywhere on the face of the globe, debauch the civil service for spoils to promote the adventure, organize a truth-suppressing censorship and demand of all citizens a suspension of judgement and their unanimous support while it chooses to continue the fighting, representative government itself is imperiled.

We propose to contribute to the defeat of any person or party that stands for the forcible subjugation of any people. We shall oppose for reëlection all who in the White House or in Congress betray American liberty in pursuit of un-American gains. We still hope that both of our great political parties will support and defend the Declaration of Independence in the closing campaign of the century.

We hold, with Abraham Lincoln, that "no man is good enough to govern another man without that man's consent. When the white man governs himself, that is self-government, but when he governs himself and also governs another man, that is more than self-government—that is despotism." "Our reliance is in the love of liberty which God has planted in us. Our defense is in the spirit which prizes liberty as the heritage of all men in all lands. Those who deny freedom to others deserve it not for themselves, and under a just God cannot long retain it."

We cordially invite the coöperation of all men and women who remain loyal to the Declaration of Independence and the Constitution of the United States.

→ DOCUMENT 14.8b ←

Speech on imperialism by Senator George F. Hoar (Massachusetts), United States Senate, January 9, 1899, in *Congressional Record*, 55th Congress, 3rd session, pp. 501–503.

At the close of the nineteenth century the American Republic, after its example in abolishing slavery has spread through the world, is asked by the Senator from Connecticut to adopt a doctrine of constitutional expansion on the principle that it is right to conquer, buy, and subject a whole nation if we happen to deem it for their good—for their good as we conceive it, and not as they conceive it.

Mr. President, Abraham Lincoln said, "No man was ever created good enough to own another." No nation was ever created good enough to own another.

No single American workman, no humble American home, will ever be better or happier for the constitutional doctrine which the Senator from Connecticut proclaims. If it be adopted here not only the workman's wages will be diminished, not only will the burden of taxation be increased, not only, like the peasant of Europe, will he be born with a heavy debt about his neck and will stagger with an armed soldier upon his back, but his dignity will be dishonored and his manhood discrowned by the act of his own Government.

The Senator from Connecticut himself acted on a different doctrine within six months. He resolved, "That the people of Cuba are, and of right ought to be, free and independent," and I think you will tell the Senate by and by that the people of Cuba are not as fit for self-government as the people of the Philippine Islands.

Mr. PLATT of Connecticut. Mr. President—

The PRESIDENT pro tempore. Does the Senator from Massachusetts yield to the Senator from Connecticut?

Mr. HOAR. Yes. I am almost through.

Mr. PLATT of Connecticut. I have not sought to interrupt the Senator, but I think he misstates my position on that resolution. I did not vote for that proposition.

Mr. HOAR. Did the Senator refrain from voting because he did not think the people of Cuba "of right ought to be free and independent," or for some other reason?

Mr. PLATT of Connecticut. Oh, no; but I simply wish to correct the misstatement of the Senator.

Mr. HOAR. I did not know but the Senator might help me a little further by saying what was his reason for not voting for the resolution. If the Senator voted against it because he thought the resolution denied the essential right to the people of Cuba to self-government, then I will withdraw the remark.

Mr. PLATT of Connecticut. The Senator is tempting me into a speech, which he would not tolerate, I think, if I should deliver it now.

Mr. HOAR. Very well. Then, if the Senator did not believe, or did not declare, six months ago "that the people of Cuba are, and of right ought to be, free and independent," if he now denies that postulate, I can not in that particular impute to him any inconsistency, and I take back anything which seems to impute it. But the Senate did. They voted that the people of Cuba of right ought to be free and independent, and I suppose the commissioners who have come back from Paris are going to tell us some time and some where that the people of Cuba are not as fit for self-government as the people of the Philippine Islands.

Mr. PLATT of Connecticut. Will the Senator permit me one word?

Mr. HOAR. Certainly.

Mr. PLATT of Connecticut. The Senator from Massachusetts upon the passage of that resolution, having voted with me against the clause that the people of Cuba were, and of right ought to be, free and independent, withheld his vote and did not vote for the resolution. Would it not be as fair for me to ask him if the reason he did not vote for the resolution was because he thought the people of Cuba ought not to be free and independent?

Mr. HOAR. The reason I did not vote for the resolution was because I thought it was an attempt to recognize a particular and pretended government there. When that was stricken out, I voted, I suppose, for the declaration on the final passage. But whoever did or whoever did not vote that way, the Senate voted that way, and the Senate will not say that the right to be free and independent belongs to the people of Cuba by reason of any special conditions, because they are white men or Americans or Christians, that does not appertain to every people the world over.

The people of the United States, through their legislative bodies and their President, have committed themselves within the last six months to the doctrine that self-government is a right, not a privilege—not "some of them." Will they attack that doctrine now?

Did they not swear at first to fight
For the King's safety and his right?
And after marched to find him out,
And charged him home with horse and foot;
And yet still had the confidence
To swear it was his defense?

I do not agree, Mr. President, that the lesson of our first hundred years is that the Declaration of Independence and the Constitution are a failure, and that America is to begin the twentieth century where Spain began the sixteenth.

The Monroe doctrine is gone. Every European nation, every European alliance, has the right to acquire dominion in this hemisphere when we acquire it in the other. The Senator's doctrine put anywhere in practice will make of our beloved country a cheap-jack country, raking after the cart for the leavings of European tyranny.

It may be that in some storm and tempest of popular delusion, a cloud may for the moment cover the great truths of our Declaration. I have within the compass of my own life encountered such a storm and tempest more than once. In 1850, after the passage of the compromise measure, the great contest for the freedom of the vast territory between the Mississippi and the Pacific seemed hopelessly lost. Senate and people, courts and State legislatures seemed all bowing in assent to the overthrow of the great principles of the Declaration. But after a few short years the cloud and storm passed by, and the eternal constellation shone out unmoved and unshaken in its glory in the sky.

I remember when the great political party swept over the North, electing in my own State every member of the legislature but two, every member of Congress, every member of the State government, based on the doctrine of denying the application of these truths to citizens of foreign birth. But again the delusion passed by, and the eternal truths shone out. I have seen like movements of popular error and delusion in more recent years. So far God has given me strength to withstand them in my humble fashion. But they were overthrown and brought to naught, not by any human strength, but because the eternal providence of God is on the side of freedom.

Our fathers dreaded a standing army; but the Senator's doctrine, put in practice anywhere, now or hereafter, renders necessary a standing army, to be reenforced by a powerful navy. Our fathers denounced the subjection of any people whose judges were appointed or whose salaries were paid by a foreign power; but the Senator's doctrine requires us to send to a foreign people judges, not of their own selection, appointed and paid by us. The Senator's doctrine, whenever it shall be put in practice, will entail upon us a national debt larger than any now existing on the face of the earth, larger than any ever known in history.

Our fathers dreaded the national taxgatherer; but the doctrine of the Senator from Connecticut, if it be adopted, is sure to make our national taxgatherer the most familiar visitant to every American home.

Our fathers respected above all the dignity of labor and rights of human nature. The one thing created by God a little lower than the angels was a man. And they meant to send abroad the American flag bearing upon its folds, invisible perhaps to the bodily eye, but visible to the spiritual discernment, the legend of the dignity of pure manhood. That legend, that charter, that fundamental truth, is written in the opening sentences of the great Declaration, and now the Senator from Connecticut would repeal them. He would repeal the great charter of our covenant. No longer, as the flag floats over distant seas, shall it bear on its folds to the downtrodden and oppressed among men the glad tidings that there is at least one spot where that beautiful dream is a living reality. The poor Malay, the poor African, the downtrodden workman of Europe, will exclaim, as he reads this new doctrine: "Good God! Is there not one place left on earth where in right of my manhood I can stand up and be a man?" Will you disregard every lesson of experience? No tropical colony was ever yet successfully administered without a system of contract labor strictly administered and enforced by the Government. I will not speak of the thirteenth amendment. In our parliamentary practice amendments fall with the original bill. This amendment will fall with the original Constitution.

Mr. President, this spasm of folly and delusion also, in my judgment, will surely pass by. Whether it pass by or no, I thank God I have done my duty, and that I have adhered to the great doctrines of righteousness and freedom, which I learned from my fathers, and in whose service my life has been spent.

Mr. PLATT of Connecticut. Mr. President—

The PRESIDENT pro tempore. The Senator will pardon the Chair for one moment. Shall the unfinished business be temporarily laid aside so that the Senator from Connecticut may proceed?

Mr. GALLINGER. I make that request.

Mr. TELLER. I ask unanimous consent that the unfinished business may be temporarily laid aside in order that the Senator from Connecticut may proceed.

The PRESIDENT pro tempore. Without objection, that order will be made.

Mr. PLATT of Connecticut. Mr. President, I can not ask the indulgence of the Senate at this time to reply extemporaneously and at length to the carefully prepared speech of the Senator from Massachusetts [Mr. HOAR]. I can only say I have listened to it with great attention and with great interest. The Senator from Massachusetts is a master of language, a master of sarcasm, and he has succeeded on this occasion in conjuring up a specter which is only a specter; to use more familiar language, he has spent a large part of his argument in creating a man of straw, and the rest of his argument in attempting to demolish his man of straw. If I have followed him correctly—and I think I have—he has not answered the argument which I had the honor to make in the Senate the other day. He has simply misrepresented what I said on that occasion.

The specter which the Senator conjures up he names Congressional despotism. He assumes and asserts that I had committed myself to the doctrine of governing territory which we may acquire, and which he says we have a right to acquire and a right to govern. He admits that.

Mr. HOAR. No. I do not: not the least in the world. If the Senator will yield to me. I deny the right.

Mr. PLATT of Connecticut. I am sorry to have my sentence broken in two, but I will yield to the Senator.

Mr. HOAR. If the Senator will pardon me. I not only denied the right of acquiring and holding territory for the purpose of governing it, but I repeated that denial twenty times; and the utterance which I imputed to the Senator from Connecticut I carefully extracted from his own speech and put in quotation marks.

Mr. PLATT of Connecticut. I think when the Senator's speech, already printed, comes to be read, he will find that I do not misquote him when I say that he admits the right to acquire territory and the right to govern it. . . .

That is a part of the argument of the Senator from Massachusetts [Mr. HOAR], and also made the other day by the Senator from Louisiana [Mr. CAFFERY], which, if I understand it, is to the effect that we can not exercise even our war power in the United

States: that we can not defend ourselves in war by going into the enemy's territory, unless we inquire beforehand whether the people of the territory that we may conquer are willing that we should go there. That is a fair statement of the argument, Mr. President, and the statement of the argument contains its answer.

I was not one who desired this war. I stood against it as long as I could. I felt that the cause of free government in Cuba might be secured by diplomacy. I thought that, if the hand of war could be stayed, the end desired might be accomplished through peace, but, Mr. President, that war came, and with it came obligations to succeed, and the moment it was declared I was for my country and for pressing that war forward to its successful conclusion.

Over in the bay of Manila there was a third of the Spanish fleet. To allow that fleet to join the home fleet of Spain and to go against our fleet would have put us perhaps at a disadvantage; certainly we would have been on no more than terms of equal advantage. The Commander in Chief of the United States sent forth the message to Admiral Dewey, "Destroy the Spanish fleet at Manila." We had no thought of the consequence. The President of the United States had no thought of the consequence. That was the one thing which in war we were obliged to do, and gloriously was it done. Is there an American citizen upon whose cheek the blush of shame would not have mantled if those ships had been called away when their work was done? It was the inevitable result of that war which I desired to avoid.

Nay, more, Mr. President, I believe that back of it all was the hand of Providence. I believe in Providence. This war might have been averted had it not been that on one night our ship, the *Maine,* lying at anchor peacefully in the harbor of Havana was, in a moment, destroyed and its crew launched into eternity. Human foresight could not have contemplated that. Human foresight could not have avoided that catastrophe. Human foresight could not foresee the consequences which were to arise from that action in Manila Bay.

I believe in Providence. I believe the hand of Providence brought about the conditions which we must either accept or be recreant to duty. I believe that those conditions were a part of the great development of the great force of Christian civilization on earth. I believe the same force was behind our army at Santiago and our ships in Manila Bay that was behind the landing of the Pilgrims on Plymouth Rock. I believe that we have been chosen to carry on and to carry forward this great work of uplifting humanity on earth. From the time of the landing on Plymouth Rock in the spirit of the Declaration of Independence, in the spirit of the Constitution, believing that all men are equal and endowed by their Creator with inalienable rights, believing that governments derive their just powers from the consent of the governed, we have spread that civilization across the continent until it stood at the Pacific Ocean looking ever westward.

Westward the course of empire takes its way.

The English-speaking people, the agents of this civilization, the agency through which humanity is to be uplifted, through which despotism is to go down, through which the rights of man are to prevail, is charged with this great mission. Providence has put it upon us. We propose to execute it. We propose to proclaim liberty in the Philippine Islands, if they are ours. We propose to proclaim liberty and justice and the protection of life and human rights wherever the flag of the United States is planted. Who denies that? Who will haul down those principles?

No, Mr. President, this is a man of straw which has been set up here, dressed up in the imagery of the Senator from Massachusetts. I did not intend to be led into any reply. I simply desire to say that there can be no false issue raised here.

We can not be accused of not loving liberty and justice and equality and the rights of men with a love as pure and as earnest and as unselfish as that of the Senator from Massachusetts. With that love in our hearts, with the traditions of the past in our eyes, and with duty ever before us, we shall meet these questions as they arise, and for one, Mr. President, I shall meet them in the spirit both of the Declaration of Independence and the Constitution of the United States.

Mr. HOAR. Mr. President, the Senator from Connecticut—

Mr. MORGAN. I should like to know how long this debate is to proceed?

Mr. HOAR. I should like only three minutes.

Mr. MORGAN. I will yield for three minutes.

Mr. HOAR. Possibly it may be four. I shall not take any great length of time.

Mr. MORGAN. All right.

The PRESIDENT pro tempore. The Senator from Massachusetts asks that the unfinished business may be temporarily laid aside in order that he may make some remarks. Is there objection? The Chair hears none.

Mr. HOAR. Mr. President, the Senator from Connecticut misunderstands my own position and misunderstands the part of his against which my argument was directed: that is, he misunderstands me as to that part of his of which I spoke. It is not about what he has lately said that I have been talking. My proposition, summed up in a nut shell, is this: I admit you have the right to acquire territory for constitutional purposes, and you may hold land and govern men on it for the constitutional purpose of a seat of government or for the constitutional purpose of admitting it as a State. I deny the right to hold land or acquire any property for any purpose not contemplated by the Constitution. The government of foreign people against their will is not a constitutional purpose, but a purpose expressly forbidden by the Constitution. Therefore I deny the right to acquire this territory and to hold it by the Government for that purpose. So when the Senator says he thought I admitted that we have the right to acquire it, he misunderstands me.

Mr. FORAKER. Will the Senator from Massachusetts allow me to ask him a question before he takes his seat?

Mr. HOAR. Yes; but not at this time. I wish to complete what I was saying.

The Senator from Connecticut undertakes to say that I misunderstood him. What I understood he said and what I commented on is in his words, quoted fully. It is not upon what principles he proposes to govern these people alone that I charge him with denying the principles of the Constitution and the Declaration. It is in his undertaking to govern them at all without their consent.

Now, I claim that under the Declaration of Independence you can not govern a foreign territory, a foreign people, another people than your own, that you can not subjugate them and govern them against their will, because you think it is for their good, when they do not: because you think you are going to give them the blessings of liberty. You have no right at the cannon's mouth to impose on an unwilling people your Declaration of Independence and your Constitution and your notions of freedom and notions of what is good. That is the proposition which the Senator asserted. He does not deny it now. If the Senator gets up and says. "I will not have those people in Iloilo subdued: I will not govern the Philippine Islands unless the people consent: they shall be consulted at every step," he would stand in a different position. That is what I am complaining of. When I asked the Senator during his speech whether he denied that just governments rested on the consent of the governed, he said, in substance, that he did deny it—that is, his answer was "some of them:" and he then went on to specify places where government did not so rest.

The Senator says, "Oh, we governed the Indians against their will when we first came here," long before the Declaration of Independence. I do not think so. I am speaking of other people. Now, the people of the Philippine Islands are clearly a nation—a people three and one-third times as numerous as our fathers were when they set up this nation. If gentlemen say that because we did what we did on finding a great many million square miles of forests and a few hundred or thousand men roaming over it without any national life, without the germ of national life, without the capacity for self-government, without self-government, without desiring self-government, was a violation of your principle. I answer if it was a violation of your principle it was wrong. It does not help us out any to say that one hundred and fifty years ago we held slaves or did something else. If it be a violation of your principle it is wrong. But if, as our fathers thought and as we all think, it was not a violation of the principle because there was not a people capable of national life or capable of government in any form, that is another thing.

But read the account of what is going on in Iloilo. The people there have got a government, with courts and judges, better than those of the people of Cuba, who, it was said, had a right to self-government, collecting their customs: and it is proposed to turn your guns on them, and say, "We think that our notion of government is better than the notion you have got yourselves." I say that when you put that onto them against their will and say that freedom as we conceive it, not freedom as they conceive it, public interest as we conceive it, not as they conceive it, shall prevail, and that if it does not we are to force it on them at the cannon's mouth—I say that the nation which undertakes that plea and says it is subduing these men for their good, when they do not want to be subdued for their good, will encounter the awful and terrible rebuke, "Beware of the leaven of the Pharisees, which is hypocrisy."

DOCUMENT 14.9a

Cartoon in magazine, "The Spanish Brute Adds Mutilation to Murder," by Grant Hamilton, in *Judge*, July 9, 1898. Culver Pictures.

DOCUMENT 14.9b

Cartoon in magazine, "Is He to Be a Despot?" artist unknown, in *The Verdict*, 1899.

IS HE TO BE A DESPOT?

→ DOCUMENT 14.10 ←

Essay by Mark Twain, "To the Person Sitting in Darkness," in *North American Review* (February 1901), pp. 461–473.

"To the Person Sitting in Darkness," February 1901

[S]hall we go on conferring our Civilization upon the peoples that sit in darkness, or shall we give those poor things a rest? Shall we bang right ahead in our old-time, loud, pious way, and commit the new century to the game; or shall we sober up and sit down and think it over first? Would it not be prudent to get our Civilization-tools together, and see how much stock is left on hand in the way of Glass Beads and Theology, and Maxim Guns and Hymn Books, and Trade-Gin and Torches of Progress and Enlightenment (patent adjustable ones, good to fire villages with, upon occasion), and balance the books, and arrive at the profit and loss, so that we may intelligently decide whether to continue the business or sell out the property and start a new Civilization Scheme on the proceeds?

Extending the Blessings of Civilization to our Brother who Sits in Darkness has been a good trade and has paid well, on the whole: and there is money in it yet, if carefully worked but not enough, in my judgment, to make any considerable risk advisable. The People that Sit in Darkness are getting to be too scarce—too scarce and too shy. And such darkness as is now left is really of but an indifferent quality, and not dark enough for the game. The most of those People that Sit in Darkness have been furnished with more light than was good for them or profitable for us. We have been injudicious.

The Blessings-of-Civilization Trust, wisely and cautiously administered, is a Daisy. There is more money in it, more territory, more sovereignty, and other kinds of emolument, than there is in any other game that is played. But Christendom has been playing it badly of late years, and must certainly suffer by it, in my opinion. She has been so eager to get every stake that appeared on the green cloth, that the People who Sit in Darkness have noticed it—they have noticed it, and have begun to show alarm. They have become suspicious of the Blessings of Civilization. More—they have begun to examine them. This is not well. The Blessings of Civilization are all right, and a good commercial property; there could not be a better, in a dim light. In the right kind of a light, and at a proper distance, with the goods a little out of focus, they furnish this desirable exhibit to the Gentlemen who Sit in Darkness:

LOVE, LAW AND ORDER, JUSTICE, LIBERTY, GENTLENESS, EQUALITY, CHRISTIANITY, HONORABLE DEALING, PROTECTION TO THE WEAK, MERCY, TEMPERANCE, EDUCATION, and so on.

There. Is it good? Sir, it is pie. It will bring into camp any idiot that sits in darkness anywhere. But not if we adulterate it. It is proper to be emphatic upon that point. This brand is strictly for Export—apparently. *Apparently*. Privately and confidentially, it is nothing of the kind. Privately and confidentially, it is merely an outside cover, gay and pretty and attractive, displaying the special patterns of our Civilization which we reserve for Home Consumption, while *inside* the bale is the Actual Thing that the Customer Sitting in Darkness buys with his blood and tears and land and liberty. That Actual Thing is, indeed, Civilization, but it is only for Export. . . .

We all know that the Business is being ruined. The reason is not far to seek. It is because our Mr. McKinley . . . [has] been exporting the Actual Thing *with the outside cover left off*. This is bad for the Game. . . .

Now, my plan is . . . let us audaciously present the whole of the facts, shirking none. . . . This daring truthfulness will astonish and dazzle the Person Sitting in Darkness. . . . Let us say to him:

"Our case is simple. On the 1st of May, Dewey destroyed the Spanish fleet. This left the [Philippine] Archipelago in the hands of its proper and rightful owners, the Filipino nation. Their army numbered 30,000 men, and they were competent to whip out or starve out the little Spanish garrison; then the people could set up a government of their own devising. Our traditions required that Dewey should now set up his warning sign, and go away. But the Master of the Game happened to think of another plan—the European plan. He acted upon it. This was, to send out an army—ostensibly to help the native patriots put the finishing touch upon their long and plucky struggle for independence, but really to take their land away from them and keep it. That is, in the interest of Progress and Civilization. The plan developed, stage by stage, and quite satisfactorily. We entered into a military alliance with the trusting Filipinos, and they hemmed in Manila on the land side, and by their valuable help the place, with its garrison of 8,000 or 10,000 Spaniards, was captured—a thing which we could not have accomplished unaided at that time. We got their help by ingenuity. We knew they were fighting for their independence, and that they had been at it for two years. We knew they supposed that we also were fighting in their worthy cause—just as we had helped the Cubans fight for Cuban independence—and we allowed them to go on thinking so. *Until Manila was ours and we could get along without them.* Then we showed our hand. Of course, they were surprised—that was natural; surprised and disappointed; disappointed and grieved. To them it looked un-American; uncharacteristic; foreign to our established traditions. And this was natural, too; for we were only playing the American Game in public—in private it was the European. It was neatly done, very neatly, and it bewildered them. They could not understand it; for we had been so friendly—so affectionate. . . .

"We and the patriots having captured Manila, Spain's ownership of the Archipelago and her sovereignty over it were at an end—obliterated—annihilated—not a rag or shred of either remaining behind. It was then that we conceived the divinely humorous idea of *buying* both of these spectres from Spain! (It is quite safe to confess this to the Person Sitting in Darkness, since neither he nor any other sane person will believe it.) In buying those ghosts for twenty millions, we also contracted to take care of the friars and their accumulations. I think we also agreed to propagate leprosy and smallpox, but as to this there is doubt. But it is not important; persons afflicted with the friars do not mind other diseases.

"With our Treaty ratified, Manila subdued, and our Ghosts secured, we had no further use for Aguinaldo and the owners of the Archipelago. We forced a war, and we have been hunting America's guest and ally through the woods and swamps ever since." . . .

Having now laid all the historical facts before the Person Sitting in Darkness, we should bring him to again, and explain them to him. We should say to him:

"They look doubtful, but in reality they are not. There have been lies; yes, but they were told in a good cause. We have been treacherous; but that was only in order that real good might come out of apparent evil. True, we have crushed a deceived and confiding people; we have turned against the weak and the friendless who trusted us; we have stamped out a just and intelligent and well-ordered republic; we have stabbed an ally in the back and slapped the face of a guest; we have bought a Shadow from an enemy that hadn't it to sell; we have robbed a trusting friend of his land and his liberty; we have invited our clean young men to shoulder a discredited musket and do bandit's work under a flag which bandits have been accustomed to fear, not to follow; we have debauched America's honor and blackened her face before the world; but each detail was for the best. We know this. The Head of every State and Sovereignty in Christendom and ninety per cent. of every legislative body in Christendom, including our Congress and our fifty State Legislatures, are members not only of the church, but also of the Blessings-of-Civilization Trust. This world-girdling accumulation of trained morals, high principles, and justice, cannot do an unright thing, an unfair thing, an ungenerous thing, an unclean thing. It knows what it is about. Give yourself no uneasiness; it is all right."

Now then, that will convince the Person. You will see. It will restore the Business. . . .

And as for a flag for the Philippine Province, it is easily managed. We can have a special one . . . : we can have just our usual flag, with the white stripes painted black and the stars replaced by the skull and cross-bones.

Confronting the Problems of Urban, Industrial America

Archive Overview

ALTHOUGH newspapers and television news programs remind us that American cities are in trouble, many of us can almost ignore urban problems because we spend so little time in the nation's central cities. And even though there are occasional scares about contaminated food or medicine, most of us expect our foods and drugs to be safe. In a similar way, we expect to work in safe, clean, and sometimes even comfortable, places.

Americans were not always able to avoid urban problems or to take for granted matters of personal safety. During the late 19th century and the first decades of the 20th century, Americans began to see some consequences of becoming an industrial, urban nation. Those who believed that conditions must change became reformers, known as *progressives*; the reform movement with which they were associated is known as *progressivism*. Despite the label, historians have disagreed about what progressivism is. Most historians mention an optimism about reform and a faith in science, efficiency, and experts, but some historians find such a definition too broad to be useful. It could describe both big businessmen and trust-busters; those who favored what would later be called "big government" and those who concentrated on the "private sector." Furthermore, it fails to illuminate the subtle power and self-interest involved in reformism.

Your main task in this archive is to explore some of the issues which concerned the progressives. What social and political problems do the sources reveal, and why did reformers find them so worrisome? Then, by examining documents drawn mostly from Hiram House, a social settlement in Cleveland, you should determine some of the strategies reformers adopted and evaluate their impact both on the reformers' working-class and immigrant clients and on the reformers themselves. What were reformers trying to accomplish, and how successful were their strategies? Your secondary task is to consider how the sources collected here relate to the historical debate about the nature of progressivism. What definitions of progressivism do these sources support? What sacrifices did reformers make in order to change their world? What signs of self-interest and a desire for power do you see?

Placing the Sources in Context

DURING the progressive era, between 1890 and the outbreak of World War I in 1914, Americans sought to improve their own and others' lives as the nation struggled with the consequences

TIMELINE

1880s–1910s	New immigration from southern and eastern Europe
1890–1910	Southern state constitutions rewritten
1890s–1920s	Migration of African-Americans from the South to northern cities
1887	College Settlement House Association founded
1889	Vida Scudder starts Denison House in Boston; Jane Addams founds Hull House in Chicago
1892	Jacob Riis's study *How the Other Half Lives* appears
1893–1897	Depression in the United States
1896	*Plessy v. Ferguson*: "separate but equal" facilities are constitutional; Hiram College students visit Cleveland
1897	Samuel Jones first elected mayor of Toledo
1899	W. E. B. Du Bois, *The Philadelphia Negro*
1901	Model tenement house bill passed in New York; Theodore Roosevelt becomes president
1906	Upton Sinclair's *The Jungle* published; Meat Inspection Act; Pure Food and Drug Act
1907–1908	Margaret Mitchell reports in Cleveland
1910	Urban League founded
1912–1916	High point of progressivism

of rapid urbanization and industrialism. Cities expanded as millions of newcomers from southern and eastern Europe and black migrants fleeing worsening racial oppression in the South crowded into them. Living conditions were often unsanitary and depressing, and city services were inadequate. Industrial work was frequently dangerous for the workers and unsafe for the consumers who bought its products. Progressive efforts ranged widely and included individuals and organizations who worked in the private sector and those who attempted to reform the machinery of government, to pass legislation improving urban living and working conditions, and to establish social justice for women, workers, and other unrepresented Americans.

Made famous by Jane Addams's Hull House in Chicago, the settlement house movement brought middle-class, native-born men and women into the city to live in working-class immigrant neighborhoods. There, residents hoped to improve the lives of their neighbors through personal interaction and education. In 1896, a group of students at Hiram College in northern Ohio attended (non-credit) lectures and discussions on reform, including social settlements. Mostly from small towns and middle-class families, the students would have come to college knowing little about the urban poor. A trip some of them took to the working-class neighborhoods of Cleveland (about 50 miles north of Hiram) was eye-opening: "We found saloons, prostitution, open sewers, and all in all everything was not very good. We went back to Hiram College with the report that Cleveland needed a settlement very bad." After graduation, seven students moved to Cleveland and put the ideas they had discussed in school into practice. Proud of their alma mater, they named the settlement Hiram House.

The settlement house movement was one approach to solving the ills of urban, industrial America. Other reformers focused on different problems and proposed political solutions. At the local level, many middle-class urbanites sought to clean up city government (controlled by a hierarchy of partisan politicians or "bosses") by electing reform-minded mayors like Samuel "Golden Rule" Jones, elected four times as an independent party mayor of Toledo, Ohio. Others favored replacing the traditional city government with a city manager form (government by appointed "experts" who were not involved in partisan politics). Still others pursued political change at the state and ultimately at the national level.

In his career as a reform politician, Theodore Roosevelt served at all levels of government. In the mid 1880s he made an unsuccessful bid to become New York City's mayor, went on to become a member of the U.S. Civil Service Commission, president of New York's police commission (1895–1897), and in 1898 the reform governor of New York. His administration so distressed the state's political bosses that they sought to get him out of state politics by engineering his nomination as President William McKinley's vice president. When McKinley was assassinated in 1901, Roosevelt became the first progressive president, and he pressed for a reform agenda on the national level. The high point of national progressivism was the election of 1912, in which all three candidates, Roosevelt, William Howard Taft, and Woodrow Wilson, adopted part of the progressive agenda.

Roosevelt's movement from state and local politics to the presidency reflected the growing conviction on the part of some progressives that problems were best dealt with at the federal level. His actions as president reinforced this point of view. Inspired by Upton Sinclair's famous muckraking novel that exposed the unsanitary nature of the meatpacking industry, Roosevelt pressed for an investigation, then for regulatory legislation to correct the practices that Sinclair had described.

Although expressing concern for a wide variety of problems plaguing American life, white middle-class reformers largely ignored African-Americans and failed to deplore the racism that kept blacks oppressed. At the same time that white, middle-class reformers were working to help European immigrants, southern whites were intensifying their efforts to segregate and repress African-Americans, instituting segregated facilities, disenfranchising black voters, and locking blacks into systems of debt slavery (see Archive 12). African-American leaders such as Ida Wells-Barnett, W. E. B. Du Bois, and others studied these worsening conditions, North and South, and sought measures of self-help to improve the lives of African-Americans.

About the Sources

YOU have several kinds of sources in this archive, most of them familiar to you. *The World's Work* (15.1), a journal launched in 1900, reported on the "activities of the newly organized world, its problems and even its romances." It featured a muckraking attack on the meatpacking industry and published the article on immigrants included here.

The first silent movies were made in the late 19th century, and by the early 20th century they had become a popular form of entertainment for a working-class and largely ethnic audience. Although progressive reformers distrusted movies, some of which—like the 1907 film *The Candidate*—ridiculed reform, they constitute a valuable source for the historian. Movie posters (15.3a and b) advertising the film version of Upton Sinclair's *The Jungle* suggest how working-class interests might mesh with reform in a form of popular entertainment.

Jacob Riis and Lewis Hines were two photographers who used their pictures to generate support for working class Americans. You should evaluate their pictures carefully for the impact they make on the viewer and the ways in which they organized their subjects and materials. Riis's photo (15.4a) shows two women and a girl doing piecework at home. Hines's picture of 16-year-old Henry McShane focuses on a boy who had lost his arm at his factory job, an accident for which he received no compensation. The other Hines photo reveals a young girl crocheting on underwear in the backyard of her Somerville, Massachusetts, home.

The scholar and activist W. E. B. DuBois, the first black to receive a Ph.D. from Harvard, studied the lives of black Philadelphians in 1899 in a pioneering work of urban sociology (15.6). Very much in the tradition of university-sponsored experts studying urban problems, Du Bois and other black leaders crusaded for rights largely ignored by white reformers.

Among the Hiram House papers are reports (15.7–15.10) made by Margaret Mitchell on her activities as a Hiram House resident in 1907 and 1908. (She was apparently no relation to the Margaret Mitchell who wrote *Gone with the Wind*.) Mitchell devotes special attention to the "On the Level" club formed by neighborhood boys under the auspices of Hiram House. When young people in the neighborhood got in trouble with the law, Hiram House worked with the local Juvenile Court to arrange for their reform and rehabilitation. Mitchell's reports also include details about working-class family life and about how the boys in the neighborhood spent their money. They also give us a sense of Mitchell's own personality and expectations, as well as indicating how settlement house workers had embraced the methods of the new discipline of social science.

List of Sources

15.1 **Magazine article on the changing character of immigration,** by Kate Claghorn, in *World's Work*, vol. 1 (1900–1901), pp. 382–387.

15.2a **Cartoon of the party boss,** undated, artist unknown. The Newberry Library, Chicago.

15.2b **Songs by Samuel "Golden Rule" Jones,** in Samuel M. Jones, Jr., *Freedom Songs* (1899–1901), Samuel Milton Jones Papers, Toledo-Lucas County Public Library, Toledo, Ohio.

15.3a **Movie poster for *The Jungle*,** 1913. Sinclair Papers, Lilly Library, Indiana University, Bloomington.

15.3b **Movie poster for *The Jungle*,** 1913. Sinclair Papers, Lilly Library, Indiana University, Bloomington.

15.4a **Photograph by Jacob Riis, *Finishing Pants*,** Jacob A. Riis Collection, microfilm image 4F4, Museum of the City of New York, New York.

15.4b **Photograph by Lewis Hines, *Henry McShane*,** 1908. Library of Congress Prints and Photographs Division, LC-DIG-nclc-01313.

15.4c **Photograph by Lewis Hines, *Annie Fedele*,** 1912. Library of Congress Prints and Photographs Division, LC-DIG-nclc-04223.

15.5 **Extract from magazine article on "Our Poorer Brother,"** by Theodore Roosevelt, 1897, in *American Ideals and Other Essays, Social and Political* (New York: Putnam, 1897), pp. 206–219.

15.6 **W. E. B. DuBois's "The Seventh Ward of Philadelphia,"** in W. E. B. DuBois, *The Philadelphia Negro: A Social Study* (Philadelphia: U. of Pennsylvania Press, 1899, reprinted 1996), pp. 58–63.

15.7 **Settlement house records on Margaret Mitchell's neighborhood visits,** around January 1907. Hiram House Records, folder 5, container 33, The Western Reserve Historical Society, Cleveland, Ohio.

15.8 **Settlement house records on Margaret Mitchell's neighborhood visits,** August 1907. Hiram House Records, folder 5, container 33, The Western Reserve Historical Society, Cleveland, Ohio.

15.9 **Settlement house records on Margaret Mitchell's neighborhood visits,** October 1907. Hiram House Records, folder 5, container 33, The Western Reserve Historical Society, Cleveland, Ohio.

15.10 **Settlement house records on Margaret Mitchell's neighborhood visits,** November 2, 1907 and January 17, 1908. Hiram House Records, folder 5, container 33, The Western Reserve Historical Society, Cleveland, Ohio.

Questions to Consider

1. Read through the first source, on immigration. How does the author describe the immigrants? What is the emotional tone of her analysis? Can you find clues to how she feels about these newcomers? What problems does she think the city poses for them? How might the situation be addressed?

2. Study the cartoon (15.2a), the songs (15.2b), the movie posters (15.3a and b), and the photographs (15.4a and b). Contrast the cartoon with the songs by Samuel Jones, mayor of Toledo, Ohio. What points does each source make? How does the character of the source, cartoon versus song, affect the content? Do you think the audience was the same for the cartoon and the songs? Now analyze the basic reform message of each of the sources. How does each image make the case for reform? Is the message accurate or exaggerated? To what kinds of people do you think the images are appealing? Do you find one of the images more powerful than the others? Why?

3. To what audience does Theodore Roosevelt appeal in his essay "How Not to Help Our Poorer Brother" (15.5)? How would you describe his philosophy of reform? Why is he so critical of socialists? In what ways does Roosevelt propose to change American life? What does he think is wrong with things as they are?

4. Looking at the first five sources, list the progressive concerns they reveal and the ways in which reformers think they might reform the problems they identify. Would you describe the problems in the same way as the progressives represented here? Which of these problems still plague American life?

5. In what ways are the problems of blacks in Philadelphia outlined by Du Bois (15.6) similar to and different from the problems of other groups documented here? How does Du Bois's analysis compare to those you have already read? For whom is Du Bois writing?

6. Carefully read Mitchell's reports (15.7–15.10). Make a list of what she does as a settlement house worker. Is her job taxing? What are the challenges? What might be the

rewards for her? How does she think and feel about her work? About her clients? What are the problems she identifies? What do you think are the major obstacles she faces in bringing about change?

7. What do Mitchell's reports reveal about the lives and work of the urban poor? About family life and relations? About leisure? About working-class young people? Compare her depiction of working-class young people with the Riis and Hines photographs.

8. The Mitchell reports on the boys' clubs suggest many questions. Were the boys seriously interested in reform, or were they putting on a show for the Hiram House staff? What caused (or causes) juvenile delinquency—inherent character flaws? Poverty? Parental tolerance of immoral behavior? The temptations posed by consumer culture? How do you think Mitchell might have answered these questions? How would her clients have answered them?

9. What approach did Hiram House take to solving the problems they found in urban life? What other approaches might they have taken instead? What do these sources tell you about progressivism?

10. Finally, after considering all the sources, how would you define progressivism? Do any of the historians' definitions fit all of the sources? Do some fit better than others? Do you see signs of self-interest and a desire for power? Of self-sacrifice? What does the progressive period reveal about the character of American reform and the desire to change the world?

→ DOCUMENT 15.1 ←

Magazine article on the changing character of immigration, by Kate Claghorn, in *World's Work*, vol. 1 (1900–1901), pp. 382–387.

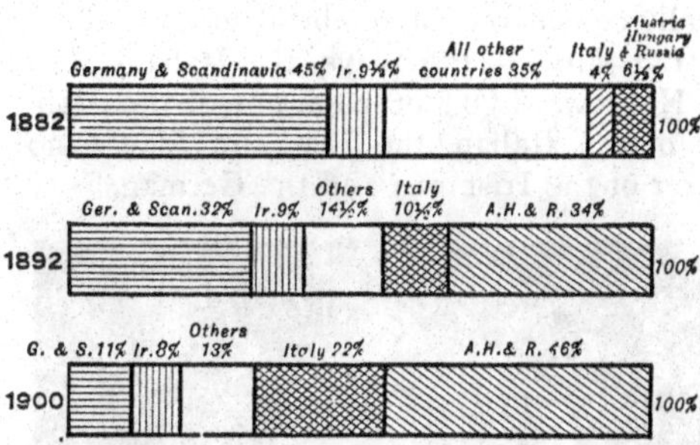

PROPORTION TO ALL IMMIGRANT ARRIVALS FOR GIVEN YEARS OF ARRIVALS FROM GIVEN COUNTRIES

The change in the composition of our immigration is made even more plain by reducing the different national elements to percentages of the total immigration in each year considered, as is shown in the diagram of immigrants from given countries.

The decreasing elements have been grouped at one side of the table, the increasing elements at the other, in shaded blocks, the unshaded blocks between the shaded blocks representing all other elements in the totals of immigration for each year.

The statistics of immigration for successive years would be even more significant, however, if the present system of classifying arrivals according to race as well as to country of residence, had been adopted sooner. The student of social matters has to thank Mr. Edward F. McSweeney, the present Assistant Commissioner of Immigration at the Port of New York, for the introduction of this better system of classification, the first results from which are given in the reports of immigration for the year ending June 30, 1899.

It is now possible to disengage the significant racial facts. For example, we can tell from last year's figures that of the 90,787 arrivals from the Russian Empire, 12,515 were Finns, 37,011 were Hebrews, 32,797 were Lithuanians and Poles, and only 1165 were "Russians" proper.

Moreover, arrivals of the same race element from different countries may be grouped together. For instance, after grouping together

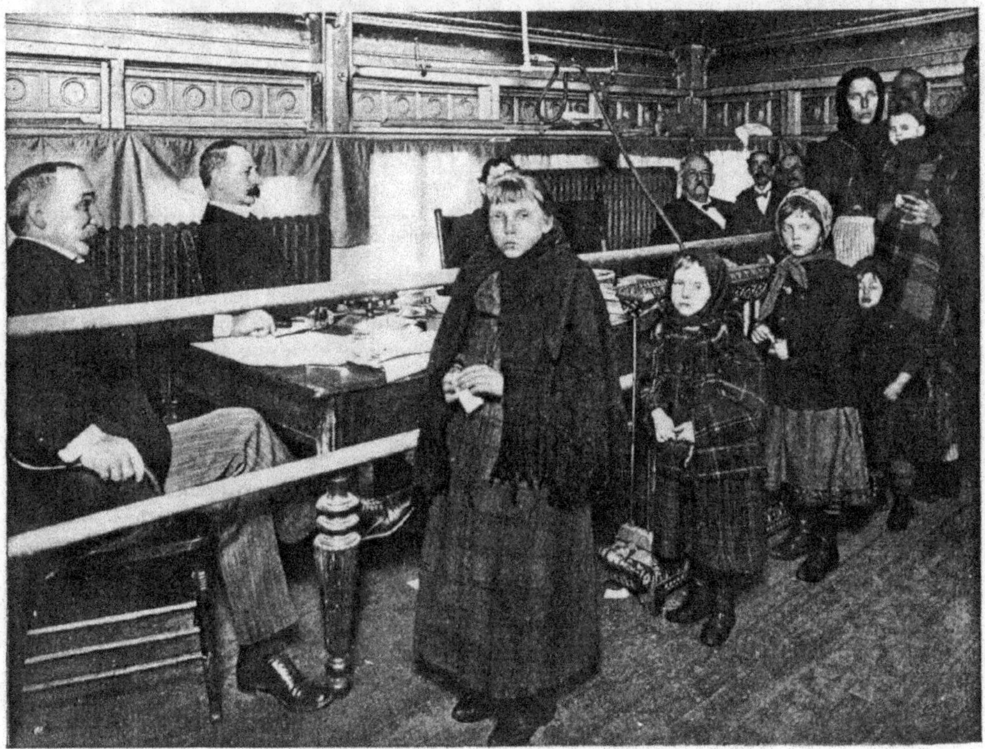

PASSING THROUGH THE BARGE OFFICE.

AN ITALIAN TYPE.

all Germans by race, while arrivals from the German Empire in 1900 were 18,507, arrivals from all countries of persons of German

A SYRIAN.

race were 29,682. Hebrew arrivals for the year were 60,764. Arranging these figures by percentages of the total immigration in a bar makes the matter plainer to the eye.

The noticeable feature in recent immigration is the predominance of three racial stocks, usually considered of doubtful social and industrial value, — the Slavs, the Italians, and the Hebrews. Our problem now is the problem of the Italian, the Jew, and Slav — no longer of the Irishman and the German.

AN IRISHWOMAN.

If we look at the human tide as it first washes our shores at the immigrant station, we shall see patient family groups — father, mother, and little children, old grandfather and grandmother, perhaps, and sturdy grown sons and daughters — as they sit beside their little possessions awaiting with eagerness the moment of their exit to a land of freedom and opportunity. The girls and women who pass the gate alone are moral and industrious peasants in the main — wives coming to husbands, sisters to brothers, or they are making the venture on their own responsibility. Even the bands of unattached men are not so bad as fancy paints them. Tall, ferocious-looking Croats and Slovacks are found, upon acquaintance with them under normal conditions, to be simple country fellows, ready to talk and sing, or to drink sociably, ready to work at anything that offers itself, planning to save the greater part of their earnings for wives and children left behind. Weather-beaten Italians, with seamed and lowering countenances, are meditating nothing darker than their chances of slipping by the inspector and gaining their foothold in the promised land.

We have practically no immigration from city slums, and very little from city populations of any sort, except the Russian Jewish immigrants, whose circumstances are peculiar, and who cannot be said, as a people, to have become infected with the characteristic slum vices. Our immigrants as a whole are a peasant population, used to the open, with the simple habits of life, the crude physical and moral health that the open air and poverty together are apt to produce. Practically all the immigration from Austria-Hungary, which has grown so considerably of late years, is from the country, as is also the immigration from Italy. The Italian mendicant, who is seldom seen here, is a member of a highly specialized class, and is as unwilling to leave his city haunts as any other specialized and privileged social product of his country would be.

A POLISH JEWESS.

READY TO BE MADE AMERICAN.

In the immigrant group as a whole are to be found poverty, ignorance, weakness, a pathetic patience, a no less pathetic hopefulness of what the future will bring, a childlike ingenuity of deceit in eluding the pains and penalties of detention and exclusion; but so little full-fledged and out-breaking viciousness that it is not worth talking about. In short, like the other class of beginners in citizenship, they come to us as little children, and claim our care and protection as such.

A REJECTED FAMILY.

But what course of training in citizenship is prepared for these grown-up children? A large proportion of them, for one reason and another, find their first homes in the slums of great cities. And so it unfortunately happens that, just as poverty and vice, ignorance and depravity, are confused together in our thought about them, so in our cities the newest immigrants, who are the most hopeful element in our slums, are brought in direct relation with the vicious and defective remnant left behind by earlier comers. The man who is climbing up the ladder stands, while still on the lowest round, with the man who has slipped down there from a higher place, or who has stood there forever.

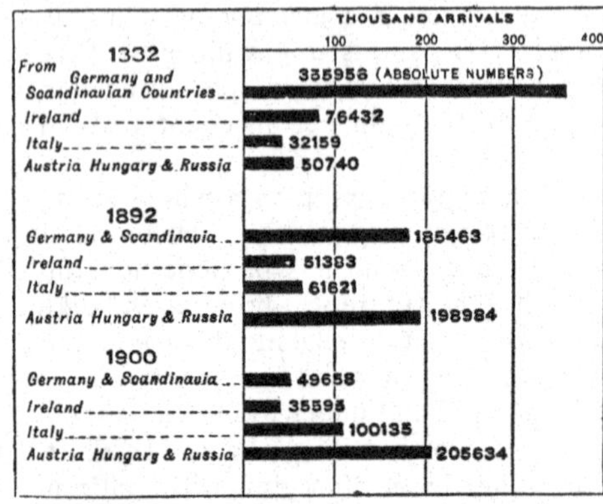

NUMBER OF ARRIVALS FROM CERTAIN COUNTRIES FOR THE YEARS ENDING JUNE 30, 1882, 1892, 1900.

When the two sets of elements — the poor and the corrupt — come in contact, some mutual impression must be made. It has to be acknowledged that in some cases the incoming of newer peoples has had a distinctly beneficial effect in the neighborhoods they have taken possession of. In New York, for example, the old Fourth and Eleventh wards, long the haunt of the drunken sailor and his vicious mate, have been to a large degree cleaned up by the incoming of Greeks, Italians, and Russian Jews. Ground-floor tenements formerly occupied by saloons and dance halls are now the lodging places of Greek pedlers, who live together in peace, quiet, and order, smoking and playing cards at home of a rainy day, neither drinking nor fighting, well thought of by that great power in tenement-house life — the "housekeeper" — and by neighboring families. Above stairs newly arrived Italians, industrious and of sober habits, have driven out the drunken Irish pauper of the second generation, to the great satisfaction of the charitable agencies that have had to struggle for so many years with the latter class.

POLACK GIRLS.

On the other hand, there are influences of tremendous force constantly at work to drag the newer immigrants down. Especially bad is the tenement house for the newly arrived immigrant. The robust physical health of the peasant fails in the poisonous air of his dwelling; such habits of cleanliness, order, and decency as the immigrant family may have brought with it are in serious danger of wreck in unsanitary and crowded quarters. Not knowing localities and prices, the immigrant takes up his abode in the parts of the city nearest his point of entry, which is, in New York, the most expensive part of the city, so far as rents are concerned. A family must not merely confine itself within as narrow limits as possible, but must, in order to meet the expense, ask another family to share the space already too narrow for itself. The moral as well as the physical evil that such crowding brings does not need to be described.

It is, perhaps, a fortunate rather than an unfortunate circumstance that as families of the newer races crowd into a given tenement, earlier comers move out. The "colony," composed of one sort of foreigners solely, representing approximately the same period of immigration, has this favorable feature, at least — it is made up of elements of similar kind. The old stager in vice and trickery is not so likely to be at hand to instruct the inexperienced new arrival in all branches of his art, nor the practised pauper, to give the

PROPORTION TO ALL IMMIGRANT ARRIVALS FOR 1900 OF ARRIVALS OF CERTAIN RACES

dangerous lesson of dependence to the normally self-helpful immigrant.

All evils, however, are favored by an institution which is the greatest evil of them all,—that is, the peculiar system of political control under which our great cities groan, "politics for profit," an organized business, run primarily for the advantage of its managers, secondarily for the benefit of their sub-agents.

The tenement house itself, with all its evils involved, was here when the immigrant came; but the continuation of the worst features of the tenement, in spite of laws enacted for its improvement, is the direct result of "politics for profit." Requirements with regard to ground space to be occupied, to the size and character of air-shafts, to other matters of construction when the building is to be erected, requirements for the lighting of hallways, to proper sanitation, to the character of inmates, after the tenement is built, are violated with impunity.

The immigrant problem is a very serious one; but we succeed with it directly in proportion to our skill or neglect in dealing with it. The material is, in the main, good raw material for American citizenship.

There has never been a sufficiently careful oversight of fresh immigrants in our crowded cities; for they ought to be regarded as civic children and cared for as such. But somehow, in haphazard ways, we assimilate them —developing the best traits in most of them but not in all, taking our chances. They take their chances, too, in coming; and the wonder is that we both survive the experiment as well as we do. The children of almost any kind of parents become American.

A FINNISH TYPE.

STARTING OUT FROM THE BARGE OFFICE.

→ DOCUMENT 15.2a ←

Cartoon of the party boss, undated, artist unknown. The Newberry Library, Chicago.

→ DOCUMENT 15.2b ←

Songs by Samuel "Golden Rule" Jones, in Samuel M. Jones, Jr., *Freedom Songs* (1899–1901), Samuel Milton Jones Papers, Toledo–Lucas County Public Library. By permisson.

FREEDOM SONGS

BY

SAMUEL M. JONES.

"Ring out a slowly dying cause
And ancient forms of party strife.
Ring in the nobler modes of life
With sweeter manners, purer laws."
—*Tennyson.*

No. 1.

DIVIDE THE DAY.

A ractical Reply to the Question, "What shall We Do for the Unemployed?

Music by Mrs. Helen Beach Jones.

Divide up the day! divide up the day!
If you're willing to help brother men on the way,
The plan is so simple that none can gainsay,
All that is needed is to split up the day.
Divide up the day, and it soon will be found
That there's plenty of food to reach all around,
When father has work, there'll be no lack of bread,
Nor innocent children go hungry to bed.

CHORUS.

Divide up the day,
Then divide up the day,
If you're willing to help brother men,
To help brother men on the way,
The plan is so simple,
That none can gainsay,
All that is needed,
Yes, all that is needed
Is—split up the day.

'Tis eight hours for work and eight hours for play,
With eight hours for rest to make the true eight hour day,
'Twas our father above that gave us this plan,
Then let us be fair with our own brother man.
Don't make him a pauper, a tramp or a shirk,
Just give him a chance at a part of your work;
No question of wages will stand in the way,
He'll be saved from this fate if we split up the day.

CHORUS—Divide up the day, etc.

Divide up the day! divide up the day!
In more ways than one 'tis a plan that will pay,
Then all who desire will have work for their hand,
And the problem is solved that darkens our land.
With millions of idle in fruitful employ,
The homes of the workers will echo with joy;
Then want and distress will flee far away,
We can bring it about just by splitting the day.

CHORUS—Divide up the day, etc.

No. 2.

INDUSTRIAL FREEDOM.

"And ye shall know the truth, and the truth shall make you free."

Tune—"Marching through Georgia."

Sing aloud the tidings that the race will yet be free,
Man to man the wide world o'er will surely brothers be;
Right to work, the right to live, let every one agree,
God freely gives to the people.

CHORUS.

Hurrah, hurrah, the truth shall make us free
Hurrah, hurrah, for dear humanity!
Right to work let all proclaim till men united be,
In God's free gift to the people.

Tell the story over to the young and to the old,
Liberty for every man is better far than gold;
In the sweat of labor eat thy daily bread, we're told,
As God's free gift to the people.

CHORUS.

Shorter days for those who toil will make more work for all,
For a shorter work day then we'll sound a trumpet call,
And thus the fruit of labor on all alike will fall,
As God's free gift to the people.

CHORUS.

Let us grant to every man the right to have a share
In the things that God has made as free as sun and air;
Let us have free land for all, then free work everywhere,
God's gift will be to the people.

CHORUS.

With justice done to everyoue, then happy shall we be,
Poverty will disappear, the prisoners will be free;
The right to work, the right to live, the love of liberty—
All God's best gifts to the people.

CHORUS.

Toledo, Ohio, Feb. 10, 1899.

DOCUMENT 15.3a

Movie poster for *The Jungle*, 1913. Sinclair Papers, Lilly Library, Indiana University, Bloomington.

DOCUMENT 15.3b

Movie poster for *The Jungle*, 1913. Sinclair Papers, Lilly Library, Indiana University, Bloomington.

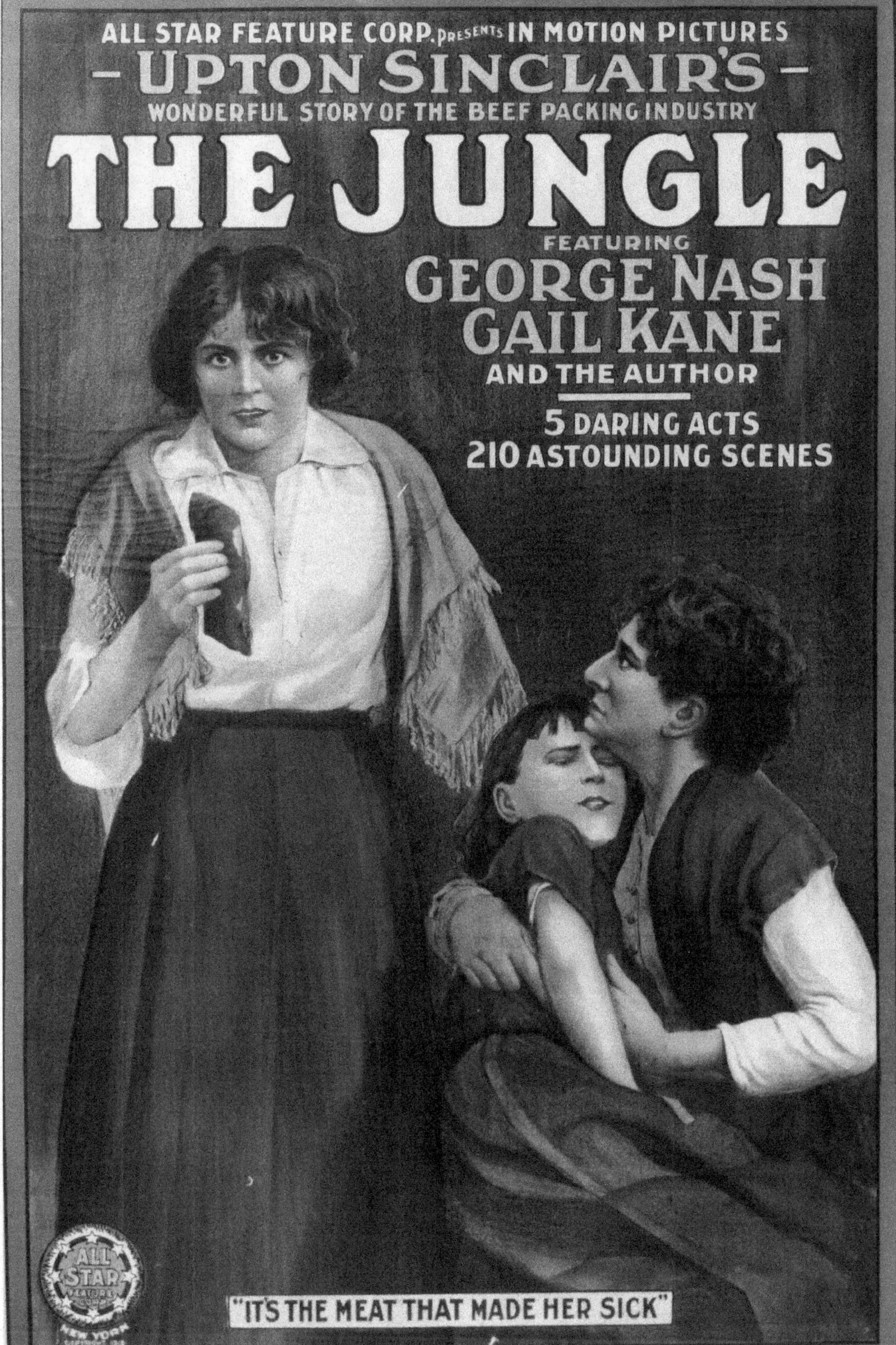

DOCUMENT 15.4a

Photograph by Jacob Riis, *Finishing Pants,* Jacob A. Riis Collection, microfilm image 4F4, Museum of the City of New York.

DOCUMENT 15.4b

Photograph by Lewis Hines, *Henry McShane*, 1908. Library of Congress Prints and Photographs Division, LC-DIG-nclc-01313.

DOCUMENT 15.4c

Photograph by Lewis Hines, *Annie Fedele,* 1912. Library of Congress Prints and Photographs Division, LC-DIG-nclc-04223.

⇢ DOCUMENT 15.5 ⇠

Extract from magazine article on "Our Poorer Brother," by Theodore Roosevelt, 1897, in *American Ideals and Other Essays, Social and Political* (New York: Putnam, 1897), pp. 206–219.

My grandfather was wealthy, and so was my father. My boyhood was spent in the idleness of a rich man's son. It was not till I was in my teens that misfortune overtook us, sent us homeless into the world, and deprived me of the thorough collegiate training my father intended for me.

At sixteen years of age I thus had to commence life moneyless, and the weary years I spent among the poor, the kindness I received in their homes, and the acquaintance I made with the hardship of their lives, gave me that profound sympathy for them which I yet retain—though I am no longer poor myself. . . .

There are plenty of ugly things about wealth and its possessors in the present age, and I suppose there have been in all ages. There are many rich people who so utterly lack patriotism, or show such sordid and selfish traits of character, or lead such mean and vacuous lives, that all right-minded men must look upon them with angry contempt; but, on the whole, the thrifty are apt to be better citizens than the thriftless; and the worst capitalist cannot harm laboring men as they are harmed by demagogues.

As the people of a State grow more and more intelligent the State itself may be able to play a larger and larger part in the life of the community, while at the same time individual effort may be given freer and less restricted movement along certain lines; but it is utterly unsafe to give the State more than the minimum of power just so long as it contains masses of men who can be moved by the pleas and denunciations of the average Socialist leader of to-day. There may be better schemes of taxation than these at present employed; it may be wise to devise inheritance taxes, and to impose regulations on the kinds of business which can be carried on only under the especial protection of the State; and where there is a real abuse by wealth it needs to be, and in this country generally has been, promptly done away with; but the first lesson to teach the poor man is that, as a whole, the wealth in the community is distinctly beneficial to him; that he is better off in the long run because other men are well off; and that the surest way to destroy what measure of prosperity he may have is to paralyze industry and the well-being of those men who have achieved success.

I am not an empiricist; I would no more deny that sometimes human affairs can be much bettered by legislation than I would affirm that they can always be so bettered. I would no more make a fetish of unrestricted individualism than I would admit the power of the State offhand and radically to reconstruct society. It may become necessary to interfere even more than we have done with the right of private contract, and to shackle cunning as we have shackled force. All I insist upon is that we must be sure of our ground before trying to get any legislation at all, and that we must not expect too much from this legislation, nor refuse to better ourselves a little because we cannot accomplish everything at a jump. Above all, it is criminal to excite anger and discontent without proposing a remedy, or only proposing a false remedy. The worst foe of the poor man is the labor leader, whether philanthropist or politician, who tries to teach him that he is a victim of conspiracy and injustice, when in reality he is merely working out his fate with blood and sweat as the immense majority of men who are worthy of the name always have done and always will have to do.

The difference between what can and what cannot be done by law is well exemplified by our experience with the negro problem, an experience of which Mr. Watson must have ample practical knowledge. The negroes were formerly held in slavery. This was a wrong which legislation could remedy, and which could not be remedied except by legislation. Accordingly they were set free by law. This having been done, many of their friends believed that in some way, by additional legislation, we could at once put them on an intellectual, social, and business equality with the whites. The effort has failed completely. In large sections of the country the negroes are not treated as they should be treated, and politically in particular the frauds upon them have been so gross and shameful as to awaken not merely indignation but bitter wrath; yet the best friends of the negro admit that his hope lies, not in legislation, but in the constant working of those often unseen forces of the national life which are greater than all legislation.

It is but rarely that great advances in general social well-being can be made by the adoption of some far-reaching scheme, legislative or otherwise; normally they come only by gradual growth, and by incessant effort to do first one thing, then another, and then another. Quack remedies of the universal cure-all type are generally as noxious to the body politic as to the body corporal.

Often the head-in-the-air social reformers, because people of sane and wholesome minds will not favor their wild schemes, themselves decline to favor schemes for practical reform. For the last two years there has been an honest effort in New York to give the city good government, and to work intelligently for better social conditions, especially in the poorest quarters. We have cleaned the streets; we have broken the power of the ward boss and the saloon-keeper to work injustice; we have destroyed the most hideous of the tenement houses in which poor people are huddled like swine in a sty; we have made parks and playgrounds for the children in the crowded quarters; in every possible way we have striven to make life easier and healthier and to give man and woman a chance to do their best work; while at the same time we have warred steadily against the pauper-producing, maudlin philanthropy of the free soup-kitchen and tramp lodging-house kind. In all this we have had practically no help from either the parlor socialists or the scarcely more noxious beer-room socialists, who are always howling about the selfishness of the rich and their unwillingness to do anything for those who are less well off. . . .

In our municipal administration here in New York we have acted with an equal hand toward wrong-doers of high and low degree. The Board of Health condemns the tenement-house property of the rich landowner, whether this landowner be priest or layman, banker or railroad president, lawyer or manager of a real estate business; and it pays no heed to the intercession of any politician, whether this politician be Catholic or Protestant, Jew or Gentile. At the same time the Police Department promptly suppresses, not only the criminal, but the rioter. In other words, we do strict justice. We feel we are defrauded of help to which we are entitled when men who ought to assist in any work to better the condition of the people decline to aid us because their brains are turned by dreams only worthy of a European revolutionist.

Many workingmen look with distrust upon laws which really would help them; laws for the intelligent restriction of immigration, for instance. I have no sympathy with mere dislike of immigrants; there are classes and even nationalities of them which stand at least on an equality with the citizens of native birth, as the last election showed. But in the interest of our workingmen we must in the end keep out laborers who are ignorant, vicious, and with low standards of life and comfort, just as we have shut out the Chinese.

Often labor leaders and the like denounce the present conditions of society, and especially of our political life, for shortcomings which they themselves have been instrumental in causing. In our cities the misgovernment is due, not to the misdeeds of the rich, but to the low standard of honesty and morality among citizens generally; and nothing helps the corrupt politician more than substituting either wealth or poverty for honesty as the standard by which to try a candidate. A few months ago a socialistic reformer in New York was denouncing the corruption caused by rich men because a certain judge was suspected of giving information in advance as to a decision in a case involving the interests of a great corporation. Now this judge had been elected some years previously, mainly because he was supposed to be a representative of the "poor man"; and the socialistic reformer himself, a year ago, was opposing the election of Mr. Beaman as judge because he was one of the firm of Evarts & Choate, who were friends of various millionaires and were counsel for various corporations. But if Mr. Beaman had been elected judge no human being, rich or poor, would have dared so much as hint at his doing anything improper.

Something can be done by good laws; more can be done by honest administration of the laws; but most of all can be done by frowning resolutely upon the preachers of vague discontent; and by upholding the true doctrine of self-reliance, self-help, and self-mastery. This doctrine sets forth many things. Among them is the fact that though a man can occasionally be helped when he stumbles, yet that it is useless to try to carry him when he will not or cannot walk; and worse than useless to try to bring down the work and reward of the thrifty and intelligent to the level of the capacity of the weak, the shiftless, and the idle. It further shows that the maudlin philanthropist and the maudlin sentimentalist are almost as noxious as the demagogue, and that it is even more necessary to temper mercy with justice than justice with mercy.

The worst lesson that can be taught a man is to rely upon others and to whine over his sufferings.

If an American is to amount to anything he must rely upon himself, and not upon the State; he must take pride in his own work, instead of sitting idle to envy the luck of others; he must face life with resolute courage, win victory if he can and accept defeat if he must, without seeking to place on his fellow-men a responsibility which is not theirs.

→ DOCUMENT 15.6 ←

W. E. B. DuBois's "The Seventh Ward of Philadelphia," in W. E. B. DuBois, *The Philadelphia Negro: A Social Study* (Philadelphia: U. of Pennsylvania Press, 1899, reprinted 1996), pp. 58–63.

14. The Seventh Ward, 1896.—We shall now make a more intensive study of the Negro population, confining ourselves to one typical ward for the year 1896. Of the nearly forty thousand Negroes in Philadelphia in 1890, a little less than a fourth lived in the Seventh Ward, and over half in this and the adjoining Fourth, Fifth and Eighth Wards:

Ward.	Negroes.	Whites.
Seventh	8,861	21,177
Eighth	3,011	13,940
Fourth	2,573	17,792
Fifth	2,335	14,619

The distribution of Negroes in the other wards may be seen by the accompanying map. (See opposite page.)

The Seventh Ward starts from the historic centre of Negro settlement in the city, South Seventh street and Lombard, and includes the long narrow strip, beginning at South Seventh and extending west, with South and Spruce streets as boundaries, as far as the Schuylkill River. The colored population of this ward numbered 3621 in 1860, 4616 in 1870, and 8861 in 1890. It is a thickly populated district of varying character; north of it is the residence and business section of the city; south of it a middle class and workingmen's residence section; at the east end it joins Negro, Italian and Jewish slums; at the west end, the wharves of the river and an industrial section separating it from the grounds of the University of Pennsylvania and the residence section of West Philadelphia.

Starting at Seventh street and walking along Lombard, let us glance at the general character of the ward. Pausing a moment at the corner of Seventh and Lombard, we can at a glance view the worst Negro slums of the city. The houses are mostly brick, some wood, not very old, and in general uncared for rather than dilapidated. The blocks between Eighth, Pine, Sixth and South have for many decades been the centre of Negro population. Here the riots of the thirties took place, and here once was a depth of poverty and degradation almost unbelievable. Even to-day there are many evidences of degradation,

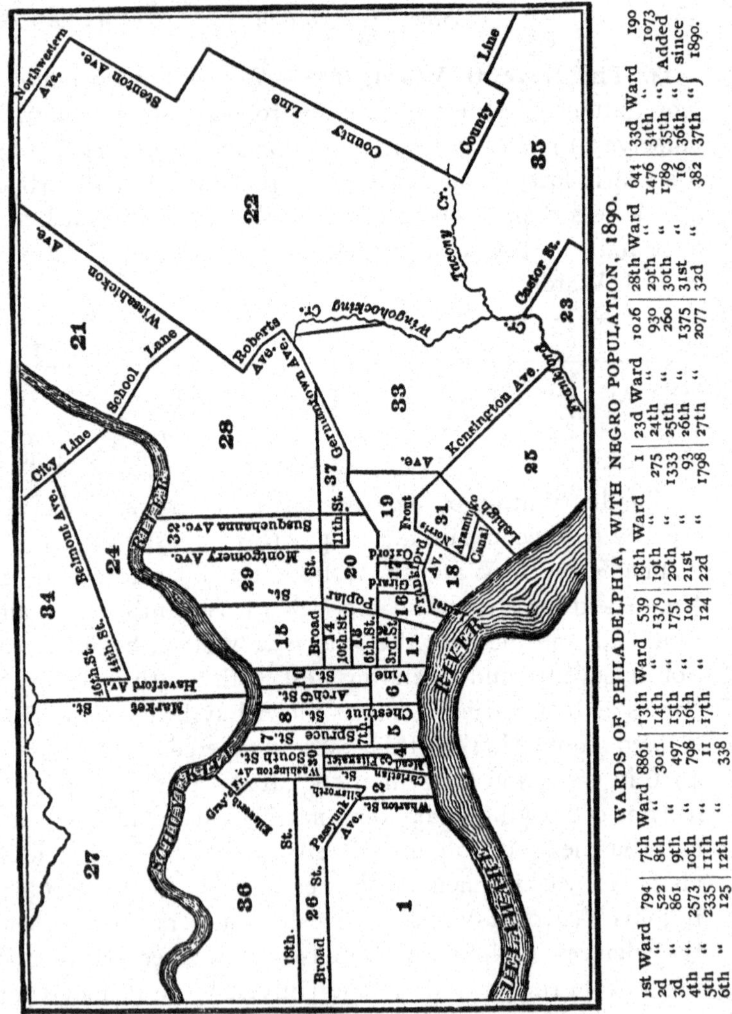

WARDS OF PHILADELPHIA, WITH NEGRO POPULATION, 1890.

Ward		Ward		Ward		Ward		Ward		Ward		Ward	
1st Ward	794	7th Ward	8861	13th Ward	539	18th Ward	1	23d Ward	1016	28th Ward	641	33d Ward	190
2d "	522	8th "	3011	14th "	1379	19th "	275	24th "	930	29th "	1476	34th "	1073
3d "	861	9th "	497	15th "	1751	20th "	1333	25th "	260	30th "	1789	35th "	Added since 1890.
4th "	2573	10th "	798	16th "	104	21st "	93	26th "	1375	31st "	16	36th "	
5th "	2335	11th "	11	17th "	124	22d "	1798	27th "	2077	32d "	382	37th "	
6th "	125	12th "	338										

although the signs of idleness, shiftlessness, dissoluteness and crime are more conspicuous than those of poverty.

The alleys[7] near, as Ratcliffe street, Middle alley, Brown's court, Barclay street, etc., are haunts of noted criminals, male and female, of gamblers and prostitutes, and at the same time of many poverty-stricken people, decent but not energetic. There is an abundance of political clubs, and nearly all the houses are practically lodging houses, with a miscellaneous and shifting population. The corners, night and day, are filled with Negro loafers—able-bodied young men and women, all cheerful, some with good-natured, open faces, some with traces of crime and excess, a few pinched with poverty. They are mostly gamblers, thieves and prostitutes, and few have fixed and steady occupation of any kind. Some are stevedores, porters, laborers and laundresses. On its face this slum is noisy and dissipated, but not brutal, although now and then highway robberies and murderous assaults in other parts of the city are traced to its denizens. Nevertheless the stranger can usually walk about here day and night with little fear of being molested, if he be not too inquisitive.[8]

Passing up Lombard, beyond Eighth, the atmosphere suddenly changes, because these next two blocks have few alleys and the residences are good-sized and pleasant. Here some of the best Negro families of the ward live. Some are wealthy in a small way, nearly all are Philadelphia born, and they represent an early wave of emigration from the old slum section.[9] To the south, on Rodman

[7] "In the Fifth Ward only there are 171 small streets and courts; Fourth Ward, 88. Between Fifth and Sixth, South and Lombard streets, 15 courts and alleys." "First Annual Report College Settlement Kitchen." p. 6.

[8] In a residence of eleven months in the centre of the slums, I never was once accosted or insulted. The ladies of the College Settlement report similar experience. I have seen, however, some strangers here roughly handled.

[9] It is often asked why do so many Negroes persist in living in the slums. The answer is, they do not; the slum is continually scaling off emigrants for other sections, and receiving new accretions from without. Thus the efforts for social betterment put forth here have often their best

The Seventh Ward of Philadelphia

The Distribution of Negro Inhabitants Throughout the Ward, and their social condition

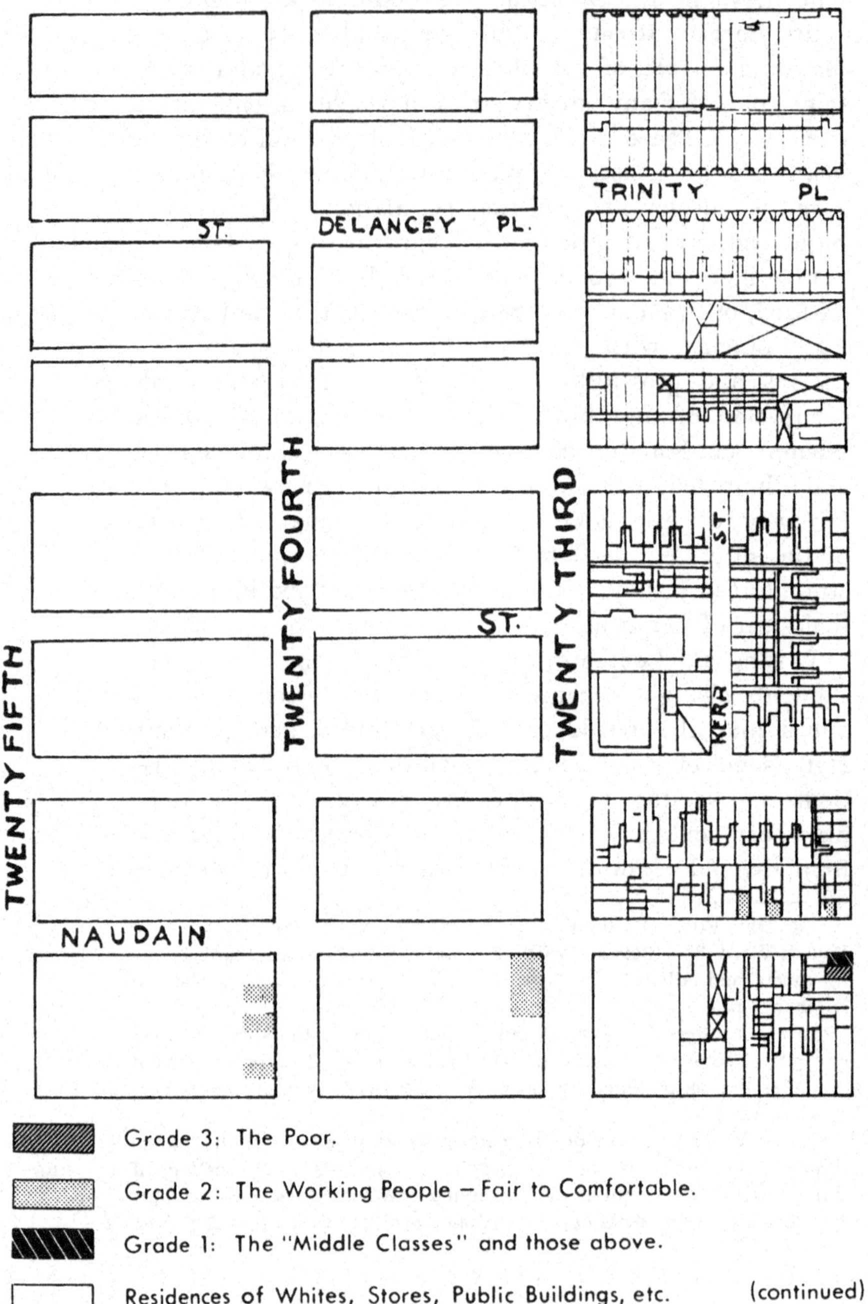

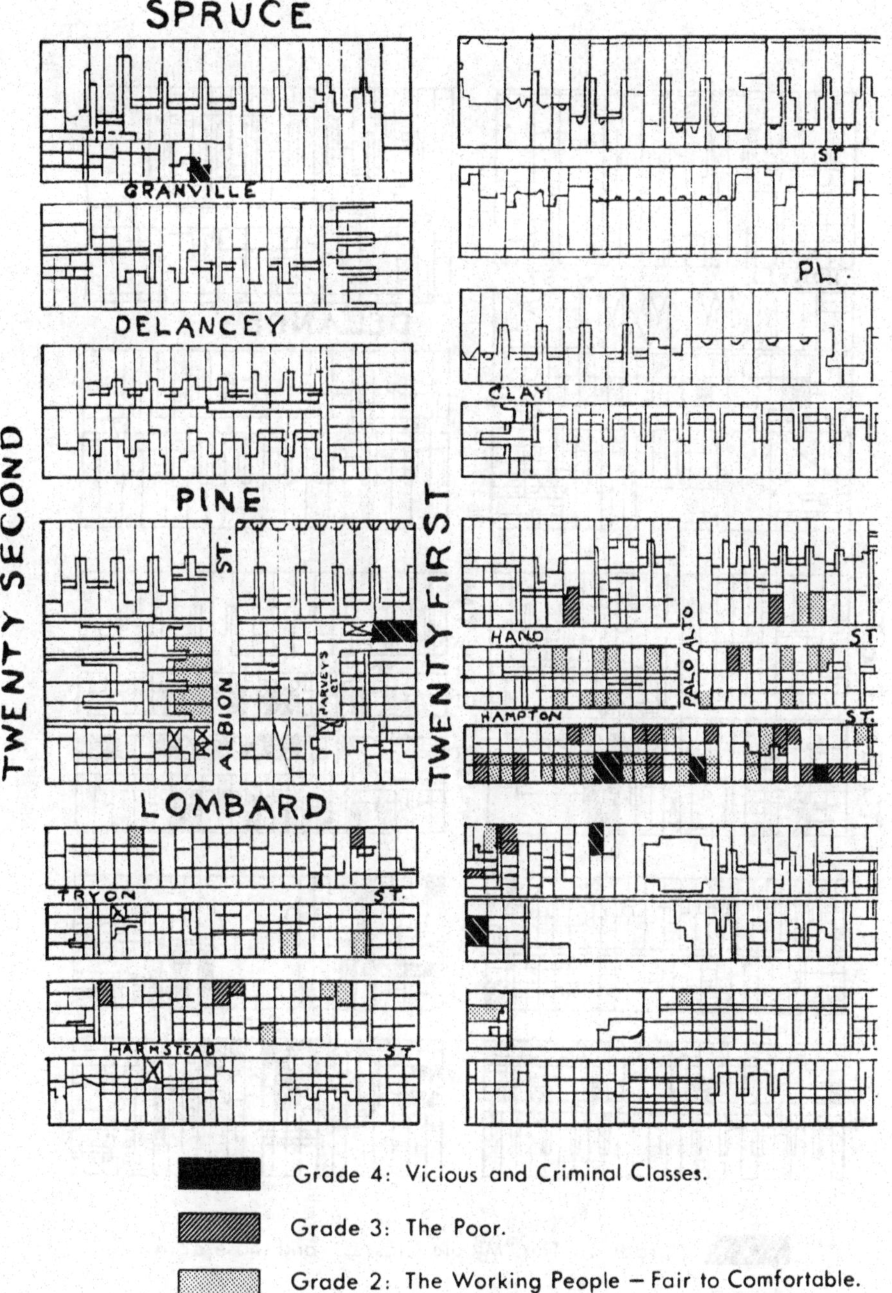

Grade 4: Vicious and Criminal Classes.

Grade 3: The Poor.

Grade 2: The Working People – Fair to Comfortable.

(For a more detailed explanation of the meaning of the different grades, see § 46, chap. xv.)

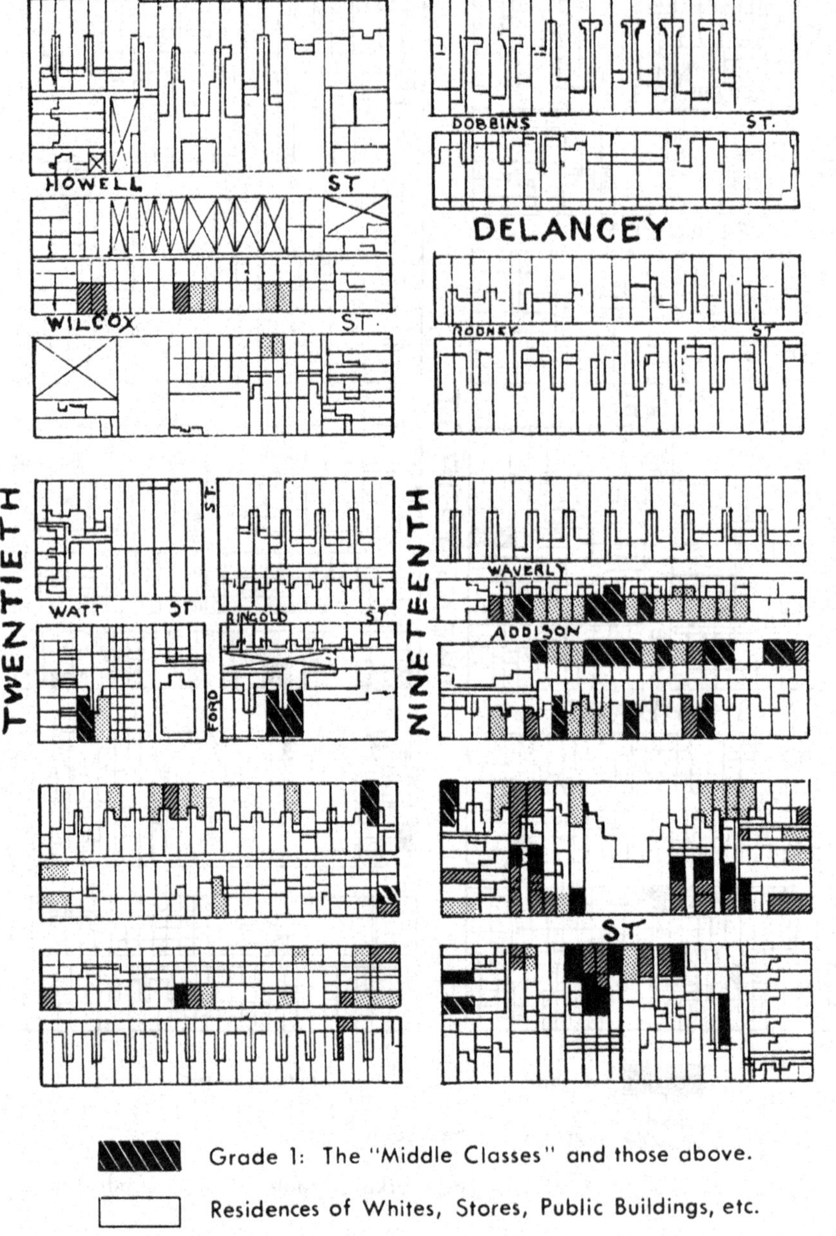

(continued)

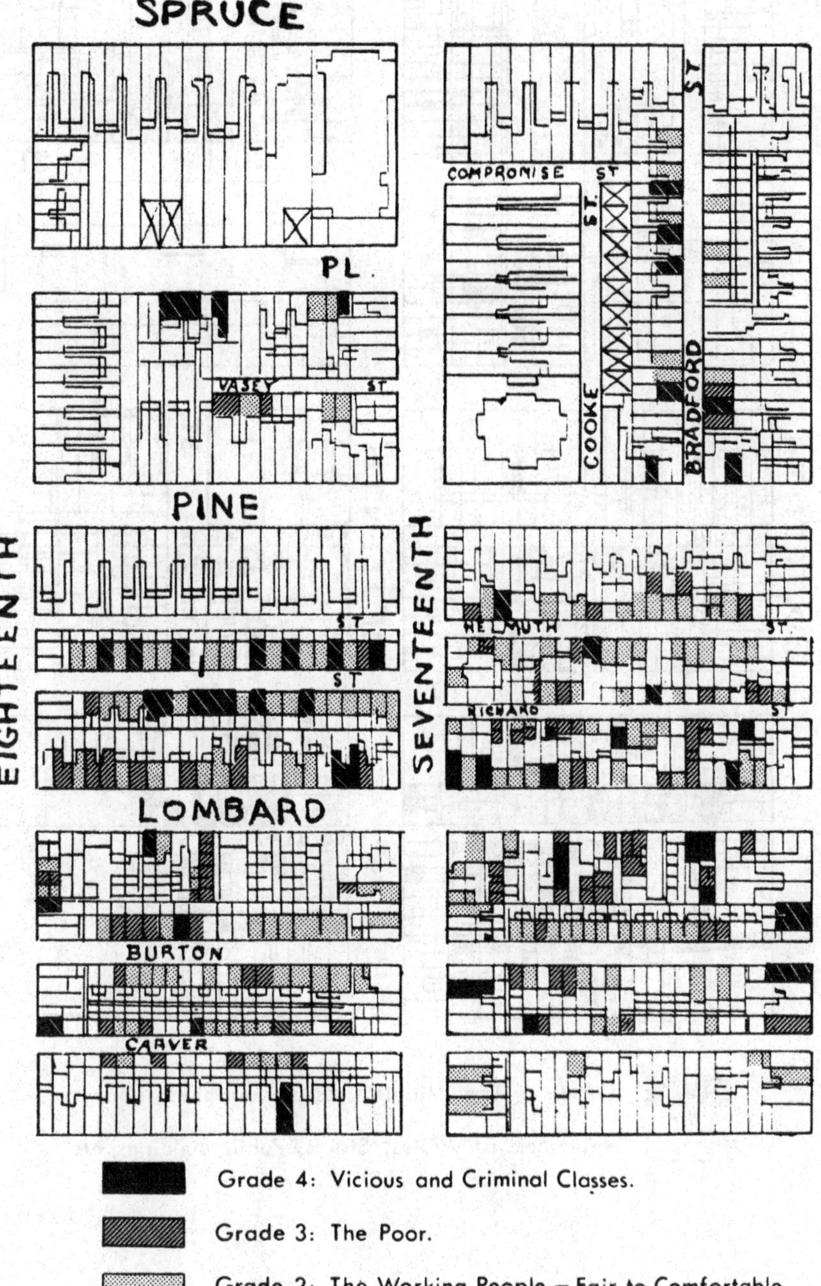

Grade 4: Vicious and Criminal Classes.

Grade 3: The Poor.

Grade 2: The Working People – Fair to Comfortable.

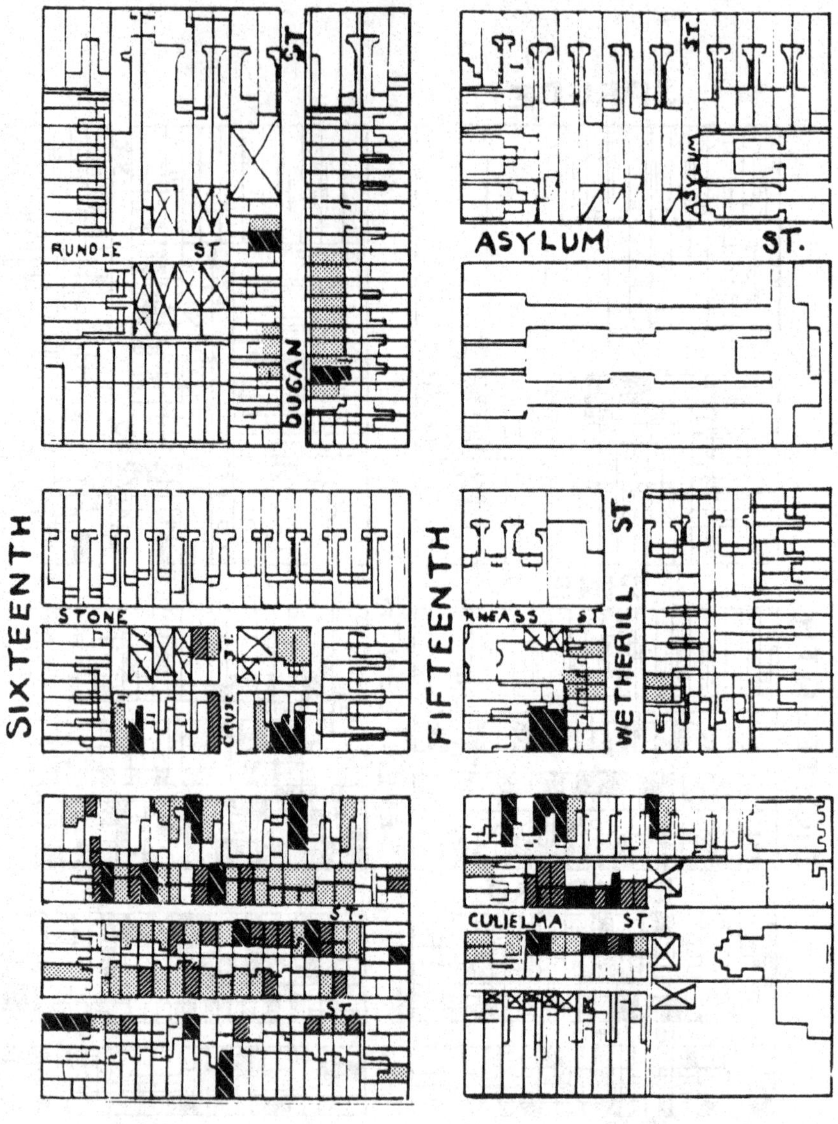

Grade 1: The "Middle Classes" and those above.

Residences of Whites, Stores, Public Buildings, etc.

(continued)

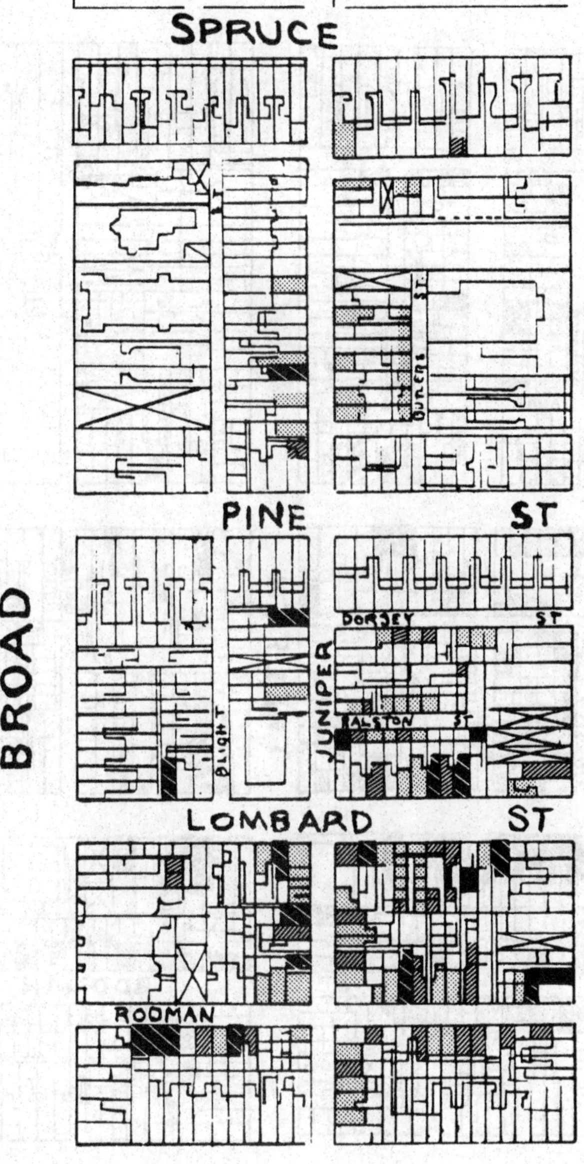

Grade 4: Vicious and Criminal Classes.

Grade 3: The Poor.

Grade 2: The Working People – Fair to Comfortable.

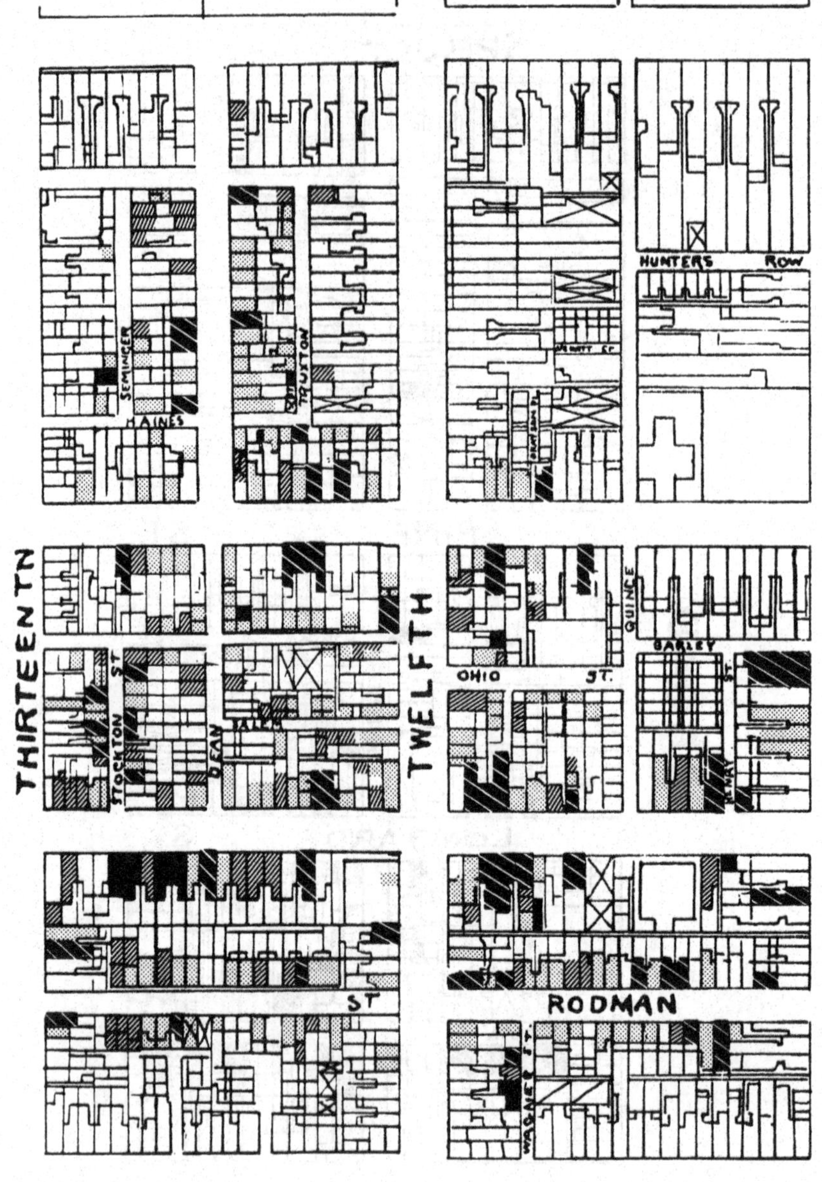

Grade 1: The "Middle Classes" and those above.

Residences of Whites, Stores, Public Buildings, etc.

(continued)

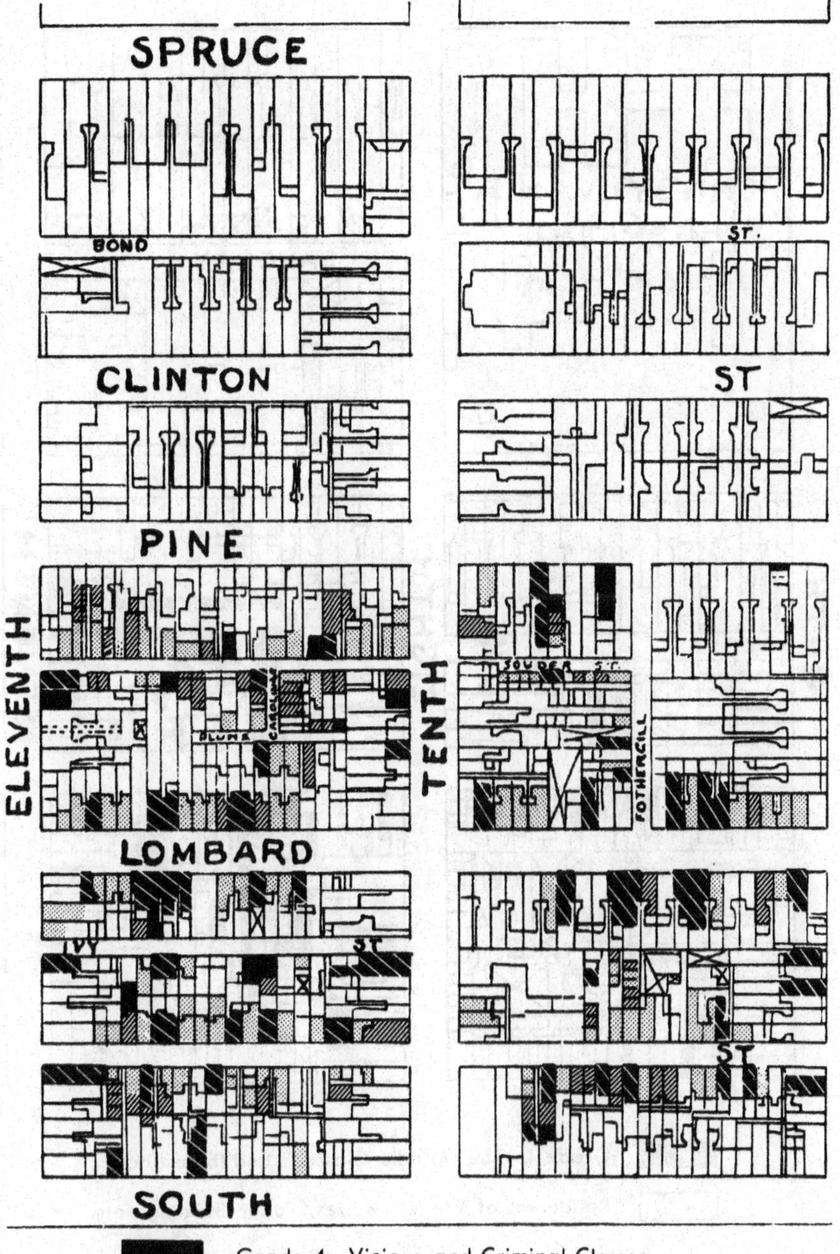

Grade 4: Vicious and Criminal Classes.

Grade 3: The Poor.

Grade 2: The Working People – Fair to Comfortable.

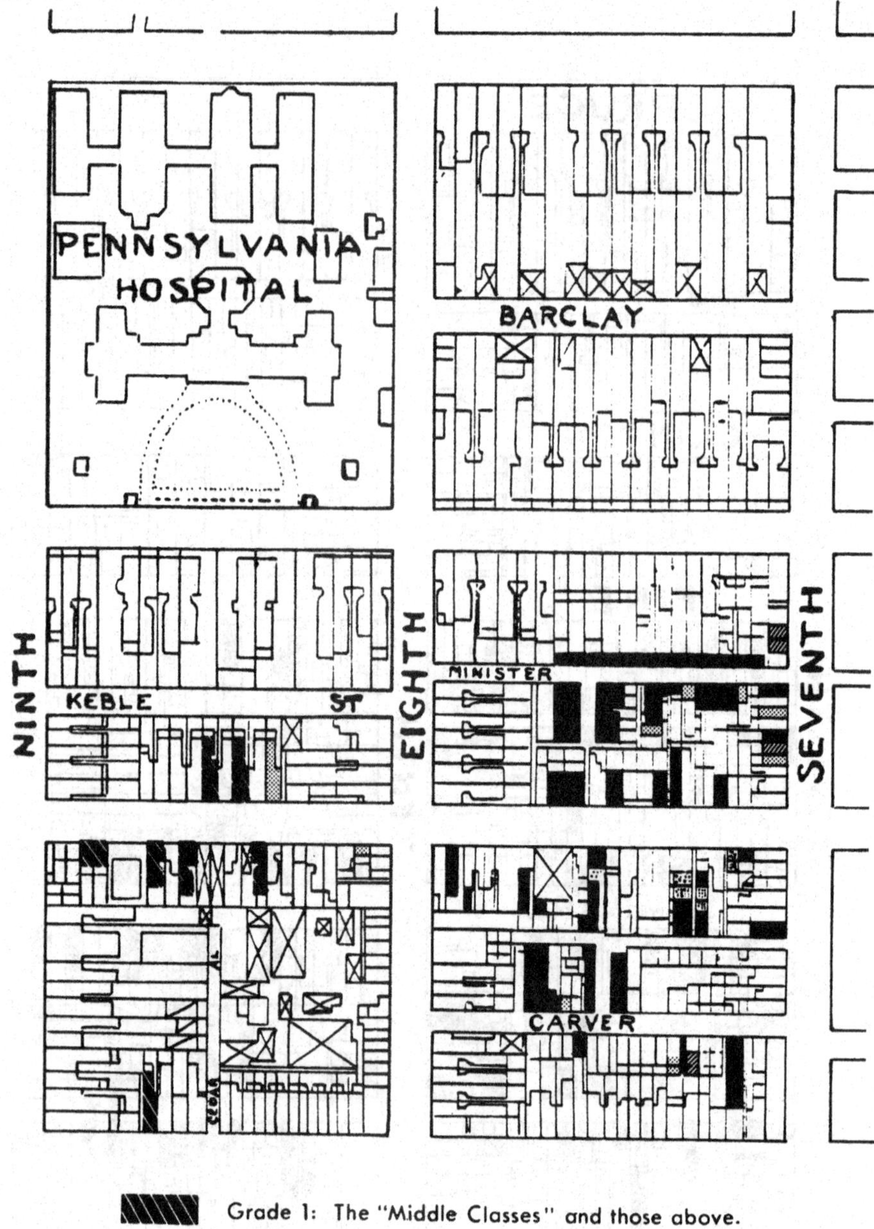

Grade 1: The "Middle Classes" and those above.

Residences of Whites, Stores, Public Buildings, etc.

street, are families of the same character. North of Pine and below Eleventh there are practically no Negro residences. Beyond Tenth street, and as far as Broad street, the Negro population is large and varied in character. On small streets like Barclay and its extension below Tenth—Souder, on Ivy, Rodman, Salem, Heins, Iseminger, Ralston, etc., is a curious mingling of respectable working people and some of a better class, with recent immigrations of the semi-criminal class from the slums. On the larger streets, like Lombard and Juniper, there live many respectable colored families—native Philadelphians, Virginians and other Southerners, with a fringe of more questionable families. Beyond Broad, as far as Sixteenth, the good character of the Negro population is maintained except in one or two back streets.[10] From Sixteenth to Eighteenth, intermingled with some estimable families, is a dangerous criminal class. They are not the low, open idlers of Seventh and Lombard, but rather the graduates of that school: shrewd and sleek politicians, gamblers and confidence men, with a class of well-dressed and partially undetected prostitutes. This class is not easily differentiated and located, but it seems to centre at Seventeenth and Lombard. Several large gambling houses are near here, although more recently one has moved below Broad, indicating a reshifting of the criminal centre. The whole community was an earlier immigration from Seventh and Lombard. North of Lombard, above Seventeenth, including Lombard street itself, above Eighteenth, is one of the best Negro residence sections of the city, centring about Addison street. Some undesirable elements have crept in even here, especially since the Christian League attempted to

results elsewhere, since the beneficiaries move away and others fill their places. There is, of course, a permanent nucleus of inhabitants, and these, in some cases, are really respectable and decent people. The forces that keep such a class in the slums are discussed further on.

[10] Gulielma street, for instance, is a notorious nest for bad characters, with only one or two respectable families.

clear out the Fifth Ward slums,[11] but still it remains a centre of quiet, respectable families, who own their own homes and live well. The Negro population practically stops at Twenty-second street, although a few Negroes live beyond.

We can thus see that the Seventh Ward presents an epitome of nearly all the Negro problems; that every class is represented, and varying conditions of life. Nevertheless one must naturally be careful not to draw too broad conclusions from a single ward in one city. There is no proof that the proportion between the good and the bad here is normal, even for the race in Philadelphia; that the social problems affecting Negroes in large Northern cities are presented here in most of their aspects seems credible, but that certain of those aspects are distorted and exaggerated by local peculiarities is also not to be doubted.

In the fall of 1896 a house-to-house visitation was made to all the Negro families of this ward. The visitor went in person to each residence and called for the head of the family. The housewife usually responded, the husband now and then, and sometimes an older daughter or other member of the family. The fact that the University was making an investigation of this character was known and discussed in the ward, but its exact scope and character was not known. The mere announcement of the purpose secured, in all but about twelve cases,[12] immediate admission. Seated then in the parlor, kitchen, or living room,

[11] The almost universal and unsolicited testimony of better class Negroes was that the attempted clearing out of the slums of the Fifth Ward acted disastrously upon them; the prostitutes and gamblers emigrated to respectable Negro residence districts, and real estate agents, on the theory that all Negroes belong to the same general class, rented them houses. Streets like Rodman and Juniper were nearly ruined, and property which the thrifty Negroes had bought here greatly depreciated. It is not well to clean a cess-pool until one knows where the refuse can be disposed of without general harm.

[12] The majority of these were brothels. A few, however, were homes of respectable people who esented the investigation as unwarranted and unnecessary.

the visitor began the questioning, using his discretion as to the order in which they were put, and omitting or adding questions as the circumstances suggested. Now and then the purpose of a particular query was explained, and usually the object of the whole inquiry indicated. General discussions often arose as to the condition of the Negroes, which were instructive. From ten minutes to an hour was spent in each home, the average time being fifteen to twenty-five minutes.

Usually the answers were prompt and candid, and gave no suspicion of previous preparation. In some cases there was evident falsification or evasion. In such cases the visitor made free use of his best judgment and either inserted no answer at all, or one which seemed approximately true. In some cases the families visited were not at home, and a second or third visit was paid. In other cases, and especially in the case of the large class of lodgers, the testimony of landlords and neighbors often had to be taken.

No one can make an inquiry of this sort and not be painfully conscious of a large margin of error from omissions, errors of judgment and deliberate deception. Of such errors this study has, without doubt, its full share. Only one fact was peculiarly favorable and that is the proverbial good nature and candor of the Negro. With a more cautious and suspicious people much less success could have been obtained. Naturally some questions were answered better than others; the chief difficulty arising in regard to the questions of age and income. The ages given for people forty and over have a large margin of error, owing to ignorance of the real birthday. The question of income was naturally a delicate one, and often had to be gotten at indirectly. The yearly income, as a round sum, was seldom asked for; rather the daily or weekly wages taken and the time employed during the year.

→ DOCUMENT 15.7 ←

Settlement house records on Margaret Mitchell's neighborhood visits, around January 1907. Hiram House Records, folder 5, container 33, The Western Reserve Historical Society, Cleveland, Ohio.

Long before trusts had come into existence, before labor was organized, ~~the~~ boys conceived a plan for mutual offense and defense – the product of this plan being the so-called "gang". Now the organized efforts of a crowd of stirring boys is no thing to be despised. If they are friendly to you all is well but if in any way you incur their displeasure, you suffer for it.

Just after the holidays, reports came to the residents of the Hiram House that there was a gang of boys known as the "Quckey gang" which was terrorizing the younger boys in our neighborhood. One boy reported that he was afraid to come to the manual training classes because these boys would always tried to hit him. At one time his mother went out to defend him against an attack, and they stoned her hurting her quite badly. He said they always hung around the Hiram House at night, tormenting boys for whom they had a dislike.

Another boy reported that the gang was after him to beat him because he refused to go with them and his father beat him if he did, learn him no alternative. Mr. Clark, principal of the Mayflower schools, when asked about the gang said they were a bad lot. He said that a few days before a boy came to him with the complaint that Gucker or Herman (or they the leader) had beaten him because he had told Mr. Clark on some members of the gang.

We knew was that something ought to be done. Their first thought was to report the leading spirits to the juvenile court authorities. But we hit upon another plan which we decided to try, namely to form a club from the gang, and to try to direct them to better avenues of escape for their energy, to appeal to their honor and make them realize they could stand for something worth while among the boys of the neighborhood.

Accordingly, the leader of the gang was visited and asked to help prepare for a party at the Hiram House to which we would invite any friends whom he might suggest. Of course he suggested the names of his gang. Each one was visited, ~~and~~ ice cream and cake being held out as an inducement to insure their attendance.

When the night appointed came, the boys all arrived long before the hour set for the meeting. When we invited them in, only part of them accepted. The rest were afraid of some scheme on our part to hand them over to the authorities. Clarence Peters, a colored boy better known as "Peck," when asked to come in said, "You needn't think you're going to get me in there. There isn't any party at all—it's a trap to get us all to Lancaster." After much coaxing they were all induced to come in, but Peck and a few other wary ones, would interpret any quick move as a ~~sign of~~ danger signal, and in spite of all our reassurances they would dart out the door and stand outside looking in until their courage returned, when they would come back in, only to rush out again. At one time the door opening into the hall was closed to keep out the noise and the boys immediately made careful investigation to see if it was locked.

The longing for ice cream and

coke however was stronger than their fears and they at last played games, ~~and~~ forgetting juvenile court and Lancaster in the excitement of "Marching to Jerusalem" and "Coach Upset."

Before the party broke up, a name was to be decided upon. Their tastes were directed into the right channels and they were left to choose their own name. "On the Level", suggested by Zhuckey, was agreed upon.

If we are successful in keeping this gang of boys "on the level" we will feel abundantly rewarded for all our efforts.

Human authority ...

Mean On the Level

Fight.

ice cream

eating on chair

Herman quickness 5¢

squaw skating

swell trick

Harry Ross.

Nemobs

Arthur Klavan

Saloon breaking

Joe Joseph in same Room

Long before trusts had come into existence, before labor was organized, boys conceived a plan for mutual offense and defense—the product of this plan being the so-called "gang." Now the organized efforts of a crowd of stirring boys is no thing to be despised. If they are friendly to you all is well but if in any way you incur their displeasure, you suffer for it.

Just after the holidays, reports came to the residents of the Hiram House that there was a gang of boys known as the "Zuckey gang" which was terrorizing the younger boys in our neighborhood. One boy reported that he was afraid to come to the manual training classes because these boys always tried to hit him. At once time his mother went out to defend him *against* an attack, and they stoned her hurting her quite badly. He said they always hung around the Hiram House at night, tormenting boys for whom they had a dislike. Another boy reported that the gang was after him to beat him because he refused to go with them, and his father beat him if he did, leaving him no alternative. Mr. Dort, principal of the Mayflower schools, when asked about the gang said they were a bad lot. He said that a few days before a boy came to him with the complaint that Zuckey or Herman Anthony the leader had beaten him because he had told Mr. Dort on some member of the gang.

We knew that something ought to be done. Our first thot [sic] was to report the leading spirits to the juvenile court authorities. But we hit upon another plan which we decided to try, namely to form a club from the gang, and to try to direct them to better avenues of escape for their energy, to appeal to their honor and make them realize they could stand for something worth while [sic] among the boys of the neighborhood.

Accordingly, the leader of the gang was visited and asked to help prepare for a party at the Hiram House to which we would invite any friends whom he might suggest. Of course he suggested the names of his gang. Each one was visited, ice cream and cake being held out as an inducement to insure their attendance.

When the night appointed came, the boys all arrived long before the hour set for the meeting. (When we invited them in, only part of them accepted. The rest were afraid of some scheme on our part to hand them over to the authorities. Clarence Peters, a colored boy better known as "Peck," when asked to come in said, "You needn't think you're going to get me in there. There isn't any party at all—it's a trap to get us all to Lancaster." After much coaxing they were all induced to come in, but Peck and a few other wary ones, would interpret any quick move as a danger signal, and in spite of all our reassurances they would dart out the door and stand outside looking in until their courage returned, when they would come back in, only to rush out again. At one time the door opening into the hall was closed to keep out the noise and the boys immediately made careful investigation to see if it was locked.

The longing for ice cream and cake however was stronger than their fears and they at last played games, forgetting juvenile court and Lancaster in the excitement of "Marching to Jerusalem" and "Crock Upset."

Before the party broke up, a name was to be decided upon. Their thots [sic] were directed into the right channels and they were left to choose their own name. "On the Level," suggested by Zuckey, was agreed upon.

If we are successful in keeping this gang of boys "on the level" we will feel abundantly rewarded for all our efforts.

Herman Anthony's sister
Mean On the Level
Fight
ice cream
eating on chair
Herman Zuicherman 25c
square dealing
swell trick
Harry Koss
[Neurds?]
Arthur Klavar
Saloon bowling
Joe Joseph in Game Room

→ DOCUMENT 15.8 ←

Settlement house records on Margaret Mitchell's neighborhood visits, August 1907. Hiram House Records, folder 5, container 33, The Western Reserve Historical Society, Cleveland, Ohio.

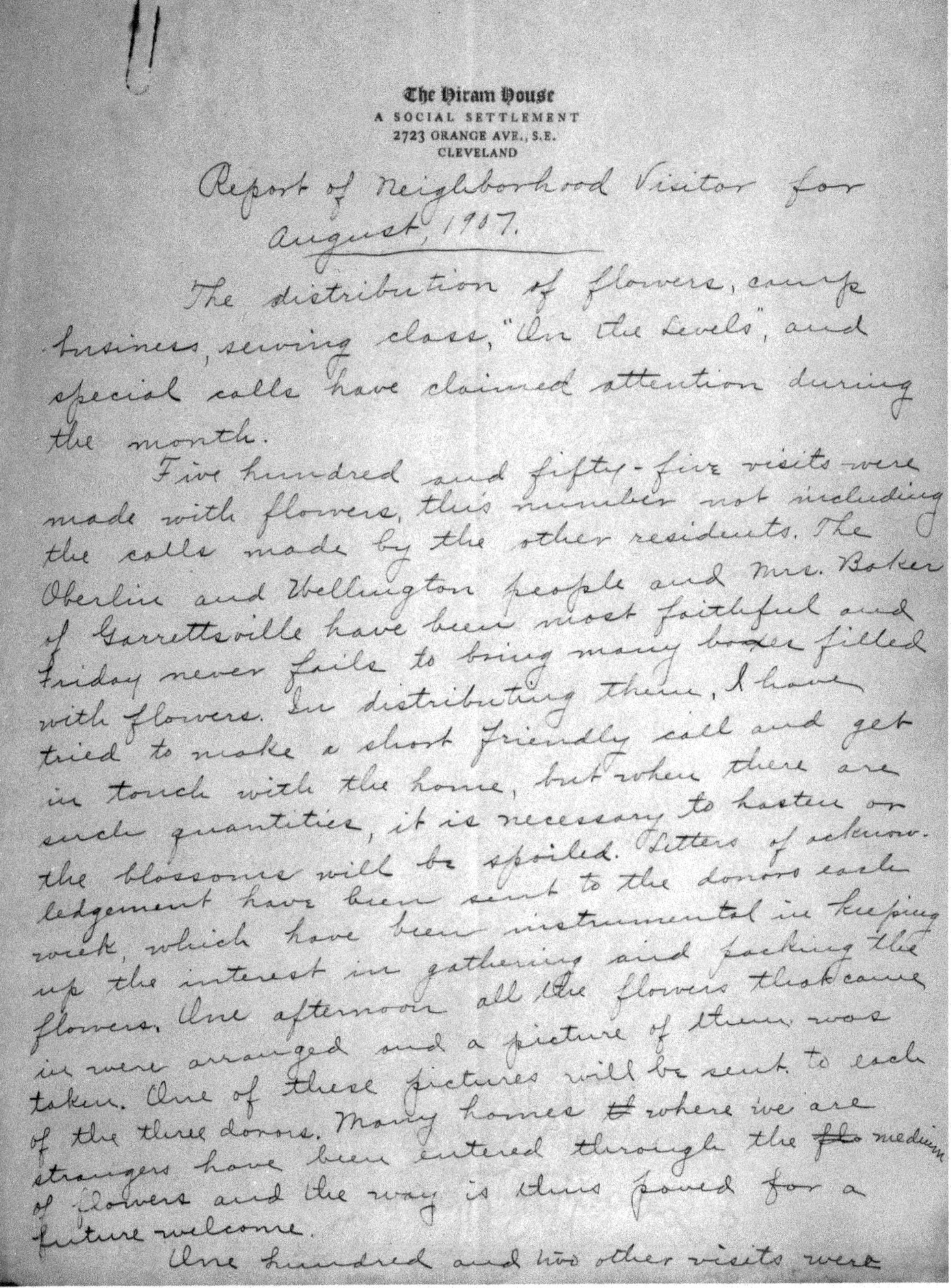

The Hiram House
A SOCIAL SETTLEMENT
2723 ORANGE AVE., S.E.
CLEVELAND

Report of Neighborhood Visitor for August, 1907.

The distribution of flowers, camp business, sewing class, "In the Levels", and special calls have claimed attention during the month.

Five hundred and fifty-five visits were made with flowers, this number not including the calls made by the other residents. The Oberlin and Wellington people and Mrs. Baker of Garrettsville have been most faithful and Friday never fails to bring many boxes filled with flowers. In distributing them, I have tried to make a short friendly call and get in touch with the home, but when there are such quantities, it is necessary to hasten or the blossoms will be spoiled. Letters of acknowledgement have been sent to the donors each week, which have been instrumental in keeping up the interest in gathering and packing the flowers. One afternoon all the flowers that came in were arranged and a picture of them was taken. One of these pictures will be sent to each of the three donors. Many homes ~~t~~ where we are strangers have been entered through the ~~flo~~ medium of flowers and the way is thus paved for a future welcome.

One hundred and two other visits were

The Hiram House
A SOCIAL SETTLEMENT
2723 ORANGE AVE., S.E.
CLEVELAND

made.

The cases of Joe Joseph, Paul Joffee, and Jake Sogolovitz were investigated in connection with brass stealing. The boys confessed that they were guilty, but did not seem overburdened with the enormity of their crime — a fact partly accounted for in the case of Paul Joffee, who was the least concerned, by the attitude of the parents, who were inclined to laugh at the sly maneuvers of the youthful thieves. It is more evident than ever that, do as much as we can "On the Levels" will occasionally slip off the level. But we know that the boys are trying and we can only work and wait. (A full account of this brass stealing episode will be handed in separately.)

Another "On the Level" has committed a theft — Arthur Covar has recently stolen $2.00 from his mother. He claims he was urged to do this by two boys who belong to a newly-organized gang called the "Loving gang." I asked the names of the two boys. At first he claimed he didn't know, but when urged to tell, he said, "I'll tell if you'll promise you won't tell Herman." I promised and he said it was Jimmy O'Donald and Tommy Olach. I asked him why he didn't want Herman to know and he said, "If Herman knew that these boys had been urging me to steal from my mother, he'd beat them up until they almost "croaked"." He said it made Herman awful mad

The Hiram House
A SOCIAL SETTLEMENT
2723 ORANGE AVE., S.E.
CLEVELAND

to have boys steal from their mothers — a rather unique sense of honor but to be admired just the same. The boys report that the new "Irving gang" are committing all sorts of depredations and the "Gookey's" are being blamed for them. They resent this, yet they can see that they have earned their bad reputation. They are censuring the other gang severely for doing the very things that they themselves were doing only a few months ago. Their better natures, dwarfed and stunted by environment are beginning to put forth buds of promise.

Harry Corse Jimmy Snyder, and "Midge" Sogolovitz were intrusted to me from juvenile where they had been summoned to answer to the charge of stealing from a five-and-ten-cent store down town. Mr. Lewis said, "Boys, go with Miss Mitchell. Go to the Hiram House and learn to do what is right. If you'll listen to them, you won't get into trouble."

Appeal was made to us from Miss Shapiro to help her to manage her brother George. She wanted us to try to induce him to come back home to live. He is only fifteen years of age, is a very bright boy, but has acquired the habit of bumming. When his sister appealed to me he hadn't been home at all for more than a week. She said they had had some trouble over a bicycle that George wanted to purchase and ~~George~~ he had left. The home was a very good

The Hiram House
A SOCIAL SETTLEMENT
2723 ORANGE AVE., S.E.
CLEVELAND

one and I felt that there must be some reason for a boy to leave such a place and sleep on the street. He very willingly came in to talk his troubles over. He felt that he had been unjustly dealt with, and I felt that he was right. For more than a week he had been sleeping in barns, coal sheds, or most anywhere and had lived on money he made peddling gum down town, contrary to law. He said he and his family couldn't agree and that he never would go home until things were made right. Then the home was again visited and the situation was frankly discussed. In the end the sister promised that if George would come home, he might buy the much-coveted wheel. He is now staying at home once more - or rather at his sister's home. He and his brothers disagree so much that he says he won't live with them. I find that there is nothing that appeals to a boy more than "fair dealing" and I believe that a sense of wronged justice is the secret of many a wayward career.

August 6 I took twelve Fresh air children to Oberlin, called on the people who have been sending us flowers, went on to Norwalk and got a crowd of Fresh air children there and brought them back to the city.

The domestic difficulties of Mrs. Corpec seemed about to overwhelm me for a few

5.

The Hiram House
A SOCIAL SETTLEMENT
2723 ORANGE AVE., S.E.
CLEVELAND

days. Two days in police court, many calls in the home, several interviews a day here — and still I couldn't make things go right. But the parish priest did, so the responsibility was taken from me.

All this month two mornings a week were spent with the Progress City sewing class. Many hours were spent the last week in helping my girls and Miss Quimby's shirt-waist girls finish some articles for the Model Cottage Exhibit. We finished two pairs of bloomers, three very pretty white aprons, three shirt waists, and a doily. The girls washed and ironed the aprons and shirt-waists under our direction and their work looked very nice, even if there wasn't much of it.

The camp work, fresh air work, and sewing classes are now over for the summer and I hope to take up more definite lines of work in my calling.

→ DOCUMENT 15.9 ←

Settlement house records on Margaret Mitchell's neighborhood visits, October 1907. Hiram House Records, folder 5, container 33, The Western Reserve Historical Society, Cleveland, Ohio.

Report of Neighborhood Visiting
for October, 1907.

Seventy visits were made during the latter part of October, the first two weeks having been spent at home. Fifty-four different families were visited.

For the most part, the section visited has been that south of Orange Avenue. Boys are more and more coming to us from the lower part of Irving and from Broadway. When we realize the wickedness of that part of the city, then we ought to be thankful that we are getting hold of at least some of the boys. Herman Anthony once said, when speaking of the neighborhood of Liberal and Broadway: "Miss Mitchell, that's an awful tough place over there. My! but the boys over there are a bad lot." No doubt Herman knew what he was talking about, too, for it was here that the Jockeys used to hang out and terrorize everyone. They were doubtless intimately acquainted with the forms of vice which flourish there. From this vicinity comes the Irving gang, or Square Deals, whose record, while by no means as bad as that of the Jockeys, is not a very clean one. But there are lots of other boys and girls whom we have not yet reached, who need all the ~~x~~ good influence that can be thrown around them.

The new Square Deals are very enthusiastic over the House and their club, as are also their parents. Mrs. Glump says she is so glad to have Fred have some place to go beside the street. She could hardly talk to me because the tobacco in her mouth interfered with her speech, and knowing the conditions in her home, I, too, was glad that Fred had a place to go. Mrs. Stironek says that Frank has an "awful glad" because of the good time he had at the Hallowe'en party. He says he isn't going to the shows any more - he's coming to the Hiram House instead. Her little boy had such a good time at the game room Hallowe'en party that he wakened his parents to tell them about it. His mother said she said to him - in emphatic if not very refined English - "By gosh! Go away and let us sleep."

Two homes have been of particular interest to me.

One evening I called on Charley Wilson - one of the "On the Levels" - and found him hurrying to get supper ready by the time his father got home from work. The kitchen was as neat and clean as could be and had an unusually homelike look. Charley's mother has been dead for years and he is the home-keeper. It is a most pathetic situation and Charley needs all the encouragement we can give him. He surely is not so hopelessly bad as the people on

3

Irving street would have us believe.

A few evenings later I called at Will Roche's—he is a member of the Square Deal club. I found him preparing supper for a family of six—his mother is dead, his sisters work in factories, and his father is a cripple. It was most pathetic to me to see this spirited boy in a home robbed of a mother's influence, trying to take her place by washing the dishes, keeping the kitchen neat and cooking the family meals. I admired him for it and at once I knew that here was a boy ~~to~~ whom it would pay to work with—there was good stuff here. He told me that he had a pupil for us to teach—a young Irishman boarding at Burke's saloon, who wishes to learn to read and write. He said he would bring him over to the Hiram House just as soon as he could. It certainly is a good sign to have boys from that district telling others of the advantages of the House and bringing them here.

→ DOCUMENT 15.10 ←

Settlement house records on Margaret Mitchell's neighborhood visits, November 2, 1907 and January 17, 1908. Hiram House Records, folder 5, container 33, The Western Reserve Historical Society, Cleveland, Ohio.

Nov. 2, 1907.

During the skating season of 1907, nearly all of
"On the Levels" appeared at the Hiram House skating
rink with fine new racing skates, costing
about $3 per pair. We wondered where they got
them all. We knew later. Arthur Cavan's mother
told me that Arthur had been helping himself to money from the cash drawer in their
saloon – she claimed he had stolen about $60
within a very short time. He spent the money
on the gang for the most part. He took them
to the theater time and again, treated them at
the restaurant, bought skates for the bunch,
and showed them a good time in general.
His father and mother suspected that he
was responsible for the steady disappearance
of money from the drawer and they set a
trap for him and caught him. Then they
beat him until he was black and blue -
then he confessed. For some time they
didn't allow ~~them~~ to go anywhere to punish
him.

Arthur told me that when he first began
stealing, he wanted to hide the money and save
it until he had enough to go West and
be a cowboy. Several times since he has taken
money but never on quite ~~so extensive a~~
so extensive a scale. At one time however he

was taken to juvenile court by his people.

The Lavdis boys, cousins of his, took money from the cash drawer in their saloon, also.

Jan. 17, '08. Arthur Covar says now that he has quit taking money from his mother, but John and Paul Lavdis still do it. Paul Lavdis has just returned to the club after four week's suspension — he had been stealing so much that he had the number of crosses against him required to suspend him. But he promises now he won't do it any more. Each time before he would report truthfully at club. The last cross he received came after a confession ~~from~~ Paul that he had been stealing corn for his pigeons.

The Americans' Experience in the Great War

Archive Overview

A hundred years ago, in the early years of the 20th century and long before NATO, most Americans confidently expected that European quarrels would have little impact on American life. They believed that their country could stand aside while Europeans resolved their differences. But then, as now, it became increasingly difficult for the United States to avoid entanglements in Europe. In 1917, after several years of witnessing the progress of what contemporaries were calling the Great War, the United States broke off diplomatic relations with Germany. Shortly thereafter, Woodrow Wilson sent his war message to Congress, and young American men were enlisting in the army, hoping before long to be on their way to fighting in France.

This archive focuses on the ways in which some Americans, mostly soldiers from Cleveland, Ohio, thought about and experienced World War I. What were the reasons for their participation in the war? How did they respond to military life and to service in France? In what ways were their experiences and attitudes similar and different? What picture of army life and the conflict do the sources in this archive reveal?

Placing the Sources in Context

WHEN the war in Europe first broke out in 1914, the policy of the United States toward the conflict was one of official neutrality. The event triggering the conflict was the assassination in Serbia of a member of the Austro-Hungarian royal family. This act of violence activated a series of military agreements that brought together Germany and Austria-Hungary as allies (the Central powers) on the one hand, and Britain, France, and Russia (the Allied powers) on the other. With the major European powers at war, Americans, Wilson warned, must "be neutral in fact as well as in name" and "impartial in thought as well as in action."

With America's rich mix of ethnic groups, Wilson believed that neutrality was a necessity; "otherwise our mixed populations would wage war on each other." In the end, the United States discovered that it could not live up to the lofty definition of neutrality Wilson espoused. While some German-Americans and Irish-Americans favored the Central powers, most Americans sympathized with Great Britain, France, and Russia. They were horrified at the German submarine campaign aimed at destroying allied shipping, and in 1915 they greeted with outrage the news that 128 American passengers had lost their lives when a German U-boat torpedoed a British liner, the *Lusitania*. Lucrative trade with and substantial loans to the Allies reinforced pro-Allied sentiments. Yet many Americans still hoped to avoid entanglement. In 1916, when Woodrow Wilson ran for reelection, he ran on the slogan "He kept us out of war." Privately, however, he was quite aware of how little power he had to keep the United States out of the conflict. After the election, Wilson tried to bring the belligerents to the conference table to conclude a peace without victory, but neither the Central powers nor the Allies showed much interest in his efforts. In January 1917 Germany announced it was resuming unrestricted submarine warfare after a period of inactivity, and in April the United States declared war.

Before Americans could have a major impact on the course of the conflict, the government had to raise and train an army.

TIMELINE

1912	Woodrow Wilson elected president
1914	World War I begins; U.S. declares neutrality
1915	Germans sink the *Lusitania*
1916	Army Reorganization Bill
1917	Germany resumes unrestricted submarine warfare; U.S. breaks off diplomatic relations with Germany; Zimmerman telegram; U.S. declares war; Selective Service Act; Espionage Act
1918	Sedition Act; Wilson's Fourteen Points; Armistice

Although thousands volunteered, the government relied on the draft to create a fighting force. The Selective Service Act required all young men between 21 and 31 (later expanded to all young men between 18 and 45) to register with their local draft board. Of the 24 million who did so, 2.8 million were drafted into military service. Women also served during the war in the Nurse Corps, in the U.S. Army Signal Corps, and in the Navy as clerks.

Because it took time to prepare recruits for war, it was almost a year before American soldiers started to make a difference in the fighting. By spring 1918, the 300,000 American soldiers in France could help to turn back a major German offensive. At the war's end in November 1918, over 2 million Americans had been involved in the defeat of Germany.

With the exception of four regiments of African-Americans who served with the French army, American soldiers were members of the American Expeditionary Force, commanded by General John J. Pershing. Distrusting British and French commanders whose decisions were responsible for the slaughter of incredible numbers of young men, Pershing was determined to keep white American troops under his own command. Partly because of his insistence on a separate force and partly because Americans were in combat for a relatively short time, American casualties were small compared to European losses. Americans who died in battle numbered 48,000, while 900,000 British and 1.4 million French were casualties of the war. Russian and German casualties were even greater.

About the Sources

DOCUMENTS in this archive include the personal writings of three Cleveland, Ohio, men who served in the military. Two kept diaries. James C. Adell, a teacher and inventor who turned 30 during the war, recopied and expanded his journal based on notes jotted down earlier (16.5). Dudley J. Hard, a colonel of field artillery in his mid forties, had a commercially printed diary with a page for each day, most of which he filled in after he left home (16.9). Rufus Ullman came from a successful Jewish family who owned one of the largest liquor distilleries in the United States; here we have several letters written to his family (16.8).

As you read the letters and journals, think about how they are similar and different. Although both diaries and letters are personal documents, for example, letters are meant to be read by others while diaries are often intended to be private. Thus each serves a different function and may well include very different kinds of materials and reflections. Because letters are usually written from time to time and diaries may be added to regularly, some even having an entry each day, the perspective of the writer toward events and the decision of what to include may also differ dramatically. You will think of further reasons for the differences as you examine the materials.

Other documents include President Wilson's war message to Congress (16.2), sheet music (16.1 and 16.4), and a poster (16.3). During the war, the government embarked on a major propaganda campaign to persuade the American people to support the war in a variety of ways, including enlisting, buying war bonds, and watching for possible spies. While posters seem a reasonable way to encourage enthusiasm, the commissioned secret report on a family of German background suggests some of the excesses that resulted from the policy to line up all Americans behind the war.

Analyze the poster and the covers of the sheet music as you would any visual source. Starting at the upper left, scan your eyes across and down the page, describing each image and asking yourself (or the members of your small group) why each image is there and what it means. Are there symbolic images in these sources?

An expression of a faith in social science as a guide, the Army Intelligence Test (16.6) was used during the war to help assign and promote soldiers. Those who could not read and write English did not take this test; they took a test based on pictures. Examiners were warned that these men "sometimes sulk and refuse to work," and they were encouraged to act "in a genial manner" with this group. Examiners told the soldiers taking the regular test, "We are not looking for crazy people. The aim is to help find out what you are best fitted to do in the Army." Officers used test results to help classify soldiers and select candidates for officer's training or special assignments. Those deemed to be "mentally inferior" would be recommended for discharge. Raw scores were translated into letter grades, and soldiers who scored lower than a middle C were rarely considered for officer's training. Some portions of the test were mathematical or abstract, but many questions tested cultural literacy or education.

Try taking the test yourself; to approximate the results from the complete test, you can score your response to the excerpt as follows:

Alpha Test	
A	26–40
B	20–25
C	5–15
D	3–4

Those scoring below 3 on the ALPHA test had to take the BETA test; those scoring below 2 on the BETA test had to be examined individually.

List of Sources

16.1 **Sheet music, "I Didn't Raise My Boy to Be a Soldier,"** by Al Piantadosi and Alfred Bryan (New York: Leo Feist, 1915). Star Sheet Music Collection, Courtesy, The Lilly Library, Indiana University, Bloomington.

16.2 **President Wilson's war message to Congress,** 1917, in Thomas G. Paterson and Dennis Merrill, *Major Problems in American Foreign Relations* (Lexington: Heath, 1995), pp. 35–37.

16.3 **War poster, "True Sons of Freedom,"** 1918, by Charles Gustrine. PP POS US J5, F32, "Negro History—WWI," negative number LC-USZC4–2426, Library of Congress, Washington, D.C.

16.4 **Sheet music, "Good Bye Alexander,"** 1918, by Creamer and Layton (Broadway Music Corporation). Star Sheet Music Collection, Courtesy, The Lilly Library, Indiana University, Bloomington.

16.5 **Journal entries of James C. Adell,** 1917–1918. James C. Adell Papers, container 2, folder 17. The Western Reserve Historical Society, Cleveland, Ohio.

16.6 **Army Intelligence Test, ALPHA, Form 5, Test 8,** in Robert M. Yerkes, ed., *Psychological Examining in the United States Army* (Washington DC: U.S. Government Printing Office, 1921), p. 227. Robert Yerkes Papers, Manuscripts and Archives, Yale University Library.

16.7 **A report on a German-American family,** undated and unsigned, probably around April 17, 1918, by Clayton Ely Emig. Leila Drumgold Emig Family Papers, The Western Reserve Historical Society, Cleveland, Ohio.

16.8 **Letters from Rufus Ullman to his family,** May 13 and August 31, 1918. Ullman Family Papers, container 1, folder 2, The Western Reserve Historical Society, Cleveland, Ohio.

16.9 **Journal entries of Dudley J. Hard,** 1918. Dudley J. Hard Papers, container 2, folder 19, The Western Reserve Historical Society, Cleveland, Ohio.

16.10 **Form letter from John J. Pershing,** February 28, 1919. In Rufus Ullman's photograph album, Ullman Family Papers, volume 1, container 1, The Western Reserve Historical Society, Cleveland, Ohio.

Questions to Consider

1. Study both the graphics and the lyrics of "I Didn't Raise My Boy to Be a Soldier" (source 16.1). What view of war do the lyrics and the graphics present? Does any cause seem to justify military action? How does the song utilize stereotypes to make an emotional appeal? What insights into antiwar sentiment in the United States does the song suggest?

2. Woodrow Wilson's war message (16.2) presents the argument that the United States must go to war. What are the main points he makes? How does he appeal to reason? To idealism? To national self-interest? How well does he make the case for war? Would those who responded to "I Didn't Raise My Boy to Be a Soldier" be swayed by Wilson's speech?

3. Study the poster (16.3). What picture of war and the enemy does the poster present? What are all the elements, both textual and visual, symbolic and realistic, that make the case for supporting the war? Why is Lincoln there? How are African-Americans depicted? This poster was not reproduced in the quantities of other pro-war posters; why not?

4. Compare "Good Bye Alexander" (16.4) to "I Didn't Raise My Boy to Be a Soldier." What are the differences between their depictions of the war, war service, and women? What views of the draft does this song suggest? What clues do the lyrics and the graphics on the cover provide to explain some of the reasons behind African-American participation in the military?

5. What does James Adell's journal (16.5) tell you about mobilization and about enthusiasm for the war? What role does class play in shaping Adell's attitude? Why does Adell change his mind about serving? What role does his mother play in his life?

6. What does the report on the Scholler family (16.7) suggest about army life and civilian life during the war? What was the government worried about in terms of civilian life?

7. Compare and contrast the experiences of Rufus Ullman and Dudley Hard (16.8 and 16.9) in France. What was war like for the men? How did they feel about serving? What did they notice and write about? In what ways would you say letters and diaries are different?

8. What picture of military service does General Pershing present in his form letter (16.10)? How does it compare to other material you have seen in this archive? Why do you think Rufus Ullman pasted the letter in his scrapbook?

9. Take the psychological exam (16.6) and score it. What does the test reveal about the army? What are the class and ethnic implications of this test?

10. Review the sources in this archive and discuss the pictures of the conflict and military service presented here. What accounts for the differences and similarities between the sources? How do these sources help you understand American participation in the Great War?

WORLD WAR I: THE WESTERN FRONT

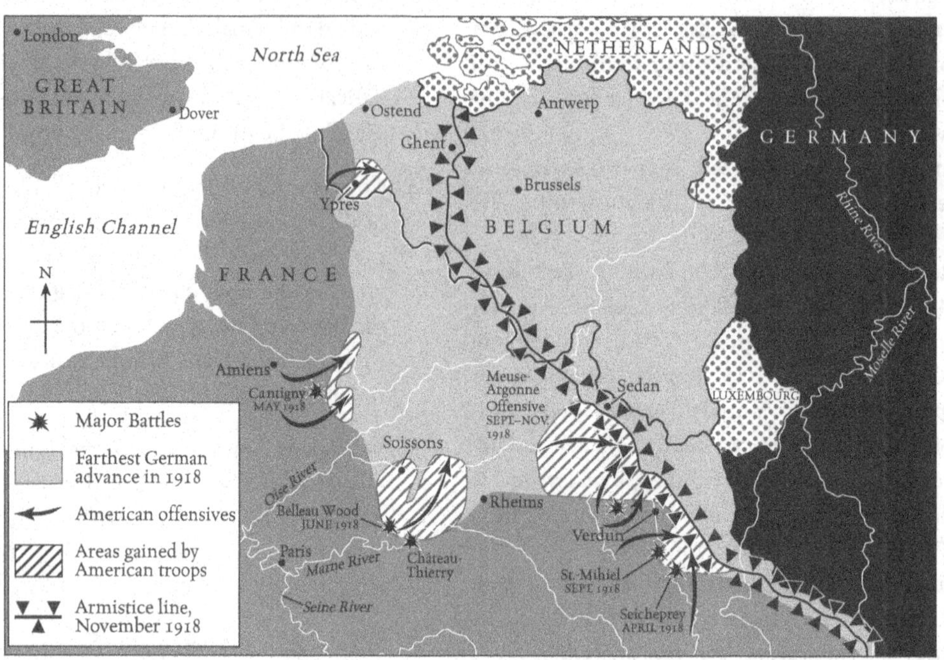

→ DOCUMENT 16.1 ←

Sheet music, "I Didn't Raise My Boy to Be a Soldier," by Al Piantadosi and Alfred Bryan (New York: Leo Feist, 1915). Star Sheet Music Collection, Courtesy, The Lilly Library, Indiana University, Bloomington.

I Didn't Raise My Boy To Be A Soldier

3
mil - lion moth - ers' hearts must break For the
vic - tor - y can bring her back All she
ones who died in vain.
cared to call her own.
marcato
Head bowed down in sor - row In her lone - ly years, I
Let each moth - er an - swer In the years to be, Re-
heard a moth - er mur - mur thro' her tears:
mem - ber that my boy be - longs to me!

CHORUS
"I did-n't raise my boy to be a sol - - dier, I
brought him up to be my pride and joy, Who
dares to place a mus-ket on his shoul - - der, To
shoot some oth-er moth-er's dar-ling boy? Let
p-f

na-tions ar - bi - trate their fut - ure trou - - bles, It's
time to lay the sword and gun a - way,
There'd
be no war to - day, If moth - ers all would say, "I
did - n't raise my boy to be a sol - dier." "I dier."
1.
2.
3190 - 4
FELLER, SONS & DORNER, NEW-YORK.

→ DOCUMENT 16.2 ←

President Wilson's war message to Congress, 1917, in Thomas G. Paterson and Dennis Merrill, *Major Problems in American Foreign Relations* (Lexington: Heath, 1995), pp. 35–37.

On the third of February last I officially laid before you the extraordinary announcement of the Imperial German Government that on and after the first day of February it was its purpose to put aside all restraints of law of humanity and use its submarines to sink every vessel that sought to approach either the ports of Great Britain and Ireland or the western coasts of Europe or any of the ports controlled by the enemies of Germany within the Mediterranean. That had seemed to be the object of the German submarine warfare earlier in the war, but since April of last year the Imperial Government had somewhat restrained the commanders of its undersea craft in conformity with its promise then given to us that passenger boats should not be sunk and that due warning would be given to all other vessels which its submarines might seek to destroy, when no resistance was offered or escape attempted, and care taken that their crews were given at least a fair chance to save their lives in their open boats. The precautions taken were meagre and haphazard enough, as was proved in distressing instance after instance in the progress of the cruel and unmanly business, but a certain degree of restraint was observed. The new policy has swept every restriction aside. Vessels of every kind, whatever their flag, their character, their cargo, their destination, their errand, have been ruthlessly sent to the bottom without warning and without thought of help or mercy for those on board, the vessels of friendly neutrals along with those of belligerents. Even hospital ships and ships carrying relief to the sorely bereaved and stricken people of Belgium, though the latter were provided with safe conduct through the proscribed areas by the German Government itself and were distinguished by unmistakable marks of identity, have been sunk with the same reckless lack of compassion or of principle.

I was for a little while unable to believe that such things would in fact be done by any government that had hitherto subscribed to the humane practices of civilized nations. International law had its origin in the attempt to set up some law which would be respected and observed upon the seas, where no nation had right of dominion where lay the free highways of the world. By painful stage after stage has that law been built up, with meagre enough results, indeed, after all was accomplished that could be accomplished, but always with a clear view, at least of what the heart and conscience of mankind demanded. This minimum of right the German Government has swept aside under the plea of retaliation and necessity and because it had no weapons which it could use at sea except these which it is impossible to employ as it is employing them without throwing to the winds all scruples of humanity or of respect for the understandings that were supposed to underlie the intercourse of the world. I am not now thinking of the loss of property involved, immense and serious as that is, but only of the wanton and wholesale destruction of the lives of noncombatants, men, women, and children, engaged in pursuits which have always, even in the darkest periods of modern history, been deemed innocent and legitimate. Property can be paid for; the lives of peaceful and innocent people cannot be. The present German submarine warfare against commerce is a warfare against mankind.

It is a war against all nations. American ships have been sunk, American lives taken, in ways which it has stirred us very deeply to learn of, but the ships and people of other neutral and friendly nations have been sunk and overwhelmed in the waters in the same way. There has been no discrimination. The challenge is to all mankind. Each nation must decide for itself how it will meet it. The choice we make for ourselves must be made with a moderation of counsel and a temperateness of judgment benefiting our character and our motives as a nation. We must put excited feeling away. Our motive will not be revenge or the victorious assertion of the physical might of the nation, but only the vindication of right, of human right, of which we are only a single champion. . . .

With a profound sense of the solemn and even tragical character of the step I am taking and of the grave responsibilities which it involves, but in unhesitating obedience to what I deem my constitutional duty, I advise that the Congress declare the recent course of the Imperial German Government to be in fact nothing less than war against the government and people of the United States; that it formally accept the status of belligerent which has thus been thrust upon it; and that it take immediate steps not only to put the country in a more thorough state of defense but also to exert all its power and employ all its resources to bring the Government of the German Empire to terms and end the war. . . .

Does not every American feel that assurance has been added to our hope for the future peace of the world by the wonderful and heartening things that have been happening within the last few weeks in Russia? Russia was known by those who knew it best to have been always in fact democratic at heart, in all the vital habits of her thought, in all the intimate relationships of her people that spoke their natural instinct, their habitual attitude towards life. The autocracy that crowned the summit of her political structure, long as it had stood and terrible as was the reality of its power, was not in fact Russian in origin, character, or purpose; and now it has been shaken off and the great, generous Russian people have been added in all their naive majesty and might to the forces that are fighting for freedom in the world, for justice, and for peace. Here is a fit partner for a League of Honour.

One of the things that has served to convince us that the Prussian autocracy was not and could never be our friends is that from the very outset of the present war it has filled our unsuspecting communities and even our offices of government with spies and set criminal intrigues everywhere afoot against our national unity of counsel, our peace within and without, our industries and our commerce. . . . That it means to stir up enemies against us at our very doors the intercepted note to the German Minister at Mexico City is eloquent evidence.

We are accepting this challenge of hostile purpose because we know that in such a government, following such methods, we can never have a friend; and that in the presence of its organized power, always lying in wait to accomplish we know not what purpose, there can be no assured security for the democratic governments of the world. We are now about to accept gauge of battle with its natural foe to liberty and shall, if necessary, spend the whole force of the nation to check and nullify its pretensions and its power. We are glad, now that we see the facts with no veil of false pretence about them, to fight thus for the ultimate peace of the world and for the liberation of its peoples, the German peoples included: for the rights of nations great and small and the privilege of men everywhere to choose their way of life and of obedience. The world must be made safe for democracy. . . .

It is a distressing and oppressive duty, Gentlemen of the Congress, which I have performed in thus addressing you. There are, it may be, many months of fiery trial and sacrifice ahead of us. It is a fearful thing to lead this great peaceful people into war, into the most terrible and disastrous of all wars, civilization itself seeming to be in the balance. But the right is more precious than peace, and we shall fight for the things which we have always carried nearest our hearts—for democracy, for the right of those who submit to authority to have a voice in their own governments, for the rights and liberties of small nations, for a universal dominion of right by such a concert of free peoples as shall bring peace and safety to all nations and make the world itself at last free. To such a task we can dedicate our lives and our fortunes, everything that we are and everything that we have, with the pride of those who know that the day has come when America is privileged to spend her blood and her might for the principles that gave her birth and happiness and the peace which she has treasured. God helping her, she can do no other.

⇝ DOCUMENT 16.3 ⇜

War poster, "True Sons of Freedom," 1918, by Charles Gustrine. PP POS US J5, F32, "Negro History—WWI," negative number LC-USZC4-2426, Library of Congress.

DOCUMENT 16.4

Sheet music, "Good Bye Alexander," 1918, by Creamer and Layton (Broadway Music Corporation). Star Sheet Music Collection, Courtesy, The Lilly Library, Indiana University, Bloomington.

Good-bye Alexander

Chorus
3
Good-bye Al-ex-an-der, Good-bye hon-ey boy Dressed up in that
un-i-form, you fills my heart with joy You aint born for mo-pin' boy, you sure can
laugh, But you left that win-dow o-pen and they got you in the draft. Al-ex-
an-der I'll save my lov-ing for you, I'll be wait-ing like Poor But-ter-
fly. So get bus-y with that gun and don't come back here till you've won
If you want to see me grin, bring me a pig-foot from Ber-lin
Al-ex-an-der good-bye. bye.
p-f
sfz
Good-bye Alexander, etc. 2

DOCUMENT 16.5

Journal entries of James C. Adell, 1917–1918. James C. Adell Papers, container 2, folder 17. The Western Reserve Historical Society, Cleveland, Ohio.

Tues. June 5, 1917 1.

While living at 1628 East 73rd, Cleveland, Cuyahoga Co., Ohio registered for military service (under the draft law) at voting booth of Precinct L, Ward 22, on June 5, 1917

At the drawing of the numbers in Washington by Sec. Baker my Serial Number was 6171 and my Order Number (in Division No. 7) was 365. Court House was jammed by men trying to get their numbers.

Thurs. August 2, '17.
Received notice to appear at Wilson School, E. 55 & White Ave., on Aug. 7 for physical examination. "Bathe before coming," was typewritten on my notice. This occasioned a great deal of merriment when I showed my notice at the luncheon hour to the other teachers in the Summer School.

Tues. Aug. 7.
Took my physical exam. It was very easy. Passed as did practically every one else. Filed claims for exemption.

Practically a week was required to get all of the affidavits of Mother, Ethel and myself fixed up and taken to the Draft Board.

Wed. Sept. 12, '17.
Received notice of Exemption from Military Service.

Sat. Dec. 15, '17.
The lottery scheme for taking men for service has been done away with. A new and scientific method of classification has been devised. Every one who registered on June 5 — and has not been sent — is required to fill out a "Questionnaire". This gives a brief summary of your training, the different kinds of work that you can do and have done, and your life history. There are also blanks for affidavits by your dependents and references must be given so that these statements can be investigated.
Received my questionnaire today. Filled it out and mailed it to Mother for her affidavit.

Mon. Dec. 17.
Was thirty years old today. The occasion was celebrated by a dinner at which "Doc" and Betty Maines were our guests. This was because Betty and I are twins. We talked mostly of the war. As all of the magazines and newspapers have been full of the horrors of the battlefield, we were pretty generally

3.

agreed that any one who went "over there" had very little chance of coming back. "Doc" said, "If they take me, I'll say 'Here goes nothing'". Every one in our crowd was anxious to escape service. "Doc" was above the age.

Ethel and Mother are very much opposed to my going and I am not very keen on the proposition myself as it looks as if I might get rich on my process for extracting manganese ores from low grade ores.

Tues. Dec. 18
Received questionnaire from Mother.

Wed. Dec. 19
Ethel ~~and~~ came over to school today and we made our affidavits as required in the questionnaire, before D. C. Meck. Meck mailed the questionnaire for me.

Spent the Holidays at Groveport and Winchester. Ethel stayed in Winchester and Mother returned to Cleveland with me for several weeks. Ethel came home and Mother went to Manhattan, Kansas, where Gertrude is expecting the stork. Mother left for Groveport Jan. 18.

Wed. Jan. 30, 1918
Received a notice today that I had been placed in Class IV A as the result of questionnaire. A couple of weeks ago I received a notice to come to the Draft Board and fill in an ommision in my questionnaire.

Sat., March 23, 1918
E. A. Bauer, Jr.

Mon. April 22,
Mother came to visit today. Ethel went to Winchester.

Alfred Bosch is trying to join the U. S. N. R. It appears to be a very interesting branch of the service. Pres. of Case spoke to the East Tech boys and girls about the U. S. N. R. There appear to be excellent chances for advancement and an urgent need for men with some education. Talked to Mother several days about the Navy. Finally obtained her consent to let me join. Then I wrote and asked Ethel what she thot of my joining. She said that she would not stand in my way.
Mother wrote Gertrude for Doc Gould's

5

address.
Went around to the recruiting office, 827 New Guardian Bldg., but could not get much information or satisfaction. Think that I did not know enough to ask intelligent questions.

Thurs. May 9,
Mother received Doc Gould's address from Desu. Sent him a very long night letter asking him for more information. As he is at Pelham Bay he ought to know all about it.

Sat. May 11

Received night letter from Doc. Gould at noon today. He advises going ahead. After lunch went to the recruiting office, was not received very enthusiastically. Had to ask the ensign for the form to take to the Draft Board. He was apparently unwilling to give me that blank form. However he did after some delay. He tried to send me to the Draft Board without the form. As it was Sat. afternoon the Draft Board was not open officially. As I did not have my draft papers I could not do anything, tho I talked with the Clerk. He had been having a rowe with the people who I were ahead of me and so was not in a pleasant frame of mind. Left him and hurried to meet Ethel who was coming home. Her train was an hour late so had to waste an hour.

Mon. May 13.

Took my Draft Card with me to the Draft Office right after school. Clerk was as pleasant as a basket of ^(surprised) chips. Saturday in reply to his insinuations about running away and deserting my family etc. I had told him who I was etc. I thot that he had forgotten who I was and that I had been in Sat. but he remembered. He talked to me as if I were his EQUAL and wanted to tell me a lot of stories about himself. I was an appreciative audience until he had all of my papers fixed after that I did not call for any more encores. Then I hustled to the New Guardian Bldg. The Ensign was more like a human being today and fixed me up without a murmur. He told me to report at the good ship Dorothea on Carnegie Ave. near 32nd Street tomorrow morning for my physical exam.

7.

Tues. May 14.

Went to school this morning until 9:30. Then went to the Good Ship Dorothea. The Ship is a brick structure about 200 feet long and 75 feet wide. A sentry was pacing back and forth in front of the gang plank. He stopped me and I had to tell him my business before I went aboard. I told him that I wanted to take my physical exam and he permitted me to pass. Before setting foot on deck I was stopped by another sentry who conducted me to the petty officer who had charge of the ship's log. My name, business and hour of arrival were recorded. Then I was directed to sit along the wall with a dozen others who were also awaiting physical examination.

The ship was strung taut with excitement for wasn't a Rear Admiral coming to inspect the old boat. The deck had been freshly scrubbed, windows and wood work washed. Caps and leggings also were newly bathed, shoes shining with black luster. The armory ~~fairly breathed~~ announced as tho thru a megaphone that it was dressed up spick and span in its

Sunday go-to-meeting attire. The men were cautioned repeatedly to use the spittoons and not the floor.
The Officer-of-the-Deck walked back and forth, occasionally killing time by looking out of the windows thru the small pair of opera glasses that hung loosely from his neck on a strap of convenient length. I learned afterwards that the opera glasses were used to label the ensign who was on duty as the Deck Officer. Other officers talked and joked. Occasionally the men were put thru an evolution or two of infantry drill without rifles. The work did not compare favorably with our rookie drilling at Ohio State.
Finally an assistant to the examining doctor came out of the Sick Bay and took us in and gave us our eye tests. The letters were very small but I passed $\frac{18}{20}$ with one eye and $\frac{19}{20}$ with the other. Then I arranged to go back to school and come in the afternoon at 3:30 for the rest of the exam.

At 3:30 the doctor's assistant told me to come back tomorrow afternoon as the doctor was too busy to take care of me.

25

Thurs. July 25

Just before supper I received this wire from Municipal Pier.

Received At 4:12 P 2D- 12:52 P

Chicago, Ill 7/25

James Claude Adell
Groveport, Ohio
Your call will be about September first or possibly later 10525
B. C. Getsinger.

Called up Uncle Elmon, read him the above message and my night letter to Lieut. Col. McPherson. He advised making it a special delivery letter as telegraphing is so uncertain. He also suggested that I ask for a commission instead of a captain's commission as I had it. Borrowed Albert Hess's typewriter and fixed up the letter in pretty good shape.

Wired Bosch the information in my message from Chicago.

Fri. July 26

Mailed my special delivery letter on the first mail this morning. Think I should get a wire tomorrow afternoon or evening. Mowed the grass and dug potatoes. It was terribly hot and I was wringing wet when I got thru. The potatoes are not turning out well this year, because it was so dry in June. My but I do miss a bathroom. Waterworks would certainly help Groveport

Fri. Aug. 2

have forwarded your letter to the Commandant of the 9th-10th-11th Naval District, Chicago, Illinois, with a request that action be taken.

C. J. McRoy
by direction.

In the afternoon and evening Albert Herr and I went out in the country selling tickets for the Groveport Chautauqua, the 8th, 9th & 10th of this month. We did fairly well.

Sat. Aug. 3.

Received a letter from Edgewood Arsenal this morning. "Colonel McPherson advises that he can not utilize your services in a commissioned capacity, but would be desirous of having you as an enlisted man, provided your induction can be arranged". Etc. Well this lets me out here. Do not believe that promotion would come as fast in this branch as in the Navy. Can not help wondering whether I'll land in the Marines or in the Naval Reserves. Ethel went to Winchester this morning. I went over this evening. Attended lodge

34

Fri. Aug. 16

Airplanes are still such a novelty that thousands and thousands of people will turn out to see them fly. As a matter of fact I saw my first airplane less than two months ago. The first one that I saw was flying over the State House.

This reminds me that fifteen years ago the autos were great curiosities. I had my first auto ride when I was a sophomore in the University. We were living up on Maynard Ave., and as I was walking to school a man came along in an electric that was about run down, he asked me to ride with him. I remember he had me get in and get out while the machine was still going as he was afraid he did not have enough current to get him to the charging station.

Sat. Aug. 17

Got off at 4:45 this afternoon expecting to get home early. But Mr. Larimer had battery trouble and we had to leave the car and go into Columbus and go home on the Scioto Valley. Got home at 7:10.

preliminary search made.
Went out to Municipal Pier.
Learned that when I report
there tomorrow morning
at eight, I shall receive
my outfit and be sent to
Great Lakes Station for
three weeks detention.
Then there will be about
three or four weeks at
the Pier. As Navigation
will soon - in December -
be closed on the Lakes, it is
rumored that we may get
our practice trip on a cruise to
South America instead of
on the Lakes. Hope this will
prove to be the case.
Blowed myself this evening
to a two dollar seat (second row)
to see "Oh Look" a very good
musical comedy.

Friday Sept. 20.

Got a good breakfast and reported
early at Municipal Pier. Over a
hundred fellows were strung out
in a line. As they were placed
in alphabetical order, I headed
the procession. We stood around
most of the morning while our
records were being checked. Fred
Kessler one of my former pupils at
Harbor High is also in my company.

Fri. Sept. 20.

The day was raw and cold and there was no heat when we stored. Most of us got quite chilly. Our room shower warmed us up quite a little. Then our clothes were almost thrown at us. We had to try everything on, then if the fit was anything near satisfactory, we took every article off and stenciled the name in it. After spending a couple of hrs. in the nude in the bitter chill, I got my outfit partially straightened out and took it upstairs. With a small library in one suit case, my civilian clothes in my norne bag, and a jammed I had a desperate struggle getting upstairs to quarters. I was of course among the first there so was given liberty about five until Sat. (tomorrow) morning at seven.

Went to the "Y" Hotel for the night. Felt very much dressed up in my uniform.

Tues. June 5, 1917

While living at 1628 East 73nd, Cleveland, Cuyahoga Co, Ohio registered for military service (under the draft law) at voting booth of Precinct L, Ward 221, on June 5, 1917.

At the drawing of the numbers in Washington by Sec. Baker my Serial Number was 6171 and my Order Number (in Division No. 7) was 365. Court House was jammed by men trying to get their numbers.

Thurs. August 2, '17

Received notice to appear at Wilson School, #. 55 & White Ave., on aug. 7 for physical examination. "Bathe before coming," was typewritten on my notice. This occasioned a great deal of merriment when I showed my notice at the luncheon hour to the other teachers in the Summer School.

Tues. Aug. 7.

Took my physical exam. It was very easy. Passed as did practically every one else. Filed claims for exemption.

Practically a week was required to get all of the affidavits of Mother, Ethel and myself fixed up and taken to the Draft Board.

Wed. Sept. 12, '17

Received notice of Exemption from Military Service.

Sat. Dec. 15 '17

The lottery scheme for taking men for service has been done away with. A new and scientific method of classification has been devised. Every one who registered on June 5—and has not been sent—is required to fill out a "Questionnaire." [sic] This gives a brief summary of your training, the different kinds of work that you can do and have done, and your life history. There are also blanks for affidavits by your dependents and references must be given so that these statements can be investigated.

Received my questionnaire today. Filled it out and Mailed it to Mother for her affidavit.

Mon. Dec. 17.

Was thirty years old today. The occasion was celebrated by a dinner at which "Doc" and Betty Maines were our guests. This was because Betty and I are twins. We talked mostly of the war. As all of the magazines and newspapers have been full of the horrors of the battlefield, we were pretty generally agreed that any one who went "over there" had very little chance of coming back. "Doc" said, "If they take me, I'll say 'Here goes nothing"'. Every one in our crowd was anxious to escape service. "Doc" was above the age.

Ethel and Mother are very much opposed to my going and I am not very keen on the proposition myself as it looks as if I might get rich on my process for extracting manganese ores from low grade ores.

Mon. April 22

Mother came to visit today. Ethel went to Winchester.

Alfred Bosch is trying to join the U.S.N.R. It appears to be a very interesting branch of the service Pres. [space left blank] of Case spoke to the East Tech boys and girls about the U.S.N.R. There appear to be excellent chances for advancement and an urgent need for men with some education. Talked to Mother several days about the Navy.

Finally obtained her consent to let me join. Then I wrote and asked Ethel what she thot [sic] of my joining. She said that she would not stand in my way.

Mother wrote Gertrude for Doc Gould's address.

Went around to the recruiting office, 827 New Guardian Bldg., but could not get much information or satisfaction. Think that I did not know enough to ask intelligent questions.

[Adell enlisted in the Naval Reserves on May 17, 1918. He was told that he would be called up in six to eight weeks, and so he quit his teaching job. By late July he still had not been called up. He wrote to the commanding officer of U.S. Naval Auxiliary Reserve School to complain that "I am going broke fast. . . . Soon I shall be up against it financially."]

Fri. July 26

. . . Mowed the grass and dug potatoes. It was terribly hot and I was wringing wet when I got thru. The potatoes are not turning out well this year, because it was so dry in June. My but I do miss a bathroom. Waterworks would certainly help Groveport.

Fri. Aug. 16

. . . There was an immense crowd on the streets and in the State House grounds. They were expecting to see an airplane exhibition. Airplanes are still such a novelty that thousands and thousands of people will turn out to see them fly. As a matter of fact I saw my first airplane less than two months ago. The first one that I saw was flying over the State House.

This reminds me that fifteen years ago the autos were great curiosities. I had my first auto ride when I was a sophomore in the University. We were living up on Maynard Ave. and as I was walking to school a man came along in an electric that was about run down, he asked me to ride with him. I remember he had me get in and get out while the machine was still going as he was afraid he did not have enough current to get him to the charging station.

[In September, he finally got his call. "Momsey felt very badly but put on a brave front."]

Friday Sept. 20

Got a good breakfast and reported early at Municipal Pier. Over a hundred fellows were strung out in a line. As they were placed in alphabetical order, I headed the procession. We stood around most of the morning while our records were being checked. Fred Kessler one of my former pupils at Harbor High is also in my company.

The day was raw and cold and there was no heat where we stood. Most of us got quite chilly. Our noon chow warmed us up quite a little. Then our clothes were almost thrown at us. We had to try everything on, then if the fit was anything near satisfactory, we took every article off and stencilled the name in it. After spending a couple of hrs. [sic] in the nude in the bitter chill, I got my out fit partially straightened out and took it upstairs. With a small library in one suit case, my civilian clothes in my [crowded?] bag, and a jammed [sic] I had a desperate struggle getting upstairs to quarters. I was of course among the first thru [sic] so was given liberty about five until Sat. (tomorrow) morning at seven.

Went to the "Y" Hotel for the night. Felt very much dressed up in my uniform.

→ DOCUMENT 16.6 ←

Army Intelligence Test, ALPHA, Form 5, Test 8, in Robert M. Yerkes, ed., *Psychological Examining in the United States Army* (Washington DC: U.S. Government Printing Office, 1921), p. 227. Robert Yerkes Papers, Manuscripts and Archives, Yale University Library.

TEST 8

Notice the sample sentence:

People hear with the eyes ears nose mouth

The correct word is **ears**, because it makes the truest sentence.

In each of the sentences below you have four choices for the last word. Only one of them is correct. In each sentence draw a line under the one of these four words which makes the truest sentence. If you can not be sure, guess. The two samples are already marked as they should be.

SAMPLES { People hear with the eyes ears nose mouth
France is in Europe Asia Africa Australia }

1 America was discovered by Drake Hudson Columbus Balboa 1
2 Pinochle is played with rackets cards pins dice 2
3 The most prominent industry of Detroit is automobiles brewing flour packing 3
4 The Wyandotte is a kind of horse fowl cattle granite 4
5 The U. S. School for Army Officers is at Annapolis West Point New Haven Ithaca .. 5

6 Food products are made by Smith & Wesson Swift & Co. W. L. Douglas B. T. Babbitt 6
7 Bud Fisher is famous as an actor author baseball player comic artist 7
8 The Guernsey is a kind of horse goat sheep cow 8
9 Marguerite Clark is known as a suffragist singer movie actress writer 9
10 "Hasn't scratched yet" is used in advertising a duster flour brush cleanser 10

11 Salsify is a kind of snake fish lizard vegetable 11
12 Coral is obtained from mines elephants oysters reefs 12
13 Rosa Bonheur is famous as a poet painter composer sculptor 13
14 The tuna is a kind of fish bird reptile insect 14
15 Emeralds are usually red blue green yellow 15

16 Maize is a kind of corn hay oats rice 16
17 Nabisco is a patent medicine disinfectant food product tooth paste 17
18 Velvet Joe appears in advertisements of tooth powder dry goods tobacco soap 18
19 Cypress is a kind of machine food tree fabric 19
20 Bombay is a city in China Egypt India Japan 20

21 The dictaphone is a kind of typewriter multigraph phonograph adding machine 21
22 The pancreas is in the abdomen head shoulder neck 22
23 Cheviot is the name of a fabric drink dance food 23
24 Larceny is a term used in medicine theology law pedagogy 24
25 The Battle of Gettysburg was fought in 1863 1813 1778 1812 25

26 The bassoon is used in music stenography book-binding lithography 26
27 Turpentine comes from petroleum ore hides trees 27
28 The number of a Zulu's legs is two four six eight 28
29 The scimitar is a kind of musket cannon pistol sword 29
30 The Knight engine is used in the Packard Lozier Stearns Pierce Arrow 30

31 The author of "The Raven" is Stevenson Kipling Hawthorne Poe 31
32 Spare is a term used in bowling football tennis hockey 32
33 A six-sided figure is called a scholium parallelogram hexagon trapezium 33
34 Isaac Pitman was most famous in physics shorthand railroading electricity 34
35 The ampere is used in measuring wind power electricity water power rainfall 35

36 The Overland car is made in Buffalo Detroit Flint Toledo 36
37 Mauve is the name of a drink color fabric food 37
38 The stanchion is used in fishing hunting farming motoring 38
39 Mica is a vegetable mineral gas liquid 39
40 Scrooge appears in Vanity Fair The Christmas Carol Romola Henry IV 40

Answer Key

1. Columbus
2. Cards
3. Automobiles
4. Fowl
5. West Point
6. Swift & Co.
7. Comic Artist
8. Cow
9. Movie Actress
10. Cleanser
11. Vegetable
12. Reefs
13. Painter
14. Fish
15. Green
16. Corn
17. Food Product
18. Tobacco
19. Tree
20. India
21. Phonograph
22. Abdomen
23. Fabric
24. Law
25. 1863
26. Music
27. Trees
28. Two
29. Sword
30. Stearns
31. Poe
32. Bowling
33. Hexagon
34. Electricity
35. Electricity
36. Toledo
37. Color
38. Farming
39. Mineral
40. The Christmas Carol

→ DOCUMENT 16.7 ←

A report on a German American family, undated and unsigned, probably around April 17, 1918, by Clayton Ely Emig. Leila Drumgold Emig Family Papers, The Western Reserve Historical Society, Cleveland, Ohio.

To The Squadron Commanding Officer.

The following 24 hour report is respectfully submitted:

THE SUBJECT: Henry A. Scholler, 28 years, a native born American of German extraction. Prior to being inducted into the Service on October 5, 1917, through local Board No. 9, Indianapolis, he lived at 241 E. Minnesota Street, Indianapolis, with his parents, brothers and sisters. Because of automobile mechanic experience, he was transferred from Camp Zachary Taylor to Kelly Field, since to the Speedway, with the 810 Aero Squadron. Last employer was Hal Motor Company, Cleveland, Ohio.

INVESTIGATION CAUSE: Recent disrespectful and obscene remarks against the Entente Allies.

HIS FAMILY: Father, Charles Scholler; Mother's maiden name, Catherine M. Merklin; a sister, Catherine; brothers, Albert, tester for the Nordyke & Marmon Mfg. Company; Frank, Press Feeder for the "Art Press", its manager,-Ray D. Barnes, 318 Century Building; and George J., a barber with a shop for many years at 1329 Madison Avenue, -- all living at 241 E. Minnesota Street.

THE INVESTIGATION: A letter was written by the local managers of a Surety Company to the Hal Motor Company, Cleveland, Ohio, copy of which is attached hereto. Such letters are very frequently written by Bonding Companies, and would arouse no suspicion nor would it create reticence. Stamped envelope enclosed, and any reply will be forwarded.

The neighborhood was found to be almost entirely German. The following surnames were noted in the indicated street square, to-wit:

Zelen.	Cartheuser.
Hermann.	Wagner.
Krauss.	Kessler.
Haverkamp.	Reimer.
Englehardt.	Zeinen.
Scholler.	Beerman.
Peters.	Geiger.

Obviously, one in uniform, making inquiries with reference to the loyalty of a particular family, of its neighbors, would be treated with suspicion, ~~and resentment~~, and a perfectly natural resentment, and probably no reliable information could thereby be obtained. Accordingly, on the evening of April 16, 1918, two young civilians, ~~naturally~~ trustworthy, discrete and patriotic, ostensibly soliciting subscriptions to the Third Liberty Loan, and equipped with official blanks and credentials, called at 241 E. Minnesota Street.

Briefly, their report follows:-

The family lives in a big, two story house, a large yard, they have a machine, and the best looking place on Minnesota Street.

They have a Service Flag hung in their window, containing two stars. On inquiry, it was learned that one of the stars represented a nephew; also a Red Cross Flag and a card, stating that "A member from this home is in the Service". No American flag was observed.

Charles Scholler, the father, has bought one $50.00 Bond through George Wagner, a neighbor, and payable at the Merchants National Bank. Frank S., son, has bought one $50.00 Bond through Wagner and the Commercial National Bank; was examined by the Draft Board April 16, 1918, and passed; was guarded in his speech with our investigators; remarked that his brother, Henry, was out at the Speedway, "living like a Prince". Said Henry was drafted last October, sent to Kelly Field, and lived, while there, mostly off of the Red Cross, because the government was not prepared to take care of her men at that time, either in food or clothes.

Has another brother, working at Nordyke & Marmon Mfg. Company, who has not bought a bond as yet, but intends doing so.

When inquiry was made of the brother, Frank, as to whether or not he passed physical examination before the Board, he shrugged, and said, "I guess so, I suppose I will go about the 27th".

Mr. Wagner was interviewed, and declared that he was personally acquainted with the entire neighborhood, and that it was patriotic, and if there were any Pro-Germans, that they had not made themselves known. Another neighbor, it was learned, was very patriotic, name unknown, son having had charge of the bond sales where he was employed, and sold some $19,000 worth. Inquiry of this lady drew forth the statement that she knew of no disloyal or unpatriotic people in the neighborhood, and observed that she thought most every one had bought a bond.

Our investigators further recommend that the women of the family, the mother and sister, be interviewed, since they went no further than the front yard, where they met Frank, who was coming around the house. Arrangements will be made by one of these two to have the Metropolitan Insurance solicitor have a casual conversation with the women of the family, and report will be made later.

Your informant called at the office of Division No. 9, and had a long, personal conversation with the chairman of that local board, Adolph Emhardt, a well known local attorney with a wide acquaintance among southside German people; was permitted to examine the questionarre of the brother, Frank; 30 years old, did not claim exemption, indicated a willingness to take evening instruction, speaks German, stated that he was in good health. Found that Mr. Emhardt has personally known this family for thirty years. He is quite sure that the family as a whole, is not, nor is any member, to his knowledge, disloyal or unpatriotic. He observed confidentially that they are rather chesty or conceited family, yet of ordinarily good character and reputation. The boys, all of them, he observed, are rather inclined to be a little bit sporty, noisy, talkative, and especially Henry, something of a "foreflusher". He thinks Henry is, if anything, more American than his brothers. Mr. Emhardt defended George J., the barber, recently in Police Court for speeding, and his acquaintanceship with the family has been such that, although not intimate, yet it would permit him to get a line upon any Pro-Germanism, if such existed. Our investigators who called at the house, after considerable thought have the opinion that either the family is entirely patriotic, or they are so wise that a front is put on that would deceive the average person.

Recently Henry Reisenberg, a prominent local citizen of German extraction, brought to this city, a well known German Professor, as I recall it now, a Dr. Bohn, who are forming all over the country, an organization known as "Friends of German Democracy", approved by the administration. A News item with reference thereto was, as I recall, contained in the Star of March 15th. Col. Richard Lieber, Military Secretary and Chief of Staff to Gov. Goodrich, it was recalled, was prominent at this meeting. Your informant called upon this gentleman, whose son is also a Staff Officer at Hattiesburg, and being courteously received, suggested to Mr. Lieber that, through the South Side Turners, one of several local German Organizations, and with whose officers Mr. Lieber was undoubtedly acquainted, inquiry as to the loyalty or Pro-Germanism of the Scholler family, be made. Consent was very willingly given, and this gentleman promised to give the matter his attention today, April 17, 1918, and will call the writer on the telephone through the Squadron Supply Office.

A brief analysis and opinion will be promptly prepared, if desired, after the receipt of the expected report from Mr. Lieber.

G-k

DOCUMENT 16.8

Letters from Rufus Ullman to his family, May 13 and August 31, 1918. Ullman Family Papers, container 1, folder 2, The Western Reserve Historical Society, Cleveland, Ohio.

Sergt R. M. Ullman
Adv. Ord. Depot #7. A. P. O. 712.

Aug. 31, 1918.

Dear Ones:- Enclose are photos taken at Aix-les-Bains in the leave area. I was there

I am writing this letter in the hotel of a large city located near the front. I am returning back to the depot having performed my duty as convoyer. Guess who was ~~one of~~ the first one I met from home at the front? Bill Marcosson? Call up his folks & tell them about him. He looks very well. The last time that I saw him was on the transport last November. I sure am seeing the boys now. Whom do you supposed signed my papers? Col. Miller of Hayden & Miller of Cleveland. He is the division ordnance officer. Do not mention to Bill Marcosson's folks that he is at the front, for probably they do not know it.

Just as it was getting dark I saw an air fight. The first one I have seen in France. It is a remarkable sight to ~~the~~ the aeroplanes manuveur & shoot at each other with their machine guns. I could describe the attack more vivid, but I think I better not. During the evening I felt a little timid about sleeping as the Boche make frequent visits & drop a handfull of bombs. He did not come over & I slept fine. I feel timid tonight again, for he comes flying around this vicinity very frequently

We are given plenty of warning so I am told to make haste for the dugouts.

In this city, I met a sergt in the artillery, who has seen much action at Chateau Thierry. He told me he sold liquor for Otto Schmidt Co. of Chicago & knew of our firm. His name is Berg. He was born in France & knows the town, as he was born only a few miles distant.

At the office here, (Adv. Depot No 1) they said that they could not send a true copy of my application for insurance, for they have none. This is what they did. They sent a letter thru military channels stating all particulars about my insurance to the War Risk Insurance Bureau. This letter shall act as a record to the Bureau. If the bureau does not think that is suffice, no doubt the bureau shall communicate the fact. The copy which should have been retained with my service record, has been lost. That is why no copy could have been made. On my service record is noted the fact that I have $10,000 insurance & states the date it was taken out.

Let me know, whether you are receiving now $20 allotment, $15 from the War Risk Insurance Bureau & $5 from the Quartermaster. Also inform me as to whether you have received the Liberty Bond made out to you. The N. Y. Federal Reserve bank, I believe, is the bank which disposes of the

the bonds.

Many thanks for the H. R. magazine & other magazines (August). Not only myself, but also the boys bunking around me, enjoy reading them.

With love & kisses

Your devoted son,

Rufus

P.S. I just thought of it. Our New Year is now drawing real close at hand. Let's pray that at the dawn of the next new year, our family may once again be reunited in America and the good U.S.A. shall establish upon earth an everlasting peace to all mankind. I hope that the coming year will find you in the best of health & contentment. Keep up your spirit & courage for I shall try and do likewise. Often do I feel depressed, but during the moments of depression, I always keep faith in God. Pray for Howard & Yourselves as well as for me in the holy sanctuary, for I might not be able to pray in a holy place. I still have the Army & Navy Prayer books which contains a few pages devoted to New Years. I hear there is a possibility for us to have a French rabbi at the depot. It sure is a shame that there are so few Jewish chaplains & consequently we have none at our depot. The Jewish Welfare Board was rather slow in making religious arrangements for our boys in France. Wishing you again a happy day. As ever, Rufus

May 13, 1918

Dear Ones:

Have been receiving your papers in bunches, about 1/2 doz came out at a time. Last night I went to the town for my pictures. The lady only printed six, two of which were no good, so next Sunday I shall get eight. Tell the folks they shall all receive one as soon as I get them. What do you think of it.

I am not in the artillery section of the warehouse anymore. Have been place [sic] in salvage which handles all the Ordnance equipment that comes back from the front. Much of it is unservicable but still there is quite a little that can be repaired.

One can hardly realize the tremendous size of this depot with its dozens of tracks & its large yards. The locomotives are operated by the soldiers.

All sorts of races & nationalities are working here. The American negroes as stevedores, the Spainiard & Chinese along the roads & tracks, & then the German prisoners guarded by the Frenchmen and Englishmen.

I don't suppose the Kaiser realized what the Americans can do. They sure shall prove their worth.

You no doubt had a good time in N.Y.

With love & kisses

Your devoted son,

Rufus

Sergt R. M. Ullman

Adv. Ord. Depot #1, A.P.O. 712

Aug. 31, 1918

Dear Ones:

Enclosed are photos taken at Aix-les-Bains in the leave area. I was there.

I am writing this letter in the hotel of a large city located near the front. I am returning to the depot, having performed my duty as convoyer. Guess who was the first one I met from home at the front?—Bill Marcosson. Call up his folks and tell them about him. He looks very well. The last time that I saw him was on the transport last November. I sure am seeing the boys now. Whom do you suppose signed my papers? Col. Miller of Hayden & Miller of Cleveland. He is the Division Ordnance Officer. Do not mention to Bill Marcosson's folks that he is at the front, for probably they do not know it.

Just as it was getting dark I saw an air fight. The first one I have seen in France. It is a remarkable sight to see the airoplanes maneuver and shoot at each other with their machine guns. I could describe the attack more vivid, but I think I better not. During the evening I felt a little timid about sleeping as the Boche make frequent visits and drop a handful of bombs. He did not come over and I slept fine. I feel timid tonight again, for he comes flying around this vicinity very frequently. We are given plenty of warning so I am told, to make haste for the dugouts.

In this city I met a Sergt. in the artillery, who has seen much action at Chateau Thierry. He told me he sold liquor for Otto Schmidt Company of Chicago and knew of our firm. His name is Bing. He was born in France and knows the town, as he was born only a few miles distant.

At the office here (Adv. Depot #1), they said that they could not send a true copy of my application for insurance, for they have none. This is what they did. They sent a letter thru. military channels stating all particulars about my insurance to the War Risk Insurance Bureau. This letter shall act as a record to the Bureau. If the bureau does not think that is suffice [sic], no doubt the bureau shall communicate the fact. The copy which should have been retained with my service record, has been lost That is why no copy could have been made. On my service record is noted the fact that I have $10,000 insurance & states the date it was taken out.

Let me know whether you are receiving now $20 allottment [sic], $ [sic] is from the War Risk Insurance Bureau & $5 from the Quartermaster. Also inform me as to whether you have received the Liberty Bond made out to you. The N.Y. Federal Reserve bank, I believe is the bank which disposes of the bonds.

Many thanks for the H.R. [Hai Resh] Magazine and other magazines (August). Not only myself, but also the boys bunking around me enjoy reading them.

With love & kisses
Your devoted son,
Rufus

P.S. I just thought of it. Our New Year is now drawing real close at hand. Let's pray that at the dawn of the next New Year, our family may once again be reunited in America and the good U.S.A. shall establish upon earth an everlasting peace to all mankind. I hope that the coming year will find you in the best of health and contentment. Keep up your spirit and courage, for I shall try and do likewise. Often do I feel depressed, but during the moments of depression, I always keep faith in God. Pray for Howard and yourselves as well as for me in the holy sanctuary, for I might not be able to pray in a holy place. I still have the Army and Navy Prayer Book, which contains a few pages devoted to New Years. I hear there is a possibility for us to have a French Rabbi at the depot. It sure is a shame that there are so few Jewish Chaplains and consequently we have none at our depot. The Jewish Welfare Board was rather slow in making religious arrangements for our boys in France.

Wishing you again a happy day.
As ever,
Rufus

→ DOCUMENT 16.9 ←

Journal entries of Dudley J. Hard, 1918. Dudley J. Hard Papers, container 2, folder 19, The Western Reserve Historical Society, Cleveland, Ohio.

a month ago today we left Sheridan.

SUNDAY, JULY 14, 1918

195 days past 170 to come

The French 4th of July. It rained throughout the day showing that the weather is no respecter of nations. Up at 1 30 bkft at 6 30 debarked at 7 15 and about 8 started on march 3½ mi thru Havre to our rest camp. The town was in gala holiday attire and looked beautiful. Bartell was on the job and got a billet for us near camp. a splendid dejeuner. Then to town with Mennicke for the parade. With the use of a little nerve we got in the grand stand the most impressive and pathetic thing was the presentation of Leg of Honor to wives, mothers sons or fathers of deceased soldiers. Very sad.

We walked around town stopped at one cafe and then wandered up at the Grand Hotel de Normandie for a rest & dinner. I was quite tired but dinner and a chance to sit down refreshed me. However I went on out to my billet and by nine oclock was in bed. The weather today spoiled any attempt to look over the town. Enough was seen to make us all fall in love with France. The people were going to Church as we marched up and they were all better dressed and cleaner than the English.

Up about 9. The gang came in late did not sleep between 1½ and 2.30. A good breakfast and then downtown for some exchange papers etc. Lunch at "The Louvre" at 1 o'clock with a major of the 342 - Interesting talk on N.G. N.A. etc. At 3 o'clock took a train for the depot - loaded at 5 P.M. Then supper with staff. Back just in time to leave at 7½. Learned we were headed for Bordeaux - Bartel and Lyon reported drunk. Will probably cost them dearly. Our first experience at real soldiering in the "Lhommes 40 - Chevaux 8" French freight cars. When we came to a stop the men would imitate a cattle train perfectly. Very humorous. They had everything except the smell. Mennecke a little embarrassed by conditions in France as compared with England. The country in the first few hours preceding dusk did not appear as well kept as England. Still Normandy is beautiful.

TUESDAY, SEPTEMBER 3, 1918

246 days past 119 to come

Watched some aeroplane flying by first Bn this afternoon but was not violently excited. Tired all day long. Dust all through my head.
Lecture on gas at 7.30 Not bad
Usual band concert. Started a letter to Tess but didn't get anywhere with it.
Usual allied victories reported to-day. Germany is surely crumbling.

Call from Dr McGaffin.

WEDNESDAY, SEPTEMBER 25, 1918

268 days past 97 to come

Enroute Perigord-Limoges-Chateauroux.

It was hard to get out of Perigueux - it was all so intensely interesting. Neal almost went nutty. A charming old Cathedral this is a Roman town and runs back to the Caesars. About the time we would make up our minds to start something else would attract us. Narrow streets about 8 ft wide. Genuine antiquity shop. Old paintings on sale. We stock up on pate de foie gras and other delicacies and finally headed for Limoges around 11 o'clock. Had a dandy lunch at Central Hotel. The town was quite American and also large. Dug up Frank Wood and got a casing through his good offices. Also a tube. We halted to go as usual but at 4 40 we hit the trail to Chateauroux arriving late (about 8 pm) and found we had gone back to Middle ages on architecture but to Broadway on life. At the hotel a party of F. officers were entertaining their "lady" friends. We are drawing nearer to Paris, it is evident. 6 fr for dinner

SATURDAY, OCTOBER 12, 1918
285 days past 80 to come

Up at 7 after a rather poor night. Capt. Rosian got away without my seeing him. Started in at Jonas to clean up Office and Kitchen. By noon the organization was beginning to go around. Got out meteorological data. Light lunch about 1:30 and then to Atton to be present at the opening of 135th's hostilities. Present were Nash "Ord" Rougier and the Majors & Adjt. Sigler fired four shots and then it happened. It developed that we were firing in a reprisal zone and the Boche opened up on the observatory. We have been under actual fire and no mistake. After six shots by Sigler I decided to cease firing as we were probably stirring the animals up. Back to Loisy.

At 3 AM awakened by Mousson. Raiding party underway on sector 36;6 Inf. Barrage called for. We fired for two hours. Nothing serious and no damage done but quite exciting the while. Got to sleep again around 6 A.M.
Heard that Germany had accepted Wilson's terms and would and were evacuating France, Belgium etc. the war may be over but we don't know it here.
Mousson bombarded last night from 7 PM to around 2 AM

MONDAY, NOVEMBER 11, 1918

315 days past 50 to come

At 845 AM this morning Brigade telephoned me that the armistice had been signed to take effect at 11 am and that all firing would immediately cease. Further that we were to remain on the alert and that we were to have no communication with the enemy. I read the announcement to the staff at breakfast. Considerable hilarity though not over much. Ordered all bns to comply. The Germans however kept the letter of the agreement and put over a heavy barrage until 10:59:55. Causing considerable casualties. Our infantry had a bad night they tried to take Beaumont and Bois de Harville without artillery preparation and were repulsed with losses. We delivered heavy fire from 5 to 5:45. Also through the night generally. At 11 oclock started out in car with Greenhalgh Nash & Gray to view front line. Saw our returning troops visited Woel, Wadonville Doncourt and St Hilaire. Couldnot get to Bois de Harville Mil Phillips. Saw battlefields and several dead Germans. A few souvenirs.

Sunday, July 14, 1918

a month today, we left Sheridan

The French 4th of July. It rained throughout the day showing that the weather is no respecter of nations. Up at 1:30 bkft at 6:30 debarked at 7:15 and about 8 started on a march $3^{1}/_{2}$ mi thru [sic] Havre to our rest camp. The town was in gala holiday attire and looked beautiful. Bartell was in the job and got a billet for us near Camp. Asplen did dejeuner. Then to town with Mennicke for the parade. With the use of a little nerve, we got in the grand stand. The most impressive and pathetic thing was the presentation of L of Honor to wives, mothers, sons or fathers of deceased soldiers. Very sad—

We walked around town stopped at one cafe and then wound up at the Grand Hotel de Normandie for a rest & dinner. I was quite tired but dinner and a chance to sit down refreshened me. However I went on out to my billet and by nine oclock was in bed. the weather today spoiled any attempt to look over the town. Enough was seen to make us all fall in love with France. The people were going to Church as we marched up and they were all better dressed and cleaner than the English.

Monday, July 15, 1918

Up about 9. The gang came in late did not sleep between 12 and 2:30. A good breakfast and then downtown for some exchange papers etc. Lunch at "The Lunes" at 1 oclock with a major of the 342. Interesting talk on [N.Y., N.Y.?] etc. At 3 oclock took a train for the depot, loaded at 5 pm. Then supper with staff. Back just in time to leave at 7:47. Learned we were headed for Bordeaux. Bartel and Lyon reported drunk. Will probably cost them dearly. Our first experience at real soldiering in the "L'homme 40—Cheveaux 8" French freight cars. When we came to a stop the men would imitate a cattle train perfectly. Very humorous. They had everything except the smell. Mennicke a little embarrassed by conditions in France as compared with England. The country in the first few hours preceding dusk did not appear as well kept as England. Still Normandy is beautiful.

Tuesday, September 3, 1918

Watch some aeroplane firing by first Bn [sic] this afternoon, but was not violently excited. Fired all day long [at the firing range]. Dust all through my head.

Lecture on gas at 9:30. Not bad. Usual band concert. Started a letter to Tess but didn't get anywhere with it.

Usual Allied victories reported today. Germany is surely crumbling.

Call from Dr McGaffin.

Wednesday, September 25, 1918

Enroute Perigord-Limoges-Chateauraux.

It was hard to get out of Perigaeux—it was all so intensely interesting. Neal almost went nutty. A charming old Cathedral. this is a Roman town and runs back to the Caesars. About the time we would make up our minds to stare something else would attract us. Narrow streets about 8 ft wide. Genuine antiquity shop. Old paintings on sale. We stock up on pate de faux gras and other delicacies and finally headed for Limoges around 11 oclock. Had a dandy lunch at Central Hotel. the town was quite American and also large. Dug up Frank Wood and got a [casing?] through his good offices. Also a tube. We hated to go as usual but at 4:40 we hit the trail to Chateau roux arriving late (about 8 pm) and found we had gone back to Middle Ages [sic] on architecture but to Broadway on life. At the hotel a party of 2 officers were entertaining their friends male female. We are drawing nearer to Paris, it is evident.

6 fr for dinner

Saturday, October 12, 1918

Up at 7 after a rather poor night Cap. Rosian got away without my seeing him. Started in at once to clean up office and kitchen. By noon the organization was beginning to go around. Got our meteorological data. Light lunch about 1:30 and then to Attn to or present at the opening of 135ths hostilities. Present were Nash Orr Rengier and the Major and Adgt. Sigler fired four shots and then it happened. It developed that we were firing on a reprisal zone and the Boche opened up on the observatory. We have been under actual fire and no mistake. After six shots by Sigler I decided to cease firing as we were probably stirring the animals up. Back to Loisy.

Sunday, October 13, 1918

At 3 am awakened by Meusson Raiding party under way on sector 366 Ingy. Barrage called for. We fired for two hours. Nothing serious, and no damage done, but quite exciting the while. Got to sleep again around 6 pm.

Heard that Germany had accepted Wilsons terms and would and were evacuating. France, Belgium etc. The war may be over but we dont know it here.

Meusson bombarded last night from 7 pm to around 2 am.

Monday, November 11, 1918

At 8:45 am this morning Brigade telephoned me that the armistice had been signed to take effect at 11 am and that all firing would immediately cease. Further that we were to remain on the alert and that we were to have no communication with the enemy. I read the announcement to the staff at breakfast. Considerable hilarity though not over much. Ordered all bns to comply. The Germans however kept the letter of the agreement and put over a heavy barrage until 10:59:55. Causing considerable casualties. Our infantry had a bad night they tried to take Bulaterelle and Bois de Harville without artillery preparation. Also were repulsed with losses. We delivered heavy fire from 5 to 5:45. Also through the night generally. At 11 oclock started out in car with Greenhalgh Nash Gray to view front line. Saw our returning troops. Visited Woel, Wadenville, Doncourt and St. Hilare. Could not get to Bois de Harville Met Phillip. Saw battlefields and several dead Germans a few souvenirs.

✧ DOCUMENT 16.10 ✧

Form letter from John J. Pershing, February 28, 1919. In Rufus Ullman's photograph album, Ullman Family Papers, volume 1, container 1, The Western Reserve Historical Society, Cleveland, Ohio.

G. H. Q.
AMERICAN EXPEDITIONARY FORCES,

GENERAL ORDERS No. 38-A.   FRANCE, *February 28, 1919.*

MY FELLOW SOLDIERS:

Now that your service with the American Expeditionary Forces is about to terminate, I can not let you go without a personal word. At the call to arms, the patriotic young manhood of America eagerly responded and became the formidable army whose decisive victories testify to its efficiency and its valor. With the support of the nation firmly united to defend the cause of liberty, our army has executed the will of the people with resolute purpose. Our democracy has been tested, and the forces of autocracy have been defeated. To the glory of the citizen-soldier, our troops have faithfully fulfilled their trust, and in a succession of brilliant offensives have overcome the menace to our civilization.

As an individual, your part in the world war has been an important one in the sum total of our achievements. Whether keeping lonely vigil in the trenches, or gallantly storming the enemy's stronghold; whether enduring monotonous drudgery at the rear, or sustaining the fighting line at the front, each has bravely and efficiently played his part. By willing sacrifice of personal rights; by cheerful endurance of hardship and privation; by vigor, strength and indomitable will, made effective by thorough organization and cordial co-operation, you inspired the war-worn Allies with new life and turned the tide of threatened defeat into overwhelming victory.

With a consecrated devotion to duty and a will to conquer, you have loyally served your country. By your exemplary conduct a standard has been established and maintained never before attained by any army. With mind and body as clean and strong as the decisive blows you delivered against the foe, you are soon to return to the pursuits of peace. In leaving the scenes of your victories, may I ask that you carry home your high ideals and continue to live as you have served—an honor to the principles for which you have fought and to the fallen comrades you leave behind.

It is with pride in our success that I extend to you my sincere thanks for your splendid service to the army and to the nation.

Faithfully,

John J. Pershing

Commander in Chief.

OFFICIAL:
ROBERT C. DAVIS,
Adjutant General.

Copy furnished to Sergt Rufus M. Ullman
Charles I. Goodhue
1st Lieut Inf. U.S.A.
Commanding.

⇢ ARCHIVE 17 ⇠

The Emergence of Modernism Between the Wars

Archive Overview

IF asked what images or generalizations come to mind when you hear the phrase "the 1920s," what would you say? Would you mention Babe Ruth, Charles Lindbergh, the Charleston, flappers, Louis Armstrong, F. Scott Fitzgerald's novel *The Great Gatsby*, and "the new woman"? While all of these—and more—certainly belong in any inventory of the 1920s, popular images of the decade sometimes called the "golden" or "roaring" twenties simplify what was a complex period. Likewise, generalizations about the 1930s that stress only depression and despair miss the subtleties of those years.

Although the United States emerged from World War I more prosperous and powerful than it had ever been, Americans faced new challenges to established norms, values, and ways of life during the interwar years. The sources in this archive illuminate some of the changes that were taking place. What areas of American life do the documents suggest were in the process of alteration? What groups or sorts of people were involved? Did some transformations have a broader impact than others? What debates and responses did the changes trigger, and why? Your task in this archive is to determine to what extent modernism and the 1920s were a roaring, golden era or a reactionary, troubled one.

Placing the Sources in Context

DURING the years between World War I and World War II, the economic, cultural, and social landscape of the United States changed enormously. For the first time, a majority of Americans lived in urban areas (defined by the census as a community of more than 2,500). Technological innovation, a maturing system of national commerce dominated by corporations, and the relatively widespread prosperity that followed World War I combined to inaugurate a new era of mass consumption. Automobiles, radios, telephone and electrical service, indoor plumbing, and some household appliances became available for the first time to many American middle-class and working-class families alike and affected the rhythms of daily life. Consumer goods industries, retail credit, and advertising all became big business.

American cultural life also changed. Artists and intellectuals were inspired and repulsed by the aesthetics of the machine age, horrified and disillusioned by the inhumanity and senselessness of the Great War and later by the Great Depression, challenged by the Prohibition experiment and the powerful new cultural media. Many broke with convention and experimented in ways that confronted traditional standards. The new style of expression became known as "modernism." Modernism also referred to "liberal" developments in Christian theology that

TIMELINE

1918 World War I ends

1919 Prohibition amendment ratified

1920 First commercial radio broadcast; Women's Suffrage amendment ratified

1921 First birth control conference

1924 Immigration Quota Act; Ku Klux Klan activity at its peak

1925 Scopes trial; Harlem Renaissance flourishes

1927 First talking movie; Babe Ruth hits 60 home runs

1928 Herbert Hoover elected president

1929 Stock market crashes

1932 Franklin Roosevelt elected president

1933 New Deal begins

1933 Prohibition repealed

1941 United States enters World War II

questioned older dogmas and fundamentalist readings of scripture—as seen in the drama of the Scopes anti-evolution case in Tennessee. In many areas, science and social science contributed to the cultural upheaval by producing new kinds of knowledge and by questioning traditional understandings of objectivity and truth.

The modernist challenge to tradition also inspired groups of people ordinarily excluded from the cultural mainstream to assert their individuality and claim their rightful place in American society. The migration of African-Americans from the rural South to cities in the North and midwest, for example, intensified agitation for basic civil rights and fed the flourishing movement in American arts and letters known as the Harlem Renaissance. Announced by the brilliant critic Alain Locke in *The New Negro* in 1925, the Harlem Renaissance was an outpouring of poetry, music, painting, dance, and other artistic expressions celebrating the black experience and black people. American women, who had won the right to vote in 1920, began to exercise their political rights, enjoyed new social freedoms, and were more likely to work, at least before marriage, than their counterparts had been at the turn of the century.

Not all Americans embraced or welcomed the social, economic, and cultural changes that were taking place in the 1920s. Many felt merely uncomfortable with the new expectations generated by new goods and an urban way of life. Others, mainly but not all southern and midwestern rural Protestants, criticized and rejected the materialism, the new attitudes and behaviors, and were offended by modernism and the questioning of conventional morals and values. The Ku Klux Klan, for example, reborn in Georgia in 1915 as anti-Catholic, anti-Jewish, and anti-Negro, gained extensive support outside the South, most notably in Indiana. Finally, the shock of the Great Depression caused many of those who embraced change as well as those who had disliked new trends to question the American way of life altogether.

About the Sources

SEVERAL sources in this archive come from popular magazines, which have provided historians with a rich mine of information about American life in this century. Advances in the technology of printing after the Civil War fostered a vast increase in the number of weekly and monthly magazines (and books), some aimed at the mass market, others at audiences specialized by class or interest. One of the selections included here was prepared for members of the Ku Klux Klan (17.3)

The most popular types of magazines included news magazines, muckraking periodicals, and domestic women's journals that flourished by means of the mass production capabilities of American industry and a system of mass distribution. Through their advertisements, these magazines, along with the movies, became primary showcases of the new consumer lifestyle, especially when color printing became affordable in the 1920s. When you study the advertisements here (17. 2), look carefully at both the graphics and the text. What messages do the images convey? In what ways does the text help sell the product? Note how text and image work together and independently.

Calling herself a "professional household efficiency engineer," Christine Frederick encouraged middle class women to apply scientific management techniques to household work. An editor of *Ladies Home Journal* and the secretary of the Associated Clubs of Domestic Science, Frederick wrote articles explaining how women could do domestic chores more efficiently by using standardized approaches to daily tasks like dishwashing and by reorganizing their workspaces. She also supported household machines like washing machines, and her pamphlet on laundry specifically promoted one particular machine. Her link with the world of advertising and consumption is evident in her 1929 book, *Selling Mrs. Consumer*. In what ways does Frederick seem modern, and in what ways tied to the past?

Langston Hughes was one of the leading poets of the Harlem Renaissance. His two poems (17.7) cry out to be read aloud; listen for the images, words, and lines that evoke a strong emotional response in you.

List of Sources

17.1 **Book excerpt on women and consumption,** 1929. Christine Frederick, *Selling Mrs. Consumer*, 1929, pp. 43–44, 46–47.

17.2a **Advertisement for a Dodge sedan,** 1922. *Ladies' Home Journal*, December 1922, p. 96. Courtesy DaimlerChrysler Corporation.

17.2b **Advertisement for a Cadillac,** 1926. *Good Housekeeping*, February 1926, p. 95.

17.2c **Advertisement for Listerine,** 1926. *Good Housekeeping*, February 1926, p. 177.

17.2d **Advertisement for Sellers kitchen cabinets,** 1926. *Good Housekeeping*, February 1926, p. 237.

17.2e **Advertisement for Lifebuoy soap,** 1935. *Ladies' Home Journal*, October 1935, III cover. Courtesy Unilever.

17.3 **The "Creed of Klanswomen,"** 1924. *The Kluxer*, March 8, 1924, p. 20.

17.4 **A criticism of prohibition,** 1922, in Fabian Franklin, *What Prohibition Has Done to America* (New York: Harcourt, Brace, 1922), pp. 66–76.

17.5 **Foreword from *The New Negro*,** 1925. Alain Locke, ed., *The New Negro: An Interpretation* (New York: Boni, 1925), pp. ix–xi.

17.6 **Photograph by James VanDerZee, *Couple in Raccoon Coats*,** 1932, in Richard J. Powell and David A. Bailey, *Rhapsodies in Black: Art and the Harlem Renaissance* (London: U. of California Press, 1997), p. 131. *Couple in Raccoon Coats*, 1932, by James VanDerZee, © Donna Mussenden VanDerZee.

17.7 **Two poems by Langston Hughes, 1926.** Langston Hughes, *The Weary Blues* (New York: Knopf, 1926), "Proem" and "Epilogue."

Questions to Consider

1. Read the excerpts from Frederick's book. How does her work reveal the growing influence of social sciences in the early 20th century? Does she use psychology in a conservative or modern way? What differences does she find between men and women? How does she apply her ideas to the worlds of advertising and consumption?

2. Study the advertisement (source 17.2). What does each ad suggest about changes in American family life? What insights into women's roles are provided? In what ways has female life changed? Stayed the same? What sorts of women are ignored? How is class used in the ads?

3. Read the texts of the ads to discover the kinds of values that are used to sell the products. Would you describe these values as traditional, modern, or a combination? What sorts of visual appeals do the pictures make? Compare these ads of the 1920s with those in other archives and consider the character of advertising in the 1920s.

4. With your new knowledge of the emergence of new norms, values, and ways of life following World War I and the responses to them, read the Ku Klux Klan piece (17.3). What sorts of anxieties does the Creed reflect? What sorts of people might respond positively to the Creed, and why?

5. What is the position of source 17.4 on Prohibition? To what values and beliefs does the writer appeal? How does he describe American culture? Do you think this description is accurate?

6. The final three sources raise issues about the "new Negro" of the 1920s. In what ways do the images and texts support the idea of a "new" Negro? What is new? Are there elements of tradition also? Describe what you see in the photograph of a couple in Harlem (17.6) and what you hear in Langston Hughes's poems (17.7).

7. To what extent does the Hughes poem "Proem" express pride in blackness, and to what extent victimization? How about "Epilogue"? How do you respond to these poems?

9. What is the relationship between African-American culture and life and the more general American culture and life? In what ways do these sources on the black experience relate to the other sources you have examined here?

9. Summarize your conclusions about the ways in which American social, cultural, and economic life was changing in the 1920s and the varied responses that these changes prompted. To what extent was the interwar period of modernism a roaring, good era and to what extent a reactionary, troubled one?

→ DOCUMENT 17.1 ←

Book excerpt on women and consumption, 1929. Christine Frederick, *Selling Mrs. Consumer,* 1929, pp. 43–44, 46–47.

V

Feminine Instincts and Buying Psychology

These are the days when the veil of woman's "mystery" is being torn off, and it is high time, for there is no real mystery in woman's psychology, although there is paradox. Woman, I must contend, cannot be expected to be wholly reasonable because of two or three facts. First fact: as a sex, woman is predominantly emotional, due to her well-authenticated greater emotionality, arising from her nature as a woman. She therefore lives a life *closer to instinct* than man. Gina Lombroso, the famous Italian woman psychologist, makes the interesting distinction that men get their satisfactions from within themselves, from more abstract and impersonal subjects. Woman's satisfactions and stimulations on the other hand, *from the objects and people immediately about her.* Doubtless this is why Mrs. Consumer is the heart and center of the merchandising world, the great family purchasing agent, who spends most of the money men earn and who is deeply concerned with all the details of ten thousand little items of merchandise, which can be more thrilling to her than men usually realize.

Second fact: women are born into an anomolous position, as second fiddle to man in the game of life. Their rôle is thus made into a psychological paradox; how to be independent, though inexorably dependent; how to be demure and "feminine" and yet aggressively attain her ends; how to retreat at the same time that she advances!

Third fact: women are not persuaded, as men are, that logic and reason are the only factors with which one should guide oneself. She has backing in this from the new psychology, which has shown that we can so very easily "rationalize" ourselves into thinking what our emotions subtly suggest that we think. The conscious brain processes are now known to be not only less powerful, but less important in making a rounded success in life. This does not mean of course, that women are using less reason and intelligence. Indeed they are using more. But emotion and instinct bulks extremely large.

23. A List of the Instincts of Woman.—The first task therefore in coming to grips with the "psychology" of Mrs. Consumer is to make some endeavor to list and rate the instincts and emotions of women, as they bear on purchasing. Woman's purchases are exceedingly near to her instincts.

The psychologists have gone a long way in recent years in studying the human emotions, and they have dug up tremendously interesting material which is especially useful in studying the feminine buyer. Psychoanalysis is something I recommend to the intensive student of the woman buyer. The basic fact of importance is the greatly added significance which our new knowledge gives to the emotional reactions (the unconscious) as contrasted with our supposedly "intellectual" or logical processes of thought. The human instincts are given a far greater dignity and power now that we have learned what Freud, Jung, Adler and even Watson have added to our knowledge. We have always assumed that men, even if not women, bought goods on a basis of logic and reason; but the findings of psychoanalysis now show that men as well as women, are thoroughly ruled by their instincts and emotions, although it is undoubtedly the truth that women are more definitely ruled by them.

24. The Error of Wrong Appeals.—I see so much advertising that is misrated in its appeals,—a kitchen device featuring mechanical ingenuity when it should be featuring sanitation; a modernistic home furnishing article featuring its foreign origin, when it should be appealing to woman's love of change and novelty. It seems to me that much selling appeal that I see, is as a result like machinery from which the power belt is slipping or which has come off entirely. The full power of the article's possible innate, instinctive appeal is not being applied, with resulting loss in sales.

In other cases the *wrong* appeal is used or given exaggerated emphasis. The case of a certain talcum powder comes to my mind; a new talcum was about to be launched on the usual, habitual appeal of "purity." But when a careful analysis of Mrs. Consumer's reactions was made it was discovered that odor was an immensely more powerful appeal; women loved their talcum perfumed. Therefore it is my urgent recommendation that all sellers of family goods leave nothing to guesswork as to which appeals are most powerful for their goods, and to specifically determine *how* powerful each is.

25. The Importance of Woman's Unconscious Self.—Psychoanalysts make much of the *unconscious*; that part of us which feels and thinks below the threshold of our conscious mind. In my belief Mrs. Consumer's mind is an especially unconscious mind. For ages women—because of the paradox of their lives I have previously mentioned—have suppressed much of themselves. They have far more "inhibitions" than man, and are content to do far more things on the basis of intuition, emotion or unconscious motive than man. Early in a girl's life her mother, teachers, church, society, outfit her with suppressions and inhibitions one after another—the heritage of our sex. She rarely parts with them even after growing up—they are part of feminine psychology. There are more words that she hates to hear mentioned; more objects, acts and ideas toward which she has a revulsion, *more things she doesn't like to do,* more limitations she imposes upon herself than man ever dreams of being bothered with. It is authenticated by psychologists that women's characteristic attitude is *dislike,* while man's is *like; women respond more quickly to appeals to their dislikes; while men respond readily to their preferences.*

For these reasons I make bold to say that the strategy of appeal to women should make frequent and full use of her unconscious self. In practice, of course, many advertisers do this (themselves often unconscious why). I learned recently, for example, that a great many young unmarried women were reading *Children,* the parents' magazine. This would puzzle you until explained with the key of the unconscious. These young women are dreaming of a home and children in their unconscious, but they wouldn't admit it. Probably if you spoke to them about it they would display a younger generation bravado and cynicism about it—but the truth, the unconscious truth, is that they are interested in reading about children. Try to bury the mother-instinct!

26. "Unconscious" Selling Campaigns.—The cigarette advertisers are subtly appealing to the unconscious with their cryptic phraseology "She's a Lucky girl," etc. and the pictures of women with men who are smoking. The *conscious* judgment of many women is that they don't like to see posters and advertisements of women smoking—even though they smoke. Here again, as in so many cases, the child enters the equation, for mothers don't want their daughters to learn to smoke at too early an age, if at all.

The Listerine advertising, a famous campaign to women, was to a degree an unconscious campaign. So have been many others. It must ever be kept in mind that woman's thought processes are not as a rule direct like a man's. Or, if this seems like characterizing women too sharply, let us say that women are not uncompromising logic-choppers like men. Being far more practical humanists and diplomats, they use more gentle strategy and circuitous methods their wonders to perform. Woman is rarely direct; she actually prefers indirection; it is more suited to her emotionality and to her anomolous position in life. Attempts to secure a direct reaction from us often rouses our anger and resentment, especially if it is in regard to a deep-lying instinct.

❖ DOCUMENT 17.2a ❖

Advertisement for a Dodge sedan, 1922. *Ladies' Home Journal*, December 1922, p. 96. Courtesy DaimlerChrysler Corporation.

DODGE BROTHERS
BUSINESS SEDAN

It is said of women that they sometimes base their choice of a motor car on the color and stripe of the upholstery.

Dodge Brothers have found, however, that the woman of today is more practical in her reasoning. She considers appearance, to be sure, but she places first emphasis on safety and utility.

She has instantly recognized, for example, the tremendous advantage of the steel body construction peculiar to this sedan. She realizes that there is an important place for such a car in her domestic affairs as well as in the routine business affairs of men.

She knows that Dodge Brothers have built the car to withstand long, hard usage.

She appreciates the durability of its Spanish leather upholstery, the lustre of its baked-on enamel finish, the removability of the rear compartment fixtures, the non-rumble qualities of its fabric roof.

She particularly admires the trim beauty of its lines, because it is a virile type of beauty that breathes strength and safety.

And so it is that she has definitely registered her approval of the car by buying it, and driving it, and recommending it enthusiastically to her friends.

The Price is $1195 f. o. b. Detroit

Patents Pending

⟡ DOCUMENT 17.2b ⟡

Advertisement for a Cadillac, 1926. *Good Housekeeping,* February 1926, p. 95.

C A D I L L A C

NEW
90
DEGREE

Prices range from $2995 for the Brougham to $4485 for the Custom Imperial. F.O.B. Detroit. Tax to be added.

. . .

Buyers on the payment plan are afforded the savings of the GMAC financing system.

. . .

General Motors Export Company, New York. Cadillac Motor Car Company of Canada, Limited, Oshawa, Ont.

Its own peculiar public—the largest following of its kind in the world—has never been won away from the Cadillac, even for a little while.

There is a strain of steadfastness in the American people when they have tested a principle, or a product, and proved it sound.

And that steadfastness has never been more significantly exemplified than in the eager enthusiasm which greeted the new 90-degree Cadillac, and the phenomenal success which has come to it.

In these days of lightning-like and disturbing changes, it is reassuring to recall this national characteristic, even in so slight a matter as the history of a motor car.

No glamor of newness, no specious appeal of any sort, has ever been able to distract public attention away from the fundamental goodness of the Cadillac.

It is true that you seem to hear, just now, more ardent praise of Cadillac than ever before.

That is because the new Cadillac has given an even more emphatic emphasis to Cadillac goodness and superlative performance.

The old thought, which has held so many owners steadfast, is now operating in a new way, and in a wider sphere.

The new Cadillac is benefiting by a national habit of hunting for things that are basically right, and, when found, holding fast to them.

CADILLAC—DIVISION OF GENERAL MOTORS CORPORATION

In using advertisements see page 6 93

DOCUMENT 17.2c

Advertisement for Listerine, 1926. *Good Housekeeping,* February 1926, p. 177.

In using advertisements see page 6 175

→ DOCUMENT 17.2d ←

Advertisement for Sellers kitchen cabinets, 1926. *Good Housekeeping,* February 1926, p. 237.

In using advertisements see page 6 235

→ DOCUMENT 17.2e ←

Advertisement for Lifebuoy soap, 1935. *Ladies' Home Journal,* October 1935, III cover. Courtesy Unilever.

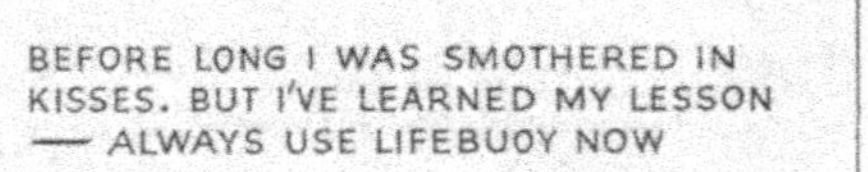

Read why millions say this

LIFEBUOY lather penetrates, *deep-cleanses* pores of clogged wastes, yet is unusually *gentle.* Scientific tests on the skins of hundreds of women show Lifebuoy is more than 20 per cent milder than many so-called "beauty soaps".

No one need be careless

We all perspire. But *only thoughtless people offend!* Bathe regularly with Lifebuoy. It purifies pores, stops "B. O." *(body odor).* Its own clean scent quickly vanishes as you rinse.

Approved by Good Housekeeping Bureau

→ DOCUMENT 17.3 ←

The "Creed of Klanswomen," 1924. *The Kluxer,* March 8, 1924, p. 20.

Creed of Klanswomen

We believe in the fatherhood of God, the brotherhood of Jesus Christ and the eternal tenets of the Christian religion, as practiced by enlightend Protestant churches.

We believe that church and state should continue separate in administration and organization, although united in their mission and purpose to serve mankind unselfishly.

We believe in the American home as the foundation upon which rests the American republic, the future of its institutions and the liberties of its citizens.

We believe in the mission of emancipated womanhood, freed from the shackles of old world traditions, and standing unafraid in the full effulgence of equality and enlightment.

We believe in the equality of men and women in political religious, fraternal civic and social affairs wherein there should be no distinction of sex.

We believe in the free public schools, where our children are trained in the principles and ideals that America the greatest of all nations.

We believe the Stars and Stripes the most beautiful flag on earth, symbolizing the purity of race, the blood of martyrs and the fidelity of patriot.

We believe that the current of pure American blood must United States and the several states, and consecrate ourselves to its preservation against all enemies at home and abroad.

We believe that the freedom of speech, of press and of worship is an inalienable right of all citizens whose allegiance and loyalty to our country is unquestioned.

We believe that principle comes before party; that justice should be firm, but impartial, and that partisanship must yield to intelligent co-operation.

We believe that the current of pure American bood must be kept uncontaminated by mongrel strains and protected from racial pollutions.

We believe that the government of the United States must be kept inviolate from the control or domination of alien races and the baleful influence of inferior peoples.

We believe that the people are greater than any foreign power or potentate, prince or prelate and that no other allegiance in America should be tolerated.

We believe that the perpetuity of our nation rests upon the solidarity and purity of our native-born, white, Gentile, Protestant men and women.

We believe that under God the Women of the Ku Klux Klan is a militant body of American freewomen by whom these principles shall be maintained, our racial purity preserved, our homes and children protected, our happiness insured and the prosperity of our community, our state and our nation guaranteed against usurpation, disloyalty and selfish exploitation.

→ DOCUMENT 17.4 ←

A criticism of prohibition, 1922, in Fabian Franklin, *What Prohibition Has Done to America* (New York: Harcourt, Brace, 1922), pp. 66–76.

Nature of the Prohibitionist Tyranny

That there are some things which, however good they may be in themselves, the majority has no right to impose upon the minority, is a doctrine that was, I think I may say, universally understood among thinking Americans of all former generations. It was often forgotten by the unthinking; but those who felt themselves called upon to be serious instructors of public opinion were always to be counted on to assert it, in the face of any popular clamor or aberration. The most deplorable feature, to my mind, of the whole story of the Prohibition amendment, was the failure of our journalists and leaders of opinion, with a few notable exceptions, to perform this duty which so peculiarly devolves upon them. . . .

What I wish to point out at present is some peculiarities of National Prohibition which make it a more than ordinarily odious example of majority tyranny.

National Prohibition in the United States—granting, for the sake of argument, that it expresses the will of a majority—is not a case merely of a greater number of people forcing their standards of life upon a smaller number, in a matter in which such coercion by a majority is in its nature tyrannical. The population of the United States is, in more than one respect, composed of parts extremely diverse as regards the particular subject of this legislation. The question of drink has a totally different aspect in the South from what it has in the North; a totally different aspect in the cities from what it has in the rural districts or in small towns; to say nothing of other differences which, though important, are of less moment. How profoundly the whole course of the Prohibition movement has been affected by the desire of the South to keep liquor away from the negroes, needs no elaboration; it would not be going far beyond the truth to say that the people of New York are being deprived of their right to the harmless enjoyment of wine and beer in order that the negroes of Alabama and Texas may not get beastly drunk on rotgut whiskey. If the South had stuck to its own business and to its traditional principle of State autonomy—a principle which the South invokes as ardently as ever when it comes to any other phase of the negro question—there would never have been a Prohibition Amendment to the Constitution of the United States; and at the same time the South would have found it perfectly possible to deal effectively with its own drink problem by energetic execution of its own laws, made possible by its own public opinion. Nor is the case essentially different as regards the West; the very people who are loudest in their shouting for the Eighteenth Amendment are also most emphatic in their praises of what Kansas accomplished by enforcing her own Prohibition law. Thus the Prohibitionist tyranny is in no small measure a sectional tyranny, which is of course an aggravated form of majority tyranny.

But what needs insisting on even more than this is the way in which the country districts impose their notions about Prohibition upon the people of the cities, and especially of the great cities. When attention is called to the wholesale disregard of the law, contempt for the law, and hostility to the law which is so manifest in the big cities, the champions of Prohibition in the press—including the New York press—never tire of saying that it is only in New York and a few other great cities that this state of things exists. But everybody knows that the condition exists not only in "a few," but in practically all, of our big cities; and for that matter that it exists in a large proportion of all the cities of the country, big and little. But if we confine ourselves only to the 34 cities having a population of 200,000 or more, we have here an aggregate population of almost exactly 25,000,000—nearly one-fourth of the entire population of the country. Is it a trifling matter that these great communities, this vast population of large-city dwellers, should have their mode of life controlled by a majority rolled up by the vote of people whose conditions, whose advantages and disadvantages, whose opportunities and mode of life, and consequently whose desires and needs, are of a wholly different nature? Could the tyranny of the majority take a more obnoxious form than that of sparse rural populations, scattered over the whole area of the country from Maine to Texas and from Georgia to Oregon, deciding for the crowded millions of New York and Chicago that they shall or shall not be permitted to drink a glass of beer?

Nor is it only the obvious tyranny of such a régime that makes it so unjustifiable. There are some special features in the case which accentuate its unreasonableness and unfairness. In the American village and small town, the use of alcoholic drinks presents almost no good aspect. The countryman sees nothing but the vile and sordid side of it. The village grogshop, the bar of the small-town hotel, in America has presented little but the gross and degrading aspect of drinking. Prohibition has meant, to the average farmer, the abolition of the village groggery and the small-town barroom. That it plays a very different part in the lives of millions of city people—and for that matter that it does so in the lives of millions of industrial workers in smaller communities—is a notion that never enters the farmer's mind. And to this must be added the circumstance that the farmer can easily make his own cider and other alcoholic drinks, and feels quite sure that Prohibition will never seriously interfere with his doing so. Altogether, we have here a case of one element of the population decreeing the mode of life of another element of whose circumstances and desires they have no understanding, and who are affected by the decree in a wholly different way from that in which they themselves are affected by it.

DOCUMENT 17.5

Foreword from *The New Negro*, 1925. Alain Locke, ed., *The New Negro: An Interpretation* (New York: Boni, 1925), pp. ix–xi. By permission of Moorland-Springarn Research Center, Howard University.

This volume aims to document the New Negro culturally and socially,—to register the transformations of the inner and outer life of the Negro in America that have so significantly taken place in the last few years. There is ample evidence of a New Negro in the latest phases of social change and progress, but still more in the internal world of the Negro mind and spirit. Here in the very heart of the folk-spirit are the essential forces, and folk interpretation is truly vital and representative only in terms of these. Of all the voluminous literature on the Negro, so much is mere external view and commentary that we may warrantably say that nine-tenths of it is *about* the Negro rather than of him, so that it is the Negro problem rather than the Negro that is known and mooted in the general mind. We turn therefore in the other direction to the elements of truest social portraiture, and discover in the artistic self-expression of the Negro to-day a new figure on the national canvas and a new force in the foreground of affairs. Whoever wishes to see the Negro in his essential traits, in the full perspective of his achievement and possibilities, must seek the enlightenment of that self-portraiture which the present developments of Negro culture are offering. In these pages, without ignoring either the fact that there are important interactions between the national and the race life, or that the attitude of America toward the Negro is as important a factor as the attitude of the Negro toward America, we have nevertheless concentrated upon self-expression and the forces and motives of self-determination. So far as he is culturally articulate, we shall let the Negro speak for himself.

Yet the New Negro must be seen in the perspective of a New World, and especially of a New America. Europe seething in a dozen centers with emergent nationalities, Palestine full of a renascent Judaism—these are no more alive with the progressive forces of our era than the quickened centers of the lives of black folk. America seeking a new spiritual expansion and artistic maturity, trying to found an American literature, a national art, and national music implies a Negro-American culture seeking the same satisfactions and objectives. Separate as it may be in color and substance, the culture of the Negro is of a pattern integral with the times and with its cultural setting. The achievements of the present generation have eventually made this apparent. Liberal minds to-day cannot be asked to peer with sympathetic curiosity into the darkened Ghetto of a segregated race life. That was yesterday. Nor must they expect to find a mind and soul bizarre and alien as the mind of a savage, or even as naive and refreshing as the mind of the peasant or the child. That too was yesterday, and the day before. Now that there is cultural adolescence and the approach to maturity,—there has come a development that makes these phases of Negro life only an interesting and significant segment of the general American scene.

Until recently, except for occasional discoveries of isolated talent here and there, the main stream of this development has run in the special channels of "race literature" and "race journalism." Particularly as a literary movement, it has gradually gathered momentum in the effort and output of such progressive race periodicals as the *Crisis* under the editorship of Dr. Du Bois and more lately, through the quickening encouragement of Charles Johnson, in the brilliant pages of *Opportunity,* a Journal of Negro Life. But more and more the creative talents of the race have been taken up into the general journalistic, literary and artistic agencies, as the wide range of the acknowledgments of the material here collected will in itself be sufficient to demonstrate. Recently in a project of *The Survey Graphic,* whose Harlem Number of March, 1925, has been taken by kind permission as the nucleus of this book, the whole movement was presented as it is epitomized in the progressive Negro community of the American metropolis. Enlarging this stage we are now presenting the New Negro in a national and even international scope. Although there are few centers that can be pointed out approximating Harlem's significance, the full significance of that even is a racial awakening on a national and perhaps even a world scale.

That is why our comparison is taken with those nascent movements of folk-expression and self-determination which are playing a creative part in the world to-day. The galvanizing shocks and reactions of the last few years are making by subtle processes of internal reorganization a race out of its own disunited and apathetic elements. A race experience penetrated in this way invariably flowers. As in India, in China, in Egypt, Ireland, Russia, Bohemia, Palestine and Mexico, we are witnessing the resurgence of a people: it has aptly been said,—"For all who read the signs aright, such a dramatic flowering of a new race-spirit is taking place close at home—among American Negroes."

Negro life is not only establishing new contacts and founding new centers, it is finding a new soul. There is a fresh spiritual and cultural focusing. We have, as the heralding sign, an unusual outburst of creative expression. There is a renewed race-spirit that consciously and proudly sets itself apart. Justifiably then, we speak of the offerings of this book embodying these ripening forces as culled from the first fruits of the Negro Renaissance.

ALAIN LOCKE.

Washington, D. C.
November, 1925.

DOCUMENT 17.6

Photograph by James VanDerZee, *Couple in Raccoon Coats,* 1932, in Richard J. Powell and David A. Bailey, *Rhapsodies in Black: Art and the Harlem Renaissance* (London: U. of California Press, 1997), p. 131. *Couple in Raccoon Coats,* 1932, by James VanDerZee, Christie's Images/Corbis.

DOCUMENT 17.7

Two poems by Langston Hughes. Langston Hughes, *The Weary Blues* (New York: Knopf, 1926), "Proem" and "Epilogue."

PROEM

I am a Negro:
  Black as the night is black,
  Black like the depths of my Africa.

I've been a slave:
  Cæsar told me to keep his door-steps clean.
  I brushed the boots of Washington.

I've been a worker:
  Under my hand the pyramids arose.
  I made mortar for the Woolworth Building.

I've been a singer:
  All the way from Africa to Georgia
  I carried my sorrow songs.
  I made ragtime.

I've been a victim:
  The Belgians cut off my hands in the Congo.
  They lynch me now in Texas.

I am a Negro:
  Black as the night is black,
  Black like the depths of my Africa.

EPILOGUE

I, too, sing America.

I am the darker brother.
They send me to eat in the kitchen
When company comes,
But I laugh,
And eat well,
And grow strong.

Tomorrow,
I'll sit at the table
When company comes.
Nobody'll dare
Say to me,
"Eat in the kitchen,"
Then.

Besides,
They'll see how beautiful I am
And be ashamed,—

I, too, am America.

ARCHIVE 18

Rural America During the New Deal

Archive Overview

THE Great Depression and memories of people's experiences during that difficult decade have influenced American life in many ways long after the depression ended. Perhaps the influence seems small—a grandfather who always turns out unnecessary lights in his house or an older relative's careful use of leftovers. The debates over the role the federal government should play in helping those in want or in intervening in the national economy have also continued. For your participation in this important contemporary discussion, a careful consideration of some New Deal programs will be most helpful.

This archive has a particular focus: the difficulties of rural life during the Great Depression of the 1930s and the New Deal programs that were designed to assist farmers. Like other New Deal measures, those that attempted to aid the nation's farmers caused controversy. Evaluations of the impact of farm policies usually started with two questions: Are these programs really helping farmers? and Do these programs violate cherished principles of American life (self-sufficiency, individualism, and local autonomy)? As you examine the materials, you should consider the different viewpoints and interests expressed in the sources and then go on to develop your own interpretation of the value and the consequences of New Deal agricultural policies.

As you read the sources, consider these important questions: What were the problems that afflicted the American countryside? What was the scope of the New Deal response, and how well did it address the basic issues of rural life and the needs of different groups of farmers? What were the intended and unintended consequences of New Deal programs? Would you rate the programs successful, partially successful, or a failure? If you decide that the programs enjoyed some success in helping farmers, consider whether they contributed to ending the depression itself. As you work out your analysis, you will be joining many others who have argued about the importance of the New Deal ever since it first took shape. Nearly all historians agree that, for better or worse, the New Deal fundamentally affected American public policy for the rest of the 20th century. At the beginning of the 21st century, as the family farm disappears and many farmers again suffer from natural and man-made disasters, variations of these questions continue to be debated in this country.

Placing the Sources in Context

IN our highly urbanized age at the start of the 21st century, it is easy to forget that nearly half of the American population lived in rural areas in the first decades of the 20th century. Although the profitability of farming differed according to where farmers

TIMELINE

1921 Farm prices decline

1929 Gross farm income at $11.9 billion; stock market crash

1930 Banks start to fail, many of them rural banks; Hawley-Smoot Tariff raises import duties; drought begins

1932 Dust storms ravage the Great Plains; gross farm income at $5.3 billion

1933 New Deal legislation relevant to agriculture:

- Farm Credit Administration (FCA)
- Agricultural Adjustment Act (AAA)
- Farm Emergency Relief Administration (FERA)
- Federal Deposit Insurance Corporation (FDIC)
- Civilian Conservation Corps (CCC)
- Tennessee Valley Authority (TVA)

1935 Resettlement Administration (later the Farm Security Administration); Rural Electrification Administration (REA)

1936 Gross farm income at about $8.5 billion

1937 Farm Security Administration (FSA)

lived and what crops and livestock they raised, the farming sector had experienced recurring problems since the late 19th century. In one respect Americans farmers were too successful. They enthusiastically increased production by enlarging their farms and using machinery, only to find that they had produced more than the market could absorb. Agricultural discontent had contributed to the rise of the Populist party in the 1890s, which sought to resolve some of the problems of the farm sector. Although the Populist party failed to win the presidency in 1896, some of the farmers' complaints were temporarily alleviated by a worldwide shortage of grain. During the first world war, life was also good because wartime demand for feeding the Allies and inflated food prices brought farmers another brief period of prosperity. New areas of the Great Plains were brought into cultivation; many farmers incurred large debts to buy land and tractors because they believed high prices would continue.

Then, during the 1920s, the agricultural sector entered a decade of severe recession, foreshadowing the Great Depression. Shattered European countries were unable to buy food from America. Farm surpluses built up, and agricultural prices plunged precipitously and rapidly. Three years after the war's end, the price of corn had fallen by 32 percent, wheat by 40 percent, hogs by 50 percent. Small farmers were especially hard hit. Unable to pay off what they owed for farm machinery or new land, they also faced the rising costs of consumer goods. Many lost their farms. Then, following the stock market crash, between 1929 and 1933, farm prices plunged by an additional two-thirds. The depression, combined with severe drought in many areas, accelerating soil erosion on the Great Plains (where about 17 percent of American farmers lived), and horrible grasshopper plagues, made an already bad situation worse for many of those who remained in farming. By 1930, American farmers were burning crops and dumping milk in ditches because of low prices. Furious at the loss of family farms through foreclosure, some even threatened to string up a federal judge. The ugly mood in America's farmlands provided a strong incentive to Franklin Roosevelt's administration to develop a farm policy for the nation's farmers.

To increase farm income as quickly as possible was the primary goal of New Deal farm policy. A second, related objective was to encourage farm families to buy more of the consumer goods being produced by struggling American industries. Increased consumption would stimulate the economy and raise the rural standard of living.

A host of agencies and programs were established to advance these goals. Like other New Deal initiatives, the federal farm programs were controversial. Under the Agricultural Adjustment Administration (AAA), the federal government encouraged farmers to reduce huge crop surpluses of wheat, cotton, hogs, rice, tobacco, and milk, thereby raising agricultural prices. For the first time in American history, the government made direct payments to farmers, in this case to farmers who took land out of production. Some farmers resisted the very idea of accepting payment for not producing and cutting back in a time when people were going hungry. Many objected when, in the summer of 1933, the AAA ordered farmers to plow up 10 million acres of cotton and to slaughter 6 million hogs. Controversy about the AAA continued when it became clear that reducing land under cultivation harmed tenant farmers and sharecroppers, who were thrown off their rented farms when acreage was taken out of production. Under the Resettlement Administration (RA), the government sought to move farm families off marginal or exhausted lands and into camps on better land—or out of farming altogether. Inadequate funding and a belief that the independent American farmer was being turned into a Soviet-style collective farmer robbed the RA of its potential impact.

Other New Deal programs were less controversial. The Rural Electrification Administration (REA) was created in 1935 to bring electric power to the countryside. The Farm Credit Administration (FCA) offered farmers low-cost loans. Other agencies encouraged practices such as agricultural terracing and digging wells to alleviate problems of drought and soil erosion, and sought to regulate the overgrazing of range lands. Many farm families participated in work relief programs as another way to provide some money.

About the Sources

THE sources in this archive will help you assess the New Deal farm programs and how they affected the lives of farmers and other rural families. They also raise the question of generalization: Can we talk about farmers as a group, or are the farmers in various regions so different that we should talk not about farmers, but about farmers in Wisconsin or Kansas?

The first document is an explanation of the 1933 AAA by Henry A. Wallace, the secretary of agriculture. Wallace, a Republican from Iowa, came to the Roosevelt cabinet with an impressive background as a plant geneticist and agricultural statistician; in the election of 1940 he would be Roosevelt's running mate. He delivered this message over the radio in May 1933, reminding us of how important this new medium was not only as a form of entertainment but also as a means of political communication. FDR, of course, used the radio for his masterful "fireside chats," in which he let the American people know what he and his administration were doing to deal with the nation's problems. The excerpt (18.10) from President Roosevelt's first fireside chat in 1936 deals with drought conditions in farm areas. It would be useful, if you are working in a small group, to have one member of the group read each speech aloud so that you can get an impression of how listeners might have heard and understood the speech without having the benefit of the written text.

The transcript of a movie newsreel (18.5) suggests the importance of another mode of communication during the New Deal: the movies. Movies continued to attract large audiences during the decade, and in addition to feature films, audiences saw newsreels. A typical newsreel contained several stories, each introduced with a "headline" followed by a narrated commentary and sometimes short interviews or vignettes. (Unlike our TV news programs, viewers heard the commentator but did not see him.) Although you can examine only the transcript, it should give some idea of how an important new media presented rural issues to a large viewing public (60 to 90 million Americans went to the movies every week). Note who appears in the story in addition to the commentator. What groups or positions do they represent? What sorts of people do not appear in the film? What do those "interviewed" say, and how much do they say? What background pictorial footage is suggested in the text, and why has it been chosen? How would you describe the point of view of the story? What messages might viewers have carried away?

The other documents fall into two categories: materials produced by farmers themselves and materials created by people observing and evaluating life on the farm. Some sources illustrate the conditions of rural life during the 1930s; others are photographs of rural conditions taken by photographers like Dorothea Lange who worked for the Historical Section of the Farm Security Administration (18.8). Remember how to read photographs, and keep in mind that these photographs were intended to make the problems of the rural sector clear and to encourage support for New Deal policies. Other sources in this archive address practical or political aspects of the New Deal farm programs.

List of Sources

18.1 **Radio broadcast by Henry A. Wallace,** May 13, 1933, in Russel Lord, ed., *Democracy Reborn: Selected from Public Papers* (New York: Reynal and Hitchcock, 1944), pp. 43–46.

18.2 **Printed handbill for a mass meeting of North Dakota farmers,** July 30, 1933. Folder: "Farm Matters, 1933–34," Official File 227, The Franklin D. Roosevelt Library.

18.3 **Report on drought conditions in western Kansas**, April 1935, by Julia L. Miller, Kansas Emergency Relief Committee. Folder RH MS 327: 48, John G. Stutz Collection, Kansas Collection, University of Kansas Libraries.

18.4 **An Open Letter to Rex Tugwell,** 1939, by Tom Burke. *The Nation*, January 22, 1936, pp. xx.

18.5 **Newsreel transcript, "The Land of Cotton,"** Partial transcript from *March of Time* newsreel (August 1936), August 1936, in H. L. Mitchell, *Roll the Union On* (Chicago: Kerr, 1987), p. 28.

18.6 **An examination of the plight of sharecroppers,** 1936, in Howard Kester, *Revolt Among the Sharecroppers* (New York: Covici Friede, 1936), pp. 48–49. Reprinted by University of Tennessee Press, 1997.

18.7 **Letter from Mr. and Mrs. W. L. Hannon to Eleanor Roosevelt,** 1939. Folder FSA-1939, Official File 1568, The Franklin D. Roosevelt Library, Hyde Park, New York.

18.8a **Photograph by Dorothea Lange, *The Trek of Bums,*** February 1936, Los Angles County, California. Library of Congress.

18.8b **Photograph by Dorothea Lange, *Dispossessed Arkansas Farmers,*** 1935, Bakersfield, California. Library of Congress.

18.8c **Photograph by Dorothea Lange of Oklahoma Dust Bowl Refugees,** June 1935, San Fernando, California. Library of Congress.

18.9 **An attack on New Deal farm policies,** 1936, in *Facts: The New Deal Versus the American System* (Chicago: Republican National Committee, 1936), pp. 53, 55, 57, 59–60.

18.10 **Radio broadcast of President Roosevelt's fireside chat,** September 6, 1936, in *The Public Papers and Addresses of Franklin D. Roosevelt* (New York, 1938), vol. 5, pp. 331–336.

Questions to Consider

1. What major problems did Wallace identify in rural America in his broadcast (18.1)? In what ways did he link rural problems to broad social and economic trends? How did he explain the nature of the new Farm Act and how it would operate? What factors did he argue would be essential for it to succeed? Note the ways in which Wallace used significant American beliefs and values to garner support for the program. What are these beliefs?

2. What does the handbill (18.2) reveal about the immediate responses of some of the nation's farmers to the Farm Act? What kind of language and values did the UFL employ?

3. What additional rural problems do "Report on drought conditions in western Kansas," "An Open Letter to Rex Tugwell," "The Land of Cotton," and "An examination of the plight of sharecroppers" (18.3–18.6) reveal? In what ways did the AAA and the relief programs improve the situation of different groups of farmers? In what ways did the program contribute to worsening their situation? How did farmers attempt to help themselves?

4. What additional insights into the impact and importance of New Deal farmers did the Hannons provide in their letter (18.7)? What impression do the photographs (18.8) make, and how do they affect your understanding of the New Deal programs?

5. How valid do you find the Republicans' attack on New Deal farm programs (18.9)? What accusations seem reasonable? Which are weak or exaggerated? What appears to be the function of the publication, and do you think it was effective?

6. In what ways is Roosevelt's discussion of conservation (18.10) different from that of the Republicans? What picture does he give of government programs and their effect? How well does Roosevelt use the radio to communicate with his audience? How does he present himself? How does he describe the nation's farmers?

7. Now for some broader questions that will help you toward an interpretation of New Deal farm policy: What values and traditions lie at the center of conflicting perspectives on the New Deal farm programs? What generalizations can

you make about the impact of the New Deal programs on the lives of rural families? What contradictions and paradoxes were encompassed in the New Deal farm programs?

8. Your evaluation of New Deal agricultural policy can help you as you consider larger historical questions about the New Deal, based on readings in your text, class lectures or discussions, and these sources. Did the New Deal improve the lives of Americans or did it create or worsen problems? Were New Deal programs primarily designed for relief, recovery, or reform? At the beginning of the 21st century, with more than seventy years of experience and hindsight, how should we judge the New Deal and its consequences?

THE UNITED STATES DURING THE DEPRESSION

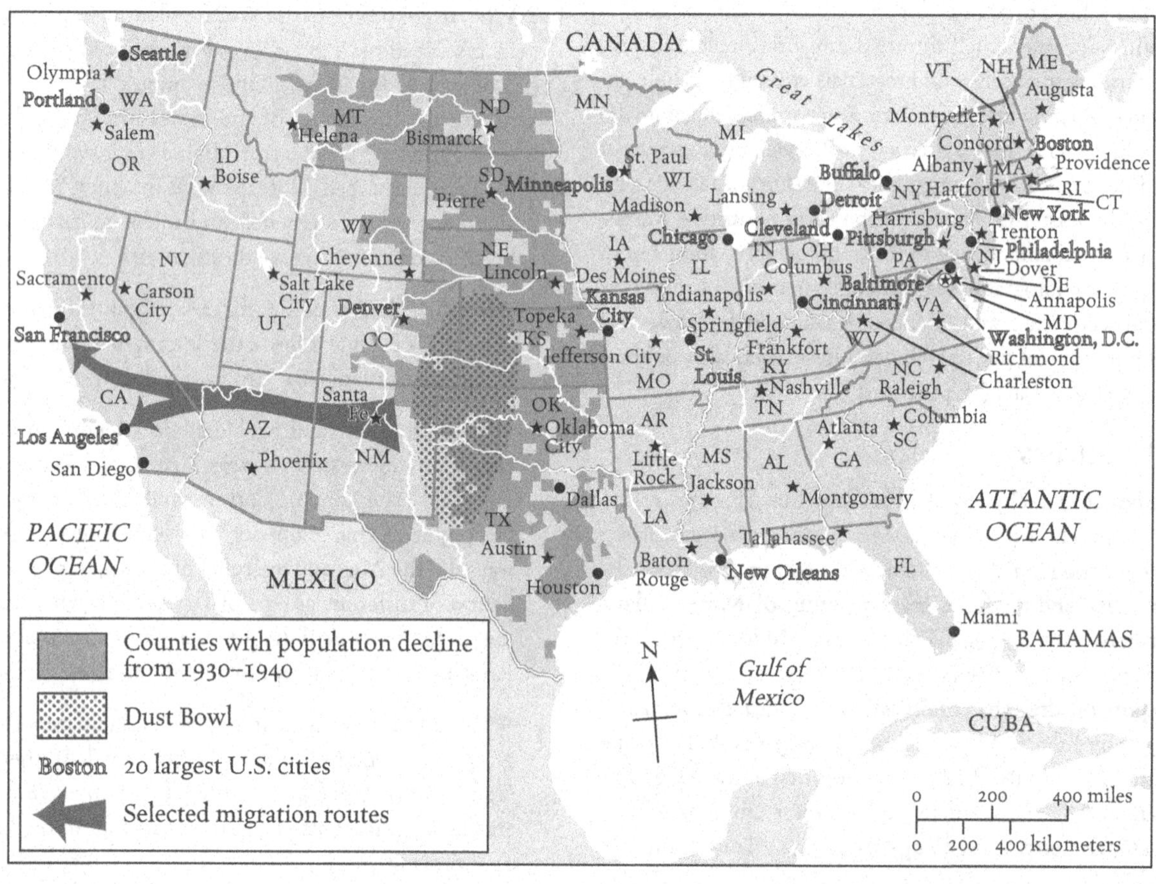

✧ DOCUMENT 18.1 ✧

Radio broadcast by Henry A. Wallace, May 13, 1933, in Russel Lord, ed., *Democracy Reborn: Selected from Public Papers* (New York: Reynal and Hitchcock, 1944), pp. 43–46.

A Declaration of Interdependence

The new Farm Act, which the President signed yesterday, initiates a program for a general advance of buying power. It is not an isolated advance in a restricted sector; it is part of a large attack on the whole problem of depression.

Agriculture and tradesmen must make their way together out of a wilderness of economic desolation and waste. This new machinery will not work itself. The farmers and the distributors of foodstuffs must use it, and make it work. The government can help map lines of march, and can see that the interest of no one group is advanced out of line with the interest of all. But government officials cannot and will not go out and work for private businesses. A farm is a private business; so is a farmers' cooperative; and so are all the great links in the food distributing chain. Government men cannot and will not go out and plow down old trails for agriculture, or build for the distributing industries new roads out of the woods. The growers, the processors, the carriers and sellers of food must do that for themselves. Following trade agreements, openly and democratically arrived at, with the consumer represented and protected from gouging, these industries must work out their own salvation. This emergency Adjustment Act makes it lawful and practical for them to get together and do so. It provides for a control of production to accord with actual need, and for an orderly distribution of essential supplies.

In the end, we envision programs of planned land use; and we must turn our thought to this end immediately; for many thousands of refugees from urban pinch and hunger are turning, with little or no guidance, to the land. A tragic number of city families are reoccupying abandoned farms, farms on which born farmers, skilled, patient, and accustomed to doing with very little, were unable to make a go of it. In consequence of this back-flow there are now thirty-two million people on the farms of the United States, the greatest number ever recorded in our history. Some of those who have returned to farming will find their place there, but most of them, I fear, will not. I look to a day when men and women will be able to do in the country the work that they have been accustomed to doing in the city; a day when we shall have more industrial workers out in the open where there is room to live. I look to a decentralization of industry; but in this respect we shall have to make haste slowly. We do not need any more farmers out in the country now. We do need there more people with some other means of livelihood, buying, close at hand, farm products; enriching and making more various the life of our open-country and village communities.

The Act authorizes the Secretary of Agriculture to apply excise taxes on the processing of these products, and to pay the money thus derived to farmers who agree to enter upon programs of planned production, and who abide by that agreement. These processing taxes will be put on gradually. Few, if any, will be levied before fall; and then we shall make them as light as we can and yet bring about the required reduction in acreage. In no case will taxes be levied on products purchased for the unemployed.

What it amounts to is an advance toward higher prices all along the line. Current proposals for government cooperation with industry are really at one with this Farm Act. Unless we can get re-employment going, lengthen pay rolls, and shorten breadlines, no effort to lift prices can last very long. Our first effort as to agriculture will be to adjust production downward, with safe margins to provide enough food for all. This effort we shall continue until such time as diminishing stocks raise prices to a point where the farmer's buying power will be as high as it was in the pre-war years, 1909 to 1914.

The reason that we chose that period is because the prices farmers got for their crops, in those years, and the prices they paid for manufactured goods and urban services most nearly approached an equitable relationship. There was thus a balance between our major producing groups. At that time there was not the terrific disparity between rural and urban purchasing power which now exists and which is choking the life out of all forms of American business.

We do not propose to reduce agricultural production schedules to a strictly domestic basis. Our foreign trade has dwindled to a mere trickle; but we still have some foreign customers for cotton, tobacco, and certain foodstuffs; we want to keep that trade and to get more foreign trade, if we can. The immediate job is to organize American agriculture to reduce its output to domestic need plus that amount which we can export at a profit. If the world tide turns and world trade revives, we still can utilize to excellent advantage our crop adjustment and controlled distribution setup. We can find out how much they really want over there, and at what price; and then we can take off the brakes and step on the gas.

The first sharp downward adjustment is necessary because during the past years we have defiantly refused to face an overwhelming reality. In consequence, changed world conditions bear down on us so heavily as to threaten our national life.

Ever since 1920, hundreds of thousands of farm families have had to do without civilized goods and services which in normal times they were glad and eager to buy. Since 1929, millions of farm people have had to patch their garments, store their cars and tractors, deprive their children of educational opportunities, and cease, as farmers, to improve their practices and their property. They have been forced to let their homes and other buildings stand bare and unpainted, eaten by time and the weather. They have been driven toward peasant, or less than peasant, standards; they have been forced to adopt frontier methods of bare sustenance at a time when, in the old surging, unlimited sense of the word, we have no longer a frontier.

When the farmer gets higher prices, he will start spending. He will have to. He needs things. He needs new shoes and clothing for all the family, so that his children can go to school in any weather with dry feet, protected bodies, and a decent American feeling of equality and pride. He needs paint and roofing, fencing, machinery and so on, endlessly.

To reorganize agriculture, co-operatively, democratically, so that the surplus lands on which men and women now are toiling, wasting their time, wearing out their lives to no good end, shall be taken out of production—that is a tremendous task. The adjustment we seek calls first of all for a mental adjustment, a willing reversal, of driving, pioneer opportunism and ungoverned *laissez-faire*. The ungoverned push of rugged individualism perhaps had an economic justification in the days when we had all the West to surge upon and conquer; but this country has filled up now, and grown up. There are no more Indians to fight. No more land worth taking may be had for the grabbing. We must experience a change of mind and heart.

The frontiers that challenge us now are of the mind and spirit. We must blaze new trails in scientific accomplishment, in the peaceful arts and industries. Above all, we must blaze new trails in the direction of a controlled economy, common sense, and social decency.

There have been delays in the passage of this Act. Meanwhile the planting season has advanced, and our assigned task of adjusting production to effective demand has become infinitely more difficult. We cannot proceed as if this were the middle of winter. Perhaps our wisest course will be to concentrate on those commodities most in need of adjustment, and on which the adjustment decided upon, this late in the season, can be practical and effective.

To help us in these determinations, we shall have here in Washington within a few days representatives of agriculture and representatives of the processing and distributing trades. Bearing their recommendations in mind, we shall decide just what action to take, and when to take it. As each decision is made we shall get it out directly and publicly to the farmers affected, and launch organization efforts throughout the Nation.

Unless as we lift farm prices we also unite to control production, this plan will not work for long. The only way we can effectively control production for the long pull is for you farmers to organize, and stick, and do it yourselves. This Act offers you promise of a balanced abundance, a shared prosperity, and a richer life. It will work, if you will make it yours, and make it work. I hope that you will come to see in this Act, as I do now, a Declaration of Interdependence, a recognition of our essential unity and of our absolute reliance one upon another.

⇢ DOCUMENT 18.2 ⇠

Printed handbill for a mass meeting of North Dakota farmers, July 30, 1933. Folder: "Farm Matters, 1933–34," Official File 227, The Franklin D. Roosevelt Library.

Farmers Mass Meeting!

AT

DATE

Speaker John G. Soltis

AND OTHERS

Subject:—Is The Farm Crisis Solved?

The farmers are facing ruin everywhere. They are fighting for the right to stay on the land. Roosevelt's "New Deal" turns out to be the same old deal for Wall St. at the expense of the farmers and workers.

The bankers and insurance companies are determined to throw the farmers off of the land, or get the last penny of profit. Come to this meeting and learn the story of the farmers struggle to live, and the program to fight against the present conditions enslaving the farmers. The Corey Gross Income Tax will also be discussed.

Auspices—
United Farmers League

STANDARD PRINTING COMPANY

→ DOCUMENT 18.3 ←

Report on drought conditions in western Kansas, April 1935, by Julia L. Miller, Kansas Emergency Relief Committee. Folder RH MS 327: 48, John G. Stutz Collection, Kansas Collection, University of Kansas Libraries.

CONDITIONS IN WESTERN KANSAS

We have 255 cases on relief rolls in Greeley County. Of this number 64 are in Tribune and 33 are in Horace. Greeley County has a population of 1900 people. The 255 cases include 980 persons, making 980 persons dependent almost entirely upon relief. Greeley County has been harder hit by drought than most any other county in this part of the country. We have had no crop for 3 years. Last fall practically no wheat was planted; thus we will need relief until a crop can be raised.

The housing problem in Greeley County is most deplorable. There are 22 families living in sod houses, and these are mostly one and two-room houses where live families from 4 to 13 in number. At least a dozen of these sod houses have one corner caved in. One 4-room sod house is braced by metal props to keep the walls from falling, here 7 are housed. Most of these sod houses are plastered with mud, or cement on inside and have cement floors. One woman has recently papered her walls with newspapers. It is clean, but lacks the attractiveness of wall paper.

We have one family of 10 living in 2 small rooms. These rooms are really squatters cabins moved together. One is higher on foundation than the other and a box a foot square forms the step up into the other room. They cook and eat in one room and in the other, 10 persons sleep in three beds placed so close together that no room is left to sweep and make the beds. This family was approved on Homestead early in December but that program has been closed through the State. He is so anxious to build a new house, of adobe block, so they can really live and entertain their friends.

We have 2 families who live in bank houses. The house extends back into a bank like a basement house, no floor only earth and dust beyond description. We have one couple who live in a chicken house, not a modern electric lighted one, but one built years ago, no windows and at 2 o'clock on a sunshiny day the woman had a lamp lighted to see to patch her husband's overalls. One family lives in a cave, not a window in it. They eat and cook in a cook shack and 6 persons sleep in this one-room hole in the ground.

In Tribune, houses are impossible to get at any price, for rent. One room cook shacks, owned by the suit case wheat farmers, who return home for the winter, rents for $5.00 and $6.00, electric lights and water are extra. We have 2 relief families living in a 4 room basement house, 2 rooms to a family. Tribune tried to prohibit the basement house being built but failed. There are 9 basement houses in town. One basement house is dug down some 5 feet and then old railroad ties piled around for the part above the ground. The cracks are daubed with mud, like the old fashioned log house. These basement houses are poorly lighted and ventilated. A number have started to build, got the basement dug and had to roof over and cement floor until conditions grow more prosperous.

The relief clients living in town expect to be assigned to city projects, while the country men are more willing to drive miles to work. The city man expects to be taken care of. The fellow living in the country, who has his cows and chickens, is no better off this year than the fellow in town, who has neither, he is really worse off because no feed was raised and to buy, takes all profit.

The only other income besides relief is the wheat allotment, this was paid regardless of whether any wheat was raised or not. Up until February, only one farmer told me he had any income from cream, and many had no milk for home use. Some have fed cotton cake. Russian thistles grew here abundantly last summer and farmers cut them for winter feed. In most cases this was the only feed provided. The cattle have steadily lost weight and many have died. In todays local paper 16 car loads of straw are advertised as from $7.50 to $8.00 per ton F.O.B. Tribune, which price is lower than last shipments. A few years ago at Topeka, choice alfalfa hay sold at $5.00 per ton.

Dust storms once or twice a week like we have had the last three weeks, when day grows dark as night, are making the farmers case look very serious. Many have everything mortgaged. To be a relief client he must have gone his mile, I mean he must have mortgaged his land, taken out all loans available, such as feed and crop loans, and cattle mortgaged and now he must have food and feed and seed to plant.

<u>Conditions as of April, 1935</u>

Julia L. Miller

→ DOCUMENT 18.4 ←

An Open Letter to Rex Tugwell, 1939, by Tom Burke. *The Nation*, January 22, 1936, pp. xx. Reprinted with permission from the January 22, 1936 issue of *The Nation*. For subscription information, call 1-800-333-8536. Portions of each week's *Nation* magazine can be accessed at http://www.thenation.com.

The Rural Resettlement Division of the Resettlement Administration of which Rexford Tugwell is administrator, is engaged in rehabilitating some 290,000 farm families taken from the relief rolls in the spring and summer of 1934. The program is designed to help these families become self-sustaining. The Resettlement administration makes small loans directly to the "rehabilitant" who purchases his goods, however, according to a budget made for him by the local representative. The following letter, which we urge upon the attention of Mr. Tugwell, relates the experience of one of these families in Alabama. Mr. Burke is assistant secretary of the Share-Croppers Unions.

—Editor, *The Nation*
—Birmingham, Alabama

Dear Mr. Tugwell:

I have just visited Mrs. Pierce White, who lives on a rehabilitation farm near Lafayette in Chambers County. Mrs. White and her four little girls had a very unhappy Christmas this year, not because they were starving on the farm—they were hardened to that—but because Mr. White had been sent to jail. I promised Mrs. White that the Share-Croppers' Union would do everything it could for her husband and family, and that is why I am writing this letter.

The local representative of the Resettlement Administration in Chambers County is Vernon Jennings, a small landowner. He is known as the field foreman. You have perhaps read about him in your special investigator's report on Chambers County.

You remember that the Rehabilitation Administration stopped advancing money for food last August and many of the people got in a pretty bad fix. Mr. White took a couple of hundred pounds of his seed cotton and sold it in order to buy food for his family. Mr. Jennings found out about it and had Mr. White arrested. When Mr. White's brother, Walton, tried to get signers for a bail bond for Pierce, he found that Mr. Jennings was going around telling everyone not to sign the bond. Of course, only the landlords are eligible to sign a bail bond and they are friends of Mr. Jennings.

To cut it short, Mr. White was held in jail until his trial and then was convicted and sent to jail for six months. Pierce White's brother Walton was arrested, too, because he had hauled the cotton. However, he appealed his case and he will be free until the spring-term court.

Pierce White has been in jail for two and a half months now, just for selling about 200 pounds of his own seed cotton. But this isn't all. After Pierce went to jail Mr. Jennings came out and took the steer (the work animal), the fertilizer distributor, the plow stock and tools, the scooter, the scrapes, and the mow boards and gear. Then Mr. Jennings took the three bales of cotton they had made and their AAA rental and parity checks; the Whites didn't get a penny out of this. A little later Mr. Jennings came and asked Mrs. White if she would need the syrup, corn, and sweet potatoes. She said she would because she had nothing else for the winter except a cow that only gave half a gallon of milk a day.

To tell you the truth, Mr. Tugwell, Mrs. White doesn't understand just how she stands because she has not received any accounting of what they were given by the government, what they owed the government, or how the government was to get it back. Mr. White must have figured that the cotton was his; so he sold a little (I haven't talked to him about it). Also the Whites believe that they had paid for the things that Mr. Jennings took away from them. You see, the cotton Mr. Jennings collected must have brought at least $150; this with the rental and parity checks would surely have paid almost all of their debt to the government. Now, Mr. Jennings has not given them any account of what they owe or any receipts for what they paid. He may have given an accounting to the Resettlement administration, but as far as the Whites are concerned, the bookkeeping system is just like the landlord's system. Mr. Jennings just takes everything and says it is for "indebtedness."

Mrs. White only got six gallons of syrup, about ten bushels of sweet potatoes, and about fifty bushels of corn, and that is all she has for the winter, along with a little milk. It is a pretty terrible diet for her little girls—the oldest is five and the youngest is four months old.

When I last saw Mrs. White she was very worried about something else, too. Mr. Paul Martin, the federal land agent, had ordered her to move. Mr. White signed the rehabilitation contract for three years, and it seems as if Mr. Jennings should be looking out for a place for the family but he isn't.

I remember Mr. R. K. Greene, the Alabama Rehabilitation Director, saying that they could not let these rehabilitated farmers get a better living than the share-croppers because all the croppers would want to be rehabilitation farmers. Well, Mr. Greene did a 100 per cent job, and there is not a rehabilitation farmer in these parts who is getting along as well as the share-croppers.

And much as Mrs. White needs help, all the other rehabilitation farmers are in almost as bad a fix. Mr. Jennings has collected almost everything they raised and intercepted the rental and parity checks and cut off the food advances; so you can see that they are in a terrible fix. Many of the rehabilitation farmers are being told to move, and Mr. Jennings isn't paying any attention to it and is letting the landlords run them off the land.

Mrs. White lives on Route I out of Lafayette, in case you want to get in touch with her.

—TOM BURKE

→ DOCUMENT 18.5 ←

Newsreel transcript, "The Land of Cotton," August 1936, in H.I. Mitchell, *Roll the Union On* (Chicago: Kerr, 1987), p.28. "The Land of Cotton," partial transcript from *March of Time* newsreel, (August 1936). By permission of HBO, New York, NY.

"The Land of Cotton"

PARTIAL TRANSCRIPT OF *March of Time* NEWSREEL (AUGUST 1936)

In all the United States, there is no parallel to the economic bondage in which cotton holds the South. Victims of this one-crop system are the five and one-half million white folk, three million Negroes, tenant farmers, sharecroppers, laborers who own no land themselves, but farm sixty percent of the South's twenty-seven million acres of cotton. Victims, too, and completely dependent on the cotton-belt's one source of income, are the planter-landlords.

Landlord to sharecropper: I know times are hard, and I know the pickin's are far from plenty, but it's the system that is all wrong. It has been handed down to us through generations. It can't be corrected overnight. You don't think I'm getting rich, do you?

Sharecropper: No, sir.

Commentator: A surplus of thirteen million bales, a whole year's production, piled up in southern warehouses. Then the New Deal stepped in, ordered every third row of the new crop plowed under. The next year increasing the program to cut forty percent of all cotton acreage. Nine-hundred thousand men and women were let off the land. Vast sums were paid out in benefits, but some of the sharecroppers failed to receive their part of the government's benefit checks, and their protest reverberated in Washington's Department of Agriculture, where three officials were fired, among them Gardner Jackson of the AAA [Agricultural Adjustment Administration].

Jackson to newspapermen: Well, one of the reasons we were fired is because Jerome Frank, Lee Pressman, and some of the rest of us tried to see to it that these sharecroppers got something approaching a square deal.

Newspaperman: What percentage of the sharecroppers do you figure got gypped?

Jackson: In darn near half the cases, the sharecroppers didn't get a nickel of the benefit payments. The landlords pocketed it all, but actually politics is in back of it. It would be political suicide to go against the planters. They are the Democrats who have the real power in the South.

Commentator: Echoing across Arkansas are the first rumblings of revolt in the Southland.

Young sharecropper: You have been sharecropping all your life and you haven't got a thing to show for it.

Speaker: We can't live on seventy-five cents a day, and I defy any planter to show me how a man can live on that wage. *[Applause]*

Blackstone (singing): Let's build the Southern Tenant Farmers Union and make our country worthwhile to live in.

Commentator: The headquarters of the Southern Tenant Farmers Union is set up in Memphis, just across the Mississippi River from the troubled region. As membership swelled to ten thousand, to twenty-five thousand, the cotton-farmers demanded that the planters sign written contracts to pay wages of $1.50 for a ten-hour day, and recognize their right to organize. Soon many a country road was peopled with families wandering aimlessly, some homeless because of curtailed production, others evicted by planters for joining Union activities. Then the Union called its members to unite for the cotton-fields' first strike.

Sharecropper organizer: Let them jail us if they want to. We'll fill every jail in Arkansas, but get out of the fields, and stay out until the bosses give in.

(Singing of "We Shall Not Be Moved.")

Commentator: Faced with the prospect of ruined profits, the Arkansas planters closed ranks.

Planter: If they haven't got enough sense to know that this Union business is going to make things worse, we've got to teach them.

(Cars of men driving down the road.)

(Claude Williams and Willie Sue Blagden are stopped on road.)

Commentator: News of the investigating expedition from Tennessee had already reached planters in the little Arkansas town of Earle.

Williams: What do you men want?

Planters: All right, now get going down that highway.

Williams led by men; one remarks: We have had enough of you Yankee agitators coming down here stirring up trouble.

(Then, having beaten Williams, the men come for Willie Sue.)

Planters: All right, come on out. You're next, sister.

Commentator: The next day the violence in the Blagden-Williams investigation came into sharp focus for the entire nation.

(Newspaper headlines—"Eastern Arkansas Planters Flog Woman and Man.")

Commentator: From Arkansas' capital at Little Rock, Governor J. Marion Futrell speaks out in defense of the planters.

Governor: I deny that there is any peonage in Arkansas, and I defy any one of these outside agitators to prove that there is.

Commentator: According to the Arkansas Governor, it is not the planter who is at fault in the Southland, but the one-crop system which has both planter and sharecropper in peonage. Gone are the days when U.S. cotton dominated the world's supply. Foreign countries stepped up production and took U.S. markets while U.S. planters were being forced to curtail their production. Gone too are King Cotton's traditional boundaries where southern wealth was born. Today one-third of all U.S. cotton grows in the new fertile stretches of Texas and Oklahoma, where large-scale industrialized farming can produce cotton forty percent cheaper than in the Old South.

(Church scene—singing of "Holy, holy, holy.")

Commentator: It is plain today that planter and sharecropper alike are the economic slaves of the South's one-crop system that only basic change can restore the one-time peace and prosperity of the Kingdom of Cotton. Time marches on.

→ DOCUMENT 18.6 ←

An examination of the plight of sharecroppers, 1936, in Howard Kester, *Revolt Among the Sharecroppers* (New York: Covici Friede, 1936), pp. 48–49. Reprinted by University of Tennessee Press, 1997.

"One great reason," writes a Georgia planter, "why cotton is so plentiful and cheap, is that on the great plantations of middle Georgia, middle Alabama, Mississippi and others of the richest regions of the South, it is grown by Negroes who get for their labor only enough to maintain a bare, brute subsistence. . . ." *What the Georgia planter failed to say is that not only Negroes who work in the cotton fields but whites as well, "get . . . only enough to maintain a bare, brute subsistence. . . ."* If all of the toilers who could verify this statement through actual experience were gotten together, they would constitute the majority of cotton workers in the fields of the South. The census for 1880 estimated the tenant farmer's income to be around $250. In off years it has gone much below that figure and in good years it has averaged a dollar a day and sometimes over. A study of Negro tenant farmers in Macon County, Alabama, in 1932, revealed that 61.7 per cent "broke even," 26.0 per cent went in the hole, while only 9.4 per cent made any profit at all. The average income of those who did make a profit ranged between $70 and $90 for the year. The average gross income of the sharecropper in Arkansas, white and colored, in 1934, is estimated by various authorities at $210. This represents his *total* gross income for his entire year's labor and includes, of course, the labor of his entire family. Can anything more than a "bare, brute subsistence" be expected from such an income?

. . .

How much did the average sharecropper in Arkansas actually make for his entire year's labor in 1933? Mr. Betts of the *St. Louis-Dispatch,* after a careful investigation, estimated his income to be $210. He arrived at his figures in the following manner. Twenty-five acres was reckoned to be the size of the average sharecropper's farm. In the rich bottom lands he would produce on an average of 1,888 pounds per acre which sold on an average for 9.4 cents per pound. The entire crop when harvested would be worth $441.90 of which the cropper's share would be $220.95. The AAA, however, forced him to plow under approximately eight acres which left only seventeen from which cotton could be harvested. This reduced his cash income to around $150. Theoretically he was to receive $60 from the Government for his share in the plow-up. This added to $150 received from the sale of the cotton which he produced amounted to $210. The record clearly shows that the majority of sharecroppers did not share in the Government benefits but that the money they were supposed to receive went to the planter. But assuming that the sharecropper did receive $60 from the Government, it would simply mean that this $210 represented the sharecropper's total income for an entire year for the labor of himself and his whole family.

→ DOCUMENT 18.7 ←

Letter from Mr. and Mrs. W. L. Hannon to Eleanor Roosevelt, 1939. Folder FSA-1939, Official File 1568, The Franklin D. Roosevelt Library.

Eldorado, Kansas

Dear Mrs. Roosevelt:

I take this liberty to tell you of the work of the Farm Security Administration in Kansas.

Many things have been said and printed against the New Deal which made me wonder why more hasn't been said and printed for the New Deal then I thought we accept all the benefactions of the New Deal without saying much about it and many times receiving these merciful benefactions and at the same time saying much against it.

I wish to write the best I can with the limited talents I possess of our actual experience and for no other reason than to show our gratitude.

In 1932 we were prosperous farmers with youth, health, and ambition. We worked hard and long hours, met all our debts promptly, and were able to accumulate a reasonable amount each year. We made well on cattle. This fired our ambition. We decided to double our herd. We would surely be able to buy the much longed for farm home.

We awoke one morning to find we owed money we never had possessed. We felt a little dazed but on every hand was consoled with the good news (it couldn't last) and by all means hold on to those cattle until prices returned.

Well the trials and tribulations of holding on to those cattle for return prices would fill a book. Droughts set in in earnest. The grass would die. Five years we had insufficient feed. I can say for endurance we couldn't be beat, for the cattle nearly died of starvation and old age before we decided prosperity wasn't just around the corner. I might add the thought of meeting a deficit at the bank had something to do with our endurance.

Finally the bankers and ourselves decided we couldn't await prosperity any longer. A sale was called. We still had a deficit of three thousand dollars and without cattle. We managed to pay rent, support our family, but could not pay interest, say nothing about the principal.

We felt a strict obligation to our debts but it began to look like we had met with the impossible. We realized interest was compounding, the principal was mounting and try our best nothing we could do about it, with crop failures and ruinous prices.

Our bankers were caught as we were facing the impossible it became too heavy a burden for them to bear. They brought in a collector to take his place, who made it his business to collect regardless. We would turn our Gov. crop checks and sell off stock not ready for market to meet his demands. Finally, we realized there was nothing more to give in his greedy taking.he had killed the goose that lay the golden egg. I am still surprised in this day of specialized training that a man so incompetent should be placed in this position. I can now see where a collector should be a man of tact and should be able to pass a high intelligence test.

We farmers of this community, while not highly educated, had common sense enough to note his egotism and lack of sympathy and also that he would have starved to death on a farm if compelled to live by his own efforts. Farmers are a little different from other classes. They do with out rather than face debt so we all felt as if we had committed the unpardonable sin. It was a skeleton in the closet. No soldier ever fought a braver battle to keep the neighbors from knowing things were not as they should be. We went with aching teeth and flirted with death rather than consult a Dr. I might add of all the many sacrifices we made our children's education was the last denial but even that came to pass.

By this time a farmer with a relative who had money would borrow or beg to pay this collector to have a chance to recuperate but alas for ourselves and many like us who had no one to turn to. We were facing the possibility of being sold out as we had signed over everything we possessed to protect the bank against this cattle loss.

We were farmers, knew no other trade, and by this time the trained city worker could not find work. We realized we had no chance in town. We were desperate. My husband's health broke under the strain of worry and overwork. I realized this was the last straw with my husband bedfast I went to this collector and asked him if we could just keep enough stock to keep off relief and plant another crop and he could take the rest. He said he would take it all and if relief was the only thing left why thousands were taking it so we would not matter. Sick and discouraged I do not like to think what might have happened had we not the Gov. to turn to.

The Gov. granted our loan, got us out from under this tyrant, reestablished us - now the result.

With peace of mind my husband's health is restored and this is no more important than his restored courage. He has taken a new lease on life, making plans in a bigger, better way and may I say here I think the loan worth the price from no other standpoint than the fact it installs a

-3-

bookkeeping which is going to make a business man of the farmer. We profit from its benefits each month and instead of trying to destroy us the Gov. loan seeks to aid us in every way.

Not a day of my life I do not thank God for President Roosevelt and his leaders who have made such a sacrifice to help the oppressed.

Oh yes! They wonder how he carries on so well and still laughs so heartily and call him America's showman No. 1. They well know what he has to content with, but the one thing they do not know is that each night as he lays these terrific burdens down he is consoled and strengthened by the fact that he has given courage and hope to thousands upon thousands and that he has fought for the oppressed with a courage no other human has ever shown. These facts account for the fact he carries on so well and can still laugh so heartily.

From a grateful farmer and his wife to whom the Farm Security Administration has given health, happiness and courage.

Mr. and Mrs. W. L. Hannon
Route 3
Eldorado, Kansas

→ DOCUMENT 18.8a ←

Photograph by Dorothea Lange of ***The Trek of Bums,*** February 1936, Los Angeles County, California. Library of Congress.

DOCUMENT 18.8b

Photograph by Dorothea Lange, *Dispossessed Arkansas Farmers*, 1935, Bakersfield, California. Library of Congress.

DOCUMENT 18.8c

Photograph by Dorothea Lange of Oklahoma Dust Bowl Refugees, June 1935, San Fernando, California. Library of Congress.

→ DOCUMENT 18.9 ←

An attack on New Deal farm policies, 1936, in *Facts: The New Deal Versus the American System* (Chicago: Republican National Committee, 1936), pp. 53, 55, 57, 59–60.

The AAA and Soil Conservation— A Program of Compulsory Regimentation

The Agricultural Adjustment Act was adopted as a means of raising farm prices to pre-war "parity." Pre-war parity may be defined as a price which will enable the farmer to exchange a unit of a commodity which he sells, such as a bushel of wheat, a hundredweight of hogs or a pound of cotton, for as much of the things which he buys as he could during the prewar period 1909–1914.

The method, as originally devised, was that of reducing the production of those commodities which were on an export basis, and which had what were considered to be price depressing surpluses. The program was intended to be wholly voluntary from the standpoint of participation by farmers. The President in his speech at Topeka on September 14, 1932, said, "The farm plan must not be coercive. It must be voluntary, and the individual producer should at all times have the opportunity of non-participation if he so desires. . . ."

But is soon became apparent that voluntary participation would not produce the desired unity of action among farmers. Compulsory regimentation began. The Bankhead Cotton Act and the Kerr Tobacco Act practically forced growers to reduce production to specified allotments by placing a prohibitive marketing tax upon the sale of cotton and tobacco in excess of quotas established under the provision of these acts. In addition to the tax, both acts provided heavy penalties for their violation.

The Potato Act of 1935 was molded along similar lines, but it went so far as to hold buyers liable for the purchase of potatoes not sold in conformity with the provisions of the Act. To an increasing extent the AAA became compulsory. To an increasing extent the American farmer lost control of the management of his farm. . . .

Rental and Benefit Payments

The great bulk of the money received by farmers was in the form of rental and benefit payments. Through March 31, 1936, these amounted to $1,135,929,072—an average of $167.00 per farm in the United States. During the same period the national debt increased by $373.00 per family in the United States. But not all farmers were equally favored in the distribution of government checks. In round numbers, only about one-half the farmers received payments. Eighty-eight per cent of the entire amount went to the producers of cotton, wheat, corn, hogs, and tobacco. Little or nothing went to the cattle raiser, the dairyman, the poultryman, the wool, fruit, and vegetable growers. This is significant when one considers that the annual value of dairy products alone is three times as great as cotton, corn and wheat combined. . . .

More significant than the reduction of production is the shifts in production from one region to another. A comparison of wheat production in 1934 and 1929 as reported by the census shows that the acres of wheat harvested increased during this five-year period in the New England, East North Central, South Atlantic and East South Central States. These increases are the more important due to the fact that wheat acreage harvested in the United States as a whole was one-third less in 1934 than it was in 1929. The year 1934 was the worst drought year in history. That year was also the one of greatest reductions under the A. A. A. Yet in the face of these deterrents, wheat production increased in most of the less specialized wheat growing regions, to the detriment of the farmer whose normal crop is wheat. Corn acreage harvested increased in 1934 over 1929 in the New England, Middle Atlantic, East North Central, South Atlantic, and East South Central States. . . .

It is clear that the paying of farmers to quit growing certain products encourages their growing other products. The result is not so much a reduction in the total farm production as it is in a shift of production from established to non-established regions.

To pay a farmer to quit growing wheat, cotton, corn and tobacco is to pay him to grow more hay and more grass. More hay and more grass means more milk, beef and mutton. Reduction of certain crops at the expense of increasing others threatens to shift distress among farmers; not eliminate it. . . .

Soil conservation is a national and non-political problem. It is of universal import. The city dweller, as well as the farmer, is interested in defending our natural resources against waste and depletion. The soil is one of the most important of these. The dust bowls of the West, the flood devastation of the East, and the ever encroaching gulleys of the South, together with the loss of fertility over wide areas, are outstanding reminders of the pressing need for corrective action. Effective action will differ markedly according to regions, and in keeping with the causes. Soil conservation on neighboring farms may call for treatment wholly unlike. It cannot be handled by a blanket formula.

The preserving of our soil resources for future generations is a long-time program. It will continue to be with us always. It should not be burdened with the temporary expedient of farm relief. It should not be made an emergency vehicle for carrying checks to farmers just before election. Its importance to the nation as a whole, demands that it not be submerged in the interests of a class, or made a political tool. . . .

Basically, the farm relief portion of the program is designed to increase farm purchasing power. Farm purchasing power is intimately related to prices of farm products. Soil conservation practices by farmers are not likely to exert an immediate influence upon farm prices. Their long-time tendency will be to shift agricultural production from certain crops to others, and to shift the production of specified crops from one region to another. But its influence as a price booster is not likely to be either great or rapid. Prices of agricultural products are dependent, in no small measure, upon such things as consumer purchasing power, which is closely associated with unemployment, which, in turn, is inseparably connected with industrial prosperity. These are matters beyond the farmers' control.

⇝ DOCUMENT 18.10 ⇜

Radio broadcast of President Roosevelt's fireside chat, September 6, 1936, in *The Public Papers and Addresses of Franklin D. Roosevelt* (New York, 1938), vol. 5, pp. 331–336.

I have been on a journey of husbandry. I went primarily to see at first hand conditions in the drought States, to see how effectively Federal and local authorities are taking care of pressing problems of relief and also how they are to work together to defend the people of this country against the effects of future droughts.

I saw drought devastation in nine States.

I talked with families who had lost their wheat crop, lost their corn crop, lost their livestock, lost the water in their well, lost their garden and come through to the end of the summer without one dollar of cash resources, facing a winter without feed or food—facing a planting season without seed to put in the ground.

That was the extreme case, but there are thousands and thousands of families on Western farms who share the same difficulties.

I saw cattlemen who because of lack of grass or lack of winter feed have been compelled to sell all but their breeding stock and will need help to carry even these through the coming winter. I saw livestock kept alive only because water had been brought to them long distances in tank cars. I saw other farm families who have not lost everything but who because they have made only partial crops must have some form of help if they are to continue farming next spring.

I shall never forget the fields of wheat so blasted by heat that they cannot be harvested. I shall never forget field after field of corn stunted, earless and stripped of leaves, for what the sun left the grasshoppers took. I saw brown pastures which would not keep a cow on fifty acres.

Yet I would not have you think for a single minute that there is permanent disaster in these drought regions, or that the picture I saw meant depopulating these areas. No cracked earth, no blistering sun, no burning wind, no grasshoppers are a permanent match for the indomitable American farmers and stockmen and their wives and children who have carried on through desperate days, and inspire us with their self-reliance, their tenacity and their courage. It was their fathers' task to make homes; it is their task to keep those homes; it is our task to help them win their fight.

First, let me talk for a minute about this autumn and the coming winter. We have the option, in the case of families who need actual subsistence, of putting them on the dole or putting them to work. They do not want to go on the dole and they are one thousand percent right. We agree, therefore, that we must put them to work for a decent wage; and when we reach that decision we kill two birds with one stone, because these families will earn enough by working, not only to subsist themselves, but to buy food for their stock, and seed for next year's planting. Into this scheme of things there fit of course the Government lending agencies which next year, as in the past, will help with production loans.

Every Governor with whom I have talked is in full accord with this program of providing work for these farm families, just as every Governor agrees that the individual States will take care of their unemployables, but that the cost of employing those who are entirely able and willing to work must be borne by the Federal Government.

If then we know, as we do today, the approximate number of farm families who will require some form of work relief from now on through the winter, we face the question of what kind of work they should do. Let me make it clear that this is not a new question because it has already been answered to a greater or less extent in every one of the drought communities. Beginning in 1934, when we also had serious drought conditions, the State and Federal Governments cooperated in planning a large number of projects, many of them directly aimed at the alleviation of future drought conditions. In accordance with that program literally thousands of ponds or small reservoirs have been built in order to supply water for stock and to lift the level of the underground water to prevent wells from going dry. Thousands of wells have been drilled or deepened; community lakes have been created and irrigation projects are being pushed.

Water conservation by means such as these is being expanded as a result of this new drought all through the Great Plains area, the Western corn belt and in the States that lie further south. In the Middle West water conservation is not so pressing a problem. Here the work projects run more to soil erosion control and the building of farm-to-market roads.

Spending like this is not waste. It would spell future waste if we did not spend for such things now. These emergency work projects provide money to buy food and clothing for the winter; they keep the livestock on the farm; they provide seed for a new crop, and, best of all, they will conserve soil and water in the future in those areas most frequently hit by drought.

If, for example, in some local area the water table continues to drop and the topsoil to blow away, the land values will disappear with the water and the soil. People on the farms will drift into the nearby cities; the cities will have no farm trade and the workers in the city factories and stores will have no jobs. Property values in the cities will decline. If, on the other hand, the farms within that area remain as farms with better water supply and no erosion, the farm population will stay on the land and prosper and the nearby cities will prosper too. Property values will increase instead of disappearing. That is why it is worth our while as a Nation to spend money in order to save money. . . .

In the drought area people are not afraid to use new methods to meet changes in Nature, and to correct mistakes of the past. If over-grazing has injured range lands they are willing to reduce the grazing. If certain wheat lands should be returned to pasture they are willing to cooperate. If trees should be planted as wind-breaks or to stop erosion they will work with us. If terracing or summer fallowing or crop rotation is called for they will carry it out. They stand ready to fit, and not to fight, the ways of Nature.

We are helping, and shall continue to help the farmer, to do those things, through local soil conservation committees and other cooperative local, State and Federal agencies of Government.

I have not the time tonight to deal with other and more comprehensive agricultural policies.

With this fine help we are tiding over the present emergency. We are going to conserve soil, conserve water and conserve life. We are going to have long-time defenses against both low prices and drought. We are going to have a farm policy that will serve the national welfare. That is our hope for the future.

→ARCHIVE 19←

"The Good War": A Diverse Nation in World War II

Archive Overview

DURING the 1930s, as ominous events were taking place in Europe and Asia, the American government pursued policies designed to keep the nation neutral. With the outbreak of war in 1939, however, the country began its long course toward involvement in yet another world conflict. When the Japanese attacked Pearl Harbor on December 7, 1941, a date that Franklin Roosevelt announced "will live in infamy," the nation went to war. "No matter how long it may take for us to overcome this premeditated invasion," Roosevelt said in his war message, "the American people in their righteous might will win through to absolute victory."

World War II became known as "the good war," a characterization that echoes strongly in our collective memory more than sixty years later. You may well have seen a film with this outlook recently, or you may have a relative who has given this sort of picture of the war. This archive allows you to explore the war and its characterization as "the good war." First, examine the sources to discover the various ways in which diverse Americans reacted to, and participated in, the war at home and abroad. How were they mobilized to support the war, and in what ways did they participate in the national effort? How did race, gender, and class shape the war experience of different Americans, what they did in the war, and how they felt about it? What were the shared experiences, and what were the distinctive ones? Your second task addresses the larger question: What was "good" about the war, and for whom was it "good"? To what extent did different Americans share equally in the burdens and benefits of World War II?

Placing the Sources in Context

DURING the 1930s, events both in Asia and in Europe seemed to point toward the possibility of another world war. In the Far East, Japan, a powerful and ambitious nation in need of raw materials, began a decade of expansion and conquest on the Asian mainland. Manchuria was taken over by Japan in 1931, and six years later Japan began a full-scale invasion of China. Japanese aggression troubled the American leadership because the United States had long seen itself as China's best friend and because Japanese expansion might threaten the Philippines, which had become an American possession during the Spanish–American War (see Archive 14).

In Europe, the rise of fascism upset the political arrangements established at the end of World War I and potentially threatened the survival of democracy there. The Italian dictator Benito Mussolini successfully defied the League of Nations with his conquest of Ethiopia in 1935, while, under the leadership of Adolf Hitler, Germany began to rearm in violation of the Treaty of Versailles. In 1938, Germany annexed Austria and occupied part of Czechoslovakia. When Hitler invaded Poland in 1939, Europe's two leading democracies, Britain and France, declared war on Germany. In the first years of the war, the Allied cause faltered badly. France fell in 1940 while Great Britain reeled under the impact of massive bombing raids. In Asia, profiting from the European chaos, Japan invaded French Indochina in 1940 and 1941.

Despite the combined threat of fascism in Europe and totalitarianism in Asia, the United States moved toward military involvement slowly. The Lend-Lease program passed by Congress

TIMELINE

1939	World War II begins
1941	FDR's Four Freedoms speech; creation of Fair Employment Practices Commission; Pearl Harbor bombed; Germany declares war on the United States
1942	Internment of Japanese-Americans; price controls and rationing
1943	Race riots in Detroit and other cities
1944	Invasion of Normandy
1945	Yalta Conference; death of Roosevelt; atomic bombs dropped on Japan; war ends

in March 1941 did provide desperately needed assistance to Great Britain and then to the Soviet Union when Germany launched an attack on that country in June 1941. It was not until the Japanese bombed Pearl Harbor on December 7, 1941, however, that Roosevelt asked Congress for a declaration of war.

Yet even before the United States formally entered the war, the terms of American participation had begun to take shape. In January 1941, President Roosevelt delivered his Four Freedoms speech to Congress. While vague about specific war aims, FDR's invocation of these key principles of American life—freedom of speech, freedom of worship, freedom from want, and freedom from fear—defined a sense of national purpose. The Four Freedoms also defined the expectations against which many Americans would come to assess their own experience of the war.

Increased production in support of the Allies began with the Lend-Lease program of March 1941, and then Pearl Harbor inaugurated full-scale national mobilization. The process of mobilizing for World War II offered new opportunities—and new challenges—to the American people. War production wiped out the lingering effects of the Great Depression. The economy boomed and jobs were plentiful. Giant firms like Ford, General Motors, and Nash Kelvinator, which had made automobiles and appliances, began manufacturing tanks, jeeps, bombs, and other war materials. African-Americans and Mexican-Americans secured jobs they had been previously denied. And because millions of men were temporarily in the armed forces, millions of women entered the workforce for the first time.

Domestic life was both chaotic and focused on winning the war. The public was constantly encouraged to contribute to the war effort by saving metals and fat, buying war bonds, growing V-for-victory vegetable gardens, volunteering, and working harder. Millions of people were on the move, migrating to regions where defense manufacturing was concentrated, and living in hastily erected housing developments. While earnings increased, consumer goods were scarce. Basic items such as food and gasoline were rationed, and it was all but impossible to buy a new car or a washing machine.

Despite the need for every available worker, and despite President Roosevelt's executive order in 1941 prohibiting job discrimination in the defense industries, prejudice and racism did not disappear. Strong group ties persisted among people of similar ethnic, racial, or religious background. Terrible race riots broke out in several cities, most notably Detroit and New York, during the summer of 1943. On the west coast, 120,000 Japanese-Americans were forcefully relocated from their homes to internment camps for the duration of the war. And of course family life was always infused with anxieties and fears about the fate of loved ones fighting, suffering, and perhaps dying thousands of miles away. The war at home was no picnic.

More than 16 million men, including Mexican-Americans, Native Americans, and African-Americans (who were placed in segregated units), and thousands of women served in the military during the war. Unlike the first world war, when most American troops were engaged in combat for a relatively short time, the average length of time soldiers spent abroad was about sixteen months. Because troops were more heavily engaged in fighting than their World War I counterparts had been, casualties were heavier: more than 405,000 soldiers lost their lives and another 670,000 were wounded. This made "the good war" the deadliest war in the nation's history after the Civil War.

All things considered, World War II was a defining moment for two generations of Americans. It was also a defining moment for the American nation, raising questions whether all Americans, women as well as men, people of color as well as whites, could share equally in the Four Freedoms announced by President Roosevelt.

About the Sources

THE sources in this archive raise broad questions about the meaning of nationhood and unity for a people at war, about race and gender, and about how and why people experience feelings of patriotism during a national crisis such as war. Considering these questions should help you identify some of the forces that encouraged Americans of different backgrounds to unite so strongly in the effort to prevail in World War II—as well as to suggest how Americans remained divided.

Many of the sources are "oral histories," transcriptions of interviews conducted years after the events described in them. Oral histories provide a rich source of information, particularly about people who might not otherwise leave written records. They help to balance a historical narrative that has often emphasized the accomplishments of powerful and articulate men and women who left an impressive paper trail for historians to follow. Yet oral history has its pitfalls. The oral historian may ask leading questions, and written transcripts of interviews may omit bad starts, repetitive yet sometimes telling phrases like "you know," and regional pronunciations or dialect. Memories are not always reliable years after the events described. As you read the oral histories, try to determine how long after the events described the interview took place, what sorts of factors (including the interviewer's questions) may have shaped what the person includes in his or her comments, and what sorts of events or feelings he or she may have omitted.

Visual sources also need to be carefully evaluated in terms of their content, purpose, and message. The wartime context must always be kept in mind, for it often shaped visual representations and their possible meanings. Some images, like Norman Rockwell's paintings of the Four Freedoms, were duplicated many times, first in a mass-circulation popular magazine, then on millions of posters. They suggest the links between art and propaganda. Others were more personal expressions of wartime experience. The family photograph, though intending no double message, reveals a great deal about the reality of life during World War II for this rural family from Wisconsin. In a similar manner, the photo of Japanese-Americans at an internment camp suggests the experiences of Asian-Americans who, despite their status as longterm residents of the United States and often as citizens, were distrusted as possible traitors. As an historian, think about how you would evaluate the function and significance of these various kinds of visual sources.

List of Sources

19.1 **Transcript of interview with Bob Barker,** January or February, 1942. Part of man-on-the-street interviews following Pearl Harbor, American Folklife Center, Library of Congress.

19.2 **Magazine illustrations depicting the Four Freedoms,** 1943, by Norman Rockwell, *The Saturday Evening Post*, February 20, 27, March 6, 13, 1943. Norman Rockwell/ Saturday Evening Post.

19.3a **War poster, *United We Win,*** 1943, based on a photograph by Alexander Liberman. Printed by Government Printing Office for the War Manpower Commission. NARA Still Picture Branch (NWDNS–44-PA–370). National Archives and Records Administration.

19.3b **War poster, *Above and Beyond the Call of Duty,*** undated, by David Stone Martin. Printed by Government Printing Office for the Office of War Information. NARA Still Picture Branch (NWDNS–208-PMP–68). National Archives and Records Administration.

19.3c **War poster, *Man the Guns—Join the Navy,*** 1942, by McClelland Barclay. Produced for the Navy Recruiting Bureau, NARA Still Picture Branch (NWDNS–44-PA–24). National Archives and Records Administration.

19.3d **War poster, *You Talk of Sacrifice,*** undated, produced by Winchester. NARA Still Picture Branch (NWDNS–179-WP–1386). National Archives and Records Administration.

19.4 **March on Washington flier,** 1941. A. Philip Randolph Papers, Manuscript Division (8-8), A. Philip Randolph Institute, Washington, DC.

19.5 **Oral interview with Robert Rasmus,** in Studs Terkel, *"The Good War": An Oral History of World War II* (New York: Pantheon, 1984), pp. 38–41.

19.6 **Oral interview with Timuel Black,** in Studs Terkel, *"The Good War": An Oral History of World War II* (New York: Pantheon, 1984), pp. 278–281.

19.7 **Photograph of the Buss family,** 1942. Private property of Kathy Frederick.

19.8 **Oral interview with Peggy Terry,** in Studs Terkel, *"The Good War": An Oral History of World War II* (New York: Pantheon, 1984), pp. 108–111.

19.9 **Photograph of women working on the fuselage of a bomber aircraft during WWII,** photo by Howard R. Hollem, October 1942. Library of Congress.

19.10a **Photograph of Japanese internment camp meal line,** June 12, 1942, Puyallup, Washington. © Seattle Post-Intelligencer Collection, Museum of History and Industry/CORBIS.

19.10b **Poem about a relocation camp,** undated, author unknown, in Deborah Gesenway and Mindy Roseman, *Beyond Words: Images from America's Concentration Camps* (Ithaca: Cornell U. Press, 1987), pp. 64–65. "That Damned Fence" from the Japanese Relocation Centers Records, #3830. By permission of the Division of Rare Book and Manuscript Collections, Cornell University Library.

19.11 **Oral interview with Peter Ota,** in Studs Terkel, *"The Good War": An Oral History of World War II* (New York: Pantheon, 1984), pp. 28–33.

19.12 **Illustration picturing the postwar world,** 1943, from *Revere's Part in Better Living*, no. 10, 1943.

Questions to Consider

1. Read the interview with Bob Barker, a farmer in Texas. What picture does he give of the attitudes of ranchers and farmers toward the war? What activities are they pursuing? What approach does he take toward the president?

2. Study the illustrations of the Four Freedoms (source 19.2). How do the pictures make the case for supporting the war? What is the war about? Who and what, do the images suggest, are threatened? What might be some of the reasons for describing a war taking place in Europe and Asia in these ways? Do the posters appeal to emotion? to reason? What sorts of people might respond to these posters? Who might not?

3. Examine the four recruiting posters (19.3). Are they in any way similar to those you have already analyzed? What sorts of Americans and what situations are shown? What seems to be the message of each poster, and how is that message conveyed? To what emotions and values does each one appeal? How would you characterize the posters here and in the first source—as art, propaganda, realism, sentimentality, or some combination of these and other attributes? What do the posters collectively suggest about the government's attempt to unite the American people behind the war?

4. After reading the recollections of Robert Rasmus and Timuel Black (19.5 and 19.6), contrast their experiences in the military and their attitudes toward the war. What might account for the similarities and the differences? How do their experiences compare with those you read about in Archive 16 on World War I? What insights into racial issues do the recollections provide? What does the "March on Washington flier" (19.4) suggest about the relation of the war to African-American consciousness?

5. Read the recollections of Peggy Terry (19.8), then study the photograph (19.9) and illustration (19.12). What do these sources reveal about women's participation in the war? What opportunities and challenges did the war pose

for them? What was life like for women during the conflict? What were their greatest concerns? How real was the war to them? What do the sources suggest about the importance of race, ethnicity, class, and gender in shaping experience?

6. For the Buss family photograph (19.7), note the date, 1942, and the age and sex of the people in the picture. What does this tell you about the realities of World War II? What are your guesses about the man to the left?

7. In the poem, the internment camp photo, and the oral history of Peter Ota (19.10 and 19.11) you have materials about Japanese-Americans during the war. What happened to them? What aspects of their experience does the photo reveal that the other sources do not? How did they feel? Why do you think Japanese-Americans were treated so harshly?

8. In what ways do the recollections of the people interviewed in the oral histories agree about the purpose of the war, its character, and its meaning? How did their actual experiences differ? What was the impact, if any, of race, gender, ethnicity, age, or class position on a person's wartime experiences?

9. How reliable or representative do the oral histories seem to be? Can you see places where the interviewer may have influenced a person's response? Are there signs in the interviews that the years and events that have occurred since the war period have affected how people tell their stories? How reliable as historical sources are these interviews? Are they more or less reliable than conventional written sources?

10. As a final question, In what ways was the second world war a good war and for whom? To what extent did diverse Americans share equally in the burdens and benefits of World War II? Are there members of your own family whom you could ask these questions?

WORLD WAR II ON THE HOME FRONT: WAR INDUSTRY AND RELOCATION

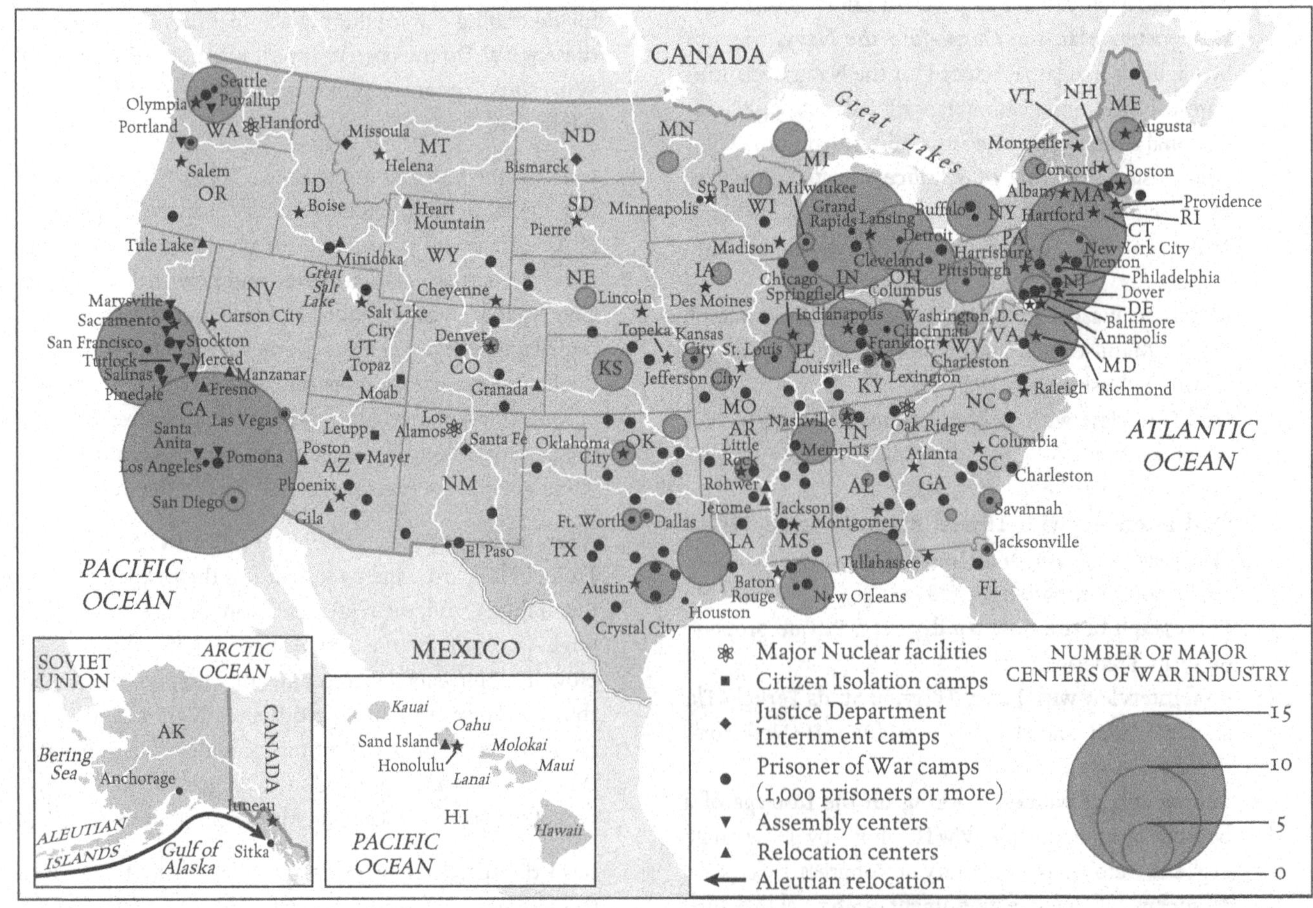

→ DOCUMENT 19.1 ←

Transcript of interview with Bob Barker, January or February, 1942. Part of man-on-the-street interviews following Pearl Harbor, American Folklife Center, Library of Congress.

Bob Barker: Mr. President, I live down here in Granbury in Hood County, Texas. This man over here says I can talk to you. Well, that's the one of the things I've always wanted to do is speak my mind to the President of the United States. Of course I never get a chance to do anything like that ordinarily, but I'm sure glad I've got this chance, and I want to talk to you. I know you're pretty busy up there in Washington, but I want to just talk to you about what I've got on my mind about this war situation.

Since the coming of Pearl Harbor, as everybody around Hood County here knows, we've been getting right in behind you Mr. President. We'll have to tell you straight before that, we was kind of wondering what you had in your mind up there. But we can see now, and we're behind you a hundred percent, and we want you to know it. The boys around Hood County, here have been joining up pretty fast, I can tell you.

I've got a son down in the state university, we've been working quite a while to save enough money so he can go to school down there, it's a fine university too. I went down there not so long ago to see him. He's going to join up, but he's got in the Naval Reserve or I believe that's what he says it is, and he can go on to school before he has to go. Now I think that's mighty fine and his mother thinks it's fine, too.

We didn't know how we was going to see him go off to war but, without an education, if he comes back at all, why, he wouldn't have a job, nor chance for a job and he'd have to get his schooling again, but he tells us he can go to school down there and get his degree, and then go on into training, and then when he gets out of the training, he'll become some kind of officer in the fleet. And we think that's mighty fine.

There's mostly ranchers and farmers around here, Mr. President. We don't amount to much, but we're real Americans, and we're real Texans. And we're right here to tell you that we're doing everything we can to help this war effort, to help you in this war effort. And we're depending on you. I was reading in the paper here the other day and we been talking about it around here, a little about how the men up there you got in Washington kind of going a little slow about this production and stuff. And we want you to get after those men and get them to working good. Now I think this man Nelson is a good man, I think he's as good a man as you could have got up there for that job. And we're just anxious to see him and his men, his workers, get after this thing, and start getting these airplanes off the line. Mass production. We want to see them in the air. My son wrote me the other day, down there at Austin, right near San Antonio where Randolph Field is, and he says they're doing lots of flying down there. He says he sees planes coming over every night, doing night flying, and so the training is going on, and those boys that are being trained have got to have the planes. And you get after those men up there and tell them to get them right out.

Besides that, we have been buying bonds down here, till the world looks level, I tell you. My wife and I have been saving as little as we can, or as much as we can, I say, as little as it is, but we're buying stamps and going to get bonds as soon as we can get enough stamps to get them. And every man I know here in Granbury and Hood County, for that matter, is doing it. My folks, my grandfather, he's an old man now, of course, but he lives out here in Thorp Springs. That's about three miles out here of Granbury, and he's buying his stamps and bonds too on the little income he's making. Money he's saved, you know, and got invested. But he's sure buying the stamps and bonds right now.

There's these cowboys out here from the ranches, we've got a few ranches around here. I see them come into Granbury nearly every Saturday afternoon. And especially on payday and they always going over to the post office and I see them coming out of there with bonds in their hands and it looks to me like, and from what I've talked to them about it, they're doing all they can. Every man around here is doing all they can to support this war effort. By buying defense stamps and bonds. Well we want you to know that. And we want you to know that when the Japs attacked us at Pearl Harbor, and when we declared war on them, we want you to know that the U.S. declared war and that Hood County declared war. And we're behind it. I sometimes think that Texas, being such a state as it is, ought to declare war, too. I mean, ought to have it in writing. But, be that as it may, we want you to know we're in the war too and we're doing everything we can and if any state in the union can do as much as Texas can we'd just like to see them get on the horse and start doing it cause we're behind this thing a hundred percent.

That's all I've got to say to you, Mr. President. I hope you stay well and healthy, during this war, and come out of it feeling fine. And I know everybody in the country will too, because we're going to win it. And we're going to win it as soon as we can.

→ DOCUMENT 19.2 ←

Magazine illustrations depicting the Four Freedoms, 1943, by Norman Rockwell, *The Saturday Evening Post*, February 20, 27, March 6, 13, 1943. Norman Rockwell/Saturday Evening Post.

Freedom of Speech

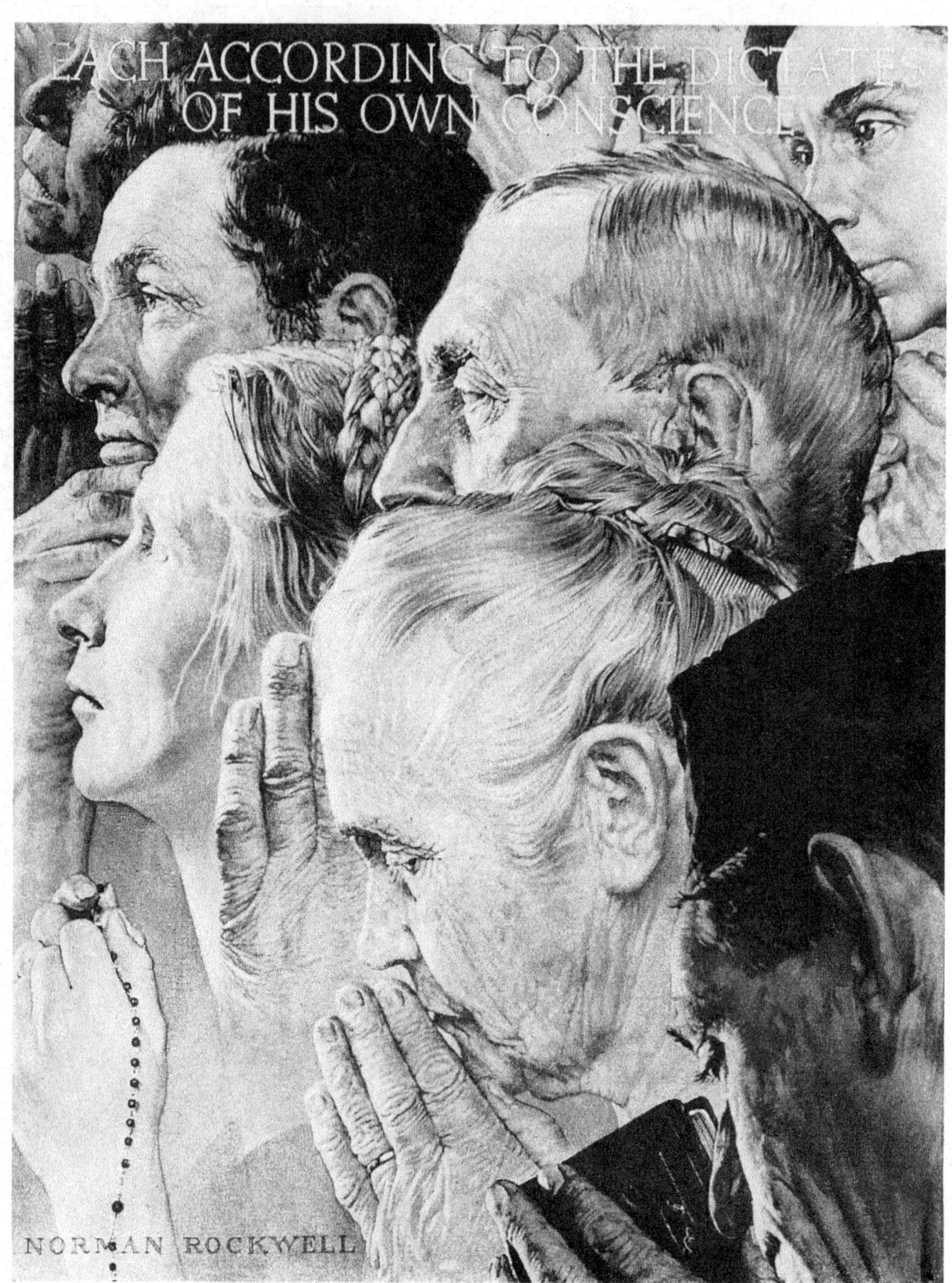

Freedom of Religion

Freedom from Want

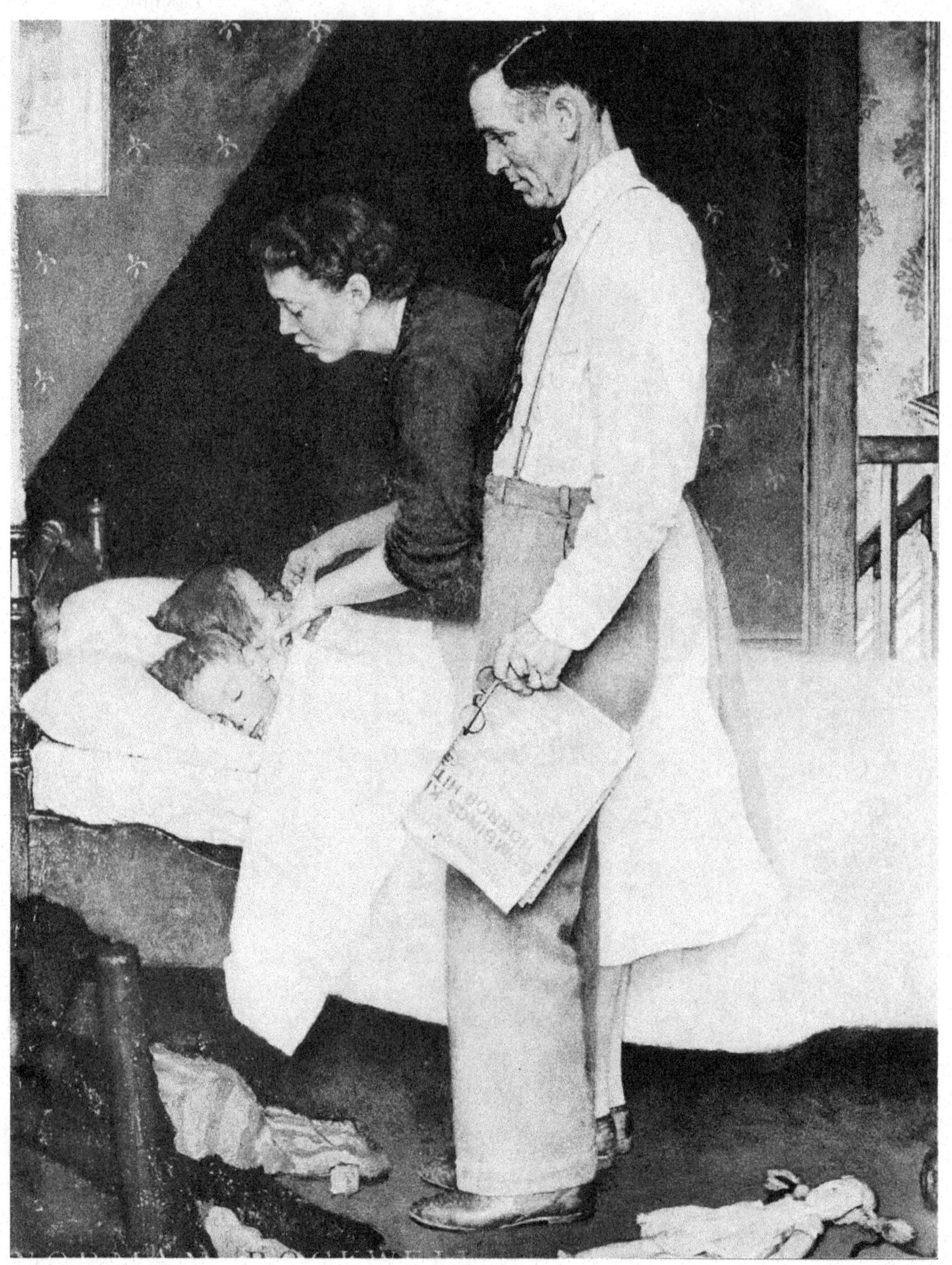

Freedom from Fear

→ DOCUMENT 19.3a ←

War poster, *United We Win,* 1943, based on a photograph by Alexander Liberman. Printed by Government Printing Office for the War Manpower Commission. NARA Still Picture Branch (NWDNS-44-PA-370). National Archives and Records Administration.

❖ DOCUMENT 19.3b ❖

War poster, *Above and Beyond the Call of Duty,* undated, by David Stone Martin. Printed by Government Printing Office for the Office of War Information. NARA Still Picture Branch (NWDNS-208-PMP-68). National Archives and Records Administration.

✧ DOCUMENT 19.3c ✧

War poster, *Man the Guns—Join the Navy,* 1942, by McClelland Barclay. Produced for the Navy Recruiting Bureau, NARA Still Picture Branch (NWDNS-44-PA-24). National Archives and Records Administration.

➛ DOCUMENT 19.3d ➛

War poster, *You Talk of Sacrifice,* undated, produced by Winchester. NARA Still Picture Branch (NWDNS-179-WP-1386). National Archives and Records Administration.

→ DOCUMENT 19.4 ←

March on Washington flier, 1941. A. Philip Randolph Papers, Manuscript Division (8-8), A. Philip Randolph Institute, Washington, DC.

WHY SHOULD WE MARCH?

15,000 Negroes Assembled at St. Louis, Missouri
20,000 Negroes Assembled at Chicago, Illinois
23,500 Negroes Assembled at New York City
Millions of Negro Americans all Over This Great Land Claim the Right to be Free!

FREE FROM WANT!
FREE FROM FEAR!
FREE FROM JIM CROW!

"Winning Democracy for the Negro is Winning the War for Democracy!" — A. Philip Randolph

What Are Our Immediate Goals?

1. To mobilize five million Negroes into one militant mass for pressure.
2. To assemble in Chicago the last week in May, 1943, for the celebration of

"WE ARE AMERICANS - TOO" WEEK

And to ponder the question of Non-Violent Civil Disobedience and Non-Cooperation, and a Mass March On Washington.

DOCUMENT 19.5

Oral interview with Robert Rasmus, in Studs Terkel, *"The Good War": An Oral History of World War II* (New York: Pantheon, 1984), pp. 38–41. By permission of Studs Terkel.

Robert Rasmus

I've lived about thirty-eight years after the war and about twenty years before. For me it's B.W. and A.W.—before the war and after the war. I suspect there are a lot of people like me. In business, there'll be times when I say, This really worries the heck out of me, but it's really minor compared to having to do a river crossing under fire. (Laughs.)

He is six feet four or five, graying. He is a business executive, working out of Chicago. Obviously he's kept himself in pretty good shape. His manner is gentle, easy, unruffled.

I get this strange feeling of living through a world drama. In September of '39 when the Germans invaded Poland, I was fourteen years old. I remember my mother saying, "Bob, you'll be in it." I was hoping she'd be right. At that age, you look forward to the glamour and have no idea of the horrors.

Sure enough, I was not only in the army but in the infantry. Step by logistic step, our division was in combat. You're finally down to one squad, out ahead of the whole thing. You're the point man. What am I doing out here—in this world-cataclysmic drama—out in front of the whole thing? (Laughs.)

You saw those things in the movies, you saw the newsreels. But you were of an age when your country wasn't even in the war. It seemed unreal. All of a sudden, there you were right in the thick of it and people were dying and you were scared out of your wits that you'd have your head blown off. (Laughs.)

I was acutely aware, being a rifleman, the odds were high that I would be killed. At one level, animal fear. I didn't like that at all. On the other hand, I had this great sense of adventure. My gosh, going across the ocean, seeing the armies, the excitement of it. I was there. . . .

When I went in the army, I'd never been outside the states of Wisconsin, Indiana, and Michigan. So when I woke up the first morning on the troop train in Fulton, Kentucky, I thought I was in Timbuktu. Of course, I was absolutely bowled over by Europe, the castles, the cathedrals, the Alps. It was wonderment. I was preoccupied with staying alive and doing my job, but it seemed, out of the corner of my eye, I was constantly fascinated with the beauty of the German forests and medieval bell towers. At nineteen, you're seeing life with fresh eyes.

The first time I ever heard a New England accent was at Fort Benning. The southerner was an exotic creature to me. People from the farms. The New York street-smarts. You had an incredible mixture of every stratum of society. And you're of that age when your need for friendship is greatest. I still see a number of these people. There's sort of a special sense of kinship. . . .

. . . I was only in combat for six weeks, but I could remember every hour, every minute of the whole forty-two days.

In Boston Harbor, we actually saw the first visible sign of the war: an Australian cruiser tied up next to the troop ship. There was a huge, jagged hole in the bow. The shape of things to come. There was a lot of bravado, kidding. . . .

I was sort of schizophrenic all through this period. I was a participant, scared out of my wits. But I was also acutely aware of how really theatrical and surreal it was.

Three days later we pulled out, crossed the Rhine, and cut off a German pocket. As we were moving out of this area of sheared-off buildings, there were courtyards with fruit trees in blossom. And there were our heavy mortars blasting away across the river. I had been seeing shadowy figures moving around. Were they infiltrators or just a bush that I was imagining? And there in sight was the Cologne cathedral amidst all this wreckage.

We've seen a little of the war now. We've seen planes dropping bombs over on the other side. We've sent out patrols, have captured prisoners. But we really hadn't been in it ourselves. It was still fun and dramatics. When the truck took us from Cologne south through Bonn, for me it was, Hey, Beethoven's birthplace! But when we crossed a pontoon bridge and I saw a balloon of fire, I knew the real combat was going to begin. I had the feeling now that we were gonna be under direct fire, some of us were gonna be killed. But I was also enormously affected by the beauty of the countryside. We were in rolling hills and great forests. It stretched out for mile after mile. I could almost hear this Wagnerian music. I was pulled in two directions: Gee, I don't wanna get killed. And, Boy, this is gorgeous country.

Our uniforms were still clean. We were still young kids who hadn't seen anything. You could see these veteran troops. Their uniforms were dirty, they were bearded, there was a look in their eyes that said they'd been through a lot. A sort of expression on their faces—You're gonna find out now. A mixture of pity and contempt for the greenhorns.

We started seeing our first dead, Germans. You drew the obvious inference: if Germans were dead, the Americans were getting killed farther up the line. Night fell, we were up within a couple of miles of where the action would begin. We were passing through our artillery emplacements. Incessant firing. It was reassuring to see how much artillery we had, but disturbing to see all these German dead. I had never seen a dead body before, except in a funeral home.

We were told that the next morning we would be on the attack. I remember the miserable cold. By this time, I had taken up cigarette smoking, wondering what my mother would think when I came back. (Laughs.) I felt sickish, I was cold, I was scared. And I couldn't even get one last cigarette.

We were awakened before dawn. I honestly don't know whether I dreamed it or whether it really happened. I've asked buddies I've seen since the war: Can you remember these ambulances and army surgeons getting their gear out? I have such an absolute recollection of it, but nobody else remembers it. It had a dreamlike quality: just seeing surgeons ready to work. Here we were still healthy, still an hour or two away from actual combat. It added to the inevitability that really bad, bad things were going to happen.

Our platoon of thirty men was to take a small town. At the time, I was a bazooka man. I'll never forget that sense of unreality as we were moving through the woods to this village, which we could just see a few hundred yards away. There were sheep grazing in the fields. By now there's gunfire: machine guns, rifle fire, mortar shells.

You'd lost your sense of direction. This was not a continuous front. These were piercing, probing actions. You'd take a town, then to the next river, then across the river and then the next one. This was the first. Now I can see actual mortar shells landing in this meadow. German 88s. They were hitting the tile roofs of these houses and barns. My initial reaction: they're not hurting anything. Oh, a few tiles being knocked loose, but it's still a beautiful sunny day. The meadow is lovely. Here we are in a medieval village. This reaction lasted three seconds. These sheep started getting hit. You were seeing blood. Immediately you say, Soon it's gonna be us torn up like these animals. You sense all these stages you've gone through. And now (laughs), the curtain has gone up and you're really in it.

We captured that town without any casualties. I think the German troops had moved out. My confidence is coming back a little. Gee, we captured a town and didn't even see a German. Later that afternoon, we were moving up to take another town. We have a sense that things aren't going too well. We seem out of radio contact with the other rifle companies. I sense an apprehension by our officers.

All of a sudden, we spotted a group of German soldiers down by the slope of this hill, perhaps fifty. We were strung out, a couple of platoons. We would be on the ground, get up on command, and start firing right into this group of Germans. We did catch them by surprise. They responded quickly, firing back, machine guns and rifles. We had them well outnumbered, our company, about 240. We did the march-and-fire. It was a new maneuver we'd never done in training. We learned. I noticed that some of our guys were getting hit. It was all in a few minutes. We killed most of the Germans. A few might have gotten away, but we wiped them out. Our guys were getting killed, too. Irony again, the first one killed was our platoon sergeant.

You have to understand the culture of our company. Most of our privates were college types. They had been dumped en masse into these infantry divisions. The cadre of noncommissioned officers were old-timers. They were mostly uneducated country types, many of them from the South. There was a rather healthy mutual contempt between the noncoms and the privates. This sergeant was the most hated man. One of the nineteen-year-olds, during maneuvers, was at the point of tears in his hatred of this man who was so unreasonable and so miserable. He'd say, "If we ever get into combat, I'm gonna kill 'im. First thing I'll do." Who's the first one killed? This sergeant. I'm sure it was enemy fire. I would bet my life on it. I'm sure the guys who said they would kill him were horrified that their wish came true.

→ DOCUMENT 19.6 ←

Oral interview with Timuel Black, in Studs Terkel, *"The Good War": An Oral History of World War II* (New York: Pantheon, 1984), pp. 278–281. By permission of Studs Terkel.

Timuel Black

A Chicago schoolteacher.

We had met on the train to Washington heading for the 1963 Civil Rights March. "This reminds me of one other experience: the liberation of Paris. The exhilaration, the exuberance of the French people. We marched down to Paris, after giving the FFI—the French Forces of the Interior—the symbolic right to free the city. As bedraggled as we were with dirty and dusty uniforms, all these people were paying tribute. Not to us, the American soldiers, but to the idea of freedom. The firin' was still going on in the streets. The FFI was chasin' the last of the German snipers. The Champs-Elysées, on that day, was an experience I'll never forget."

I was drafted in 1943, right after the Chicago and Detroit riots. We had this influx of war workers, both white and black, from the South, especially in Detroit. The tensions continued to mount until they exploded. We weren't talking about integration. Should the blacks or whites have the Brewster Homes? That was the new housing project in Detroit. There was no place for black young men, who'd been ignored, left to the side. Suddenly, they were soldiers. In a very segregated army, of course.

My father said, "What the hell are you goin' to fight in Europe for. The fight is here. You should be goin' up to Detroit." He was a militant kind of guy. He would've gone with me. We couldn't get to Detroit, though we had relatives there. The buses and trains were carefully screened. The roads were blocked. Right after that, they began to sweep the streets clean of all eligible young black people by the draft. They had just begun to let blacks in the navy in menial positions.

I went to Camp Custer, Michigan, for induction and then to Camp Lee in Virginia. All officers were white. We had done well enough on the AGCT, the Army General Classification Test. We believed we should have been officers. If you scored over a certain level, you could apply to OCS. I took one of those tests and I know I did well. We knew all our scores. Very often, our noncoms had access to those records and we'd find out. We could look at the records and see that we'd scored well on our first attempt. All black soldiers got was one attempt. Some of our superior officers had taken the exam two or three times. Can you imagine the kind of tensions set up between the white guy who is giving you orders and the black guy who has to take those orders, when both of them know the black guy has superior qualifications?

Most black GIs were put in the Quartermaster Corps. I was. We handled supplies: food, clothing, equipage. In Europe, we handled ammunition, too. We were really stevedores. Many of those young blacks wanted to be in combat units. I went into Normandy with combat troops. We serviced them.

Generally they made illiterate blacks from the South the noncommissioned officers to be over us, who had more education. Most of us were from the North. Here you have a somewhat resentful southern black guy, glad to have a chance to kick this arrogant northern city slicker around. (Laughs.) Deep underneath, those of us who came from New York, Chicago, and Detroit did consider ourselves a little better than our southern less-well-educated brothers. We did carry that attitude of haughtiness.

We were shipped overseas. On board, blacks had their quarters and the whites had theirs. We didn't associate with one another. Different mess halls, different everything. We zigzagged our way all across the Atlantic, because of the German subs. We stayed in Wales, getting ready for the invasion.

Black soldiers and white soldiers could not go to the same town. The ordinary British were absolutely amazed, looking at these two armies. I guess they hadn't thought about their two armies, too: the colonial and the regular. But they were chagrined by this racial situation, which they'd never seen. White soldiers would say, Don't have anything to do with those niggers. They have tails, they howl at night, all kinds of funny stories. Very often if we got into fights, the British guys and gals would be on our side. (Laughs.)

Blacks were given the least desirable towns to go to. Often, some of our more aggressive young men would say, I'm goin' to the nice town. I'm not gonna go to that crummy town. They'd have a conflict. We were fightin' a war before we went to the real war.

If a young black fellow, eighteen years old, would get together with a British girl, sixteen, that girl would be encouraged to say she was raped. We had a number of young black soldiers who were hanged. We had one in our outfit who was hanged.

We're getting ready now for the main battle. We're taken down now close to Southampton in great secrecy. Our outfit was originally assigned to go in D-Day, but they took another QM group. Our guys were disappointed, except me. I didn't want to do that. (Laughs.) Two days later, we went in. We went into Utah Beach. Omaha was the hot one, but Utah was hot enough for me.

It was a weird experience. Young men cryin' for their mothers, wetting and defecating themselves. Others tellin' jokes. Most of us were just solemn. I was thinking, Boy, if I get through this, it'll never happen to me again. What happens when you finally get off this LST? All you know is you wade into that beach. You hear the big guns.

The Germans aimed at our supplies. We were direct targets. I been on six-by-six trucks many nights when the Luftwaffe was strafing us. We had good air cover. But it didn't feel good when they were droppin' those small bombs and firin' those machine guns at us. We lost a few fellas.

We were responsible for keeping the German saboteurs from blowing up our ammunition dump. If they had gotten us, we would have been pushed right back into the beach. The Germans had dropped young fellas who lived in places like New York and Chicago and spoke perfect English. They could talk about the Brooklyn Dodgers and the White Sox. You couldn't distinguish them from Americans. You didn't know whether the white person was an American soldier or a German saboteur. They were really crack troops.

They had to take all the white American soldiers off the streets at night and use the black soldiers to do patrol duty. If there was a white person on the street at night, we had orders to pick him up or shoot him. We were doing double duty. Keep the supplies movin' and patrol at night. My whole outfit was decorated with the Croix de Guerre.

We stayed in Normandy until Patton came through. We went from Normandy to Brittany and moved toward Paris. And we came there on this beautiful day. How can I describe it? Know how I know they'd retained hope and dreams? They'd buried their jazz records of people like Louis Armstrong and Duke Ellington and Coleman Hawkins. (Laughs.) They said, (tries a French accent) "M'sieur, ze music, le jazz." They hugged and embraced us. It was the feeling of acceptance. I seriously considered not returning to the United States. They respected something from my own culture so openly, jazz music. I said, God, what kind of craziness am I involved in? It was an eye-opening experience.

We were in Belgium during the Battle of the Bulge. We were at one time feeding three million soldiers: the First, the Third, the Ninth, and the British Seventh. We used German prisoners to do our loading. Some weren't bad, but there were a lot who were arrogant, who considered us inferior.

Often white officers accepted their interpretation. It was frustrating. One time I had a bale of fatigues that had to be carried from one place to another. This German chap refused. I knew he was friendly with our lieutenant. He said, "You can't tell me what to do, you're a black man." I insisted. He resisted. I put the bale on his back, as he was at the top of the stairs, and I put my foot to his behind. He tumbled all the way down, and the bale followed him very quickly. I was reprimanded by the officers for mistreating a prisoner. But they never considered his mistreatment of me as his superior in this situation.

Guys like me were constantly on the spot. On one end, some of my black brothers felt I was endangering them. They were getting away with things by sneaking around, and I wanted to do things because I was an American soldier and wanted fair treatment. On the other end, the officers resented what I did. It was very lonely.

⟡ DOCUMENT 19.7 ⟡

Photograph of the Buss family, 1942. Private property of Kathy Frederick.

→ DOCUMENT 19.8 ←

Oral interview with Peggy Terry, in Studs Terkel, *"The Good War": An Oral History of World War II* (New York: Pantheon, 1984), pp. 108–111. By permission of Studs Terkel.

Peggy Terry

She is a mountain woman who has lived in Chicago for the past twenty years. Paducah, Kentucky is her hometown. She visits it as often as her meager purse allows.

The first work I had after the Depression was at a shell-loading plant in Viola, Kentucky. It is between Paducah and Mayfield. They were large shells: anti-aircraft, incendiaries, and tracers. We painted red on the tips of the tracers. My mother, my sister, and myself worked there. Each of us worked a different shift because we had little ones at home. We made the fabulous sum of thirty-two dollars a week. (Laughs.) To us it was just an absolute miracle. Before that, we made nothing.

You won't believe how incredibly ignorant I was. I knew vaguely that a war had started, but I had no idea what it meant.

Didn't you have a radio?

Gosh, no. That was an absolute luxury. We were just moving around, working wherever we could find work. I was eighteen. My husband was nineteen. We were living day to day. When you are involved in stayin' alive, you don't think about big things like a war. It didn't occur to us that we were making these shells to kill people. It never entered my head.

There were no women foremen where we worked. We were just a bunch of hillbilly women laughin' and talkin'. It was like a social. Now we'd have money to buy shoes and a dress and pay rent and get some food on the table. We were just happy to have work.

I worked in building number 11. I pulled a lot of gadgets on a machine. The shell slid under and powder went into it. Another lever you pulled tamped it down. Then it moved on a conveyer belt to another building where the detonator was dropped in. You did this over and over.

Tetryl was one of the ingredients and it turned us orange. Just as orange as an orange. Our hair was streaked orange. Our hands, our face, our neck just turned orange, even our eyeballs. We never questioned. None of us ever asked, What is this? Is this harmful? We simply didn't think about it. That was just one of the conditions of the job. The only thing we worried about was other women thinking we had dyed our hair. Back then it was a disgrace if you dyed your hair. We worried what people would say.

We used to laugh about it on the bus. It eventually wore off. But I seem to remember some of the women had breathing problems. The shells were painted a dark gray. When the paint didn't come out smooth, we had to take rags wet with some kind of remover and wash that paint off. The fumes from these rags—it was like breathing cleaning fluid. It burned the nose and throat. Oh, it was difficult to breathe. I remember that.

Nothing ever blew up, but I remember the building where they dropped in the detonator. These detonators are little black things about the size of a thumb. This terrible thunderstorm came and all the lights went out. Somebody knocked a box of detonators off on the floor. Here we were in the pitch dark. Somebody was screaming, "Don't move, anybody!" They were afraid you'd step on the detonator. We were down on our hands and knees crawling out of that building in the storm. (Laughs.) We were in slow motion. If we'd stepped on one. . . .

Mamma was what they call terminated—fired. Mamma's mother took sick and died and Mamma asked for time off and they told her no. Mamma said, "Well, I'm gonna be with my mamma. If I have to give up my job, I will just have to." So they terminated Mamma. That's when I started gettin' nasty. I didn't take as much baloney and pushing around as I had taken. I told 'em I was gonna quit, and they told me if I quit they would blacklist me wherever I would go. They had my fingerprints and all that. I guess it was just bluff, because I did get other work.

I think of how little we knew of human rights, union rights. We knew Daddy had been a hell-raiser in the mine workers' union, but at that point it hadn't rubbed off on any of us women. Coca-Cola and Dr. Pepper were allowed in every building, but not a drop of water. You could only get a drink of water if you went to the cafeteria, which was about two city blocks away. Of course you couldn't leave your machine long enough to go get a drink. I drank Coke and Dr. Pepper and I hated 'em. I hate 'em today. We had to buy it, of course. We couldn't leave to go to the bathroom, 'cause it was way the heck over there.

We were awarded the navy E for excellence. We were just so proud of that E. It was like we were a big family, and we hugged and kissed each other. They had the navy band out there celebrating us. We were so proud of ourselves.

First time my mother ever worked at anything except in the fields—first real job Mamma ever had. It was a big break in everybody's life. Once, Mamma woke up in the middle of the night to go to the bathroom and she saw the bus going down. She said, "Oh my goodness, I've overslept." She jerked her clothes on, throwed her lunch in the bag, and was out on the corner, ready to go, when Boy Blue, our driver, said, "Honey, this is the wrong shift." Mamma wasn't supposed to be there until six in the morning. She never lived that down. She would have enjoyed telling you that.

My world was really very small. When we came from Oklahoma to Paducah, that was like a journey to the center of the earth. It was during the Depression and you did good having bus fare to get across town. The war just widened my world. Especially after I came up to Michigan.

My grandfather went up to Jackson, Michigan, after he retired from the railroad. He wrote back and told us we could make twice as much in the war plants in Jackson. We did. We made ninety dollars a week. We did some kind of testing for airplane radios.

Ohh, I met all those wonderful Polacks. They were the first people I'd ever known that were any different from me. A whole new world just opened up. I learned to drink beer like crazy with 'em. They were all very union-conscious. I learned a lot of things that I didn't even know existed.

We were very patriotic and we understood that the Nazis were someone who would have to be stopped. We didn't know about concentration camps. I don't think anybody I knew did. With the Japanese, that was a whole different thing. We were just ready to wipe them out. They sure as heck didn't look like us. They were yellow little creatures that smiled when they bombed our boys. I remember someone in Paducah got up this idea of burning everything they had that was Japanese. I had this little ceramic cat and I said, "I don't care, I am not burning it." They had this big bonfire and people came and brought what they had that was made in Japan. Threw it on the bonfire. I hid my cat. It's on the shelf in my bathroom right now. (Laughs.)

In all the movies we saw, the Germans were always tall and handsome. There'd be one meanie, a little short dumpy bad Nazi. But the main characters were good-lookin' and they looked like us. The Japanese were all evil. If you can go half your life and not recognize how you're being manipulated, that is sad and kinda scary.

I do remember a nice movie, *The White Cliffs of Dover.* We all sat there with tears pouring down our face. All my life, I hated England, 'cause all my family all my life had wanted England out of Ireland. During the war, all those ill feelings just seemed to go away. It took a war.

I believe the war was the beginning of my seeing things. You just can't stay uninvolved and not knowing when such a momentous thing is happening. It's just little things that start happening and you put one piece with another. Suddenly, a puzzle begins to take shape.

My husband was a paratrooper in the war, in the 101st Airborne Division. He made twenty-six drops in France, North Africa, and Germany. I look back at the war with sadness. I wasn't smart enough to think too deeply then. We had a lotta good times and we had money and we had food on the table and the rent was paid. Which had never happened to us before. But when I look back and think of him. . . .

Until the war he never drank. He never even smoked. When he came back he was an absolute drunkard. And he used to have the most awful nightmares. He'd get up in the middle of the night and start screaming. I'd just sit for hours and hold him while he just shook. We'd go to the movies, and if they'd have films with a lot of shooting in it, he'd just start to shake and have to get up and leave. He started slapping me around and slapped the kids around. He became a brute.

→ DOCUMENT 19.9 ←

Photograph of women working on the fuselage of a bomber aircraft during WWII, photo by Howard R. Hollem, October 1942. Library of Congress.

→ DOCUMENT 19.10a ←

Photograph of Japanese internment camp meal line, June 12, 1942, Puyallup, Washington. © Seattle Post-Intelligencer Collection, Museum of History & Industry/CORBIS.

→ DOCUMENT 19.10b ←

Poem about a relocation camp, undated, author unknown, in Deborah Gesenway and Mindy Roseman, *Beyond Words: Images from America's Concentration Camps* (Ithaca: Cornell U. Press, 1987), pp. 64–65. "That Damned Fence" from the Japanese Relocation Centers Records, #3830. By permission of the Division of Rare Book and Manuscript Collections, Cornell University Library.

THAT DAMNED FENCE

They've sunk in posts deep into the ground,
They've strung wires all the way around.
With machine gun nests just over there,
And sentries and soldiers everywhere!

We're trapped like rats in a wired cage
To fret and fume with impotent rage;
Yonder whispers the lure of the night
But that DAMNED FENCE assails our sight.

We seek the softness of the midnight air,
But that DAMNED FENCE in the floodlight glare
Awakens unrest in our nocturnal quest,
And mockingly laughs with vicious jest.

With nowhere to go and nothing to do,
We feel terrible, lonesome, and blue;
That DAMNED FENCE is driving us crazy,
Destroying our youth and making us lazy.

Imprisoned in here for a long, long time,
We know we're punished though we've committed no crime
Our thoughts are gloomy and enthusiasm damp;
To be locked up in a concentration camp.

Loyalty we know and patriotism we feel,
To sacrifice our utmost was our ideal.
To fight for our country, and die, mayhap;
Yet we're here because we happen to be a Jap.

We all love life, and our country best,
Our misfortune's to be here in the west;
To keep us penned behind that DAMNED FENCE
Is someone's notion of National Defense!!!

—Anonymous

→ DOCUMENT 19.11 ←

Oral interview with Peter Ota, in Studs Terkel, "*The Good War*": *An Oral History of World War II* (New York: Pantheon, 1984), pp. 28–33. By permission of Studs Terkel.

Peter Ota

He is a fifty-seven-year-old Nisei. His father had come from Okinawa in 1904, his mother from Japan. He's an accountant. His father had worked on farms and in the coal mines of Mexico. After thirty-seven years building a fruit and vegetable business, he had become a successful and respected merchant in the community. He was a leader in the Japanese Chamber of Commerce of Los Angeles.

On the evening of December 7, 1941, my father was at a wedding. He was dressed in a tuxedo. When the reception was over, the FBI agents were waiting. They rounded up at least a dozen wedding guests and took 'em to county jail.

For a few days we didn't know what happened. We heard nothing. When we found out, my mother, my sister, and myself went to jail. I can still remember waiting in the lobby. When my father walked through the door, my mother was so humiliated. She didn't say anything. She cried. He was in prisoner's clothing, with a denim jacket and a number on the back.

The shame and humiliation just broke her down. She was into Japanese culture. She was a flower arranger and used to play the *biwa,* a Japanese stringed instrument. Shame in her culture is worse than death. Right after that day she got very ill and contracted tuberculosis. She had to be sent to a sanitarium. She stayed behind when we were evacuated. She was too ill to be moved. She was there till she passed away.

My father was transferred to Missoula, Montana. We got letters from him—censored, of course—telling us he was all right. It was just my sister and myself. I was fifteen, she was twelve. In April 1942, we were evacuated to Santa Anita. At the time we didn't know where we were going, how long we'd be gone. We didn't know what to take. A toothbrush, toilet supplies, some clothes. Only what you could carry. We left with a caravan.

Santa Anita is a race track. The horse stables were converted into living quarters. My sister and I were fortunate enough to stay in a barracks. The people in the stables had to live with the stench. Everything was communal. We had absolutely no privacy. When you went to the toilet, it was communal. It was very embarrassing for women especially. The parent actually lost control of the child. I had no parents, so I did as I pleased. When I think back what happened to the Japanese family. . . .

We had orders to leave Santa Anita in September of 1942. We had no idea where we were going. Just before we left, my father joined us. He was brought into camp on the back of an army state truck, he and several others who were released from Missoula. I can still picture it to this day: to come in like cattle or sheep being herded in the back of a pickup truck bed. We were near the gate and saw him come in. He saw us. It was a sad, happy moment, because we'd been separated for a year.

He never really expressed what his true inner feelings were. It just amazes me. He was never vindictive about it, never showed any anger. I can't understand that. A man who had worked so hard for what he had and lost it overnight. There is a very strong word in Japanese, *gaman.* It means to persevere. Old people instilled this into the second generation: You persevere. Take what's coming, don't react.

He had been a very outgoing person. Enthusiastic. I was very, very impressed with how he ran things and worked with people. When I saw him at Santa Anita, he was a different person.

We were put on a train, three of us and many trains of others. It was crowded. The shades were drawn. During the ride we were wondering, what are they going to do to us? We Niseis had enough confidence in our government that it wouldn't do anything drastic. My father had put all his faith in this country. This was his land.

Oh, it took days. We arrived in Amache, Colorado. That was an experience in itself. We were right near the Kansas border. It's a desolate, flat, barren area. The barracks was all there was. There were no trees, no kind of landscaping. It was like a prison camp. Coming from our environment, it was just devastating.

School in camp was a joke. Let's say it was loose. If you wanted to study, fine. If you didn't, who cared? There were some teachers who were conscientious and a lot who were not. One of our basic subjects was American history. They talked about freedom all the time. (Laughs.)

After a year, I was sent out to Utah on jobs. I worked on sugar beet farms. You had to have a contract or a job in order to leave camp. The pay was nominal. We would have a labor boss, the farmer would pay us through him. It was piecework. Maybe fifteen of us would work during the harvest season. When it was over, we went back to camp.

If you had a job waiting, you could relocate to a city that was not in the Western Defense Command. I had one in Chicago, as a stock boy in a candy factory. It paid seventy-five cents an hour. I was only in camp for a year. My sister was in until they were dismantled, about three and a half years. My father was in various camps for four years.

I went from job to job for a year. I had turned draft age, so I had to register. It's ironic. Here I am being drafted into the army, and my father and sister are in a concentration camp waiting for the war to end.

I was in the reserve, not yet inducted, in the middle of 1944, when I received a wire from my father saying that my mother was very ill. I immediately left Chicago for Amache, Colorado, to get my clearance from the Western Defense Command. It took several days. While I was waiting, my mother passed away.

Since we wanted her funeral to be at the camp where my father and sister were, I decided to go on to California and pick up her remains. At Needles, California, I was met at the train by an FBI agent. He was assigned to me. He was with me at all times during my stay there. Whether I went to sleep at night or whether I went to the bathroom, he was by my side.

As soon as we stepped off the train at the Union Station in Los Angeles, there was a shore patrol and a military police who met me. They escorted me through the station. It was one of the most . . . (He finds it difficult to talk.) I don't even know how to describe it. Any day now, I'd be serving in the same uniform as these people who were guarding me. The train stations at that time were always filled. When they marched me through, the people recognized me as being Oriental. They knew I was either an escaped prisoner or a spy. Oh, they called out names. I heard "dirty Jap" very distinctly.

After we got to the hotel, the FBI agent convinced the military that it wasn't necessary for them to stay with me. But he had to. He was disgusted with the whole situation. He knew I was in the reserve, that I was an American citizen. He could see no reason for him to be with me. But he was on assignment. We spoke personal things. His wife was having a baby, he couldn't be with her. He thought it was ridiculous.

I was in the armored division at Fort Knox. We were sent to Fort Mead for embarkation when the European war ended. They didn't know what to do with us Japanese Americans. We were in our own units. Should they send us to the Pacific side? They might not be able to tell who was the enemy and who was not. (Laughs.)

The war ended while I was at Fort McDowell on San Francisco Bay. That was the receiving point for Japanese prisoners captured in the war. I went back with a boatload of them. I didn't know how they'd react to me. I was very surprised. The professional soldiers who were captured during the early days of the war in Guadalcanal, Saipan, never believed the war ended. They would always say, when the subject came up, it was propaganda. The civilian soldiers were very different. We could get along with them. They were very young—*boheitai,* boy soldiers. We could relate to them as to children. They were scared. They had nothing to go back to. Okinawa was devastated. A lot of them lost their families.

My furloughs were spent in camp, visiting my father and sister. Going to camp was like going home for me, to see my family. We made the best of what we had. We celebrated Christmas in the American fashion. We tried to make our lives go easy.

We came back to Los Angeles at the end of the war, believing that there was no other way but to be American. We were discouraged with our Japanese culture. My feeling at the time was, I had to prove myself. I don't know why I had to prove myself. Here I am, an ex-GI, born and raised here. Why do I have to prove myself? We all had this feeling. We had to prove that we were Americans, okay?

✧ DOCUMENT 19.12 ✧

Illustration picturing the postwar world, 1943, from *Revere's Part in Better Living,* no. 10, 1943.

"After total war
can come total living"

→ ARCHIVE 20 ←

Social and Cultural Life in a Mass Society

Archive Overview

THE United States emerged from World War II victorious, prosperous, and with astounding productive capacity. As the hot war turned into the Cold War, mass consumption, high materialistic expectations, and strong pressures for social conformity turned America into a mass society. It was in this society that your grandparents or perhaps your parents grew up, so you may have your own sources who can tell you what it was like to see Elvis Presley on the Ed Sullivan show, to hear the Supremes on the radio, and to see James Dean on the movie screen. You already know what it is like to get a hamburger at McDonald's—which started the fast food chain restaurant mania in the mid 1950s.

What is a "mass society" and what does "mass culture" look like? The sources in this archive will allow you to define the meanings of mass society and mass culture in the 1950s. As you move toward this definition, consider how the following questions contribute to your efforts to understand these two phenomena. What kinds of evidence suggest conformity and homogeneity in certain areas of American life, and what kinds hint at difference and disagreement? What insights do the sources reveal about the hopes, fears, and values of Americans in the 1950s? To what extent do you find signs of tensions between confidence and insecurity, between high art and popular art, between the individual and society? How does a consideration of race affect ideas of conformity and "mass culture"?

Placing the Sources in Context

IN 1941 Henry Luce, publisher of *Time*, *Life*, and *Fortune* magazines, advised readers to prepare for "the American Century." As "the most powerful and vital nation in the world," Luce declared, the United States must "exert upon the world the full impact of our influence, for such purposes as we see fit." Following the allied victory in World War II and the return to a peacetime economy, the country pursued Luce's objective.

America at midcentury undoubtedly was a mass society. Soldiers returned from the European and Pacific fronts, rejoined their families or married, went to college on the GI Bill, built homes of their own in suburban tract developments, and joined what the sociologist David Riesman called "the lonely crowd." Most people adapted to the urban, industrial, and large-scale character of American life, accepted the impersonality that went along with it, and shared a common set of cultural experiences conveyed by the mass media, especially television.

TIMELINE

1944	GI Bill
1948	Harry Truman elected president
1949	Soviet Union tests its first nuclear bomb
1950	The McCarran Act; Korean War begins; David Riesman et al., *The Lonely Crowd*
1951	Levittown completed
1952	Dwight D. Eisenhower elected president
1954	Army–McCarthy hearings televised *Brown v. Board of Education*
1955	First McDonald's restaurant opens; Montgomery Bus Boycott
1956	Interstate Highway Act; Chuck Berry's, "Roll Over Beethoven"; Elvis Presley's "Heartbreak Hotel" no. 1 on Hit Parade; Allen Ginsberg's "Howl"
1957	Jack Kerouac's *On the Road*; Russians launch *Sputnik* Desegregation of Little Rock High School
1960	John F. Kennedy elected president; 75 percent of all Americans own TVs

With the maturation of the country's system of mass production and distribution and the forms of mass communication, the distinctive culture of consumption, born earlier in the century, reached ever more deeply into society and characterized ever more people's actual life experiences. Fueled initially by tens of billions of dollars in wartime savings, the twenty-five years after the war was a period of unprecedented affluence for Americans. Real purchasing power (adjusted for inflation) rose by 22 percent between 1946 and 1960, and in 1960 nearly every family owned at least one car, three-quarters of all families had a television set (compared to fewer than 20,000 in 1946), and one-quarter of all existing homes were less than ten years old. These trends fueled the expectation that the consumption of material goods would continue and increase.

Major social changes combined with broad-based consumerism to shape this mass society. The postwar "baby boom" created the largest generational cohort in American history—a demographic reality that will continue to affect American society well into the 21st century. The baby boom meant that many of the women who had entered the workforce during the war now returned to their homes to raise children. Even so, by 1960, 30 percent of married women were employed outside the home. Each year during the 1950s more than a million farmers left agriculture to find other employment.

By the middle of that decade, a majority of American workers had white-collar jobs in corporate, government, and institutional bureaucracies rather than manual jobs in the manufacturing or farm sectors. In conjunction with these employment trends, college enrollments more than doubled, thanks to the GI Bill, between 1940 and 1960. Finally, in search of comfort, security, and friendship with like-minded people, millions of American families, nearly all of them white, moved to the new suburbs, leaving poor, non-white families behind in the inner cities. By 1960, one-third of all Americans lived in suburbs, and central cities were beginning to suffer public neglect and deterioration. Freeways on the new interstate highway system were built around and over urban slums, which rendered the urban poor invisible. All of these changes contributed to the texture of a seemingly homogeneous mass society.

But was social and cultural experience in this mass society actually homogeneous? Did people who lived in similar houses in similar suburbs, who worked at similar kinds of jobs, who watched the same television programs and read the same magazines become a faceless, undifferentiated mass? What about those who did not live in suburbs, work in white-collar jobs, or read mainstream magazines like *Time*, *Life*, *Reader's Digest*, and *The Saturday Evening Post?*

The 1950s also witnessed the beginnings of the Civil Rights movement. In 1954 the Supreme Court ruled that separate or segregated schools were not equal. The following year the Montgomery Bus Boycott began. Racial progress was slow, especially in terms of integrating southern public schools. In 1957, nine black students were barred from Little Rock High School upon the orders of the Arkansas governor, Orval Faubus. When the federal government intervened, the black students were allowed into the school. But the next year, Little Rock voters overwhelmingly decided to close the public high schools in order to block further integration. The schools did not reopen until the following year. In what ways does the emergence of the Civil Rights movement change the ways we might understand "mass society" and "mass culture"?

It may be easy to identify the marks of a mass society; defining what that concept actually means is another matter. These sources will provoke you to think about this problem.

About the Sources

THE first source, drawn from a published essay by the prominent sociologist C. Wright Mills, offers an analysis of mass society. Mills's observations on power, politics, and society attracted much attention. As a Cornell University political scientist explained, "If Mills does not solve the pressing problems of our age, at least he tells us what they are."

Several sources suggest how the widespread availability of different forms of communication linked people together in shared experiences. Popular magazines were one means of mass communication. *The Saturday Evening Post* (20.4b and 20.5b), a large-format, colorful magazine filled with features expressing "the values of ordinary men—cozy domesticity, a sense of humor, a belief in decency and common sense, and faith in free enterprise,"[1] sold between 4 and 5 million copies weekly during the 1950s; only *Reader's Digest*, at 10 million-plus, had a greater circulation. *Time* magazine, the venerable news weekly also represented here (20.4a and 20.6a), had a circulation in the neighborhood of 2 million during this period. Cookbooks (20.2) targeted one segment of American society: women who were in charge of cooking for their families while *Vogue* targeted the fashion conscious. A television script (20.7) and a picture of Elvis Presley (20.6c), whose career received a boost when he appeared live on the Ed Sullivan show, point to the growing importance of this means of communication as increasing numbers of American families acquired TVs. Radio retained its popularity particularly among teens who listened to rock and roll (20.6b) on the radio and who also bought their favorite songs as "singles."

Market research helped to stimulate mass consumption in a mass society. The piece by Ray Kroc (20.3) shows how he adopted and adapted the notion of mass marketing to hamburgers and thereby helped create the fast food industry.

[1] *Time*, January 17, 1969, p. 48.

The final sources focus on the integration of Central High School in Little Rock, Arkansas. Two newspaper photographs (20.8a and b) reveal some of the incidents surrounding the efforts of nine black students to attend the high school. The letter (20.9) from Daisy Miller, president of the Arkansas chapter of the NAACP, describes other difficulties the students faced.

List of Sources

20.1 **C. Wright Mills's analysis of mass media,** from "Mass Media and Public Opinion," in C. Wright Mills, *Power, Politics and People: The Collected Essays of C. Wright Mills* (New York: Oxford U. Press, 1963), pp. 581–585.

20.2 **Cookbook excerpts,** 1948, from Ruth Berolzheimer, ed., *Culinary Arts Institute Encyclopedic Cookbook* (New York: Perigree Books, 1988), pp. 4–7, 64–65. Copyright © 1988 by Perigee. Used by permission of Perigee Books, a division of Penguin Putnam, Inc.

20.3 **An account of the birth of McDonald's,** in Ray Kroc, *Grinding It Out* (Chicago: H. Regnery, 1977), pp. 6–9, 84–86.

20.4a **Magazine advertisement for McCall's showing family togetherness.** *Time*, January 9, 1956, p. 93. Courtesy Gruner + Jahr USA Publishing.

20.4b **Magazine advertisement for International Harvester trucks picturing an American family,** in *The Saturday Evening Post*, June 22, 1957, p. 63. Courtesy International Truck and Engine Corporation. ATA Foundation, Inc., logo appears by permission of American Trucking Associations, Inc.

20.5a **Newspaper advertisement for Halo shampoo,** 1954. *Sunday News*, 1954.

20.5b **Magazine advertisement for Powers fluid foundation,** 1953. *Vogue*, November 1, 1953.

20.6a **Magazine article on the younger generation.** *Time*, November 5, 1951, pp. 46–47. Time Life Syndication.

20.6b **Rock and roll lyrics, "Yakety Yak,"** 1958, words and music by Jerry Leiber and Mike Stoller; sung by the Coasters, "The Coasters' Greatest Hits," Gusto-PO-310.

20.6c **Photograph of Elvis Presley singing on stage,** June 22, 1956, Hollywood, California. ©Bettmann/CORBIS.

20.7 **A television script, "Living 1950—The Children of Strangers,"** November–December 1950, pp. 2–3, 16–19. Papers of Ben Grauer, Box 55, Columbia University Rare Book and Manuscript Library, New York.

20.8a **Photograph of crowd action at Central High School,** 1957. Photograph by Will Counts for *Arkansas Democrat*, September, 1957.

20.8b **Photograph of Elizabeth Eckford waiting for the bus,** 1957. Photograph by Will Counts for *Arkansas Democrat*, September, 1957.

20.9 **Holograph letter from Daisy Bates to Ray Wilkens,** December 17, 1957. NAACP Collection, Manuscript Division (9–18a), Library of Congress.

Questions to Consider

With such a wide variety of sources at hand, keep in mind the basic questions that you normally ask of a document: Who produced it and for what purpose? Who was the target audience, and how was that audience likely to interpret it? Did the source accurately reflect widely shared sentiment, public opinion, or cultural attitudes? While you are often asked to work with one or two documents at once, in this archive you will be working through all the documents to answer specific questions that will help you to assess the meanings of mass society and mass culture.

1. Read the selection from C. Wright Mills carefully. List the features of mass society as he understood it. How did he feel about mass society? What forces did he see as being primarily responsible for the emergence of mass society?

2. Read through the rest of the sources and find evidence to support the features of mass society Mills describes. Are there signs of the forces he identifies as being responsible for its emergence?

3. Now consider what aspects of the sources do not support Mills's analysis. Do these features properly belong in a definition of mass society, or do they suggest the need to modify our understanding of the scope and meaning of mass society?

4. Which sources provide support for the ideas of conformity and homogeneity in lifestyles, beliefs, and values in the 1950s? How do the sources shed light on gender and age issues? How do the sources present their ideas? Do visuals and text deliver consistent messages?

5. What signs of hopes and fears do the sources give? Choose one source to analyze in detail, showing how it reveals hopes and fears.

6. Can you find evidence for difference and disagreement in the sources? If so, how do you reconcile this evidence with the notions of mass society and mass culture?

7. What does it mean to say that America was a mass society in the 1950s? How would you compare the 1950s with the 1920s (Archive 17)?

8. Would you say that America is a mass society today? Does that concept mean the same thing today as it meant in the 1950s?

MID-20TH CENTURY MASS SOCIETY: THE INTERSTATE HIGHWAY SYSTEM

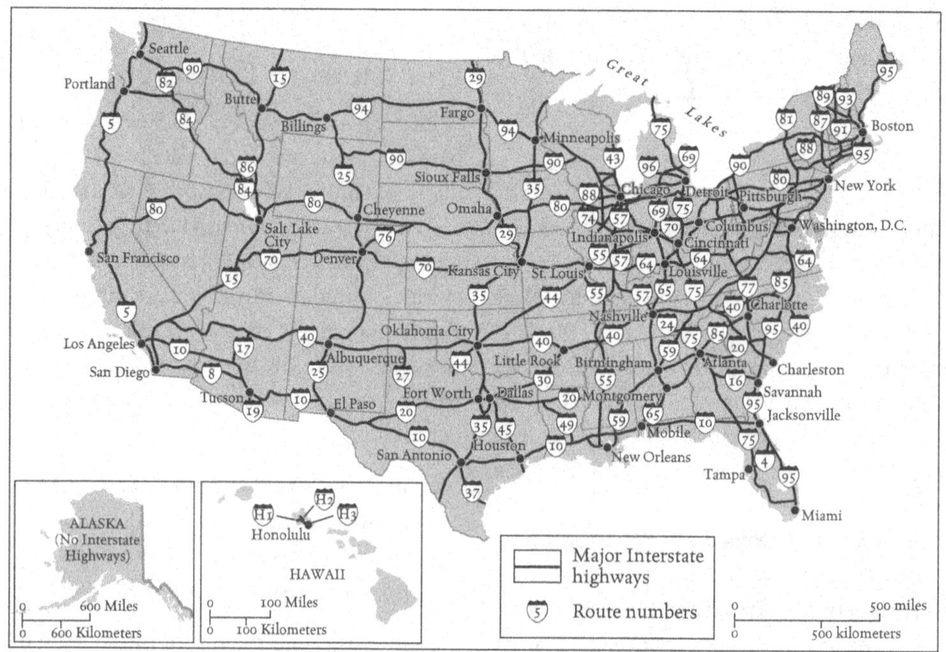

→ DOCUMENT 20.1 ←

C. Wright Mills's analysis of mass media, from "Mass Media and Public Opinion," in C. Wright Mills, *Power, Politics and People: The Collected Essays of C. Wright Mills* (New York: Oxford U. Press, 1963), by C. Wright Mills, edited by Irving Louis Horowitz (New York: Oxford U. Press, 1963), pp.580-585.

. . . [I]t was with the rise of totalitarian states in the twentieth century, in particular with the rise of Naziism, that another view of the public and of public opinion was formed.

The rise of the mass media, especially radio and motion pictures, had already been accompanied by an immense enlargement of the scale of economic and political institutions, and by the apparent relegation of primary face-to-face relationships to secondary place. Institutions become centralized and authoritarian; and media markets gain ascendancy over primary publics. There is, again, an historical parallel between the commodity market in the economic sphere and the public of public opinion in the sphere of opinion. In brief, there is a movement from widely scattered little powers and laissez-faire, to concentrated powers and attempts at monopoly control from powerful centers. And in both centers, economic and opinion, power is partially hidden; they are centers of manipulation as well as of authority.

The small shop serving a small neighborhood is replaced by the anonymity of the national corporation; mass advertisement replaces the personal influence of opinion between merchant and customer. The political leader hooks up his speech to a national network and speaks, with appropriate personal touches, to a million people he never saw and never will see. Entire brackets of professions and industries are in the "opinion business," impersonally manipulating the public for hire.

In the simple democratic society of primary publics, competition of opinions and ideas goes on between people holding the various views which service their special interests and their reasoning. But in the mass society of media markets, competition goes on between the crowd of manipulators with their mass media on the one hand, and the people receiving their communications on the other. "Answering back" by the people is systematically unavailable.

Under such conditions, it is not surprising that a conception of public opinion as a mere impressment or as a reaction—we cannot say "response"—to the content of the mass media should arise. In this view, the public is merely the collectivity of individuals each rather passively exposed to the mass media and rather helplessly opened up to the suggestions and manipulations that flow from these media. The fact of manipulation from centralized points of control constitutes, as it were, an expropriation of the information and change of opinion participated in by the old multitude of little opinion producers and consumers operating in a free and balanced market.

Decisions are made by those in authority. These decisions are then set forth in the media of mass communication. They are impressed upon members of the media markets. They are acted out by official agents of the authorities, but if it is needed to obtain action from others, that action, too, is organized by the authorities in terms of their decision; crowds, selected out from the mass, organized by the authorities, act as adjuncts of the official agents.

Technical conditions of the media make a selection of speakers necessary and, by determining the low ratio of speakers to hearers, limit the chances to answer back. In addition, the authorities of the mass society, which is congruent with the predominance of media markets, attempt to organize *all* communication processes. Public opinion then consists of reactions to what is presented in the formal media of communication; personal discussion does not affect the opinion formulated; each man is an isolated atom reacting alone to the orders and suggestions of the monopolized mass media.

With centralized authority, opinion managers first monopolize the formal means of communication, then strive to set up enforced listening and reading groups. They try to unite media markets and monopolized media so as to insure a disciplined response from the people on the media markets.

But the propagandist with authority is by no means content by his work in the media market. He would enter the primary publics as well. In fact, he may use his authority to terrorize it. He organizes and monopolizes the management of its voluntary organizations. Any institutions or even informal situations which might become the forum of a free discussion circle is broken up. He would atomize those areas of it which are not amenable to his own organizational control. By terrorization and by rules enforced by threats and use of violence, he tries to fragment the public, in order that each individual stands naked of social relations before the media of the authoritative propagandists. Enforce conformity, *Gleichshaltung,* bring them to heel; associate violent threats with standardized, simple symbols or emblems; then surround the individual with these emblems of menace—in this way act constantly on the mass and reinvoke in them the menace. Initiate in the media the menace of propaganda by the deed. This is the mechanism of intimidation, which is skillfully used by various media of communication, from radio to billboard, from movie to sidewalk chalking.

The aim of the regimenters of opinion is to keep the underlying population in continuous emotional subjection, this being more important than the inculcation of specific beliefs; for if the frame of the mind is set for docility in opinion, for obedience in will, the people will be ready to believe and to feel any number of specific beliefs. In this the regimenters work deeper than specific views and emotions; they are trying to modify the basic ideological predisposition of the person. And they want to do this on a mass scale: to make all the population alike in their ideological predisposition, in order that they will all think as it is desired that they think. So, the volume of assertion becomes "stunning;" from all sides and through all senses it converges upon the isolated individual. All power and all social initiative is exercised from above downward.

A mass society involves more than mass communications. The idea implies that multitudes of people participate in various public activities, but that they do so only formally and passively. Action and opinion are one again, and both are rigorously controlled by monopolized media. The authorities provide the opinions and the channels for their realization in activity. People on the media markets hold by mass, the lines of their action being parallel by virtue of their monogeneous opinion, homogeneously impressed by the media. More drastic action may occur when the mass becomes at selected points a temporary crowd, but in all cases public or collective action is guided by institutional authorities. The people, even as they act, are more like spectators than actors. The public of mass society acts, but only by acclamation, by plebiscite. It passively allows; it actively acclaims. Its activity does not spring from its autonomous decision and initiative; it is an implanted reaction to a controlled stimulus presented by centralized management.

Since the public of a mass society is a media market and an activated mass, the discussion phase of the process of opinion formation is virtually eliminated. In it there is less social or informal group cohesion; the institutionalized means of free and informal discussion are fragmentalized; individuals are atomized. There is an affinity between dispersed mass and contagiously juxtaposed crowd. In neither are men joined; opinions, emotions, and drives to act converge by virtue of the common denominator, the homogeneity of readiness to react planlessly to the exciting jerk of symbols and slogans. With the destruction of primary publics and voluntary associations, both the mass and the crowd come into their own.

There are at least four things which taken together characterize the mass ideal-type of "public" in a mass society: (1) The role of mass media is increased and that of discussion circles is decreased. In the extreme, the mass communication industry, pumping opinions to huge media markets, displaces the face-to-face communication systems composed of a multiplicity of primary publics. (2) There is thus a definitive centralization of the opinion process; discussion circles are necessarily small and decentralized; media markets are huge and centralized. (3) The way opinions *change* is more authoritative and manipulative. There is little or no self-regulation on the part of the public. The people in this media market are propagandized: they cannot answer back to the print in the column, the voice on the radio; they cannot even answer back to the media in their immediate circle of co-listeners with ease and without fear. (4) The use of physical and institutional sanctions are involved in opinion process. As Kurt Riezler has remarked: without Himmler's powerful grip, Goebbel's manipulations of opinion would have quickly failed.

Official opinion is thus monopolized by virtue of the centralization and control of mass media, and by enforced listening and reading by means of street mikes, radio jamming, etc. Unofficial opinion is atomized by the fragmentalization of all institutions and occasions for discussion, by the infiltration of every block with opinion fixers, that is, agents of the central authority, and by the systems of "blackmailing" carried on by mutually fearful informers. Recall the headlines: "Nazi Plan of Terror Control of Public Revived in Berlin; Vicious Block System of Tyranny under 40,000 Quasi-Officials . . ." or: "Secret Societies in Japan Unmasked . . . Records Showing that Neighborhood Spies Controlled Thought . . ." Not only people as media markets, but also people as primary publics must be organized in order to make a mass out of a public, and to arrange an opinion process in full accord with such a mass conception.

Any modern society may be regimented into a total mass, or may drift into a mass-like set of performances. To paraphrase Goebbels, in the transition to mass society, the private formation of public opinion, as in the democratic image, is replaced by the public formation of even private opinion. The mass media, as it were, expropriate from individuals in discussion the formulation of opinion.

❖ DOCUMENT 20.2 ❖

Cookbook excerpts, 1948, from Ruth Berolzheimer, ed., *Culinary Arts Institute Encyclopedic Cookbook* (New York: Perigee Books, 1988), pp. 4–7, 64–65.

The Personality of a Cookbook is as apparent as it is important. It is composed of known and stable ingredients with unknown and elusive ones to make a mixture as familiar, friendly and exhilarating as a pine woods early on a summer morn.

The Stable Ingredients are compounded of a sound knowledge of what the homemaker needs for herself and her family; an easy handling of all fundamental facts on preparing and serving foods, based on the science of nutrition up to the date of publication, and on the presentation of those facts in a simple, concise, explicit, well organized, specific, easy-to-follow, step-by-step procedure that gives a comforting feeling of confidence in the final product.

The Elusive Charm of this personality stems from clear overtones: a light touch —a sense of humor—a flair for the clever idea in cooking and serving that results in something called style, but above all a feeling for the kind of beauty that women want about them in their work-a-day world.

Most of This Beauty has been made possible by the cooperation and confidence of colleagues in the food and equipment industry, whose constant flow of inspiring ideas has resulted in illustrations of glorious usefulness. For these the editors are deeply indebted to:

Aluminum Cooking Utensil Company, American Can Company, American Cranberry Exchange, American Dairy Association, American Fruit Growers, Inc., American Gas Association, American Institute of Baking, American Meat Institute, American Molasses Company, American Spice Trade Association, Angelus-Campfire Company, Appalachian Apple Service, Inc., Armour and Company, Ball Brothers Company, Biscuit and Cracker Manufacturers Association, Blueberry Cooperative Association, Booth Fisheries Corporation, Brazil Nut Advertising Fund, Brown County Pottery, Bureau of Industrial Service, Inc., California Extension Service, California Fig Institute, California Food Research Institute, California Fruit Growers Exchange, California Lima Bean Growers Associaton, Campbell Soup Company, Canned Salmon Industry, Carnation Company, Cookware Associates, Corning Glass Works, Corn Products Refining Company, Cranberry Canners, Inc., Cranberry Growers, Inc., Cudahy Packing Company, Cultivated Mushroom Institute of America, Inc., Dixie Vortex Company, Dow Chemical Company, Florida Citrus Commission, Foley Manufacturing Company, Fostoria Glass Company, Frosted Food Sales Co., Gaper Catering Company, Gebhardt Chili Powder Company, General Foods Corporation, Hawaiian Pineapple Company, Hecker Products Corporation, H. J. Heinz Company, Hershey Estates, Hotpoint, Idaho Potato Growers, International Harvester Company, International Silver Company, Evaporated Milk Association, John F. Jelke Company, Kalamazoo Vegetable Parchment Company, Kerr Glass Manufacturing Company, Kraft Foods Company, Land O' Lakes Creameries, Inc., Lenox, Inc., Louisiana State University, Lunt Silversmiths, McGraw Electric Company, Maine Development Commission, Beatrice Foods Co., Miami Beach Gas Company, Milk Foundation, Mirro Aluminum, John Morrell and Company, Muench Kreuzer Candle Company, Inc., National Association Service, National Biscuit Company, National Dairy Council, National Kraut Packers Association, Inc., National Live Stock and Meat Board, National Peach Council, National Peanut Council, National Presto Industries, Inc., National Shrimp Canners Association, New Mexico College of Agriculture and Mechanical Arts, Northwestern Yeast Company, Ohio State University, Oklahoma Agricultural and Mechanical College, Oneida Community, The Palmer House, Pendleton and Dudley, Pennsylvania State College, Peoples Gas Light and Coke Company, Pet Milk Company, Pillsbury Flour Mills, Poultry and Egg National Board, Publicity Associates, Purdue University, Quaker Oats Company, Reed and Barton, Reynolds Metals Company, Robertshaw Thermostat Company, Rumford Chemical Works, St. Charles Custom Kitchens, San Antonio Public Service Company, Sealtest Laboratory Kitchen, South Dakota State College, Standard Brands, Inc., State of Wisconsin, Wisconsin Department of Agriculture, Sunsweet, The Best Foods, Inc., The Borden Company, The Junket Folks, The Kellogg Company, 3-Squares-a-Day Cooking School, United Brewers Industrial Foundation, U. S. Bureau of Human Nutrition and Home Economics, U. S. Bureau of Fisheries, University of Georgia, University of Illinois, University of Minnesota, University of Wisconsin, Utah State Agricultural College, VanCamp Sea Food Company, Vernon Kilns, Washington State Apple Commission, Wesson Oil & Snowdrift Sales Co., West Bend Aluminum Company, Wheat Flour Institute, Wine Institute, Winter Pear Bureau.

Ruth Berolzheimer

The American Family and the American Community have always been food conscious . . . In every section of the country there are special food festivals . . . Fish Frys in the South, Barbecues and Chuck Wagon days in the West, Clambakes in the East and Steak Frys and Weiner Roasts in the North . . . All happy occasions are celebrated with food . . . often very colorfully . . . The etched inserts on the Chapter Title Pages are a salute to many of these occasions. They are warm-hearted reminders of the richness of the American scene.

DEFINITIONS

APPETIZER—A small serving of food or beverage served before or as the first course of a meal.

ARTICHOKE—A vegetable. The Jerusalem artichoke looks like a potato. The globe artichoke is cylindrical in shape, with a tapering "heart" covered with fibrous green leaves.

ASPIC—A transparent jelly, usually made of meat stock, which has been boiled down sufficiently to become firm when cold. Also applies to meat, fish or vegetable stock which has been thickened with gelatin.

BATTER—A mixture of liquid, flour, etc., that can be beaten or stirred.

BISQUE—A rich thick cream soup usually made from fish. Also a rich frozen dessert, usually containing powdered nuts or macaroons.

BONBON—A sweet made of or dipped into fondant.

BOUILLABAISE—A chowder made of several varieties of fish and white wine.

Meat, fish or vegetables molded in aspic and served on chicory are found on many a luncheon plate

BOUILLON—Clear delicately seasoned soup usually made from lean beef stock.

CAFFEINE—An alkaloidal substance found in the coffee bean, coffee leaf, tea leaf, yerba mate, cacao bean, etc. The content in a cup of coffee is 1.5 grains; in tea less than 1 grain.

CANAPÉ—An appetizer made of a small piece of bread spread with a highly seasoned food.

CARAMEL—Burnt sugar sirup used for coloring and flavoring. Also a chewy candy.

CAVIAR—Salted roe (fish eggs). Originally from sturgeon.

CAPON—A castrated male chicken. Grows large and has tender meat.

CHARLOTTE OR CHARLOTTE RUSSE—Usually a gelatin dessert with flavored whipped cream molded in a form lined with cake or ladyfingers.

CHICORY—The root of a plant that is cut into slices, dried and roasted as coffee. Leaves of plant are used for salad and sometimes called curly endive.

CHOWDER—A dish made of fresh fish, or clams, pork, crackers, onions, etc., stewed together.

CIDER—The juice pressed from apples used as a beverage or to make vinegar.

COBBLER—A deep-dish fruit pie with a rich biscuit dough used instead of pastry.

COCKTAIL—(a) An appetizer served before or as the first course of a meal. (b) An alcoholic beverage usually served before dinner. (c) Fruit or vegetable juice. (d) Cut fruit or shellfish with tart sauce served as first course.

COMPOTE—Sweetened stewed fruit, cooked to keep the fruit as whole as possible.

CONDIMENTS—Food seasonings such as salt, vinegar, herbs and spices.

CONSOMMÉ—A highly seasoned clear soup made from one or a combination of meats.

CRACKLINGS—Crisp particles left after fat has been fried out.

CREAM SAUCE—A white sauce made with cream.

CROQUETTES—A mixture of chopped or ground cooked food held together by eggs on a thick sauce, shaped, dipped into egg and crumbs and fried.

CROUTONS—Cubes of toasted or fried bread served with soup.

CUSTARD—A cooked or baked mixture mainly of eggs and milk. It may be sweetened to use as a dessert or flavored with cheese, fish, etc., as an entrée.

CUTLET—A small piece of meat cut from the leg or rib of veal or pork, or a croquette mixture made into the shape of a cutlet.

DEEP-DISH PIE—A fruit pie with top crust only, baked in a deep dish.

DOUGH—A mixture of liquid, flour, etc., that is stiff enough to be handled or kneaded.

DRIPPINGS—Fat and liquid resulting from cooking meat.

ENTRÉE—The main dish of an informal meal or a subordinate dish served between main courses.

FONDANT—A sugar and water mixture cooked to the soft-ball stage (234°F.), cooled and kneaded.

FONDUE—A baked food similar to a soufflé but including bread or cracker crumbs.

FRAPPÉ—Sweetened fruit juice frozen until of mushy consistency.

FRITTERS—Fruit, meat, vegetables or fish covered with batter or chopped and mixed with batter. Usually fried in deep fat.

FROSTING—A cooked or uncooked sugar mixture used to cover and decorate cakes, cookies and other foods.

GELATIN—A purified protein found in connective tissues and bones of animals.

GIBLETS—The heart, liver and gizzard of poultry.

GOULASH—A thick meat stew originating in Hungary.

HOLLANDAISE—A rich sauce made of eggs and butter, served hot with vegetables and fish.

HORS D'OEUVRES—Salty, tart or crisp foods served as appetizers, such as canapés, fish, pickles, olives, celery, sausages, etc.

ICE—A frozen mixture of fruit juice, sugar and water.

INFUSION—Liquid extracted from coffee, tea or herbs.

JULIENNE—Food cut into match-like strips.

MACEDOINE—A mixture of vegetables or fruits.

MARINADE—An oil and acid mixture as French dressing in which food is allowed to stand to give flavor to meats and salads.

MARZIPAN—A paste of sweet almonds and sugar.

MERINGUE—A mixture of stiffly beaten egg whites, flavoring and sugar. Used on pies, etc.

MINESTRONE—A thick Italian vegetable soup.

MOCHA—A flavoring made with coffee infusion or with coffee infusion and chocolate.

MOUSSE—A mixture of whipped cream, sugar and flavoring frozen without stirring. Or flavored thin cream and gelatin combined with meat, fruits or vegetables.

MUFFIN—A drop batter baked in individual pans and served as a quick bread.

PARFAIT—A frozen dessert made of a foundation of beaten egg whites or yolks cooked with hot sirup, sometimes with whipped cream added. Also applied to ice cream and sirup served in parfait glasses.

PURÉE—A smooth thick liquid made by pressing cooked fruit or vegetables through a sieve.

RAGOUT—A thick highly seasoned stew.

RELISH—A highly seasoned food used as an accompaniment.

ROE—Eggs of fish.

SHERBET—Frozen mixture of fruit juice, sugar, egg whites and milk or water.

SKEWER—A long strong pin of wood or metal used to hold food in shape while cooking.

STOCK—A rich extract of soluble parts of meat, fish, poultry, etc. A basis for soups or gravies.

VEGETABLE MARROW—An egg-shaped gourd about 8 to 10 inches long. A vegetable.

PROCESSES

BAKE—To cook by dry heat, usually in an oven.

BARBECUE—To roast or broil whole, as a hog, fowl, etc. Usually done on a revolving frame over coals or upright in front of coals. To cook thin slices of meat in a highly seasoned vinegar sauce.

BASTE—To moisten roasting meat or other food while baking by pouring melted fat, drippings or sauces over it.

BEAT—To make a mixture smooth and introduce air by a brisk regular motion that lifts mixture over and over.

BLANCH—To pour boiling water over a food, then drain and rinse with cold water. Used to

Hollandaise sauce is decorative and delicious on vegetables and fish

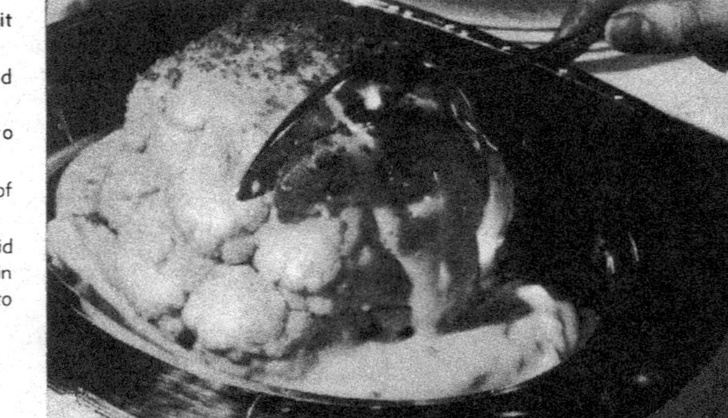

Scrambled Eggs in Sautéed Bologna Cups, 288
Wilted Lettuce Salad
Rhubarb Cream Sherbet
V V V

Egg and Spring Onion Salad, 531
Cucumber Tomato Rye Sandwiches
Peach Bavarian Cream
V V V

Sliced Pickled Tongue, 404
Julienne Green Beans
Hot Lettuce Bowl with Sour Cream Dressing
Banana Fritters with Lemon Sauce
V V V

Scalloped Potatoes with Peas, 486
Celery Radishes
Cracked Wheat Muffins
Stewed Rhubarb
V V V

Veal Birds, 391
Cheese Stuffed Prunes on Orange Slices
Strawberry Ice
V V V

Liver Patties Wrapped in Bacon, 232, 240
Macedoine Luncheon Salad with Horse-radish Dressing
Meringue Spongecake with Banana Custard Filling
V V V

Club Sandwiches, 207, 210
Berry Fluff
Tea Milk
V V V

Oysters Louisiana, 924 in Potato Nests, 489
Spiced Beets
Grapefruit and Orange Salad
Cheese Sticks
V V V

Stuffed Hard-cooked Eggs, 307
Toasted Whole-wheat Rolls
Lettuce with Thousand Island Dressing
Strawberry Milk Mallobet
Tea Milk
V V V

Ham Asparagus Rolls with Cheese Sauce, 223, 278
Celery
Spring Onions
Coconut Cake

APRIL FOOL'S LUNCHEON

Hard-cooked Eggs in Jellied Bouillon
Meat Loaf in Blanket, 355 with Mushroom Sauce, 278
Vegetable Salad
Fresh Strawberry Tarts
V V V

Cottage Cheese and Olive Sandwiches, 179
Celery Pickle Slices
Fruit Soufflé
V V V

Sliced Cold Meats, 552
Hot Potato Salad
Stuffed Celery
Orange Nut Bread
V V V

Crab-meat Salad Sandwiches, 182
Sweet Pickles Celery
Frozen Pear and Cheese Salad
V V V

Swiss Chard Ring, 260 with Creamed Eggs, 298
Celery Curls Pickle Fans
Hot Bran Muffins
Fresh Pineapple Wedges
V V V

Cream of Asparagus Soup, 111
Lettuce and Egg Salad
Strawberries
Hot Cross Buns

SMÖRGÅSBORD

Pickled Herring
Ripe Olives Filled Celery
Herring Salad, 553
Jellied Veal Loaf, 389
Swedish Meat Balls, 362
Braised Liver
Red Cabbage Salad
Potato Salad, 538, 540
Apple Salad, 525
Molded Fruit Salad
Assorted Cheese
Swedish Hardtack, 147
Limpa, 137
Continental Soup Calla Lilies
Coffee
V V V

SUNDAY NIGHT SUPPERS

Jellied Salmon Ring with Cucumber Dressing, 545, 865
Potato Chips
Lemon Mallobet
Hot Coffee Milk
V V V

Fresh Asparagus Tips and Poached Eggs on Toast with Cream Sauce, 294, 852
Chocolate Refrigerator Cake
Coffee Milk

Hail the opening of the berry season with luscious shortcake

Fish on the menu at least once a week should be garnished and served attractively

May Dinners

Tomato Juice
Spiced Ham Loaf, 380
Mustard Greens
Buttered Beets
Lettuce with Russian Dressing
Glazed Strawberry Tarts
V V V

Planked Shad with Duchess Potatoes, 315, 494
Green Beans Cooked with Bacon
Jellied Apricot Salad
Cheese Cake
Coffee Milk
V V V

Lamb en Brochette with Grilled Tomato and Bacon, 369, 513
Buttered New Peas
Pineapple Celery Salad with Mint French Dressing
Chocolate Bread Pudding
Iced Coffee
V V V

Vegetable Juice Cocktail
Shrimp Asparagus Casserole, 340
Garlic Bread
Lettuce Salad
Banana Butterscotch Pie
Coffee Milk
V V V

Pineapple Juice
Charcoal Broiled Steak, 352
Grilled Tomato Halves
Creamed New Potatoes
Mashed Turnips
Strawberry Ice Cream

Pineapple and Strawberry Juice
Roast Beef, 352
Franconia Potatoes
Cooked Cabbage
Molded Tomato Salad
Jellied Apricot Pie
Coffee Milk
V V V

Fresh Fruit Cup
Chicken Fricassee, 417
Hominy
Buttered Peas
Hot Biscuits
Rhubarb Upside-down Cake
Coffee Milk
V V V

Breaded Fillets of Whitefish with Bacon, 320, 374
Parsley Potato Balls
Green Beans with Egg Sauce
Marinated Tomato Slices
Spring Onions
Chocolate Mallow Pie
Coffee Milk
V V V

Braised Veal, 393
Fried Potatoes
Asparagus Tips with Hollandaise Sauce
Lettuce Cucumber Salad Bowl
Strawberry Shortcake
Coffee Milk
V V V

Apricot Juice
Baked Ham and Pineapple, 379
Baked Potatoes
Chopped Spinach
Sliced Tomatoes, French Dressing
Rhubarb and Banana Pudding
Coffee Milk

Tomato Consommé de Luxe
Baked Stuffed Fish, 316
Baked Potatoes
Chopped Spinach
Grated Carrots and Cucumbers in Sour Cream
Pineapple Marlow
V V V

Apple Juice
Salisbury Steak with Onions, 361
Mashed Potatoes
Buttered Green Beans
Floating Island
V V V

Cream of Tomato Soup
Pan-broiled Liver and Bacon, 401, 513
Mashed Potatoes
Buttered Beets
Green Pepper and Cottage Cheese Salad
Rhubarb Cream Pie
V V V

Pineapple Juice
Chicken and Dumplings, 416
Buttered Asparagus
Tomato and Cucumber Salad
Peaches
Daffodil Cake
Coffee Milk
V V V

Jellied Fruit Cocktail Salad
Veal Fricassee, Jardinière, 389
Curried Rice
Sliced Tomatoes
Burnt Almond Parfait
Coffee Milk
V V V

Sauerkraut Juice
Stuffed Pork Chops, 378
Mustard Greens
Baked Tomatoes
Strawberries and Cream

✧ DOCUMENT 20.3 ✧

An account of the birth of McDonald's, in Ray Kroc, *Grinding It Out* (Chicago: Regnery, 1977), pp. 6–9, 84–86.

I flew out to Los Angeles one day and made some routine calls with my representative there. Then, bright and early the next morning, I drove the sixty miles east to San Bernardino. I cruised past the McDonald's location about 10 A.M., and I was not terrifically impressed. There was a smallish octagonal building, a very humble sort of structure situated on a corner lot about 200 feet square. It was a typical, ordinary-looking drive-in. As the 11 o'clock opening time approached, I parked my car and watched the helpers begin to show up—all men, dressed in spiffy white shirts and trousers and white paper hats. I liked that. They began to move supplies from a long, low shed at the back of the property. They trundled four-wheeled carts loaded with sacks of potatoes, cartons of meat, cases of milk and soft drinks, and boxes of buns into the octagonal building. Something was definitely happening here, I told myself. The tempo of their work picked up until they were bustling around like ants at a picnic. Then the cars began to arrive, and the lines started to form. Soon the parking lot was full and people were marching up to the windows and back to their cars with bags full of hamburgers. Eight Multimixers churning away at one time began to seem a lot less farfetched in light of this steady procession of customers lockstepping up to the windows. Slightly dazed but still somewhat dubious, I got out of my car and took a place in line.

"Say, what's the attraction here?" I asked a swarthy man in a seersucker suit who was just in front of me.

"Never eaten here before?" he asked.

"Nope."

"Well, you'll see," he promised. "You'll get the best hamburger you ever ate for fifteen cents. And you don't have to wait and mess around tipping waitresses."

I left the line and walked around behind the building, where several men were hunkered down in the shade baseball-catcher style, resting their backs against the wall and gnawing away on hamburgers. One wore a carpenter's apron; he must have walked over from a nearby construction site. He looked up at me with an open, friendly gaze; so I asked him how often he came there for lunch.

"Every damned day," he said without a pause in his chewing. "It sure beats the old lady's cold meatloaf sandwiches."

It was a hot day, but I noticed that there were no flies swarming around the place. The men in the white suits were keeping everything neat and clean as they worked. That impressed the hell out of me, because I've always been impatient with poor housekeeping, especially in restaurants. I observed that even the parking lot was being kept free of litter.

In a bright yellow convertible sat a strawberry blond who looked like she had lost her way to the Brown Derby or the Paramount cafeteria. She was demolishing a hamburger and a bag of fries with a demure precision that was fascinating. Emboldened by curiosity, I approached her and said I was taking a traffic survey.

"If you don't mind telling me, how often do you come here?" I asked.

"Anytime I am in the neighborhood," she smiled. "And that's as often as possible, because my boyfriend lives here."

Whether she was teasing or being candid or simply using the mention of her boyfriend as a ploy to discourage this inquisitive middle-aged guy who might be a masher, I couldn't tell, and I cared not at all. It was not her sex appeal but the obvious relish with which she devoured the hamburger that made my pulse begin to hammer with excitement. Her appetite was magnified for me by the many people in cars that filled the parking lot, and I could feel myself getting wound up like a pitcher with a no-hitter going. This had to be the most amazing merchandising operation I had ever seen!

I don't remember whether I ate a hamburger for lunch that day or not. I went back to my car and waited around until about 2:30 in the afternoon, when the crowd dwindled down to just an occasional customer. Then I went over to the building and introduced myself to Mac and Dick McDonald. They were delighted to see me

("Mr. Multimixer" they called me), and I warmed up to them immediately. We made a date to get together for dinner that evening so they could tell me all about their operation.

I was fascinated by the simplicity and effectiveness of the system they described that night. Each step in producing the limited menu was stripped down to its essence and accomplished with a minimum of effort. They sold hamburgers and cheeseburgers only. The burgers were a tenth of a pound of meat, all fried the same way, for fifteen cents. You got a slice of cheese on it for four cents more. Soft drinks were ten cents, sixteen-ounce milk shakes were twenty cents, and coffee was a nickel.

After dinner, the brothers took me over to visit their architect, who was just completing work on the design of a new drive-in building for them. It was neat. The building was red and white with touches of yellow, and had snazzy looking oversized windows. It had some improved serving area features over those being used in the McDonald's octagonal structure. And it had washrooms in back. In the existing building, customers had to walk to the back of the lot to the long, low building that was a combination warehouse, office, and washrooms. What made the new building unique was a set of arches that went right through the roof. There was a tall sign out front with arches that had neon tubes lighting the underside. I could see plenty of problems there. The arches of the sign looked like they would topple over in a strong wind, and those neon lights would need constant attention to keep them from fading out and looking tacky. But I liked the basic idea of the arches and most of the other features of the design, too.

That night in my motel room I did a lot of heavy thinking about what I'd seen during the day. Visions of McDonald's restaurants dotting crossroads all over the country paraded through my brain. In each store, of course, were eight Multimixers whirring away and paddling a steady flow of cash into my pockets.

The next morning I got up with a plan of action in mind. I was on the scene when McDonald's windows opened for business. What followed was pretty much a repeat of the scenario that had played the previous day, but I watched it with undiminished fascination. I observed some things a lot more closely, though, and with more awareness, thanks to my conversation with the McDonald brothers. I noted how the griddleman handled his job; how he slapped the patties of meat down when he turned them, and how he kept the sizzling griddle surface scraped. But I paid particular attention to the french-fry operation. The brothers had indicated this was one of the key elements in their sales success, and they'd described the process. But I had to see for myself how it worked. There had to be a secret something to make french fries that good.

Now, to most people, a french-fried potato is a pretty uninspiring object. It's fodder, something to kill time chewing between bites of hamburger and swallows of milk shake. That's your ordinary french fry. The McDonald's french fry was in an entirely different league. They lavished attention on it. . . .

The experience with the Waukegan store and the others we opened during the summer and fall of 1956 brought home to me the fact that I needed a good operations man in corporate headquarters. I was committed in each franchise agreement to furnish the licensee with experienced help to train his crew and get the McDonald's system working in his store. I couldn't afford to bring Art Bender from California each time, and I couldn't spare Ed MacLuckie from the Des Plaines store very often, so I had to give some of the operators a $100 discount in lieu of the promised assistance. This was not good at all, because insistence on quality has to be emphasized in every procedure, and every crew member must be drilled in the McDonald's method of providing service. These basic elements will insure success for a store, unless its location is unspeakably bad, and we have had only a few instances of that in more than twenty years. But the fundamentals do not spring forth, self-evident and active, from the brow of every former grocery clerk, soda jerk, military man, or specialist in one of the hundreds of other callings who join the ranks of McDonald's operators. Quite the contrary; the basics have to be stressed over and over. If I had a brick for every time I've repeated the phrase *QSC and V* (Quality, Service, Cleanliness, and Value), I think I'd probably be able to bridge the Atlantic Ocean with them. And the operators need the stress on fundamentals as much as their managers and crews. This is especially true of a new location.

→ DOCUMENT 20.4a ←

Magazine advertisement for *McCall's* showing family togetherness. *Time*, January 9, 1956, p. 93. Courtesy Gruner + Jahr USA Publishing.

Today...togetherness
inspires the decision

Today—togetherness is the *accepted* way of family living.
And because women and their families live and play and plan together...
Togetherness is inspiring *women* in more and more buying decisions.
From carpets and floor coverings to automobiles to appliances.
From food to drug products to fashions!

You can influence *more* of these buying decisions *your way*...
in more than 4,500,000 homes . . . through advertising in the *only* magazine
edited to the ideal of Togetherness and
addressed to the Woman in terms of her family.
Ask your McCall's representative for the full story.

The Magazine of Togetherness in more than **4,500,000 HOMES** *each month*

TIME, JANUARY 9, 1956 93

DOCUMENT 20.4b

Magazine advertisement for International Harvester trucks picturing an American family, in *The Saturday Evening Post*, June 22, 1957, p. 63. Courtesy International Truck and Engine Corporation. ATA Foundation, Inc., logo appears by permission of American Trucking Associations, Inc.

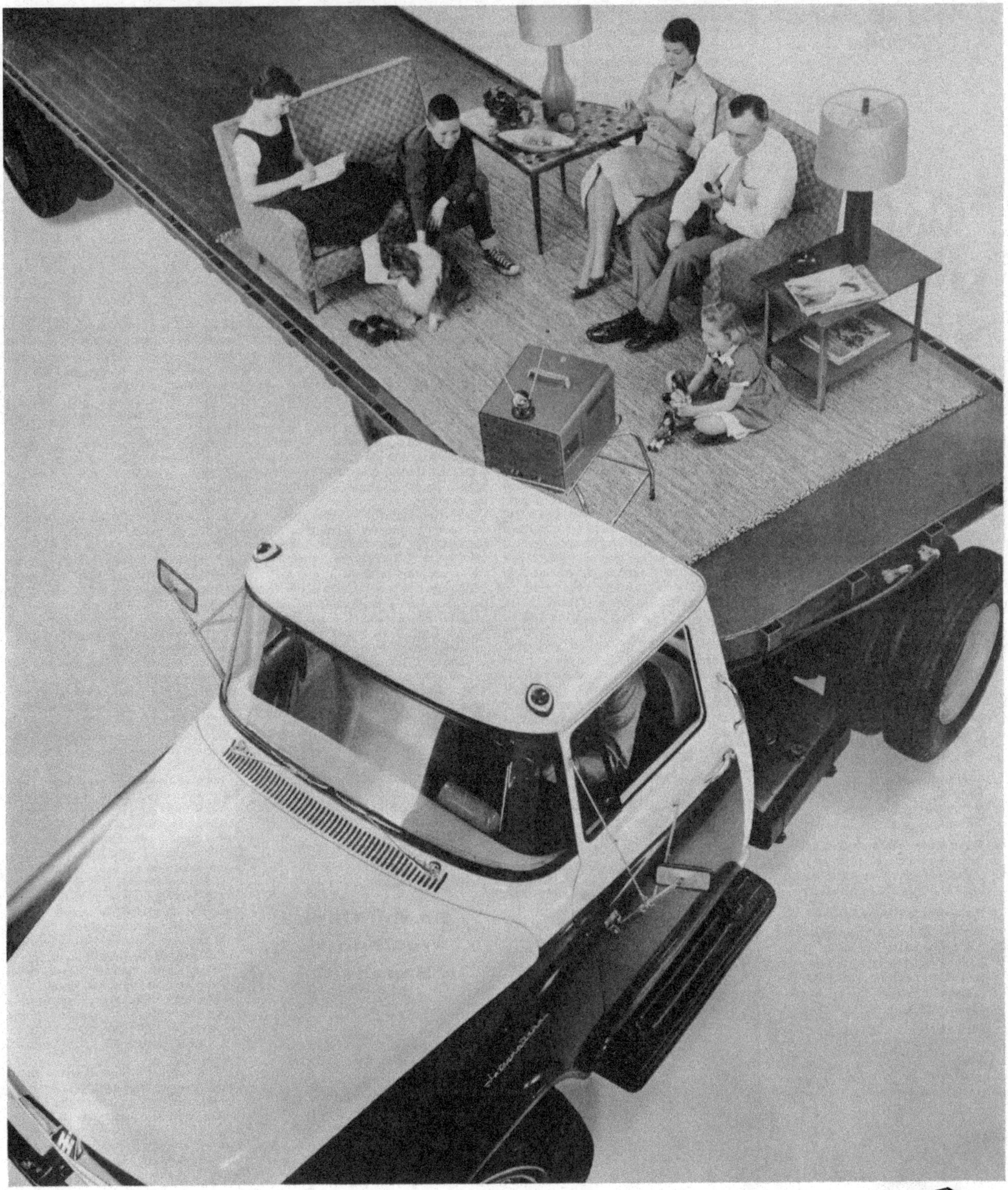

It takes a lot of trucking to make life easier!

Almost 170 million Americans live better today because motor trucks bring so many good things into their lives. You name it—trucks deliver it! Internationals have been delivering to American homes for 50 years. Motor trucks make a real contribution to the better living and greater security of all Americans.

INTERNATIONAL HARVESTER

AMERICAN TRUCKING INDUSTRY

Washington 6, D. C.

→ DOCUMENT 20.5a ←

Newspaper advertisement for Halo shampoo, 1954. *Sunday News*, 1954.

→ DOCUMENT 20.5b ←

Magazine advertisement for Powers fluid foundation, 1953. *Vogue*, November, 1, 1953.

ADVERTISEMENT

ABOUT THE AUTHOR . . .

Head of the famous Powers Model Agency for more than thirty years, John Robert Powers knows *what* makes a woman beautiful, and he knows how she can *make* herself beautiful and keep that beauty through the years. He has taught literally thousands of girls and women how to do it. Here he tells the Powers Girls' most precious beauty secrets . . . and how *you* can use them, too, to make the most of your own "natural resources" and look lovelier than ever before.

What Makes a Woman Beautiful?

(Second of a series)

by John Robert Powers

Every woman would like to be beautiful, I'm sure. I'm always a little sad when I hear someone envy my lovely Powers models, sighing, "Oh, wouldn't it be wonderful to be born beautiful like that!"

Because I know most of the Powers Girls weren't born any more beautiful than millions of other women. They've just learned how to make the most of their "natural resources," to create their own individual illusion of beauty. And I'm going to tell you a couple of their precious beauty secrets that will help *you* to do the same.

The Powers models have always been admired for the youthful *naturalness* of their beauty. And one of the basic reasons for this is the fact that their foundation and make-up colors are keyed scientifically to each individual skintone.

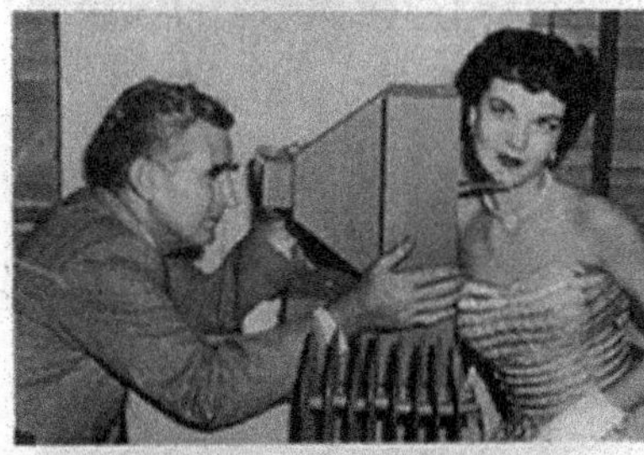

Above: John Robert Powers determines the true skintone of Powers Model Caroline O'Connor, using his patented Cosmetiscope. *Right:* Powers Model Olga Nicholas, always radiant in makeup color-keyed to her lovely blond complexion.

The wrong color foundation makes any woman look older, unattractive, obviously "made up." Yet most women today do use the wrong shade because they must choose it by guesswork, and because most cosmetic lines offer only a limited number of colors, recommended according to some vague grouping of hair or skin coloring.

The Powers models, however, have their best color determined scientifically by the John Robert Powers patented Cosmetiscope. This amazing invention is the *only* known method for identifying which of the *26* known skintones is yours, and which shade of Powers Fluid Foundation and other cosmetics will create the most flattering make-up harmony for you.

Then, when you apply your Powers Fluid Foundation, it blends so beautifully, covers so smoothly, gives such a dewy-fresh and flawless look, it doesn't look like make-up at all. You just seem to have a *naturally* young and beautiful complexion.

And here's the secret that will help you *keep* that radiant, youthful look and stave off the ravages of passing years . . . the Beauty Fluid that has done more than any other to help the Powers models keep their complexions clear, firm and young-looking long after their contemporaries are frantic over wrinkles, sagging jowls and crepy throats.

It's Powers Fluid Gold, my amazing skin "normalizer," the *only* treatment known that simultaneously corrects both dry and oily skin, restoring the proper acid-alkaline balance needed for fresh, young-skin beauty.

Fluid Gold provides the mild lubrication normal or slightly dry skin requires, and helps supply the moisture that makes tired and aging skin look fresher, smoother, younger. It quickly relieves that taut, tired feeling, helps to banish puffiness and age lines, and firm drooping contours.

The Powers models have been using my Fluid beautifiers for years, but only recently have these cosmetics been made available to a limited number of the finest department stores. If you are unable to obtain Powers Fluid Gold in your city, you may order from the John Robert Powers Products Co., Inc., 681 Fifth Avenue, Dept. 8, New York 22, N. Y. A three months' supply costs $5 plus 20% federal tax. With each order, I will enclose a copy of my fascinating new booklets, "The Story of Fluid Gold" and "Beauty Secrets of the Powers Girls."

→ DOCUMENT 20.6a ←

Magazine article on the younger generation. *Time*, November 5, 1951, pp. 46–47. Time Life Syndication.

THE YOUNGER GENERATION

IS it possible to paint a portrait of an entire generation? Each generation has a million faces and a million voices. What the voices say is not necessarily what the generation believes, and what it believes is not necessarily what it will act on. Its motives and desires are often hidden. It is a medley of good and evil, promise and threat, hope and despair. Like a straggling army, it has no clear beginning or end. And yet each generation has some features that are more significant than others; each has a quality as distinctive as a man's accent, each makes a statement to the future, each leaves behind a picture of itself.

What of today's youth? Some are smoking marijuana; some are dying in Korea. Some are going to college with their wives; some are making $400 a week in television. Some are sure they will be blown to bits by the atom bomb. Some pray. Some are raising the highest towers and running the fastest machines in the world. Some wear blue jeans; some wear Dior gowns. Some want to vote the straight Republican ticket. Some want to fly to the moon.

TIME's correspondents across the U.S. have tried to find out about this younger generation* by talking to young people, and to their teachers and guardians. What do the young think, believe, and read? Who are their heroes? What are their ambitions? How do they see themselves and their time? These are some of the questions TIME's correspondents asked; the masses of answers—plus the correspondents' interpretation—contain many clashing shades of opinion, but nevertheless reveal a remarkably clear area of agreement on the state of the nation's youth.

Youth today is waiting for the hand of fate to fall on its shoulders, meanwhile working fairly hard and saying almost nothing. The most startling fact about the younger generation is its silence. With some rare exceptions, youth is nowhere near the rostrum. By comparison with the Flaming Youth of their fathers & mothers, today's younger generation is a still, small flame. It does not issue manifestoes, make speeches or carry posters. It has been called the "Silent Generation." But what does the silence mean? What, if anything, does it hide? Or are youth's elders merely hard of hearing?

They Are Grave and Fatalistic

Listen to their voices, in a college bull session:

"I think the draft has all the fellows upset . . . They can't start figuring in high school or even in college what they want to do . . . First thing you know, Uncle Sam has tagged them off base."

"The boys are upset about the Korean business because they can't tell from one day to the next what they are going to be doing, going into the Army or what."

"Sure, the boys say, 'What's the use? I'd just get started and whammo, I'm gone.'"

"It's hard to get married when you don't know what the deal is. Maybe your husband is off to Korea or somewhere, and there you are."

"With maybe a baby on the way."

"It's better to get a job and wait."

"That's the worst part."

The "Korean business"—and a lot of other business that may follow—is the dominant fact in the life of today's youth. "I observe that you share the prevailing mood of the hour," Yale's President A. Whitney Griswold told his graduating class last June, "which in your case consists of bargains privately struck with fate—on fate's terms." The hand of fate has been on the U.S. with special gravity since World War I; it has disturbed the lives of America's youth since the '30s, through depression and war. The fear of depression has receded; the fear of war remains. Those who have been to war and face recall, and those who face the draft at the end of their schooling, know that they may have to fight before they are much older.

* TIME's working definition of the younger generation: 18 to 28.

But youth is taking its upsetting uncertainties with extraordinary calm. When the U.S. began to realize how deeply it had committed itself in Korea, youngsters of draft age had a bad case of jitters; but all reports agree that they have since settled down to studying or working for as long as they can. The majority seem to think that war with Russia is inevitable sooner or later, but they feel that they will survive it. Reports TIME's Los Angeles Bureau: "Today's youth does have some fear of the atomic age. But he does not feel as though he is living on the brink of disaster, nor does he flick on the radio (as was done in the '40s) and expect his life to be changed drastically by the news of the moment. There is a feeling that the world is in a ten-round bout, and that there will be no quick or easy knockout."

Hardly anyone wants to go into the Army; there is little enthusiasm for the military life, no enthusiasm for war. Youngsters do not talk like heroes; they admit freely that they will try to stay out of the draft as long as they can. But there is none of the systematized and sentimentalized antiwar feeling of the '20s. Pacifism has been almost nonexistent since World War II; so are Oxford Oaths. Some observers regard this as a sign of youth's passivity. But, as a student at Harvard puts it: "When a fellow gets his draft notice in February and keeps on working and planning till June, instead of boozing up every night and having a succession of farewell parties, he has made a very difficult, positive decision. Most make that decision today."

They Are Conventional and Gregarious

On a sunny Sunday not long ago, Sociology Professor Carr B. Lavell of George Washington University took one of his students on a fishing trip. He is a brilliant student, president of his class, a big man on campus, evidently with a bright future in his chosen field, medicine. In the bracing air, professor and student had a quiet talk. Why had he gone into medicine? asked the professor. Answer: medicine looked lucrative. What did he want to do as a doctor? Get into the specialty that offered biggest fees. Did he think that a doctor owed some special service to the community? Probably not. "I am just like anyone else," said the student. "I just want to prepare myself so that I can get the most out of it for me. I hope to make a lot of money in a hurry. I'd like to retire in about ten years and do the things I really want to do." And what are those? "Oh," said the brilliant student, "fishing, traveling, taking it easy."

Then they stopped talking, because the student had a nibble.

Perhaps more than any of its predecessors, this generation wants a good, secure job. This does not mean that it specifically fears a depression, as some aging New Dealers claim. The feeling is widespread that anyone who wants to work can find a decent job; the facts confirm that feeling (and the starting pay is better than ever). But youth's ambitions have shrunk. Few youngsters today want to mine diamonds in South Africa, ranch in Paraguay, climb Mount Everest, find a cure for cancer, sail around the world, or build an industrial empire. Some would like to own a small, independent business, but most want a good job with a big firm, and with it, a kind of suburban idyll.

An official of the placement bureau at Stanford University finds college graduates mostly interested in big companies—and choosy about which ones they will work for. "Half the time a guy will turn down a good job because he has to work in the city [meaning San Francisco]. They all figure there's no future in being holed up in a little apartment in town for ten years or getting up at 6 in the morning to commute to work and then not getting home until after dark. So they all want to work down on the peninsula where they can have a little house in the country and play golf or tennis and live the good life."

Says one youthful observer who still likes his dreams bigger: "This generation suffers from lack of worlds to conquer. Its fathers, in a sense, did too well. Sure, there are slums left—but another Federal housing project can clean up the worst. Most of the fights in labor have simmered down to arguments around the bargaining table. Would-be heroes find themselves padded from harm—and hope—like lunatics in a cell. In business, the tax structure, social security and pension plans promise to soften the blow of depression or personal misfortune—and forbid the building of new empires. In science there is the great corporation (or the Government) glad to furnish the expensive machinery now necessary for the smallest advance—and to give its name, or that of its group research boss, to the new process, while plowing back the profits. A man goes bounding, with no visible bruises, among the pads of an over-organized society."

The facts are that the U.S. is a highly organized society, must be, and will get more rather than less organized; that the big corporation is here to stay (and is a progressive instrument of U.S. capitalism). What is discouraging to some observers is not so much that youth has accepted life within the well-padded structure of organized society and big corporations, but that it seems to have relatively little ambition to do any of society's organizing. What is even more disturbing is youth's certainty that Government will take care of it—a feeling which continues despite a good deal of political distrust of Government. Reports TIME's Seattle Bureau: "The Pacific Northwest is only yesterday removed from the frontier, but the 'root, hog, or die' spirit has almost disappeared. Into its place has moved a curious dependence on the biggest new employer—Government. A 28-year-old aerodynamics specialist at Boeing says: 'I hope to work toward an income of $500 or $600 a month, after taxes. You know, only on a sliding scale for inflation. I'd just like to net $600, and then my family would always be O.K. You start earning more than that, and it's taxed away from you, so what the hell.' "

Says a 26-year-old promotion manager in Dallas: "Sure, I'd like to do something on my own, but I want to get well fixed first—make plenty of money and then maybe start some innovations."

This cautious desire to be "well fixed" and a little more has many causes: the war; the lingering shock of the Big Depression (which this younger generation felt or heard about in its childhood); and the hard-to-kill belief (still expounded in some college economics courses) that the frontiers of the U.S. economy have been reached.

There is also the feeling that it is neither desirable nor practical to do things that are different from what the next fellow is doing. Said a girl in Minneapolis: "The individual is almost dead today, but the young people are unaware of it. They think of themselves as individuals, but really they are not. They are parts of groups. They are unhappy outside of a group. When they are alone, they are bored with themselves. There is a tendency now to date in foursomes, or sixsomes. Very few dates are just a boy & girl together. They have to be with a crowd. These kids in my group think of themselves as individuals, but actually it is as if you took a tube of toothpaste and squeezed out a number of little distinct blobs on a piece of paper. Each blob would be distinct—separated in space—but each blob would be the same."

The Girls Want a Career—and Marriage

At the corner of Manhattan's Lexington Avenue and 63rd Street stands a 23-story building populated entirely by women, in which men are not permitted above the first floor. This does not mean that its inhabitants are not interested in men. The Barbizon hotel for women is considered a good, respectable address for out-of-town girls who have come to make a name for themselves in New York. In the small green lobby, through which moves a constant stream of eager young women carrying an air of determination, one aspiring young actress from Providence, R.I. said: "The men in New York are all the same. They're out for what they can get. I have a boy friend from home who comes to see me about every three weeks. He's a real home-town boy, all-American, clean-cut. He wouldn't speak the same language as these New York men. They're all trying to be big shots. I go out with them when he isn't here, but since I've been in New York I haven't met one man I can call a friend . . . I won't marry until I've convinced myself that I've gotten everything I can out of acting. Back home, everybody's a home-body, wants to raise big families. I'm not ready for that yet. If I married this fellow from home, I know I'd have to quit acting right away. He just wouldn't stand for it. I don't think I could do both, anyway."

American young women are, in many ways, the generation's most serious problem: they are emotional D.P.s. The granddaughters of the suffragettes, the daughters of the cigarette-and-short-skirt crusaders, they were raised to believe in woman's emancipation and equality with man. Large numbers of them feel that a home and children alone would be a fate worse than death, and they invade the big cities in search of a career. They ride crowded subways on which men, enjoying equality, do not offer them seats. They compete with men in industry and the arts; and keep up with them, Martini for Martini, at the cocktail parties.

There is every evidence that women have not been made happy by their ascent to power. They are dressed to kill in femininity. The bosom is back; hair is longer again; office telephones echo with more cooing voices than St. Mark's Square at pigeon-feeding time. The career girl is not ready to admit that all she wants is to get married; but she has generally retreated from the brassy advance post of complete flat-chested emancipation, to the position that she would like, if possible, to have marriage and a career, both. In the cities, she usually lives with a roommate (for respectability and lower rent) in a small apartment, fitted with chintz slipcovers, middlebrow poetry and a well-equipped kitchenette. Rare and fortunate is the bachelor who has not been invited to a "real, home-cooked dinner," to be eaten off a shaky bridge table, by a young woman who during the daytime is a space buyer or a dentist's assistant.

Says a Minneapolis priest: "The young American male is increasingly bewildered and confused by the aggressive, coarse, dominant attitudes and behavior of his women. I believe it is one of the most serious social traits of our time—and one that is certain to have most serious social consequences."

Their Morals Are Confused

The shrieking blonde ripped the big tackle's shirt from his shoulder and Charlestoned off through the crowded room, fan-dancing with a ragged sleeve. In her wake, shirts fell in shreds on the floor, until half the male guests roared around bare to the waist. Shouts and laughs rose above the full-volume records from *Gentlemen Prefer Blondes*. The party, celebrating the departure of a University of Texas coed who had flunked out, had begun in midafternoon some three hours earlier. In one corner, four tipsily serious coeds tried to revive a passed-out couple with more salty dog (a mixture of gin, grapefruit juice and salt). About 10 p.m., a brunette bounded on to the coffee table, in a limited striptease. At 2 a.m., when the party broke up, one carload of youngsters decided to take off on a two-day drive into Mexico (they got there all right, and sent back picture postcards to the folks).

The younger generation can still raise hell. The significant thing is not that it does, but how it goes about doing it. Most of today's youngsters never seem to lose their heads; even when they let themselves go, an alarm clock seems to be ticking away at the back of their minds; it goes off sooner or later, and sends them back to school, to work, or to war. They are almost discreet about their indiscretions, largely because (unlike their parents) they no longer want or need to shock their elders. The generation has "won its latchkey." It sees no point or fun in yelling for freedom to do as it pleases, because generally no one keeps it from doing as it pleases. It is not rebellious—either against convention or instruction, the state or fate, Pop or Mom. Toward its parents, it exhibits an indulgent tolerance. As one young New Yorker put it with a shrug: "Why insult the folks?"

The younger generation seems to drink less. "There is nothing glorious or inglorious any more about getting stewed," says one college professor. Whether youth is more or less promiscuous than it used to be is a matter of disagreement. Fact is that it is less showy about sex. Whatever its immoralities, it commits them on the whole because it enjoys them, and not because it

→ DOCUMENT 20.6b ←

Rock and roll lyrics, "Yakety Yak," 1958, words and music by Jerry Leiber and Mike Stoller; sung by the Coasters, "The Coasters' Greatest Hits," Gusto-PO-310.

YAKETY YAK

Take out the papers and the trash
Or you don't get no spendin' cash
If you don't scrub that kitchen floor
You ain't gonna rock and roll no more
Yakety yak (don't talk back)

Just finish cleanin' up your room
Let's see that dust fly with that broom
Get all that garbage out of sight
Or you don't go out Friday night
Yakety yak (don't talk back)

You just put on your coat and hat
And walk yourself to the laundromat
And when you finish doin' that
Bring in the dog and put out the cat
Yakety yak (don't talk back)

[chiefly sax instrumental]

Don't you give me no dirty looks
Your father's hip; he knows what cooks
Just tell your hoodlum friend outside
You ain't got time to take a ride
Yakety yak (don't talk back)

Yakety yak, yakety yak
Yakety yak, yakety yak
Yakety yak, yakety yak

FADE
Yakety yak, yakety yak

✧ DOCUMENT 20.6c ✧

Photograph of Elvis Presley singing on stage, June 22, 1956, Hollywood, California. ©Bettmann/CORBIS.

DOCUMENT 20.7

A television script, "Living 1950—The Children of Strangers," November–December 1950, pp. 2–3, 16–19. Papers of Ben Grauer, Box 55, Columbia University Rare Book and Manuscript Library, New York.

-2-

nearly 100 years ago.

NARR: Greetings, America. Walt Whitman said it: "This is not a nation but a teeming nation of nations."

(MUSIC: THEME....IN AND UNDER NARRATION)

cut We're a Scotch broth, an Hungarian goulash, a Mulligatawny stew of every nation under the sun. Walk down the street -- one out of every eight adults you meet may be foreign-born. Visit almost any public school and listen to the roll call.

TEACHER: (ON CUE Mary Adams.

GIRL: Here.

TEACHER: Jo Barranco.

BOY: Here.

TEACHER: Ann Cabot

GIRL: Here

TEACHER: David Cohen

BOY: Here.

NARR: What has America meant to its Barrancos and Cohens, its De Solas and Kaboulians and O'Malleys? To all its people who came here as strangers from other lands? More important what does it mean today to their children and their children's children? Have we given them a feeling of belonging, a full participation in our democracy? Or do they remain on the outer rim of American life--still to us THE CHILDREN OF STRANGERS?

(ROLL CALL FADES UNDER)

TEACHER: Josephine De Sola

GIRL: Here.

TEACHER: George Kaboulian

BOY: Here.

TEACHER: Margaret O'Malley

GIRL: Here.

(MUSIC: THEME UP & FADING BEHIND)

BOY: (RECITING PAINSTAKINGLY) We hold these truths to be self-evident. That all men are created equal. That they are endowed by their Creator with certain .. certain in .. inalienable rights, among which are life, liberty and the pursuit of happiness.....Wh-e-ew! I said inalienable right that time, didn't I, Teach?

(MUSIC: ACCENT & UNDER)

NARR: The preamble to the Constitution of the United States. Words that every school-boy knows today. Words grown shop-worn with useage. But once, once they flashed across the world like a new comet in the sky.

BOY: (REPEATS) Life, liberty, and the pursuit of happiness.

MAN: (SLIGHT ACCENT) Life, liberty, and the pursuit of happiness.

NARR: This was the promise. This was what we offered to the Barrancos and the Cohens, the De Solas, the Kaboulians, and the O'Malleys. To all the people of the Old World, worn thin by poverty, ground down by racial and religious strife. Often they translated the promise into more simple terms.

MAN: (ACC.) In America a man can get ahead.

WOMAN: (ACC.) In America nobody is afraid of anybody.

BOY: (ACC.) In America every-body has ice-cream every day.

NARR: Whatever personal meaning he gave to the promise, every newcomer who streamed through the portals of Ellis Island felt a sense of something new beginning.

~~(BABBLE OF VOICES)~~

WOMAN 2: (FILTER) Be a good mother. Use our talcum powder.

(MUSIC: ACCENT)

NARR: By new world standards of success, father, to the child, often represented failure. He looked elsewhere for his heroes and found them in the card-board men of the ads -- in the celluloid people of the cheap movie houses.

(POUNDING HOOVES.....FILTER)

(SHOTS FIRED........DITTO)

MAN: (SLIGHT FILTER) Okay, Two-gun. You got away from me this time. But you won't again. Remember this. Nobody gets away from Smilin' Sam but once.

(MUSIC: QUICK BRIDGE...HORSE OPERA)

BOY: (SLIGHT FILTER) Okay, Two-gun, you got away from me this time. But you won't again. Remember this. Nobody...

TEACHER: (OVER DAY-DREAM) George!...George!...George, I'm speaking to you.

BOY: Huh ... Oh.. Oh, was you talking to me, Miss Phillips?

TEACHER: I certainly was. For the third time, what is the Monroe Doctrine?

(MUSIC: ACCENT & BEHIND)

NARR: It is our failure, not their's, if our second generation Americans have sometimes sold their birthright for a mess of pottage (PAUSE)

But what of the third generation, the boys and girls of today, the grand-children of our immigrant peoples? By the third generation, sociologists tell us, the process of assimilation has been more or less completed.

(MORE)

NARR: (CONTD) Psychologically, the tie with the old world that plagued their fathers has been dissolved. Few of the third generation have any interest in the land of their forebears. Few know any language but English. They dress American, talk American, eat American. In so far as they are able to they become one of us. But in many cases there is still a wall between these children and other Americans. A wall of our making.

OLDER BOY: Dad, there's something I have to tell you. You're not going to like it. But...

MAN: What is it, Joseph?

OLDER BOY: I...I want to change my name. I've been turned down by three colleges already. I'll never get to be a doctor with a name like our's. Don't look like that, Dad. Try to understand. I'm not ashamed of you. I... I..

(MUSIC: ACCENT)

NARR: In America today, for all our progress, it is still more comfortable to be light tanned than dark, more comfortable to be Protestant than Catholic, or Jewish, more comfortable to be called Smith than Ivanovich or ~~Hadad~~ Zybeiko.

(MUSIC: STING & HOLD)

OLDER GIRL: So I don't get the job.

MAN: I'm sorry. It's not me, it's just the policy of the management. Your qualifications are excellent, but...

OLDER GIRL: But you don't like my face.

(MUSIC: STING & HOLD)

MAN: I'm sorry. All our apartments are taken.

OLDER BOY: But the sign said.

MAN: I'm sorry.

OLDER BOY: I get it. You're restricted.

(MUSIC: STING & SEGUE TO NARRATIVE THEME)

NARR: This is not the whole picture. There are colleges in America that have taken a stand against discrimination. There are employers, too. And there are newspapers that refuse to print discriminatory ads. Eight of our states have passed fair employment practice legislation, which makes it a crime to discriminate in hiring, job tenure, or conditions of employment because of race, color, creed or national origin.

In some of our public schools, too, where classes are not too big, teachers not too over-worked and weary, Americanism is being taught in a new way.

BOY 1: I'm a one hundred percent American. My father told me so.

TEACHER: Just what is a one hundred percent American, Bobby?

BOY 1: Why it's...it's. Well, it's people like me. People who aren't foreigners. (PAUSE) Well, isn't it?

TEACHER: You sound to me, Bobby, like you think America is a little plot of ground with a fence around it and a no trespassing sign. We're a great big giant of a country. In the past we've been big enough to make room for people from every country in the world.

BOY 1: That's the trouble, my father says. He says we've been too big-hearted letting just everybody in.

WOMAN: Democracy is not just a word, a catch-phrase. A child must experience democracy to believe in it.

NARR: Yes, a child must experience democracy to believe in it.

GIRL 1: (FADES ON) Acka, baka, Soda-cracker,
Acka, baka, Boo.
If your father chews tobacco,
Out go YOU.

VOICES: You're IT, Irene. You're IT.

GIRL 2: (FADING ON) Hey, Mary, I want to play. Let me play, too.

GIRL 1: You can't Josephine. We got too many already.

GIRL 2: Okay, but will you come to my house after school? (PAUSE) Will you?

GIRL 1: I guess not.

GIRL 2: Why not?

GIRL 1: My mother said I should play just with Americans.

GIRL 2: Well, I'm an American. I was born here the same as you were.

GIRL 1: Your folks weren't. They're foreigners.

GIRL 2: I don't care if they are. I'm an American. Everybody came from somewhere in the beginning. Even George Washington's folks, I bet.

(MUSIC: BRIDGE & TO THEME:)

NARR: Everybody came from somewhere in the beginning. Mary's people landed at Plymouth Rock. Josephine's at Castle Garden. What's the difference? We are not a nation, but a teeming nation of nations.

TEACHER: (ROLL CALL) Mary Adams.

GIRL: Here.

TEACHER: Jo Barranco.

BOY: Here.

TEACHER: ~~John~~ Jim Cabot.

BOY: Here.

NARR: Only ~~when~~ we can educate our children to take full pride in the rich and varied threads that make American life the tapestry that it is, only then will the promise be fulfilled. Only then will all our children have a feeling of belonging, none The Children of Strangers.

(ROLL CALL UNDER:)

TEACHER: Josephine De Sola.

GIRL: Here.

TEACHER: George Kaboulian.

BOY: Here.

TEACHER: Margaret O'Malley.

GIRL: Here.

→ DOCUMENT 20.8a ←

Photograph of crowd action at Central High School, 1957. Photograph by Will Counts for *Arkansas Democrat*, September, 1957.

✧ DOCUMENT 20.8b ✧

Photograph of Elizabeth Eckford waiting for the bus, 1957. Photograph by Will Counts for *Arkansas Democrat*, September, 1957.

→ DOCUMENT 20.9 ←

Holograph letter from Daisy Bates to Ray Wilkens, December 17, 1957. NAACP collection, Manuscript Division (9–18a), Library of Congress.

"The Paper That's Published For Its Readers"

P. O. BOX 2179

Little Rock, Arkansas

December 17, 1957

Mr. Roy Wilkins
20 West 40th Street
New York, N. Y.

Dear Mr. Wilkins:

Conditions are yet pretty rough in the school for the children. Last week, Minnie Jean's mother, Mrs. W. B. Brown, asked me to go over to the school with her for a conference with the principal, and the two assistant principals. Subject of conference:"Firmer disciplinary measures, and the withdrawal of Minnie Jean from the glee club's Christmas program." The principal had informed Minnie Jean in withdrawing her from the program that "When it is definitely decided that Negroes will go to school here with the whites, and the troops are removed, then you will be able to participate in all activities." We strongly challenged this statement, which he denied making in that fashion.

We also pointed out that the treatment of the children had been getting steadily worse for the last two weeks in the form of kicking, spitting, and general abuse. As a result of our visit, stronger measures are being taken against the white students who are guilty of committing these offenses. For instance, a boy who had been suspended for two weeks, flunked both six-weeks tests, and on his return to school, the first day he knocked Gloria Ray into her locker. As a result of our visit, he was given an indefinite suspension.

The superintendent of schools also requested a conference the same afternoon. Clarence and I went down and spent about two hours. Here, again we pointed out that a three-day suspension given Hugh Williams for a sneak attack perpetrated on one of the Negro boys which knocked him out, and required a doctor's attention, was not sufficient punishment. We also informed him that our investigation revealed that there were many pupils willing to help if given the opportunity, and that President Eisenhower was very much concerned about the Little Rock crisis. He has stated his willingness to come down and address the student body if invited by student leaders of the school. This information was passed on to the principal of the school, but we have not been assured that leadership would be given to children in the school who are willing to organize for law and order. However, we have not abandoned the idea. Last Friday, the 13th, I was asked to call Washington and see if we could get FBI men placed in the school December 16-18.

ARCHIVE 20

Thanks for sending Clarence to help. I don't know how I would have made it without him. I am enclosing a financial statement, and as you can see, we are in pretty bad shape financially. On December 18, we will probably have to make bond for three of our officials from the North Little Rock Branch. December 18, midnight, is the deadline for filing names and addresses of members and contributors. I have talked with Mrs.Birdie Williams, and we are attempting to have them spend the night away from their homes, because we have been informed that they plan to arrest them after midnite.

I am suggesting that a revolving fund be set up here of $1,000.00 to take care of emergencies, and an accounting could be given at the end of each month. We are having trouble getting cost bonds executed on the North Little Rock suit. We had to put up $510.00 collateral plus three co-signers. We informed Bob Carter of our difficulty, and he asked Jack to see what could be done on that end. Please check with him.

I have not heard anything from the scholarship trust papers. We have deposited the money received for the scholarship. Mrs. A. L. Mothershed, 1313 Chester street, mother of one of the children, is serving as trustee.

I would appreciate hearing from you pertaining to the above mentioned matters at your earliest convenience.

I plan to attend the board meeting on January 6.

Sincerely,

Daisy Bates

LCB:j

cc: Mr. Current

ARCHIVE 21

The United States and the Vietnam War

Archive Overview

BETWEEN 1961 and 1973, the United States engaged in the longest military conflict in its national history. The costs were high: 58,000 Americans dead, $613 billion spent for a war that ended in defeat, bitter disagreements over whether the country should be involved in a war so far away, and growing cynicism on the part of many Americans about the ways in which their leaders justified the war and evaluated its progress. Although the United States finally pulled out of South Vietnam in 1973, the war left behind many legacies, one of them being suspicion and even rejection of the Cold War policy of containment and a deepening distrust of the federal government.

This archive can only begin to suggest some aspects of the American involvement in Vietnam. The first set of documents raises questions about why American policy makers concerned themselves with Vietnam, a small and seemingly insignificant country far from those areas of the world where the United States had clear and significant interests. What was the frame of reference of American policy makers? Why did they have any interest in Vietnam? How much did they really know about the country? As you read two Vietnamese documents, you should consider how well the analysis of American policy makers meshed with Vietnamese realities. After you have considered these issues, you'll find testimony from several American soldiers who served in Vietnam. What were their views of the conflict? How did they think the war was being conducted? What was the personal impact on them of their participation in the war? How well does their testimony shed light on the war and on Americans' feelings about it? When you have reflected on these questions, consider the ways in which policy makers and private citizens agreed and disagreed about the country's involvement in Vietnam.

TIMELINE

1867	French colonize Indochina
1940–1941	Japanese occupy Indochina
1941	Viet Minh organized
1945	Viet Minh establishes Democratic Republic of Vietnam
1946	French return to Vietnam; war against the French begins in Vietnam
1950	U.S. provides military aid to the French
1952	Eisenhower elected president
1954	French lose control of Indochina; "temporary" partition into Republic of South Vietnam (RSV) and Democratic Republic of Vietnam (DRV); U.S. begins support of South Vietnam
1959	North Vietnam begins support of communists in RSV
1960	Kennedy elected president; National Liberation Front (Vietcong) established in RSV
1961	Kennedy increases assistance to South Vietnam
1963	Lyndon Johnson becomes president
1964	Gulf of Tonkin Resolution
1965	American military escalation in Vietnam
1968	Tet offensive; Nixon elected president
1969	Nixon Doctrine
1973	Ceasefire in Vietnam
1975	South Vietnam falls to North Vietnam

Placing the Sources in Context

THE length of the chronology below suggests the complexity of American involvement in Vietnam as well as that country's long struggle for freedom from foreign domination. While many Americans, at the time of the war and later, viewed the conflict primarily from an American perspective, it is difficult to understand this country's debacle in Vietnam without some consideration of the Vietnamese history and point of view.

The Vietnamese effort to end French colonialism in Indochina was only one episode in a long struggle to assert the region's independence from powerful neighbors like China and Japan, and from western imperialists like the French. When the Japanese invaded French Indochina in 1940 (see Archive 19), nationalist forces called the Viet Minh, led by Ho Chi Minh, carried on guerrilla warfare against the Japanese. Ho Chi Minh, who had joined the Communist Party years before, attracted by its opposition to colonialism, was less a doctrinaire communist than a nationalist who was intent on making his country independent. During the war, Ho had little problem collaborating with the American Office of Strategic Services in the shared struggle against the Japanese, and he enthusiastically discussed American ideals with members of the OSS. As one interpreter noted, Ho was "sure America would be on his side" once the war was over. Ho's communications with Washington indicated clearly his desire for American support. When the Viet Minh announced the formation of the Democratic Republic of Vietnam in 1945, their Declaration of Independence was modeled on ours and paid obvious tribute to American ideals.

The United States, however, failed to back Vietnamese independence, and France returned to the country. Guerrilla warfare against the French commenced almost at once. Because the United States was concerned about the stability of western Europe in the early days of the Cold War, it did not want to see the French weakened by the Indochina conflict, and eventually the United States gave France substantial financial support. By 1954, the year in which the French were defeated, the United States was footing more than 75 percent of the cost of the French military effort.

After the French defeat, the country was divided into North Vietnam, controlled by Ho Chi Minh and the Viet Minh, and South Vietnam, where a supposedly democratic government was established. The Cold War framework encouraged American policymakers to view Ho Chi Minh as a dangerous communist and the South as the bastion of freedom. In fact, the South Vietnamese government was dictatorial, inept, and unpopular. Nevertheless, American aid flowed to the South. Gradually the United States established a modest military presence there.

Under President Lyndon Johnson, military escalation began in earnest. In 1965 the number of American soldiers ballooned from 25,000 to 184,000. By 1967 there were 385,000 Americans in Vietnam, the next year more than half a million. Despite the numbers and the vast amounts of military hardware and dollars devoted to the struggle, the war went badly. Endless and futile "search and destroy" missions into the jungle, disastrous defeats facing a supposedly weaker enemy, the amazing success of the Vietcong in the 1968 Tet offensive, the horrifying massacre of Vietnamese civilians at the village of My Lai, and the demoralization of American troops by drugs, defeat, and opposition at home all turned the war in Vietnam into a national nightmare.

About the Sources

SEVERAL sources in this archive (21.1, 21.3, and 21.4) present the Vietnamese point of view. As the American phase of the war for independence has receded into the past, Vietnamese documents have become available and Americans have been able to visit the country. (Some of the materials here were collected by one of the authors on a recent trip to that country.)

Not only did the war lead Americans at home to violent differences of opinion about the importance and the morality of the country's participation, but there was also disagreement among those who served about the wisdom of the war and the ways in which it was being waged. In 1971, the Vietnam Veterans Against the War, an organization speaking for 11,000 veterans, staged three days of hearings in Detroit, Michigan. More than one hundred veterans, all honorably discharged from service, testified about the brutality of American conduct in Vietnam. As you read some of the testimony (21.6–21.8), keep in mind that the purpose of the hearing was to increase pressure on the government to get out of Vietnam and to arouse sympathy for this goal among the public. The testimony was placed in the *Congressional Record* by Senator Hatfield, who also forwarded it to the Department of Defense and the Department of State, urging "in accord with . . . stated policy, that the evidence and allegations it contains be fully investigated."

List of Sources

21.1 **Declaration of Independence for the Democratic Republic of Vietnam,** September 2, 1945, in Ho Chi Minh, *Selected Works* (Hanoi, 1960–1962), vol. 3, pp. 17–21.

21.2a **Policy statement about American objectives in Southeast Asia,** June 25, 1952, in *The Pentagon Papers* (Boston: Beacon Press, 1971), vol. 2, pp. 286–288.

21.2b **Report by Vice President Johnson on his visit to Asian countries,** May 23, 1961. *The Pentagon Papers* as published by the *New York Times*. (New York: Quadrangle Books, 1971), pp.133–135.

21.2c **Magazine advertisement about the dangers of socialism.** *The Saturday Evening Post*, April 5, 1952, p. 78.

21.3 **General Vo Nguyen Giap's reflections on the people's war,** 1961, in Thomas G. Paterson and Dennis Merrill, *Major Problems in American Foreign Relations* (Lexington, 1995), vol. 2, pp. 538–539.

21.4a **Photograph of Vietnamese resistance measures,** 1965, by Duong Thanh Phong. Postcard reproduction, personal collection of Julie Roy Jeffrey.

21.4b **Photograph of tunnel construction,** 1965, by Duong Thanh Phong. Postcard reproduction, personal collection of Julie Roy Jeffrey.

21.4c **Photograph of making weapons from unexploded American bombs,** 1965, by Duong Thanh Phong. Postcard reproduction, personal collection of Julie Roy Jeffrey.

21.4d **Photograph of a Cu Chi female guerrilla,** 1965, by Duong Thanh Phong. Postcard reproduction, personal collection of Julie Roy Jeffrey.

21.4e **Photograph of making bamboo traps,** 1965, by Duong Thanh Phong. Postcard reproduction, personal collection of Julie Roy Jeffrey.

21.5 **Cartoon about the war,** 1964, by William Mauldin, November 25, 1964. Mauldin, reprinted with special permission from the Chicago Sun-Times, Inc. © 2000.

21.6 **Testimony by marine William Crandell at the Winter Soldier Investigation,** January 31 and February 1, 1971. The Sixties Project, sponsored by Viet Nam Generation, Inc., and the *Advanced Institute of Advanced Technology in the Humanities*, the University of Virginia.

21.7 **Testimony by members of the First Marine Division at the Winter Soldier Investigation,** January 31 and February 1, 1971. The Sixties Project, sponsored by Viet Nam Generation, Inc., and the *Advanced Institute of Advanced Technology in the Humanities*, the University of Virginia.

21.8 **Testimony by members of the Twenty-fifth Infantry Division at the Winter Soldier Investigation,** January 31 and February 1, 1971. The Sixties Project, sponsored by Viet Nam Generation, Inc., and the *Advanced Institute of Advanced Technology in the Humanities*, the University of Virginia.

21.9a **Photograph of American soldiers wading in rice paddy,** 1966, Bong Son, South Vietnam. © Bettmann/CORBIS.

21.9b **Photograph of U.S. soldiers jumping from helicopters,** by Bill Hall, November 16, 1967, Dak To, South Vietnam. © Bettmann/CORBIS.

21.9c **Photograph of U.S. troops in action in South Vietnam,** February 22, 1968, Hue, South Vietnam. © Bettmann/CORBIS.

21.9d **Photograph of an American patrol stopping Vietnamese civilians,** November 1969, photograph by Bob Lindgren, in Vietnam War Internet Project Image Library. Courtesy Bob Lindgren.

21.9e **Photograph of an American soldier with Vietnamese police,** December 1969. Cpl. Robert J. Lindgren accompanying South Vietnamese National Police on an operation, in Vietnam War Internet Project Image Library. Courtesy Bob Lindgren.

Questions to Consider

1. What American ideals and documents does the Vietnamese Declaration of Independence (21.1) use to support the case for independence from France? Is the case a convincing one? What might have been the reasons why the declaration used such language? What insights does the document give into the events in Indochina during the period of the war? What insight into the thinking of the leadership of the Viet Minh?

2. After reading the policy statement by the National Security Council (21.2a) and the memo from Vice President Lyndon Johnson (21.2b), describe the chain of reasoning that made American policy makers decide that the French should be supported in Indochina. Are there indications that Americans had a detailed knowledge of Vietnam or of the Viet Minh? Using your text, if necessary, speculate on the ways in which the interest in Vietnam fit into American cold war concerns outside of Asia. What light does the advertisement throw on the cold war climate of opinion in which policymakers operated?

3. Having in mind the document by General Giap (21.3) and the photographs (21.4), discuss the ways in which "the people" opposed the American and South Vietnamese forces. What values and beliefs made this kind of opposition possible? Remembering the sources you examined in Archive 20 on mass society, how might an American respond to Giap's piece?

4. Analyze the cartoon (21.5). What is going on? What does the figure leaning against the tree represent? What point do you think Mauldin is making? Is there humor here? Do you consider that this cartoon offers a serious criticism of American involvement in South Vietnam?

5. Study the testimony by the U.S. soldiers (21.6, 21.7, 21.8). What is the purpose of the hearings? How do the witnesses describe American military actions? Do they offer convincing evidence for their statements? How much credence should we give to their testimony? When you consider what they say in light of Giap's description of the People's Army, the Vietnamese photographs, and the American photographs (21.9), can you see why American soldiers may have had extreme reactions to the Vietnamese villagers and the kind of opposition they encountered?

6. Focus on the American photographs. How do they fit with the testimony provided by the veterans at the hearing? How are they different?

7. What picture do these sources (21.6–21.9) give of the emotional and psychological impact of the war on American combatants?

8. Based on all the sources, what generalizations would you make about the character of the war, its impact on participants, and the different perspectives of policymakers and American soldiers?

9. What is your historical interpretation of the Vietnam War?

→ DOCUMENT 21.1 ←

Declaration of Independence for the Democratic Republic of Vietnam, September 2, 1945, in Ho Chi Minh, *Selected Works* (Hanoi, 1960–1962), Vol. 3, pp. 17–21.

Declaration of Independence, Democratic Republic of Vietnam

[September 2, 1945]

"All men are created equal. They are endowed by their Creator with certain inalienable rights, among these are Life, Liberty, and the pursuit of Happiness"

This immortal statement was made in the Declaration of Independence of the United States of America in 1776. In a broader sense, this means: All the peoples on the earth are equal from birth, all the peoples have a right to live, to be happy and free.

The Declaration of the French Revolution made in 1791 on the Rights of Man and the Citizen also states: "All men are born free and with equal rights, and must always remain free and have equal rights." Those are undeniable truths.

Nevertheless, for more than eighty years, the French imperialists, abusing the standard of Liberty, Equality, and Fraternity, have violated our Fatherland and oppressed our fellow-citizens. They have acted contrary to the ideals of humanity and justice. In the field of politics, they have deprived our people of every democratic liberty.

They have enforced inhuman laws; they have set up three distinct political regimes in the North, the Center and the South of Vietnam in order to wreck our national unity and prevent our people from being united.

They have built more prisons than schools. They have mercilessly slain our patriots—they have drowned our uprisings in rivers of blood. They have fettered public opinion; they have practised obscurantism against our people. To weaken our race, they have forced us to use opium and alcohol.

In the fields of economics, they have fleeced us to the backbone, impoverished our people, and devastated our land.

They have robbed us of our rice fields, our mines, our forests, and our raw materials. They have monopolised the issuing of bank-notes and the export trade.

They have invented numerous unjustifiable taxes and reduced our people, especially our peasantry, to a state of extreme poverty.

They have hampered the prospering of our national bourgeoisie; they have mercilessly exploited our workers.

In the autumn of 1940, when the Japanese Fascists violated Indochina's territory to establish new bases in their fight against the Allies, the French imperialists went down on their bended knees and handed over our country to them.

Thus, from that date, our people were subjected to the double yoke of the French and the Japanese. Their sufferings and miseries increased. The result was that from the end of last year to the beginning of this year, from Quang Tri province to the North of Vietnam, more than two million of our fellow-citizens died from starvation. On March 9, the French troops were disarmed by the Japanese. The French colonialists either fled or surrendered, showing that not only were they incapable of "protecting" us, but that, in the span of five years, they had twice sold our country to the Japanese.

On several occasions before March 9, the Vietminh League urged the French to ally themselves with it against the Japanese. Instead of agreeing to this proposal, the French colonialists so intensified their terrorist activities against the Vietminh members that before fleeing they massacred a great number of our political prisoners detained at Yen Bay and Cao Bang.

Not withstanding all this, our fellow-citizens have always manifested toward the French a tolerant and humane attitude. Even after the Japanese putsch of March 1945, the Vietminh League helped many Frenchmen to cross the frontier, rescued some of them from Japanese jails, and protected French lives and property.

From the autumn of 1940, our country had in fact ceased to be a French colony and had become a Japanese possession.

After the Japanese had surrendered to the Allies, our whole people rose to regain our national sovereignty and to found the Democratic Republic of Vietnam.

The truth is that we have wrested our independence from the Japanese and not from the French.

The French have fled, the Japanese have capitulated, Emperor Bao Dai has abdicated. Our people have broken the chains which for nearly a century have fettered them and have won independence for the Fatherland. Our people at the same time have overthrown the monarchic regime that has reigned supreme for dozens of centuries. In its place has been established the present Democratic Republic.

For these reasons, we, members of the Provisional Government, representing the whole Vietnamese people, declare that from now on we break off all relations of a colonial character with France; we repeal all the international obligation that France has so far subscribed to on behalf of Vietnam and we abolish all the special rights the French have unlawfully acquired in our Fatherland.

The whole Vietnamese people, animated by a common purpose, are determined to fight to the bitter end against any attempt by the French colonialists to reconquer their country.

We are convinced that the Allied nations which at Tehran and San Francisco have acknowledged the principles of self-determination and equality of nations, will not refuse to acknowledge the independence of Vietnam.

A people who have courageously opposed French domination for more than eighty years, a people who have fought side by side with the Allies against the Fascists during these last years, such a people must be free and independent.

For these reasons, we, members of the Provisional Government of the Democratic Republic of Vietnam, solemnly declare to the world that Vietnam has the right to be a free and independent country and in fact it is so already. The entire Vietnamese people are determined to mobilize all their physical and mental strength, to sacrifice their lives and property in order to safeguard their independence and liberty.

→ DOCUMENT 21.2a ←

Policy statement about American objectives in Southeast Asia, June 25, 1952, in *The Pentagon Papers* (Boston: Beacon Press, 1971), vol. 2, pp. 286–288.

25 June 1952

Statement of Policy by the National Security Council on United States Objectives and Courses of Action with Respect to Southeast Asia[1]

Objective

1. To prevent the countries of Southeast Asia from passing into the communist orbit, and to assist them to develop the will and ability to resist communism from within and without and to contribute to the strengthening of the free world.

General Considerations

2. Communist domination, by whatever means, of all Southeast Asia would seriously endanger in the short term, and critically endanger in the longer term, United States security interests.

a. The loss of any of the countries of Southeast Asia to communist control as a consequence of overt or covert Chinese Communist aggression would have critical psychological, political and economic consequences. In the absence of effective and timely counteraction, the loss of any single country would probably lead to relatively swift submission to or an alignment with communism by the remaining countries of this group. Furthermore, an alignment with communism of the rest of Southeast Asia and India, and in the longer term, of the Middle East (with the probable exceptions of at least Pakistan and Turkey) would in all probability progressively follow. Such widespread alignment would endanger the stability and security of Europe.

b. Communist control of all of Southeast Asia would render the U.S. position in the Pacific offshore island chain precarious and would seriously jeopardize fundamental U.S. security interests in the Far East.

c. Southeast Asia, especially Malaya and Indonesia, is the principal world source of natural rubber and tin, and a producer of petroleum and other strategically important commodities. The rice exports of Burma and Thailand are critically important to Malaya, Ceylon and Hong Kong and are of considerable significance to Japan and India, all important areas of free Asia.

d. The loss of Southeast Asia, especially of Malaya and Indonesia, could result in such economic and political pressures in Japan as to make it extremely difficult to prevent Japan's eventual accommodation to communism.

3. It is therefore imperative that an overt attack on Southeast Asia by the Chinese Communists be vigorously opposed. In order to pursue the military courses of action envisaged in this paper to a favorable conclusion within a reasonable period, it will be necessary to divert military strength from other areas thus reducing our military capability in those areas, with the recognized increased risks involved therein, or to increase our military forces in being, or both.

4. The danger of an overt military attack against Southeast Asia is inherent in the existence of a hostile and aggressive Communist China, but such an attack is less probable than continued communist efforts to achieve domination through subversion. The primary threat to Southeast Asia accordingly arises from the possibility that the situation in Indochina may deteriorate as a result of the weakening of the resolve of, or as a result of the inability of the governments of France and of the Associated States to continue to oppose the Viet Minh rebellion, the military strength of which is being steadily increased by virtue of aid furnished by the Chinese Communist regime and its allies.

[1]Southeast Asia is used herein to mean the area embracing Burma, Thailand, Indochina, Malaya and Indonesia.

5. The successful defense of Tonkin is critical to the retention in non-Communist hands of mainland Southeast Asia. However, should Burma come under communist domination, a communist military advance through Thailand might make Indochina, including Tonkin, militarily indefensible. The execution of the following U.S. courses of action with respect to individual countries of the area may vary depending upon the route of communist advance into Southeast Asia.

6. Actions designed to achieve our objections in Southeast Asia require sensitive selection and application, on the one hand to assure the optimum efficiency through coordination of measures for the general area, and on the other, to accommodate to the greatest practicable extent to the individual sensibilities of the several governments, social classes and minorities of the area. . . .

Courses of Action

8. With respect to Indochina the United States should:

a. Continue to promote international support for the three Associated States.

b. Continue to assure the French that the U.S. regards the French effort in Indochina as one of great strategic importance in the general international interest rather than in the purely French interest, and as essential to the security of the free world, not only in the Far East but in the Middle East and Europe as well.

c. Continue to assure the French that we are cognizant of the sacrifices entailed for France in carrying out her effort in Indochina and that, without overlooking the principle that France has the primary responsibility in Indochina, we will recommend to the Congress appropriate military, economic and financial aid to France and the Associated States.

d. Continue to cultivate friendly and increasingly cooperative relations with the Governments of France and the Associated States at all levels with a view to maintaining and, if possible, increasing the degree of influence the U.S. can bring to bear on the policies and actions of the French and Indochinese authorities to the end of directing the course of events toward the objectives we seek. Our influence with the French and Associated States should be designed to further those constructive political, economic and social measures which will tend to increase the stability of the Associated States and thus make it possible for the French to reduce the degree of their participation in the military, economic and political affairs of the Associated States.

e. Specifically we should use our influence with France and the Associated States to promote positive political, military, economic and social policies, among which the following are considered essential elements:

(1) Continued recognition and carrying out by France of its primary responsibility for the defense of Indochina.

(2) Further steps by France and the Associated States toward the evolutionary development of the Associated States.

(3) Such reorganization of French administration and representation in Indochina as will be conducive to an increased feeling of responsibility on the part of the Associated States.

(4) Intensive efforts to develop the armies of the Associated States, including independent logistical and administrative services.

(5) The development of more effective and stable Governments in the Associated States.

(6) Land reform, agrarian and industrial credit, sound rice marketing systems, labor development, foreign trade and capital formation.

(7) An aggressive military, political, and psychological program to defeat or seriously reduce the Viet Minh forces.

(8) US-French cooperation in publicizing progressive developments in the foregoing policies in Indochina.

→ DOCUMENT 21.2b ←

Report by Vice President Johnson on his visit to Asian countries, May 23, 1961. *The Pentagon Papers* as published by the *New York Times*. (New York: Quadrangle Books, 1971), pp. 133–135.

I took to Southeast Asia some basic convictions about the problems faced there. I have come away from the mission there—and to India and Pakistan—with many of those convictions sharpened and deepened by what I saw and learned. I have also reached certain other conclusions which I believe may be of value as guidance for those responsible in formulating policies. These conclusions are as follows:

1. The battle against Communism must be joined in Southeast Asia with strength and determination to achieve success there—or the United States, inevitably, must surrender the Pacific and take up our defenses on our own shores. Asian Communism is compromised and contained by the maintenance of free nations on the subcontinent. Without this inhibitory influence, the island outposts—Philippines, Japan, Taiwan—have no security and the vast Pacific becomes a Red Sea.

2. The struggle is far from lost in Southeast Asia and it is by no means inevitable that it must be lost. In each country it is possible to build a sound structure capable of withstanding and turning the Communist surge. The will to resist—while now the target of subversive attack—is there. The key to what is done by Asians in defense of Southeast Asian freedom is confidence in the United States.

3. There is no alternative to United States leadership in Southeast Asia. Leadership in individual countries—or the regional leadership and cooperation so appealing to Asians—rests on the knowledge and faith in United States power, will and understanding.

4. SEATO is not now and probably never will be the answer because of British and French unwillingness to support decisive action. Asian distrust of the British and French is outspoken. Success at Geneva would prolong SEATO's role. Failure at Geneva would terminate SEATO's meaningfulness. In the latter event, we must be ready with a new approach to collective security in the area.

We should consider an alliance of all the free nations of the Pacific and Asia who are willing to join forces in defense of their freedom. Such an organization should:

a. have a clear-cut command authority

b. also devote attention to measures and programs of social justice, housing, land reform, etc.

5. Asian leaders—at this time—do not want American troops involved in Southeast Asia other than on training missions. American combat troop involvement is not only not required, it is not desirable. Possibly Americans fail to appreciate fully the subtlety that recently-colonial peoples would not look with favor upon governments which invited or accepted the return this soon of Western troops. To the extent that fear of ground troop involvement dominates our political responses to Asia in Congress or elsewhere, it seems most desirable to me to allay those paralyzing fears in confidence, on the strength of the individual statements made by leaders consulted on this trip. This does not minimize or disregard the probability that open attack would bring calls for U.S. combat troops. But the present probability of open attack seems scant, and we might gain much needed flexibility in our policies if the spectre of combat troop commitment could be lessened domestically.

6. Any help—economic as well as military—we give less developed nations to secure and maintain their freedom must be a part of a mutual effort. These nations cannot be saved by United States help alone. To the extent the Southeast Asian nations are prepared to take the necessary measures to make our aid effective, we can be—and must be—unstinting in our assistance. It would be useful to enunciate more clearly than we have—for the guidance of these young and unsophisticated nations—what we expect or require of them.

7. In large measure, the greatest danger Southeast Asia offers to nations like the United States is not the momentary threat of Communism itself, rather that danger stems from hunger, ignorance, poverty and disease. We must—whatever strategies we evolve—keep these enemies the point of our attack, and make imaginative use of our scientific and technological capability in such enterprises.

8. Vietnam and Thailand are the immediate—and most important—trouble spots, critical to the U.S. These areas require the attention of our very best talents—under the very closest Washington direction—on matters economic, military and political.

The basic decision in Southeast Asia is here. We must decide whether to help these countries to the best of our ability or throw in the towel in the area and pull back our defenses to San Francisco and [a] "Fortress America" concept. More important, we would say to the world in this case that we don't live up to treaties and don't stand by our friends. This is not my concept. I recommend that we move forward promptly with a major effort to help these countries defend themselves. I consider the key here is to get our best MAAG people to control, plan, direct and exact results from our military aid program. In Vietnam and Thailand, we must move forward together.

> *a.* In Vietnam, Diem is a complex figure beset by many problems. He has admirable qualities, but he is remote from the people, is surrounded by persons less admirable and capable than he. The country can be saved—if we move quickly and wisely. We must decide whether to support Diem— or let Vietnam fall. We must have coordination of purpose in our country team, diplomatic and military. The Saigon Embassy, USIS, MAAG and related operations leave much to be desired. They should be brought up to maximum efficiency. The most important thing is imaginative, creative, American management of our military aid program. The Vietnamese and our MAAG estimate that $50 million of U.S. military and economic assistance will be needed if we decide to support Vietnam. This is the best information available to us at the present time and if it is confirmed by the best Washington military judgment it should be supported. Since you proposed and Diem agreed to a joint economic mission, it should be appointed and proceed forthwith.
>
> *b.* In Thailand, the Thais and our own MAAG estimate probably as much is needed as in Vietnam—about $50 million of military and economic assistance. Again, should our best military judgment concur, I believe we should support such a program. Sarit is more strongly and staunchly pro-Western than many of his people. He is and must be deeply concerned at the consequence to his country of a communist-controlled Laos. If Sarit is to stand firm against neutralism, he must have—soon—concrete evidence to show his people of United States military and economic support. He believes that his armed forces should be increased to 150,000. His Defense Minister is coming to Washington to discuss aid matters.

The fundamental decision required of the United States—and time is of the greatest importance—is whether we are to attempt to meet the challenge of Communist expansion now in Southeast Asia by a major effort in support of the forces of freedom in the area or throw in the towel. This decision must be made in a full realization of the very heavy and continuing costs involved in terms of money, of effort and of United States prestige. It must be made with the knowledge that at some point we may be faced with the further decision of whether we commit major United States forces to the area or cut our losses and withdraw should our other efforts fail. We must remain master in this decision. What we do in Southeast Asia should be part of a rational program to meet the threat we face in the region as a whole. It should include a clear-cut pattern of specific contributions to be expected by each partner according to his ability and resources. I recommend we proceed with a clear-cut and strong program of action.

I believe that the mission—as you conceived it—was a success. I am grateful to the many who labored to make it so.

DOCUMENT 21.2c

Magazine advertisement about the dangers of socialism. *The Saturday Evening Post*, April 5, 1952, p. 78.

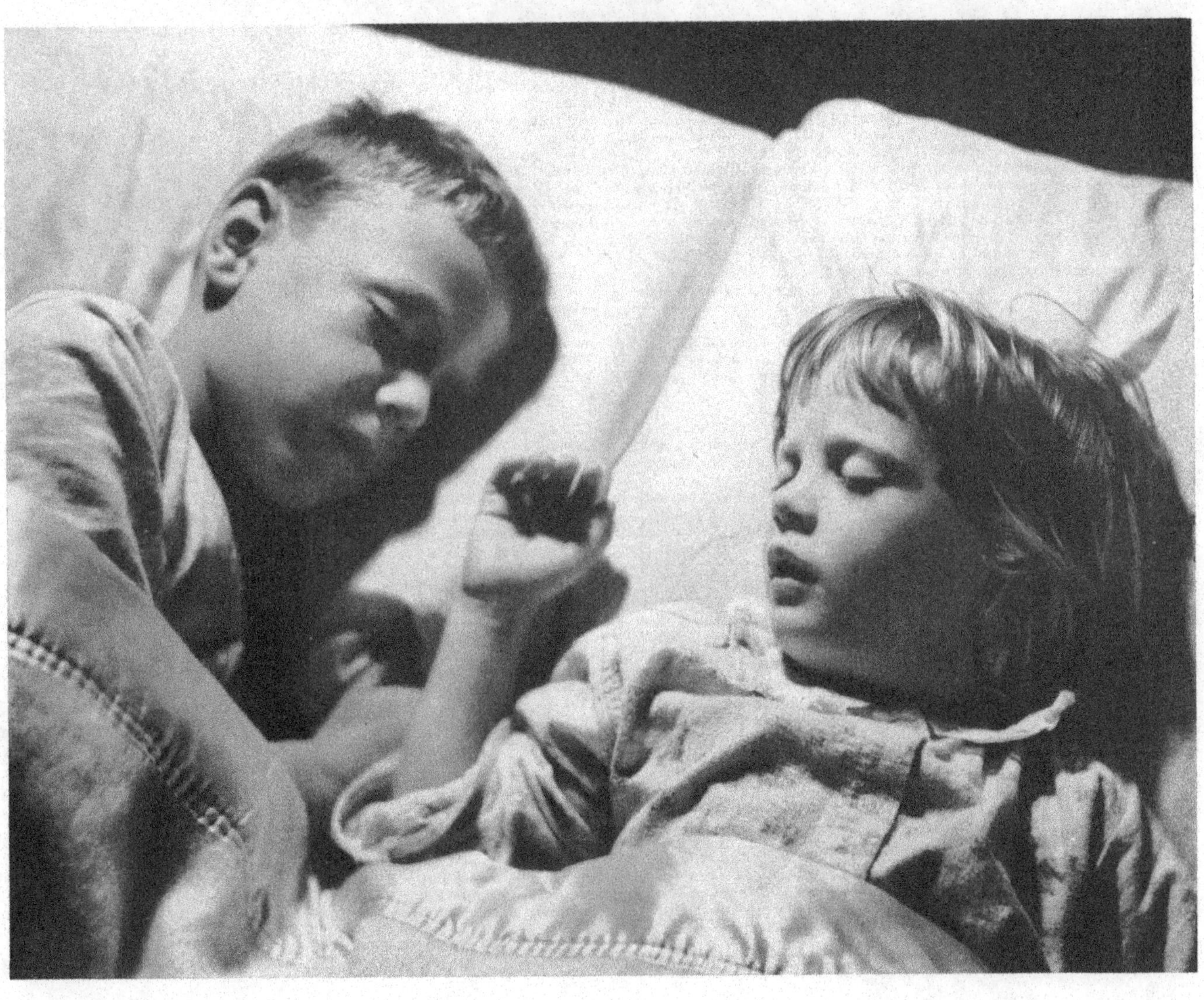

Will they inherit socialism?

You wouldn't want to leave a socialistic America to your children. Most Americans wouldn't.

But you may — without realizing it. For socialism wears many false faces. You can't always tell it at a glance.

It's socialism, for example, when the federal government takes over for keeps the rights and responsibilities of its citizens on any pretext.

It's socialism when the government steps into and takes over a business or industry.

It's socialism when people urge you to give up the freedom to run your own life and let the government run it for you.

Today in America, there are people who would like to see an all-powerful federal government own and operate our railroads, our medical profession, our electric light and power companies and other businesses and services. Perhaps they're not all socialists, but what they suggest is socialism — even though they never call it that.

And they'll have their way unless you act now. Here's what you can do: Start thinking of your future and your children's. Exercise your rights as a citizen. Discuss this danger with your friends and neighbors. Use your ballot wisely. And above all, learn to recognize socialism behind the many false faces it wears.

• • • •

America's *business*-managed, tax-paying ELECTRIC LIGHT AND POWER COMPANIES* publish this advertisement to expose some of the many disguises behind which socialism operates in this country.

**Names on request from this magazine*

Electric power is the key to U. S. production strength. We need more and more of it to produce more steel, aluminum and other materials, and to make them into more planes, ships, tanks and guns.

America's electric light and power companies have planned ahead to have enough electricity ready on time to meet foreseeable demands.

They'll *have* it ready...*if* their suppliers can get the steel and other materials they need to finish the new power plants, new lines and equipment they've started.

"MEET CORLISS ARCHER"
ABC—Sundays
9:15 P. M., Eastern Time;

Look for the
"ELECTRIC THEATRE"
on Television.

→ DOCUMENT 21.3 ←

General Vo Nguyen Giap's reflections on the people's war, 1961, in Thomas G. Paterson and Dennis Merrill, *Major Problems in American Foreign Relations* (Lexington: D.C. Heath, 1995), vol.2, pp.538-539.

The Vietnamese people's war of liberation was a just war, aiming to win back the independence and unity of the country, to bring land to our peasants and guarantee them the right to it, and to defend the achievements of the August Revolution. That is why it was first and foremost a people's war. To educate, mobilise, organise and arm the whole people in order that they might take part in the Resistance was a crucial question.

The enemy of the Vietnamese nation was aggressive imperialism, which had to be overthrown. But the latter having long since joined up with the feudal landlords, the anti-imperialist struggle could definitely not be separated from antifeudal action. On the other hand, in a backward colonial country such as ours where the peasants make up the majority of the population, a people's war is essentially a peasant's war under the leadership of the working class. Owing to this fact, a general mobilisation of the whole people is neither more nor less than the mobilisation of the rural masses. The problem of land is of decisive importance. From an exhaustive analysis, the Vietnamese people's war of liberation was essentially a people's national democratic revolution carried out under armed form and had [a] twofold fundamental task: the overthrowing of imperialism and the defeat of the feudal landlord class, the anti-imperialist struggle being the primary task.

A backward colonial country which had only just risen up to proclaim its independence and install people's power, Viet Nam only recently possessed armed forces, equipped with still very mediocre arms and having no combat experience. Her enemy, on the other hand, was an imperialist power [France] which has retained a fairly considerable economic and military potentiality despite the recent German occupation [during World War II] and benefited, furthermore, from the active support of the United States. The balance of forces decidedly showed up our weaknesses against the enemy's power. The Vietnamese people's war of liberation had, therefore, to be a hard and long-lasting war in order to succeed in creating conditions for victory. All the conceptions born of impatience and aimed at obtaining speedy victory could only be gross errors. It was necessary to firmly grasp the strategy of a long-term resistance, and to exalt the will to be self-supporting in order to maintain and gradually augment our forces. . . .

From the point of view of directing operations, our *strategy and tactics had to be those of a people's war and of a long-term resistance.*

Our strategy was, as we have stressed, to wage a long-lasting battle. A war of this nature in general entails several phases; in principle, starting from a stage of contention, it goes through a period of equilibrium before arriving at a general counter-offensive. In effect, the way in which it is carried on can be more subtle and more complex, depending on the particular conditions obtaining on both sides during the course of operations. Only a long-term war could enable us to utilise to the maximum our political trump cards, to overcome our material handicap and to transform our weakness into strength. To maintain and increase our forces, was the principle to which we adhered, contenting ourselves with attacking when success was certain, refusing to give battle likely to incur losses to us or to engage in hazardous actions. We had to apply the slogan: to build up our strength during the actual course of fighting.

The forms of fighting had to be completely adapted that is, to raise the fighting spirit to the maximum and rely on heroism of our troops to overcome the enemy's material superiority. In the main, especially at the outset of the war, we had recourse to guerilla fighting. In the Vietnamese theatre of operations, this method carried off great victories: it could be used in the mountains as well as in the delta, it could be waged with good or mediocre material and even without arms, and was to enable us eventually to equip ourselves at the cost of the enemy. Wherever the Expeditionary Corps came, the entire population took part in the fighting; every commune had its fortified village, every district had its regional troops fighting under the command of the local branches of the Party and the people's administration, in liaison with the regular forces in order to wear down and annihilate the enemy forces.

Thereafter, with the development of our forces, guerilla warfare changed into a mobile warfare—a form of mobile warfare still strongly marked by guerilla warfare—which would afterwards become the essential form of operations on the main front, the northern front. In this process of development of guerilla warfare and of accentuation of the mobile warfare, our people's army constantly grew and passed from the stage of combats involving a section or company, to fairly large-scale campaigns bringing into action several divisions. Gradually, its equipment improved, mainly by the seizure of arms from the enemy—the materiel of the French and American imperialists.

From the military point of view, *the Vietnamese people's war of liberation proved that an insufficiently equipped people's army, but an army fighting for a just cause, can, with appropriate strategy and tactics, combine the conditions needed to conquer a modern army of aggressive imperialism.*

→ DOCUMENT 21.4a ←

Photograph of Vietnamese resistance measures, 1965, by Duong Thanh Phong. Postcard reproduction, personal collection of Julie Roy Jeffrey.

✧ DOCUMENT 21.4b ✧

Photograph of tunnel construction, 1965, by Duong Thanh Phong. Postcard reproduction, personal collection of Julie Roy Jeffrey.

✧ DOCUMENT 21.4c ✧

Photograph of constructing weapons from unexploded American bombs, 1965, by Duong Thanh Phong. Postcard reproduction, personal collection of Julie Roy Jeffrey.

→ DOCUMENT 21.4d ←

Photograph of a Cu Chi female guerrilla, 1965, by Duong Thanh Phong. Postcard reproduction, personal collection of Julie Roy Jeffrey.

→ DOCUMENT 21.4e ←

Photograph of making bamboo traps, 1965, by Duong Thanh Phong. Postcard reproduction, personal collection of Julie Roy Jeffrey.

✧ DOCUMENT 21.5 ✧

Cartoon about the war, 1964, by William Mauldin, November 25, 1964. Mauldin, reprinted with special permission from the Chicago Sun-Times, Inc. © 2000.

"What's so funny, Monsieur? I'm only trying to find my way."

November 25, 1964

→ DOCUMENT 21.6 ←

Testimony by Marine William Crandell at the Winter Soldier Investigation, January 31 and February 1, 1971. The Sixties Project, sponsored by Viet Nam Generation, Inc., and the *Advanced Institute of Advanced Technology in the Humanities,* the University of Virginia.

OPENING STATEMENT OF *WILLIAM CRANDELL*

"Over the border they send us to kill and to fight for a cause they've long ago forgotten." These lines of Paul Simon's recall to Vietnam veterans the causes for which we went to fight in Vietnam and the outrages we were part of because the men who sent us had long ago forgotten the meaning of the words.

We went to preserve the peace and our testimony will show that we have set all of Indochina aflame. We went to defend the Vietnamese people and our testimony will show that we are committing genocide against them. We went to fight for freedom and our testimony will show that we have turned Vietnam into a series of concentration camps.

We went to guarantee the right of self-determination to the people of South Vietnam and our testimony will show that we are forcing a corrupt and dictatorial government upon them. We went to work toward the brotherhood of man and our testimony will show that our strategy and tactics are permeated with racism. We went to protect America and our testimony will show why our country is being torn apart by what we are doing in Vietnam.

In the bleak winter of 1776 when the men who had enlisted in the summer were going home because the way was hard and their enlistments were over, Tom Paine wrote, "Those are the times that try men's souls. The summer soldier and the sunshine patriot will in this crisis shrink from the service of his country, but he that stands it now deserves the love and thanks of man and woman." Like the winter soldiers of 1776 who stayed after they had served their time, we veterans of Vietnam know that America is in grave danger. What threatens our country is not Redcoats or even Reds; it is our crimes that are destroying our national unity by separating those of our countrymen who deplore these acts from those of our countrymen who refuse to examine what is being done in America's name.

The Winter Soldier Investigation is not a mock trial. There will be no phony indictments; there will be no verdict against Uncle Sam. In these three days, over a hundred Vietnam veterans will present straightforward testimony—direct testimony—about acts which are war crimes under international law. Acts which these men have seen and participated in. Acts which are the inexorable result of national policy. The vets will testify in panels arranged by the combat units in which they fought so that it will be easy to see the policy of each division and thus the larger policy. Each day there will be a special panel during the hours of testimony. Today, a panel on weaponry will explain the use and effects of some of the vicious and illegal weapons used in Vietnam. Tomorrow there will be a panel on prisoners of war composed of returned POWs, parents of a POW, American POW interrogators and vets who served in our own military stockades. Every witness throughout the three days will be available for cross-examination by the press after their initial statements and questioning by their fellow-vets who are acting as moderators. . . .

It has often been remarked but seldom remembered that war itself is a crime. Yet a war crime is more and other than war. It is an atrocity beyond the usual barbaric bounds of war. It is legal definition growing out of custom and tradition supported by every civilized nation in the world including our own. It is an act beyond the pale of acceptable actions even in war. Deliberate killing or torturing of prisoners of war is a war crime. Deliberate destruction without military purpose of civilian communities is a war crime. The use of certain arms and armaments and of gas is a war crime. The forcible relocation of population for any purpose is a war crime. All of these crimes have been committed by the U.S. Government over the past ten years in Indochina. An estimated one million South Vietnamese civilians have been killed because of these war crimes. A good portion of the reported 700,000 National Liberation Front and North Vietnamese soldiers killed have died as a result of these war crimes and no one knows how many North Vietnamese civilians, Cambodian civilians, and Laotian civilians have died as a result of these war crimes.

But we intend to tell more. We intend to tell who it was that gave us those orders; that created that policy; that set that standard of war bordering on full and final genocide. We intend to demonstrate that My Lai was no unusual occurrence, other than, perhaps, the number of victims killed all in one place, all at one time, all by one platoon of us. We intend to show that the policies of Americal Division which inevitably resulted in My Lai were the policies of other Army and Marine Divisions as well. We intend to show that war crimes in Vietnam did not start in March 1968, or in the village of Son My or with one Lt. William Calley. We intend to indict those really responsible for My Lai, for Vietnam, for attempted genocide. General Westmoreland said in 1966:

> I'd like to say that let one fact be clear. As far as the U.S. Military Assistance Command in Vietnam is concerned, one mishap, one innocent civilian killed, one civilian wounded, or one dwelling needlessly destroyed is too many.
>
> By its very nature war is destructive and historically civilians have suffered. But the war in Vietnam is different; it is designed by the insurgents and the aggressors to be fought among the people many of whom are not participants in or closely identified with the struggle. People more than terrain are the objectives in this war and we will not and cannot be callous about those people. We are sensitive to these incidents and want no more of them. If one does occur, mistake or accident, we intend to search it carefully for any lesson that will help us improve our procedures and our controls. We realize we have a great problem and I can assure you we are attacking it aggressively.

We need not judge Westmoreland's bland assurances nor need we pass responsibility for these crimes. You who hear or read our testimony will be able to conclude for yourselves who is responsible.

We are here to bear witness not against America, but against those policy makers who are perverting America. We echo Mark Twain's indictment of the war crimes committed during the Philippine insurrection:

> We have invited our clean young men to soldier a discredited musket and do bandit's work under a flag which bandits have been accustomed to fear not to follow. We cannot conceal from ourselves that privately we are a little troubled about our uniform. It is one of our prides: it is acquainted with honor; it is familiar with great deeds and noble. We love it; we revere it. And so this errand it is on makes us uneasy. And our flag, another pride of ours, the chiefest. We have worshipped it so and when we have seen it in far lands, glimpsing it unexpectedly in that strange sky, waving its welcome and benediction to us, we have caught our breaths and uncovered our heads for a moment for the thought of what it was to us and the great ideals it stood for. Indeed, we must do something about these things. It is easily managed. We can have just our usual flag with the white stripes painted black and the stars replaced by the skull and crossbones. We are ready to let the testimony say it all.

⟡ DOCUMENT 21.7 ⟡

Testimony by members of the First Marine Division at the Winter Soldier Investigation, January 31 and February 1, 1971. The Sixties Project, sponsored by Viet Nam Generation, Inc., and the *Advanced Institute of Advanced Technology in the Humanities*, the University of Virginia.

MODERATOR. We'd like to ask a few questions of the gentlemen up here. Mr. Craig, on that thing with the convoy, the people you saw a convoy run down an old man—it was an old woman—okay, who is the, or did the convoy commander—what was his rank and did he do anything about it? Did he try and slow the convoy down or did they just run right over her?

CRAIG. The convoy was moving pretty slow and the old woman, like, most of the civilians over there sort of ignore the military people going down the road. And it didn't seem—like he didn't beep the horn or like do anything—like, he just moved up to the old woman and started nudging her and then I saw her fall out of the way. When the convoy had completely passed, like she was on the road, really like squashed.

MODERATOR. How many—was it a large convoy?

CRAIG. No, it was about five trucks, maybe six.

MODERATOR. Five or six trucks. Did anybody stop from the convoy and see . . .

CRAIG. No, they kept moving. They were loaded.

MODERATOR. They kept moving. Also, did you ever see the mistreatment of prisoners that we had taken? *Viet Cong* suspects or *NVA?*

CRAIG. Yes, I did. These people were only suspects taken from a village after we had a mine sweep team that was wiped out and I guess people more or less went out to pick up these suspects on a grudge basis. When they brought them back in they were loading them on a truck to take them to (?) and they were making a game out of it by grabbing their feet and their hands and swinging them up in the air to see how high they could throw them and land in the back of a duce-and-a-half truck which had a steel bed.

MODERATOR. Okay. Were there any senior *NCOs* present?

CRAIG. There was a Staff Sergeant present.

MODERATOR. Staff Sergeant—that's a staff NCO?

CRAIG. Yes, sir.

. . .

MODERATOR. You have some testimony here on the burning of villages, cutting off of ears, cutting off of heads, calling in artillery on villages for games, women raped, napalm on villages, all sorts of testimony of crimes against the civilians. Could you go into just a few of these to let the people know how you treat the Vietnamese civilian?

CRAIG. All right. The calling in of artillery for games, the way it was worked would be the mortar forward observers would pick out certain houses in villages, friendly villages, and the mortar forward observers would call in mortars until they destroyed that house and then the artillery forward observer would call in artillery until he destroyed another house and whoever used the least amount of artillery, they won. And when we got back someone would have to buy someone else beers. The cutting off of heads—on Operation Stone—there was a Lt. Colonel there and two people had their heads cut off and put on stakes and stuck in the middle of the field. And we were notified that there was press covering the operation and that we couldn't do that anymore.

. . .

MODERATOR. Were these primarily civilians or do you believe that they were, or do you know that they were actual NVA?

CAMILE. The way that we distinguished between civilians and VC, VC had weapons and civilians didn't and anybody that was dead was considered a VC. If you killed someone they said, "How do you know he's a VC?" and the general reply would be, "He's dead," and that was sufficient. When we went through the villages and searched people the women would have all their clothes taken off and the men would use their penises to probe them to make sure they didn't have anything hidden anywhere and this was raping but it was done as searching.

MODERATOR. As searching. Were there officers present there?

CAMILE. Yes, there were.

MODERATOR. Was this on a company level?

CAMILE. Company level.

MODERATOR. The company commander was around when this happened?

CAMILE. Right.

. . .

MODERATOR. Did the men in your outfit, or when you witnessed these things, did they seem to think that it was all right to do anything to the Vietnamese?

CAMILE. It wasn't like they were humans. We were conditioned to believe that this was for the good of the nation, the good of our country, and anything we did was okay. And when you shot someone you didn't think you were shooting at a human. They were a *gook* or a Commie and it was okay. And anything you did to them was okay because, like, they would tell you they'd do it to you if they had the chance.

MODERATOR. This was told you all through your training, then, in boot camp, in advanced training, and so forth and it was followed on then, right on through it?

CAMILE. Definitely.

MODERATOR. Mr. Campbell, you were, I believe, in the same unit that Mr. Camile was. There was a period of perhaps two months separating the time that he left and the time you came. Was this same unit type policy, was this carried on?

CAMPBELL. Some of the policy was not carried on because of an incident that happened in Quang Tri Province that Scott Camile witnessed and there was a big stink about it. There was some kind of investigation into it and I heard about it when I got to Nam and all the guys that were there before me talked about it and things were kind of cooled down and so a lot of this stuff when I first got there wasn't actually carried out. Bravo Company was to cool it for a while. The whole Battalion, actually, because we had a bad mark against us from the incident previous to the time I got there.

MODERATOR. One more question on that. The training—What did you consider the Vietnamese? Were they equal with you?

CAMPBELL. The Vietnamese were gooks. We didn't just call the VC or the NVA gooks. All Vietnamese were gooks and they were slant eyes. They were zips. They were Orientals and they were inferior to us. We were Americans. We were the civilized people. We didn't give a ______ about those people.

MODERATOR. Mr. Eckert, you stated that you witnessed an old Vietnamese woman shot by security guards in Quang Tri Province. Could you elaborate and tell us if she was a VC or a civilian?

ECKERT. I was up in Quang Tri visiting a friend of mine who was on security, which is like a rat patrol. They go out in the little jeeps and patrol the perimeter. We were out about five o'clock in the morning, just about coming in, when they spotted this old woman about—she looked about fifty but she was probably about twenty-five—and she was running across some trees and everyone in the jeep—no one was supposed to be out there, of course, it was not a *free fire zone* but from the hours from dusk to dawn there's not supposed to be anybody out there, and if there is, you're supposed to stop them, check them out, and eliminate them if you have to. So these guys decided that they would kind of play a little game and they let her run about fifty yards and they'd fire in front of her so she'd have to turn around, and then they'd let her run another direction and then they'd cut her off. This went on about a half hour until the time the sun started to come up. So then they decided it best to eliminate her as soon as possible, so they just ripped her off right there, and then the guy, the corporal that was in charge, he decided that they'd better check her out for an ID card just to be safe about it and they went over and, of course, she didn't have an ID card; she didn't have anything. Her only crime was being out probably tending to her buffalo before the time she should have been. These guys just took it upon themselves to waste her.

MODERATOR. What was the general attitude of the men in your unit toward the Vietnamese? Was this a common experience?

ECKERT. I think the feeling was pretty wide spread that these people were inferior to us and based on the training we received these people were not looked upon as even humans. If they had slanted eyes they were the enemy and the only good one was a dead one. And that was for the majority of the people in my unit, that was the only way they looked at it.

→ DOCUMENT 21.8 ←

Testimony by members of the Twenty-fifth Infantry Division at the Winter Soldier Investigation, January 31 and February 1, 1971. The Sixties Project, sponsored by Viet Nam Generation, Inc., and the Advanced Institute of Advanced Technology in the Humanities, the University of Virginia.

MODERATOR. We'd like to move along to a panel on information specialists and on press censorship. Larry Rottmann.

ROTTMANN. My name is Larry Rottmann. I served as Assistant Information Officer for the 25th Infantry Division, based at Cu Chi, Vietnam from June 5th, 1967 till March 9th, 1968. My duties were to be officer in charge of the division newspaper, *Tropic Lightning News,* the *Lightning Two Five* monthly news magazine, and the Lightning Two Five ARVN radio program. I was also in charge of division press releases including photos, officer in charge of visiting newsmen including television network crews, and a frequent briefer of the division staff on all civilian news media and information matters. I'd like to introduce the rest of the members of the information panel: Mike McCusker, who was information specialist with the Marines; Larry Craig, who was information specialist at *Brigade* level in the 25th Division; Vernon Shibla, who was an information specialist on the Brigade level; Alex Primm, who was an information specialist at the 1st Logistical Command Headquarters. Those men will identify themselves and give you a little background. Mike, do you want to start out?

MCCUSKER. My name is Mike McCusker. I was a Sergeant in the Marine Corps and I served in Vietnam in 1966 and '67 with the 1st Marine Division as what they call an Infantry Combat Correspondent. This meant that I went out with every unit of the Infantry that was stationed, generally in Chu Lai, but I ended up all over the *I Corps* with almost every Marine infantry unit and also reconnaissance unit because I was also reconnaissance qualified. These things that the men from the 25th told you were covered up. None of these instances were generally reported. Most of the stories that we wrote generally appeared in such publications as *Stars and Stripes,* a paper we had in I Corps area called *Sea Tiger,* various other military news services, and the civilian press. They appeared in ways that we did not even write them. Information in them was either deleted or added. Quite often what we had written, what we had seen, what we had covered, just didn't come out in the stories. It was something entirely different. The general policy of being an Informational Services man (that's what the Marine Corps calls its reporters, the Informational Services Office). The only thing we had to do with information, I believe, is to cover it up, disguise it, or deny it. Some of the things that we could not write about, and if we did write about them they were always redlined from our stories, were the amount of American dead. Now they'd always go into light casualties, medium casualties, or heavy casualties. However, heavy casualties were never reported upon because when they got to Da Nang—and if they mention casualties in the Da Nang press center, if a platoon went out and got wiped out, they would measure platoon by battalion strength and that would, of course, be light casualties. And play those little games. Every Vietnamese dead was naturally a Viet Cong dead; even six month old babies, 99 year old men and women. If they are dead, they are Viet Cong, which is a misnomer, at any rate.

We could never really write about the Vietnamese life style, or how the Vietnamese viewed their life in their universe, because it's so contrary to how we viewed Vietnam and the purpose of Vietnam. And the dichotomy would be very apparent in any story. We could not write of taking souvenirs—souvenirs that we witnessed being taken such as ears and teeth. You can't help but notice it because it happens all the time and if you did write of it, it would be redlined and, of course, you'd be on the carpet if your Information Services Office could find you out on the field. You could not write of villages being burned, of crops destroyed. You could not write of defoliation, of the use of tear gas. The use of tear gas on at least three occasions—I witnessed tear gas pumped into caves and people running out and shot down as they run out of those caves. When the story of tear gas being used in 7th Marines in 1965 was exploded, through Colonel ______ ______ the regimental commander at the time said it was only for humane purposes. And I witnessed a few of those humane purposes and I did write it in the story, infuriated, and it was redlined. The use of napalm; you can't even use the term napalm any more. It's called incindergel, like Jello. You could not write of women guerrillas, women prisoners; especially the deaths of women, children, old men and women. You could not write of H & I fire which is harassment and interdiction. This was supposedly to keep the Viet Cong on their toes. What they would do is just throw rounds out in every direction every night. It didn't matter where. There was no set plan, just throw them out. Anything in the way, that's a shame. Also free fire zones; a setup. Free fire zones essentially means anything within that zone is dead. Anything moving is fair game. We could not write of these things. One particular instance of the free fire zone was a village that was supposedly pacified and I had to cover it for the division. This colonel went in with a bunch of newsmen—into this one particular village. The medical team that had preceded him has a chow team and they had set up hot chow. They passed out the Band Aids and the Kool-Aid and they only gave medical supplies enough for two days in any particular village because they figured if they gave these medical supplies to a village lasting longer than two days, the *NLF* would get to those supplies and use them. So, therefore, though the medical teams might not visit a particular village for a period of a month, maybe, they would only leave supplies for two days.

→ DOCUMENT 21.9a ←

Photograph of American soldiers wading in rice paddy, 1966, Bong Son, South Vietnam. © Bettmann/CORBIS.

→ DOCUMENT 21.9b ←

Photograph of U.S. soldiers jumping from helicopters, by Bill Hall, November 16, 1967, Dak To, South Vietnam. © Bettmann/CORBIS.

→ DOCUMENT 21.9c ←

Photograph of U.S. troops in action in South Vietnam, February 22, 1968, Hue, South Vietnam.

DOCUMENT 21.9d

Photograph of an American patrol stopping Vietnamese civilians, November 1969, photograph by Bob Lindgren, in Vietnam War Internet Project Image Library. Courtesy Bob Lindgren.

DOCUMENT 21.9e

Photograph of an American soldier with Vietnamese police, December 1969. Cpl. Robert J. Lindgren accompanying South Vietnamese National Police on an operation, in Vietnam War Internet Project Image Library. Courtesy Bob Lindgren.

→ ARCHIVE 22 ←

Experiencing the "Sixties"

Archive Overview

STUDENTS remain fascinated by the actions of their peers of the 1960s, who are now almost in their sixties. Many students today could probably recite a list of the major events, assassinations, rock concert sites, music groups, songs, and slogans from that decade: sit-ins, freedom rides, Birmingham, "We Shall Overcome," JFK, Martin Luther King, Jr., Malcolm X, César Chávez, grape boycotts, the Great Society, urban riots in Detroit, Newark, and other cities, "Black Power," antiwar demonstrations, the Free Speech movement, hippies and Haight-Ashbury, "Drop out and tune in," "Don't trust anyone over 30," SNCC, SDS, NOW, the Beatles, the Rolling Stones, Peter, Paul and Mary, Bob Dylan, "The Times They Are A-Changin," Jimi Hendrix, Janis Joplin, Woodstock, Kent State. The list goes on and on.

The question this archive poses is somewhat different from the sorts of questions you explored in previous archives. In the face of the issues and the tone revealed by this collection of sources from the 1960s, how—if at all—would you have participated in the events of that decade? Would you have been a radical political activist or a moderate? Or would you have been a hippie dropout, a member of the "counterculture"? Or would you have scorned both political and cultural radicalism and joined the Young Americans for Freedom or another conservative group? Or would you have concentrated entirely on getting ahead with your life and career? What choices would you have made about the draft? Who would you have voted for in 1968?

Let these sources take you back to experiencing a taste of the Sixties and guide you in making these decisions. There is a danger, however: In attempting to relive the Sixties (or any

TIMELINE

1960	John F. Kennedy elected president; sit-ins south and north; founding of SDS (Students for a Democratic Society) and SNCC (Student Nonviolent Coordinating Committee)
1961	Freedom rides; voter registration drives; Berlin Wall erected; Bay of Pigs failed invasion of Cuba
1962	SDS approves the Port Huron Statement; Cuban missile crisis
1963	Birmingham; March on Washington; King's "I Have a Dream" speech; Kennedy assassinated; Betty Friedan's *The Feminist Mystique*
1964	LBJ defeats Barry Goldwater for the presidency; Civil Rights Act; National Farm Workers Union organizes grape boycotts; Free Speech movement at Berkeley
1965	Selma to Montgomery march; Voting Rights Act; Assassination of Malcolm X; Watts riots; first antiwar "teach-in" at University of Michigan; The Great Society
1966	Founding of NOW (National Organization for Women); Black Panthers; "Black Power"; SNCC changes name to Student *National* Coordinating Committee
1967	Antiwar march on the Pentagon; urban riots/civil disorders in Newark, Detroit, and other cities; Beatles' "Magical Mystery Tour"
1968	Kerner report on "Civil Disorders"; Tet offensive in Vietnam; assassinations of King and Robert Kennedy; more urban riots; Chicago Democratic Party convention; riots and student demonstrations at Columbia University and other college campuses; Peace and Freedom Party; Richard Nixon elected president
1969	People's Park fight in Berkeley; bombings of more ROTC buildings
1970	Invasion of Cambodia; Kent State and Jackson State protesters killed; publication of *Sisterhood Is Powerful: An Anthology of Writings from the Women's Liberation Movement*, edited by Robin Morgan
1971	*Our Bodies, Our Selves: A Book by and for Women*

historical period), one is tempted to romanticize the past. While the 1960s were an exciting time packed with memorable political and cultural events, they also presented extremely difficult questions and decisions that all Americans, and especially young people, had to face.

Placing the Sources in Context

THE election in 1960 of the young, handsome, idealistic-sounding John F. Kennedy set the tone for the Sixties. In his inaugural address in 1961, Kennedy pronounced that "the torch has been passed to a new generation" and asked his fellow (and younger) Americans to "ask not what your country can do for you" but rather "what you can do for your country." But the "Camelot" dream ended rather abruptly with a number of serious challenges to the Kennedy presidency. The failure of the American-backed attempt to invade Cuba in 1961 at the Bay of Pigs, the decision of communist leaders to erect the Berlin Wall to prevent East Germans from fleeing to the West in 1961, and increasingly tough diplomatic talk from the Soviets seriously tested Kennedy's image and leadership. He also faced subtle pressures to increase the American presence in Vietnam and violent southern white resistance to the struggle for civil rights. His image was salvaged, if temporarily, by his tragic assassination on November 22, 1963.

The middle years of the Sixties were dominated by continued struggles for civil rights and justice, powerful southern resistance, the escalating war in Vietnam (see Archive 21), and the imposing force of Lyndon Johnson. His attempt to create a Great Society through a "war on poverty" and other liberal measures, however, was increasingly pushed aside by the war in Vietnam and the commitment of more American troops and planes to combat the guerrilla forces of the Viet Cong and their North Vietnamese allies. More soldiers meant more dependence on the selective service system (the draft), which touched the lives of more and more 18- to 22-year-olds. In 1966 the Civil Rights movement entered a militant (northern) phase, influenced by the legacy of the slain Malcolm X, and turned away from civil rights in the south to black nationalist liberation and "Black Power" in the north. Women and students were increasingly mobilizing on behalf of a growing sense of their own oppressed status.

In 1964, as Betty Friedan's *Feminine Mystique* was raising women's consciousness, *Time* magazine's "man of the year" was youth. That year marked the coming of age of the "baby boomers," conceived at the end of World War II and turning 18–20 years old in the middle Sixties. The Free Speech movement at the University of California at Berkeley in the fall of 1964, which closed the mega-university, signaled the power of young people. This new force would show itself the rest of the decade, not only in the politics of protest but also in musical tastes, purchasing power, and experimental lifestyle habits. The technological developments of the birth-control pill, stereo phonographs, and music-amplification systems, combined with mind-altering drugs such as marijuana and LSD, stimulated frenzied partying, sexual openness, and huge rock concerts at Woodstock (New York), Altamont (California), and elsewhere.

Although most young people in the Sixties could not help but be influenced by both political and cultural developments, they tended to divide into three groups: political activists, counter-cultural (lifestyle) radicals, and those who avoided both. Political activists demonstrated for and against the war in Vietnam, advocated numerous causes at colleges and universities, and joined organizations like the Students for a Democratic Society (SDS), the Student Nonviolent Coordinating Committee (SNCC), and other "radical" civil rights and antiwar organizations. Conservative students opposed them by joining such groups as the Young Americans for Freedom (YAF).

Black youth in SNCC (and their elders in Dr. King's Southern Christian Leadership Conference) had been involved in civil rights protests since Rosa Parks refused to give up her bus seat and sparked the Montgomery bus boycott in 1955. The movement escalated with the sit-ins in 1960, the freedom rides in 1961, voter registration campaigns, and freedom school efforts throughout the deep south. Actions focused on Birmingham in 1963, Selma in 1965, and many other cities. Northern white activists participated in boycotts, picketing, and other demonstrations against racism and went south for the Mississippi Freedom Summer in 1964 to help register blacks to vote.

Young political activists manifested different degrees of commitment and risk-taking. Cultural radicals, too, varied in the intensity of their experimentation with drugs, sexual freedom, and "dropping out." Still others focused on pursuing their studies, on developing relationships, on launching their careers. However, the fact that political activists and cultural radicals shared the typical interests of youth makes it difficult to generalize about young people in the Sixties. (Imagine trying to categorize youth today!)

By the late Sixties, concepts of liberation had expanded to include Chicano farm workers in California and Texas, American Indians, gays and lesbians, and feminist women of all ages. With the threat of the draft, forcing agonizing choices for men 18–25 years old, more and more students were swept up into these movements, which rocked college campuses. Antiwar demonstrators and advocates for black liberation grew more militant, at least in their rhetoric, and occasionally more violent. The Black Panthers and the Weathermen, a fringe group of SDS, both gained far more public attention than their small numbers warranted. A few violent incidents and bombings brought a reaction from mainstream Americans, who elected Richard Nixon president in 1968 on a law and order platform. Some date the end of the Sixties with the killing of four students at Kent State by the Ohio National Guard during an antiwar demonstration on May 4, 1970.

About the Sources

The sources in this archive reveal some of the causes that college students and other young people supported during the 1960s and suggest their far-ranging concerns. They also suggest that the widespread agreement about American foreign policy and the social, political, racial, generational, and cultural arrangements that seemed to characterize the 1950s was breaking down. In fact, some historians have argued that the conflicts of the 1960s were the most serious the nation has experienced since the Civil War.

You have evidence here of student assessments, from both the conservative and radical points of view (22.2 and 22.3) of the challenges facing the country in the early 1960s. Other sources reveal Civil Rights activism in the south and the growing militancy of black activists in the north (22.4). Huey Newton and Bobby Seale were two of the founders of the Black Panther Party for Self-Defense, an organization that was established in Oakland, California, in 1966. Aspects of student struggles on campus (22.5) give some idea of how conflicts over free speech and even administrative building projects played themselves out on the local level. The antiwar or peace movement (22.6) involved thousands of students. Their efforts included teach-ins, demonstrations outside induction centers, public burnings of draft cards, and marches. Most Americans did not join student demonstrations, and several pictures point to the anger that student activism generated among different groups in the country.

One of the aspects of the 60s that many Americans found troubling was the emergence of a counterculture that rejected middle-class norms of behavior. Several sources (22.7a and b) touch on aspects of the counterculture that shocked parents and politicians alike.

Although feminism became a force in the 1970s, its roots lay in the previous decade (22.8). Think about the ways in which the different causes of the 1960s were intertwined.

At this point in the term, we have confidence that you know how to read primary sources in depth, questioning the authenticity of documents, considering contexts, and asking questions that deepen the meaning of a source. You will also note the variety of sources and know how to "read" visual clues as well as written ones.

Although some of these sources were pertinent to Americans of all ages, the focus of the selection in this archive is on sources that describe the lives and choices of young people during the Sixties. They include oral histories and photographs of activist and counter-cultural youth, the buttons they wore, the petitions they signed (or refused to sign), and the manifestoes from the left and the right that they endorsed, and the music they listened to. These sources should be studied within the context of the larger historical events young Americans both reacted to and helped to make.

List of Sources

22.1 **Political and protest buttons,** 1960s. Personal collection of Peter Frederick.

22.2 **"The Port Huron Statement" of the Students for a Democratic Society,** drafted by Tom Hayden, June 1962, in Ronald Lora, ed., *America in the '60s: Cultural Authorities in Transition* (New York: Wiley, 1974), pp. 259–270.

22.3a **Issues paper no. 7, "Student Subversion, the Majority Replies,"** 1965, Young Americans for Freedom. Personal collection of Peter Frederick.

22.3b **Pamphlet, "What Can *I* Do? to Combat Communism,"** about 1965, Students Associated Against Totalitarianism, Berkeley, California, Christian Anti-Communism Crusade. Personal collection of Peter Frederick.

22.4a **Oral history of the civil rights activist Lawrence Guyot,** in Howell Raines, *My Soul Is Rested: Movement Days in the Deep South Remembered* (New York: Bantam, 1978), pp. 258–263.

22.4b **Enclosure in letter from SNCC: "SNCC Does Not Wish to Become A New Version of the White Man's Burden,"** *I. F. Stone's Weekly*, June 6, 1966. Personal collection of Peter Frederick.

22.4c **Black Panther Flyer, "If You're Not Part of the Solution You're Part of the Problem,"** 1968. Social Movements Collection, University of Virginia.

22.4d **Black Panther Flyer, "Racist Dog Policemen,"** 1968. Social Movements Collection, University of Virginia.

22.4e **Black Panther Flyer, "We Will Not Sit Back and Let the Fascists Murder Chairman Bobby in the Electric Chair,"** no date. Social Movements Collection, University of Virginia.

22.5a **Oral history of a student activist, James Seff,** in Peter Joseph, *Good Times: An Oral History of America in the Nineteen Sixties* (New York: Charterhouse, 1973).

22.5b **Photograph of students and professors in a brawl at Columbia University,** April 28, 1968, New York, New York. © Bettmann/CORBIS.

22.6a **Antiwar appeal from teachers, "Help Stop the War in Vietnam,"** 1967. Personal collection of Peter Frederick.

22.6b **Photograph of Vietnam War Protestors outside the White House,** November 30, 1965, Washington, DC © Hulton-Deutsch Collection/CORBIS.

22.6c **Photograph, "Stop the Vietnam War" rally, Central Park, NYC,** 1968. Photograph by Elliott Landy, 1968.

22.6d **Photograph, "Along the March Route," Washington, DC,** 1967. Photograph by Elliott Landy, 1967.

22.6e **Photograph, "Pentagon Peace Demonstration," Washington, DC,** 1967. Photograph by Elliott Landy, 1967.

22.6f **Photograph, "Pro-war Demonstrator," New York City,** 1968. Photograph by Elliott Landy, 1968.

22.7a **Oral History of cultural rebellion of Erika Taylor,** in Peter

Joseph, *Good Times: An Oral History of America in the Nineteen Sixties* (New York: Charterhouse, 1973).

22.7b **Flyer, "Love: A Psychedelic Celebration, Tompkins Square Park,"** October 6, 1966. Social Movements Collection, University of Virginia.

22.8 **Book covers, *Our Bodies Our Selves: A Book by and for Women,*** 1971 and 1998, by the Boston Women's Health Book Collective, Inc.

Questions to Consider

1. What do the buttons (22.1) suggest about student causes in the 1960s? What do they suggest about the ways in which students made their loyalties known to others?

2. In what ways does the Port Huron Statement (22.2) set apart the students from their parents' generation? How radical were their goals for the nation? What is idealistic about this statement? What kind of a country did the founders of the SDS want to create? What changes did they envision for the university? Are you sympathetic to this statement of beliefs and goals?

3. Contrast the principles and beliefs expressed in the Sharon Statement (22.3a), generated by Young Americans for Freedom, and the pamphlet by the Students Associated Against Totalitarianism (22.3b) with the Port Huron Statement (22.2). What are the crucial differences? Are there any similarities? What do these sources suggest about student opinion in the 1960s? What is appealing about the conservative position?

4. Describe the difficulties facing Lawrence Guyot (22.4a) as he attempted to register blacks to vote. How dangerous was his work? How successfully did the white community resist the efforts of the SNCC workers? In what ways do the other sources suggest the growing radicalization of the Civil Rights movement? What kind of language and images did the Black Panthers exploit? How might white northerners respond to the process of radicalization we see here?

5. How does James Seff (22.5a) describe the Free Speech movement on the Berkeley campus? What were the students doing? Why did the police and administration respond as they did to what was a nonviolent protest? Why do you think the Free Speech movement generated the "foul speech movement?" What does the Columbia picture suggest could happen when students protested?

6. In what ways does the antiwar appeal from teachers (22.6a) condemn the war? How does it urge people to end the war? What other activities of the antiwar movement appear in the photograph (22.5b)? How might the publication of such pictures affect those who supported the war? Would they be persuasive to those who were beginning to question the wisdom of American policy? Why were the military police involved in the Pentagon peace demonstration? What can we learn about those who thought American military involvement in Vietnam was the correct policy for the United States?

7. Use the various sources on the counterculture (22.7) as the basis for a description of the activities and values of those who participated in it. What mainstream values were rejected? What were the new standards of behavior?

8. What role in general did the Civil Rights movement play in generating the radicalism of the 1960s? How were the different forms of activism connected?

9. How would you characterize the 1960s? Do you agree with the view that that decade witnessed a virtual civil (or perhaps uncivil) war? What aspects of modern life can we trace to the 1960s? How successful were the activists of the 1960s in transforming American life?

DOCUMENT 22.1

Political and protest buttons, 1960s. Personal collection of Peter Frederick.

NO TUITION
TAX
WAR PROFITS
OUT
NOW.
PEACE
PAZ
PEACE
SHALOM
WORK FOR PEACE
NOV 13 & 14
OUT
NOW.
april
OUT
NOW
15
SMC
Free
DAN
and
PHIL
BRING
THE
TROOPS
HOME
NOW!
READ THE NEWSLETTER
THOREAU
war
is not
healthy
for
children
and
other
living
things
DEC.
4
THE
RESISTANCE
HOW
MANY
MORE?

→ DOCUMENT 22.2 ←

"The Port Huron Statement" of the Students for a Democratic Society, drafted by Tom Hayden, June 1962, in Ronald Lora, ed., *America in the '60s: Cultural Authorities in Transition* (New York: Wiley, 1974), pp. 259–270. By permission of Tom Hayden.

The Port Huron Statement

Introduction: Agenda for a Generation

We are people of this generation, bred in at least modest comfort, housed now in universities, looking uncomfortably to the world we inherit.

When we were kids the United States was the wealthiest and strongest country in the world; the only one with the atom bomb, the least scarred by modern war, an initiator of the United Nations that we thought would distribute Western influence throughout the world. Freedom and equality for each individual, government of, by, and for the people—these American values we found good, principles by which we could live as men. Many of us began maturing in complacency.

As we grew, however, our comfort was penetrated by events too troubling to dismiss. First, the permeating and victimizing fact of human degradation, symbolized by the Southern struggle against racial bigotry, compelled most of us from silence to activism. Second, the enclosing fact of the Cold War, symbolized by the presence of the Bomb, brought awareness that we ourselves, and our friends, and millions of abstract "others" we knew more directly because of our common peril, might die at any time. We might deliberately ignore, or avoid, or fail to feel all other human problems, but not these two, for these were too immediate and crushing in their impact, too challenging in the demand that we as individuals take the responsibility for encounter and resolution.

While these and other problems either directly oppressed us or rankled our consciences and became our own subjective concerns, we began to see complicated and disturbing paradoxes in our surrounding America. The declaration "all men are created equal . . ." rang hollow before the facts of Negro life in the South and the big cities of the North. The proclaimed peaceful intentions of the United States contradicted its economic and military investments in the Cold War status quo.

We witnessed, and continue to witness, other paradoxes. With nuclear energy whole cities can easily be powered, yet the dominant nation-states seem more likely to unleash destruction greater than that incurred in all wars of human history. Although our own technology is destroying old and creating new forms of social organization, men still tolerate meaningless work and idleness. While two-thirds of mankind suffers undernourishment, our own upper classes revel amidst superfluous abundance. Although world population is expected to double in forty years, the nations still tolerate anarchy as a major principle of international conduct and uncontrolled exploitation governs the sapping of the earth's physical resources. Although mankind desperately needs revolutionary leadership, America rests in national stalemate, its goals ambiguous and tradition-bound instead of informed and clear, its democratic system apathetic and manipulated rather than "of, by, and for the people."

Not only did tarnish appear on our image of American virtue, not only did disillusion occur when the hypocrisy of American ideals was discovered, but we began to sense that what we had originally seen as the American Golden Age was actually the decline of an era. The worldwide outbreak of revolution against colonialism and imperialism, the entrenchment of totalitarian states, the menace of war, overpopulation, international disorder, supertechnology—these trends were testing the tenacity of our own commitment to democracy and freedom and our abilities to visualize their application to a world in upheaval.

Our work is guided by the sense that we may be the last generation in the experiment with living. But we are a minority—the vast majority of our people regard the temporary equilibriums of our society and world as eternally functional parts. In this is perhaps the outstanding paradox: we ourselves are imbued with urgency, yet the message of our society is that there is no viable alternative to the present. Beneath the reassuring tones of the politicians, beneath the common opinion that America will "muddle through," beneath the stagnation of those who have closed their minds to the future, is the pervading feeling that there simply are no alternatives, that our times have witnessed the exhaustion not only of Utopias, but of any new departures as well. Feeling the press of complexity upon the emptiness of life, people are fearful of the thought that at any moment things might be thrust out of control. They fear change itself, since change might smash whatever invisible framework seems to hold back chaos for them now. For most Americans, all crusades are suspect, threatening. The fact that each individual sees apathy in his fellows perpetuates the common reluctance to organize for change. The dominant institutions are complex enough to blunt the minds of their potential critics, and entrenched enough to swiftly dissipate or entirely repel the energies of protest and reform, thus limiting human expectancies. Then, too, we are a materially improved society, and by our own improvements we seem to have weakened the case for further change.

Some would have us believe that Americans feel contentment amidst prosperity—but might it not better be called a glaze above deeply felt anxieties about their role in the new world? And if these anxieties produce a developed indifference to human affairs, do they not as well produce a yearning to believe there *is* an alternative to the present, that something *can* be done to change circumstances in the school, the workplaces, the bureaucracies, the government? It is to this latter yearning, at once the spark and engine of change, that we direct our present appeal. The search for truly democratic alternatives to the present, and a commitment to social experimentation with them, is a worthy and fulfilling human enterprise, one which moves us and, we hope, others today. On such a basis do we offer this document of our convictions and analysis: as an effort in understanding and changing the conditions of humanity in the late twentieth century, an effort rooted in the ancient, still unfulfilled conception of man attaining determining influence over his circumstances of life.

VALUES

Making values explicit—an initial task in establishing alternatives—is an activity that has been devalued and corrupted. The conventional moral terms of the age, the politician moralities—"free world," "people's democracies"—reflect realities poorly, if at all, and seem to function more as ruling myths than as descriptive principles. But neither has our experience in the universities brought us moral enlightenment. Our professors and administrators sacrifice controversy to public relations; their curriculums change more slowly than the living events of the world; their skills and silence are purchased by investors in the arms race; passion is called unscholastic. The questions we might want raised—what is really important? can we live in a different and better way? if we wanted to change society, how would we do it?—are not thought to be questions of a "fruitful, empirical nature," and thus are brushed aside.

Unlike youth in other countries we are used to moral leadership being exercised and moral dimensions being clarified by our elders. But today, for us, not even the liberal and socialist preachments of the past seem adequate to the forms of the present. Consider the old slogans: Capitalism Cannot Reform Itself, United Front Against Fascism, General Strike, All Out on May Day. Or, more recently, No Cooperation with Commies and Fellow Travelers, Ideologies are Exhausted, Bipartisanship, No Utopias. These are incomplete, and there are few new prophets. It has been said that our liberal and socialist predecessors were plagued by vision without program, while our own generation is plagued by program without vision. All around us there is astute grasp of method, technique—the committee, the *ad hoc* group, the lobbyist, the hard and soft sell, the make, the projected image—but, if pressed critically, such expertise is incompetent to explain its implicit ideals. It is highly fashionable to identify oneself by old categories, or by naming a respected political figure, or by explaining "how we would vote" on various issues.

Theoretic chaos has replaced the idealistic thinking of old—and, unable to reconstitute theoretic order, men have condemned idealism itself. Doubt has replaced hopefulness—and men act out a defeatism that is labeled realistic. The decline of utopia and hope is in fact one of the defining features of social life today. The reasons are various: the dreams of the older left were perverted by Stalinism and never recreated; the congressional stalemate makes men narrow their view of the possible; the specialization of human activity leaves little room for sweeping thought; the horrors of the twentieth century, symbolized in the gas ovens and concentration camps and atom bombs, have blasted hopefulness. To be idealistic is to be considered apocalyptic, deluded. To have no serious aspirations, on the contrary, is to be "tough-minded."

In suggesting social goals and values, therefore, we are aware of entering a sphere of some disrepute. Perhaps matured by the past, we have no sure formulas, no closed theories—but that does not mean values are beyond discussion and tentative determination. A first task of any social movement is to convince people that the search for orienting theories and the creation of human values is complex but worthwhile. We are aware that to avoid platitudes we must analyze the concrete conditions of social order. But to direct such an analysis we must use the guideposts of basic principles. Our own social values involve conceptions of human beings, human relationships, and social systems.

We regard *men* as infinitely precious and possessed of unfulfilled capacities for reason, freedom, and love. In affirming these principles we are aware of countering perhaps the dominant conceptions of man in the twentieth century: that he is a thing to be manipulated, and that he is inherently incapable of directing his own affairs. We oppose the depersonalization that reduces human beings to the status of things—if anything, the brutalities of the twentieth century teach that means and ends are intimately related, that vague appeals to "posterity" cannot justify the mutilations of the present. We oppose, too, the doctrine of human incompetence because it rests essentially on the modern fact that men have been "competently" manipulated into incompetence—we see little reason why men cannot meet with increasing skill the complexities and responsibilities of their situation, if society is organized not for minority, but for majority, participation in decision-making.

Men have unrealized potential for self-cultivation, self-direction, self-understanding, and creativity. It is this potential that we regard as crucial and to which we appeal, not to the human potentiality for violence, unreason, and submission to authority. The goal of man and society should be human independence: a concern not with image of popularity but with finding a meaning in life that is personally authentic; a quality of mind not compulsively driven by a sense of powerlessness, nor one which unthinkingly adopts status values, nor one which represses all threats to its habits, but one which has full, spontaneous access to present and past experiences, one which easily unites the fragmented parts of personal history, one which openly faces problems which are troubling and unresolved; one with an intuitive awareness of possibilities, an active sense of curiosity, an ability and willingness to learn.

This kind of independence does not mean egotistic individualism—the object is not to have one's way so much as it is to have a way that is one's own. Nor do we deify man—we merely have faith in his potential.

Human relationships should involve fraternity and honesty. Human interdependence is contemporary fact; human brotherhood must be willed, however, as a condition of future survival and as the most appropriate form of social relations. Personal links between man and man are needed, especially to go beyond the partial and fragmentary bonds of function that bind men only as worker to worker, employer to employee, teacher to student, American to Russian.

Loneliness, estrangement, isolation describe the vast distance between man and man today. These dominant tendencies cannot be overcome by better personnel management, nor by improved gadgets, but only when a love of man overcomes the idolatrous worship of things by man. As the individualism we affirm is not egoism, the selflessness we affirm is not self-elimination. On the contrary, we believe in generosity of a kind that imprints one's unique individual qualities in the relation to other men, and to all human activity. Further, to dislike isolation is not to favor the abolition of privacy; the latter differs from isolation in that it occurs or is abolished according to individual will.

We would replace power rooted in possession, privilege, or circumstance by power and uniqueness rooted in love, reflectiveness, reason, and creativity. As a *social system* we seek the establishment of a democracy of individual participation, governed by two central aims: that the individual share in those social decisions determining the quality and direction of his life; that society be organized to encourage independence in men and provide the media for their common participation.

In a participatory democracy, the political life would be based in several root principles:

That decision-making of basic social consequence be carried on by public groupings.

That politics be seen positively, as the art of collectively creating an acceptable pattern of social relations.

That politics has the function of bringing people out of isolation and into community, thus being a necessary, though not sufficient, means of finding meaning in personal life.

That the political order should serve to clarify problems in a way instrumental to their solution; it should provide outlets for the expression of personal grievance and aspiration; opposing views should be organized so as to illuminate choices and facilitate the attainment of goals; channels should be commonly available to relate men to knowledge and to power so that private problems—from bad recreation facilities to personal alienation—are formulated as general issues.

The economic sphere would have as its basis the principles:

That work should involve incentives worthier than money or survival. It should be educative, not stultifying; creative, not mechanical; self-directed, not manipulated, encouraging independence, a respect for others, a sense of dignity and a willingness to accept social responsibility, since it is this experience that has crucial influence on habits, perceptions and individual ethics.

That the economic experience is so personally decisive that the individual must share in its full determination.

That the economy itself is of such social importance that its major resources and means of production should be open to democratic participation and subject to democratic social regulation.

Like the political and economic ones, major social institutions—cultural, educational, rehabilitative, and others—should be generally organized with the well-being and dignity of man as the essential measure of success.

In social change or interchange, we find violence to be abhorrent because it requires generally the transformation of the target, be it a human being or a community of people, into a depersonalized object of hate. It is imperative that the means of violence be abolished and the institutions—local, national, international—that encourage nonviolence as a condition of conflict be developed.

These are our central values, in skeletal form. It remains vital to understand their denial or attainment in the context of the modern world.

The Students

In the last few years, thousands of American students demonstrated that they at least felt the urgency of the times. They moved actively and directly against racial injustices, the threat of war, violations of individual rights of conscience and, less frequently, against economic manipulation. They succeeded in restoring a small measure of controversy to the campuses after the stillness of the McCarthy period. They succeeded, too, in gaining some concessions from the people and institutions they opposed, especially in the fight against racial bigotry.

The significance of these scattered movements lies not in their success or failure in gaining objectives—at least not yet. Nor does the significance lie in the intellectual "competence" or "maturity" of the students involved—as some pedantic elders allege. The significance is in the fact the students are breaking the crust of apathy and overcoming the inner alienation that remain the defining characteristics of American college life.

If student movements for change are still rareties on the campus scene, what is commonplace there? The real campus, the familiar campus, is a place of private people, engaged in their notorious "inner emigration." It is a place of commitment to business-as-usual, getting ahead, playing it cool. It is a place of mass affirmation of the Twist, but mass reluctance toward the controversial public stance. Rules are accepted as "inevitable," bureaucracy as "just circumstances," irrelevance as "scholarship," selflessness as "martyrdom," politics as "just another way to make people, and an unprofitable one, too."

Almost no students value activity as citizens. Passive in public, they are hardly more idealistic in arranging their private lives: Gallup concludes they will settle for "low success, and won't risk high failure." There is not much willingness to take risks (not even in business), no setting of dangerous goals, no real conception of personal identity except one manufactured in the image of others, no real urge for personal fulfillment except to be almost as successful as the very successful people. Attention is being paid to social status (the quality of shirt collars, meeting people, getting wives or husbands, making solid contacts for later on); much, too, is paid to academic status (grades, honors, the med school rat race). But neglected generally is real intellectual status, the personal cultivation of the mind.

"Students don't even give a damn about the apathy," one has said. Apathy toward apathy begets a privately constructed universe, a place of systematic study schedules, two nights each week for beer, a girl or two, and early marriage; a framework infused with personality, warmth, and under control, no matter how unsatisfying otherwise.

Under these conditions university life loses all relevance to some. Four hundred thousand of our classmates leave college every year.

But apathy is not simply an attitude: it is a product of social institutions, and of the structure and organization of higher education itself. The extracurricular life is ordered according to *in loco parentis* theory, which ratifies the administration as the moral guardian of the young.

The accompanying "let's pretend" theory of student extracurricular affairs validates student government as a training center for those who want to spend their lives in political pretense, and discourages initiative from the more articulate, honest, and sensitive students. The bounds and style of controversy are delimited before controversy begins. The university "prepares" the student for "citizenship" through perpetual rehearsals and, usually, through emasculation of what creative spirit there is in the individual.

The academic life contains reinforcing counterparts to the way in which extracurricular life is organized. The academic world is founded on a teacher-student relation analogous to the parent-child relation which characterizes *in loco parentis*. Further, academia includes a radical separation of the student from the material of study. That which is studied, the social reality, is "objectified" to sterility, dividing the student from life—just as he is restrained in active involvement by the deans controlling student government. The specialization of function and knowledge, admittedly necessary to our complex technological and social structure, has produced an exaggerated compartmentalization of study and understanding. This has contributed to an overly parochial view, by faculty, of the role of its research and scholarship, to a discontinuous and truncated understanding, by students, of the surrounding social order; and to a loss of personal attachment, by nearly all, to the worth of study as a humanistic enterprise.

There is, finally, the cumbersome academic bureaucracy extending throughout the academic as well as the extracurricular structures, contributing to the sense of outer complexity and inner powerlessness that transforms the honest searching of many students to a ratification of convention and, worse, to a numbness to present and future catastrophes. The size and financing systems of the university enhance the permanent trusteeship of the administrative bureaucracy, their power leading to a shift within the university toward the value standards of business and the administrative mentality. Huge foundations and other private financial interests shape the under-financed colleges and universities, not only making them more commercial, but less disposed to diagnose society critically, less open to dissent. Many social and physical scientists, neglecting the liberating heritage of higher learning, develop "human relations" or "morale-producing" techniques for the corporate economy, while others exercise their intellectual skills to accelerate the arms race. . . .

There are no convincing apologies for the contemporary malaise. While the world tumbles toward the final war, while men in other nations are trying desperately to alter events, while the very future qua future is uncertain—America is without community, impulse, without the inner momentum necessary for an age when societies cannot successfully perpetuate themselves by their military weapons, when democracy must be viable because of the quality of life, not its quantity of rockets.

The apathy here is, first, *subjective*—the felt powerlessness of ordinary people, the resignation before the enormity of events. But subjective apathy is encouraged by the *objective* American situation—the actual structural separation of people from power, from relevant knowledge, from pinnacles of decision-making. Just as the university influences the student way of life, so do major social institutions create the circumstances in which the isolated citizen will try hopelessly to understand his world and himself.

The very isolation of the individual—from power and community and ability to aspire—means the rise of a democracy without publics. With the great mass of people structurally remote and psychologically hesitant with respect to democratic institutions, those institutions themselves attenuate and become, in the fashion of the vicious circle, progressively less accessible to those few who aspire to serious participation in social affairs. The vital democratic connection between community and leadership, between the mass and the several elites, has been so wrenched and perverted that disastrous policies go unchallenged time and again. . . .

→ DOCUMENT 22.3a ←

Issues paper no. 7, "Student Subversion, the Majority Replies," 1965, Young Americans for Freedom. Personal collection of Peter Frederick. Reprinted by permission of Young Americans for Freedom.

ISSUES PAPER NUMBER 7

STUDENT SUBVERSION

the majority replies

YOUNG AMERICANS FOR FREEDOM

The Sharon Statement

Adopted at the Founding Conference of Young Americans for Freedom at Sharon, Connecticut, September 9-11, 1960.

IN THIS TIME of moral and political crisis, it is the responsibility of the youth of America to affirm certain eternal truths.

WE as young conservatives, believe:

THAT foremost among the transcendent values is the individual's use of his God-given free will, whence derives his right to be free from the restrictions of arbitrary force;

THAT liberty is indivisible, and that political freedom cannot long exist without economic freedom;

THAT the purposes of government are to protect these freedoms through the preservation of internal order, the provision of national defense, and the administration of justice;

THAT when government ventures beyond these rightful functions, it accumulates power which tends to diminish order and liberty;

THAT the Constitution of the United States is the best arrangement yet devised for empowering government to fulfill its proper role, while restraining it from the concentration and abuse of power;

THAT the genius of the Constitution—the division of powers—is summed up in the clause which reserves primacy to the several states, or to the people, in those spheres not specifically delegated to the Federal Government;

THAT the market economy, allocating resources by the free play of supply and demand, is the single economic system compatible with the requirements of personal freedom and constitutional government, and that it is at the same time the most productive supplier of human needs;

THAT when government interferes with the work of the market economy, it tends to reduce the moral and physical strength of the nation; that when it takes from one man to bestow on another, it diminishes the incentive of the first, the integrity of the second, and the moral autonomy of both;

THAT we will be free only so long as the national sovereignty of the United States is secure; that history shows periods of freedom are rare, and can exist only when free citizens concertedly defend their rights against all enemies;

THAT the forces of international Communism are, at present, the greatest single threat to these liberties;

THAT the United States should stress victory over, rather than coexistence with, this menace; and

THAT American foreign policy must be judged by this criterion: does it serve the just interests of the United States?

Application for Membership

Young Americans for Freedom, Inc.
1221 Massachusetts Avenue, N. W.
Washington, D. C. 20005

I am in agreement with the Sharon Statement and I wish to apply for membership.

I enclose my membership dues of: (box checked at right).

NAME . . . .
Please print

MAILING ADDRESS . . . .

CITY . . . . STATE . . . . ZIP . . . .

AGE . . . . SCHOOL OR OCCUPATION . . . .

Write For Other Issues Papers:

1 Social Security: fraud on young people
2 The Minimum Wage: crime against the negro
3 The Draft: there is an alternative
4 East-West Trade: committing national suicide
5 Victory in Viet Nam: the American imperative
6 National Student Association: a smear against students
7 Student Subversion: the majority replies

Check One

- ☐ Student $3.00*
- ☐ Student $1.00 (Does not include New Guard)
- ☐ Non-Student $3.00 (Under 40)*
- ☐ Non-Student $1.00 (Does not include New Guard)
- ☐ Joint Membership for Married Couples $4.00 (Under 40)*
- ☐ Associate Membership $10.00 (Over 40)*
- ☐ I enclose a contribution in the amount of $ . . . .
- ☐ I would like more information about YAF

*I understand that $2.50 of my dues is for a subscription to The New Guard for one year.

> "No more marches. No more rallies. No more speeches. The dialogue is over, baby. Tolerance of rational dissent has become an insidious form of repression. The goal is to disrupt an insane society." —Paul Krassner, Editor, The Realist.

THE AMERICAN CAMPUS is under attack. Leftist revolutionaries dedicated to the destruction of the American society are disrupting campus activities around the country and attempting to silence the majority by force.

THE STUDENTS FOR a Democratic Society proclaim "One, Two, Many Columbias" as their slogan for the new school year. They have even gone so far as to slate more than two hundred schools as targets for violence and disruption.

THE RIOTS AND DISRUPTIONS that swept so many campuses last spring were neither spontaneous nor accidental. They were planned and initiated by dedicated fanatics bent upon the destruction of our society. These people are not reformers trying to improve campus conditions but radical revolutionaries trying to destroy order and rational debate. The grievances they protest are grievances to be exploited tactically rather than alleviated.

STUDENTS ON CAMPUS after campus have seen leftist minorities shout down speakers, disrupt classes and deny the rights of others that they so vigorously claim themselves. This has to stop. We of YOUNG AMERICANS FOR FREEDOM believe that the campus should be a forum open to all. We feel that people expressing diverse opinions must be protected in their right to speak or meet on our campuses. We believe most emphatically that a radical minority should not be allowed to disrupt and destroy the open forum. Physical force must not be allowed to replace rational debate on our campuses.

WHAT AMAZES most of us is not so much the leftist desire to force its will on the rest of us, as its insistence that such action constitutes a rational and legitimate exercise of the right of free speech. Leftist professors, such as San Diego's Herbert Marcuse, have endorsed such action. They have, in fact, advocated force and reveled in it. Any legitimate claim to fair treatment and respect was lost by the left when it adopted this course of action.

What Lies Ahead?

"Students for a Democratic Society is slated to be taken out of undergraduate leadership, molded into the 'Movement for a Democratic Society' and meshed closely with the international Marxist-Leninist apparatus. Guided by members and affiliates of the Socialist Scholars Conference, the new MDS and Youth International Party (Yippies) . . . will be used as 'detonators.' . . .Whoever wins (the Presidency), the Socialist Scholars intend to continue their Marxist-Leninist revolutionary struggle at home and abroad, acting as a fuse to human detonators to set off social explosions."

"A Report on the Fourth Conference of Socialist Scholars," BARRON's, 16 Sept. 1968.

MANY CAMPUS ADMINISTRATIONS have failed to protect the integrity of the campus forum. They have allowed leftists to shout down their opponents and disrupt campus activities. Administrative reprisals against the left have been half-hearted and inadequate. The American university, thus, is in crisis. If university administrations don't come to the defense of the responsible majority, chaos and anarchy will inevitably result.

WE OF YOUNG AMERICANS FOR FREEDOM believe in free rational discussion. We believe that all groups should be allowed to air their views on our campuses. But we do not believe that groups dedicated and acting to destroy freedom and rational discussion can be tolerated. Groups and individuals denying the rights of others can claim none for themselves.

WE THEREFORE URGE university and college administrations to take all action necessary to see to it that the radical leftist minority not be allowed to disrupt campus life. Such action should where necessary include the dismissal of individual students, and the barring of certain groups from the campus.

THESE ARE STEPS that should have been taken long ago. We insist that they be taken now. We feel strongly that if our campus administrators do not or can not maintain order, that responsible students and organizations will be forced to come together to act in their own defense. If this proves necessary in individual situations, we support student action required to force our administrations to maintain order and to guarantee the education contracted for by the student from the university.

⇝ DOCUMENT 22.3b ⇜

Pamphlet, "What Can *I* Do? to Combat Communism," about 1965, Students Associated Against Totalitarianism, Berkeley, California, Christian Anti-Communism Crusade. Personal collection of Peter Frederick.

Communist plan for WORLD CONQUEST

COMMUNIST THREAT

"Whether you like it or not, history is on our side. We will bury you."

—Nikita Khrushchev

COMMUNIST BLUEPRINT:

"War to the hilt between Communism and Capitalism is inevitable. Today, of course, we are not strong enough to attack. Our time will come in twenty to thirty years. To win we shall need the element of surprise. The bourgeois will have to be put to sleep, so we shall begin by launching the most spectacular peace movement on record. There will be electrifying overtures and unheard of concessions. The Capitalist countries, stupid and decadent, will rejoice to cooperate in their own destruction. They will leap at another chance to be friends. As soon as their guard is down, we shall smash them with our clenched fist."

—Dimitry A. Manuilsky
Speech—1930

ENCIRCLEMENT plus DEMORALIZATION = SURRENDER

COMMMUNIST PROGRESS

1903	Bolshevism began	— 17 Supporters
1917	Russian Revolution	— 40,000 Revolutionists
1945	Major World Power	— 175,000,000 Under control
1960	Epidemic Progress	—1,000,000,000 Slaves
?	World Enslavement	—2,800,000,000 Population

COMMUNIST TIMETABLE:

In 1953 Mao-Tse-Tung and Joseph Stalin, according to reliable reports, in their last conference, expressed the belief that it would take two five year plans to consolidate their strength in the far east and two more five year plans to encircle and degenerate the United States, resulting in their surrender without an Atomic Hydrogen War, making the tentative date for World Conquest ABOUT THE YEAR

Strategy & Tactics for Victory over Communism

ALTERNATIVES

1. Atomic Annihilation
2. Surrender
3. Victory over Communism without War

REQUIREMENTS FOR VICTORY

Ⓟ People

Ⓚ Knowledge

Ⓜ Motivation

Ⓟ+Ⓚ−Ⓜ=Pessimism

Ⓟ−Ⓚ+Ⓜ=Fanaticism

Ⓟ+Ⓚ+Ⓜ=Victory

● ● ● ● ● ● ● ● ● ● ● ● ● ●

Action without knowledge breeds confusion and chaos.

ORGANIZATIONAL STRUCTURE

Our strength is not in UNITY, as one united group can be easily infiltrated, subverted or smeared. We need 10,000 "American Fronts"!

Mobilize Multiple Motivations

Lenin started in 1903 with but 17 dedicated supporters. Ten thousand groups of 17 each (170,000) matching the dedication of the Communist and armed with the truth of God, even at this late hour, could change our nation's defensive position to an offensive force and ultimate VICTORY.

● ● ● ● ● ● ● ● ● ● ● ● ● ●

Freedom is not every man's right, but instead every man's Responsibility!

TO COMBAT COMMUNISM

POLITICAL

CHURCH

EDUCATION

CIVIC

POLITICAL

1. Have you completed the necessary registration required to enable you to vote?

__ __
Yes No

2. Did you go to a precinct meeting this year?

__ __
Yes No

3. Did you vote intelligently in all of the primaries, runoff, and general elections this year

__ __
Yes No

● ● ● ● ● ● ● ● ● ● ● ● ● ●

Unfortunately, actions are not generally taken in our governmental headquarters based on what is right and wrong, but instead on what is politically expedient.

4. Have you written your Senator and Congressman in Washington during the past 60 days?

__ __
Yes No

5. Have you contacted in person or written your State Legislator in the past 60 days?

__ __
Yes No

6. Can you intelligently discuss the voting record of your senators and representatives on Major Bills in the last or present legislative session?

__ __
Yes No

● ● ● ● ● ● ● ● ● ● ● ● ● ● ●

Bad Politicans Are Elected by Good People That Stay Home!

CHURCH

1. Do you take an active part in your church?

   ___ ___
   Yes No

2. Are you regularly and systematically studying and memorizing God's word, the Bible, as you would study physics, chemistry, etc?

   ___ ___
   Yes No

3. Have you written a Missionary of your church in the past 30 days that you might be enlightened as to the Missionary opportunities as well as to display an interest in the Missionaries work?

   ___ ___
   Yes No

● ● ● ● ● ● ● ● ● ● ● ● ● ● ● ●

"Study to show thyself approved unto God, a workman that needeth not to be ashamed, rightly dividing the word of truth." II Tim. 2:15

4. Have you recently prayed for a specific Missionary for a specific need?

   ___ ___
   Yes No

5. Did you make a contribution designated for use in church's Foreign Missionary program last month?

   ___ ___
   Yes No

6. Would you like to support a full time worker dedicated to Christian Anti-Communism work in India for $15.00 per month?

   ___ ___
   Yes No

Basic Battleground

God	vs.	Anti-God
Spiritual Values	vs.	Material Values
Heaven	vs.	Hell
Christ	vs.	Satan

● ● ● ● ● ● ● ● ● ● ● ● ● ● ●

"Go Ye Into All the World and Preach the Gospel to Every Creature" Mark 16:15

EDUCATION

1 Have you obtained study material from U.S. Government Printing Office, Washington, D.C., to give you facts and information for intelligent action?

— — Yes No

2. Have you read Dr. Fred C Schwarz's books on communism? (You can order from Christian Anti-Communism Crusade.)

— — Yes No

3. Have you visited your local library to obtain books; such as "Masters of Deceit" by J. Edgar Hoover; "The Witness" by Whitaker Chambers and the writings of such men as Edward Hunter, Herb Philbrick, Cleon Skousen, and Louis Budenz, Dr Fred Schwarz and many others?

— — Yes No

● ● ● ● ● ● ● ● ● ● ● ● ● ●

"For those who want to understand Communism, we prescribe, not a 15 day trip to Russia, but 15 days in a Library studying the Communist conspiracy" —American Bar Association

4. Have you delivered a set of Dr. Schwarz's books to your neighbor, business associate, church missionaries, and other friends in an endeavor to broaden their education on the subject?

Yes No

5. Have you ordered any of Dr. Fred Schwarz's speeches before The Texas Legislature prepared to be used as envelope stuffers, distributed as tracts, etc.? (**$15.00 per M imprinted with your name and brief message; $2.00 per C standard message. Please send check with order**)

Yes No

6. Have you given a copy of "Masters of Deceit" by J. Edgar Hoover or "You Can Trust the Communists" by Dr. Fred Schwarz as a gift to a member of your family, or to a friend for their birthday anniversary, at Christmas, for graduation, or similar occasion?

— — Yes No

● ● ● ● ● ● ● ● ● ● ● ● ● ● ●

"All That Is Necessary for the Triumph of Evil Is for Good Men To Do Nothing." Edmund Burke

CIVIC

1. Have you arranged for the review of a Pro-American and Anti-Communism book before your civic club, P.T.A., women's club, etc.?

    ___ ___
    Yes No

2. Have you written a letter to the editor of magazines and newspapers that print such letters, to disseminate important information not normally carried in regular press service?

    ___ ___
    Yes No

3. Have you assisted in the bringing of a nationally prominent Pro-American and Anti-Communism speaker to your city for a speaking engagement or seminar?

    ___ ___
    Yes No

● ● ● ● ● ● ● ● ● ● ● ● ● ●

Write to the Christian Anti-Communism Crusade for information as to how to plan such a seminar in your city.

4. Have you offered to speak or write an article to disseminate the information you know to your civic club, church group, sorority, fraternity, etc.?

    ___ ___
    Yes No

5. Does the civic group to which you belong give primacy to the human and spiritual rather than the material values of life? Do they by precept and example endeavor to develop a more intelligent, aggressive and serviceable citizenship?

    ___ ___
    Yes No

6. Would you consider organizing a neighborhood study group to use tape recordings and films of some of the world's outstanding authorities on the subject to gain the knowledge for intelligent action?

    ___ ___
    Yes No

● ● ● ● ● ● ● ● ● ● ● ● ● ●

Write to the Crusade for a Manual to Assist You in the Formation of a Study Group.

WHERE TO BEGIN

Freedom will only win if every American who reads this makes his decision NOW to accept his individual responsibility to take effective, positive action for the preservation of freedom.

"We can defeat Communist ideology and, at the same time, reinforce the structure of our own democracy by the combined process of exposure and education."

J. EDGAR HOOVER
Director, F.B.I.

"Our people must understand and recognize the enemy we face: his nature, objectives, tactics, strategy, who he is, and how he works in our midst everyday."

VICE ADMIRAL WALTER G. SCHINDLER
U.S.N. retired

HOW TO BEGIN

Action without knowledge breeds confusion and chaos. Once this is realized, education on the true nature of Communism becomes the first logical step to victory.

The Christian Anti-Communism Crusade, a non-profit, tax exempt organization having as its foundational structure evangelism, education, and dedication has created a "Local Study Group Program" as the vehicle for knowledge followed by intelligent action.

Over 300 hours of tape recorded lectures and films are available from the Crusade at a nominal cost featuring some of the leading experts in the world. Typical listings follow on pages 18 and 19. The material covered starts with Communist philosophy and carries the student through to Communist activities in foreign and economic affairs as well as in our everyday life. These tapes and films are in use in public schools, churches, civic clubs, homes, military units, as well as in radio and television programming. Manuals are available on request giving detailed listings of material and suggestions on formation of a study group (price $.50) plus a meeting manual (price $.50) outlining the program schedule, objectives, and ultimate goals.

TAPE LIBRARY

—over 300 hours available

SAMPLE LISTING

"Communist Doctrines" . . . . Dr. Fred C. Schwarz
"Communist Thought Control" . . . Herbert Philbrick
"Communism in Government" . . . . Richard Arens
"Brainwashing, Personal Experience" . Rev. Leslie Millin
"I Was A Slave In Russia" . . . John Noble
"Subversion in U.S.A." . . . . Martin Dies
"Communism in Education" . . . . W. Cleon Skousen
"Communism in Foreign Affairs" . . . . Walter Judd
"Brainwashing Techniques" . Edward Hunter
"P.O.W. Indoctrination" . . . Major William Mayer
"We Are At War" . . Adm. Walter Schindler
"Communism in China" . . . . Rev. C. S. Dunker, C.M.
"Communist Expansion" . . . . . Dr. Anthony Bouscaren
"What Can I Do?" . . . . . W. P. Strube, Jr.

Public Service Radio Tapes Also Available

Tapes (Two, one hour messages) $5.00 per tape

FILM LIBRARY

over 50 available

SAMPLE LISTING

Title—16mm sound films	Producer
Crimson Shadow	Christian Anti-Communism Crusade
Dead Men on Furlough	World Vision Inc.
Red Plague	World Vision Inc.
A Look at Socialism	Harding College
A Look at Capitalism	Harding College
Security and Freedom	Harding College
American Responsibility of Citizenship	Harding College
Communist Blueprint for Conquest	U. S. Army
Communist Weapon of Allure	U. S. Army
The Hucksters	U. S. Navy

Slide and strip film with tape recording

Communism on the Map . . . National Education Program
Communist Blueprint for Conquest
Christian Anti-Communism Crusade

Films Available—Freewill Offering or Rental Basis

NOW... BEGIN!

1. Procure one tape, borrow tape recorder.
2. Invite friends for "coffee and doughnuts" and play tape. Distribute free literature available.
3. Schedule organizational meeting.
4. Second meeting: select name, chairman, secretary, and listen to tape. Establish telephone committee.
5. Write U.S. Government printing office requesting your name be added to the mail list for new issues and for listing plus a listing on all available material on Anti-Communism.
6. Each participant write Allen-Bradley Company, Milwaukee, Wisconsin, for 25 free copies "The Communist Mind" for distribution. (P.S.: Write individual thank you letters to Allen-Bradley Co. after receiving material for their contribution to freedom.)
7. Procure 1000 of this "What Can I Do?" pamphlets with your study group advertisement on back cover, and distribute to your community to help form other groups. (1000 with your ad $15.00 post paid. Please send check with order.)

Order From

Christian Anti-Communism Crusade
P. O. Box 6422, Houston 6, Texas

CHRISTIAN ANTI-COMMUNISM CRUSADE

Organized: May 12, 1953 in Waterloo, Iowa

Tax Exempt Status: Granted by U. S. Treasury Dept. Sept. 18, 1956

Officers: President: Fred C. Schwarz, M.D.
Physician and Surgeon, Sydney, Australia
One of the world's leading authorities on Communist ideology

Vice President: George Westcott, M.D.
Physician and Surgeon,
Ypsilanti, Michigan
formerly Medical Missionary to Africa

Vice President: Robert Sackett, Morris Printing Company, Waterloo, Iowa

Vice President: Jim D. Colbert, B.D.
Missionary Director Christian Anti-Communism Crusade

Secretary: W. P. Strube, Jr., President
Mid-American Life Insurance Company,
Houston, Texas

Offices: Long Beach, California (P. O. Box 890)
San Francisco, California (582 Market St.)
Houston, Texas (P. O. Box 6422)
Sydney, Australia (142 Concord Rd.)

Affiliated works: Formosa, Korea, Japan, India, Africa, Philippines, South America

References: Organizations or individuals listed
Dun and Bradstreet
Retail Credit Corp.
Better Business Bureaus in cities having Crusade offices

Financial Statements: Abbreviated report furnished upon request.
C.P.A. Audit available for observation.

"WE WILL BURY YOU!"
—Nikita Khrushchev

The communist say their victory is certain because the average American is so

INTELLECTUALLY LAZY

INTOXICATED WITH ENTERTAINMENT

LIMITED IN HIS HORIZON

INHERENTLY SELFISH

That he won't have the conviction or dedication to do that which is necessary to stop them.

If you think you are "too busy" to take action, examine your life in the light of Hungary, Tibet, Poland, and Czechoslovakia. Just for one week prepare a 24 hour a day schedule sheet and keep track of your activities including sleeping, eating, working, etc., and see if you can't rearrange the schedule to find some time to fulfill your responsibilities in this battle for the preservation of your freedom.

ETERNAL VIGILANCE IS
THE PRICE OF LIBERTY

CITIZEN'S CODE OF CONDUCT

"I will never forget that I am an American Citizen, responsible for my actions, and dedicated to the principles that made my country free. I will Trust in God and in the United States of America."

Christian Anti-Communism Crusade
P. O. Box 6422, Houston 6, Texas

DOCUMENT 22.4a

Oral history of the civil rights activist Lawrence Guyot, in Howell Raines, *My Soul Is Rested: Movement Days in the Deep South Remembered* (New York: Bantam, 1978), pp. 258–263.

Lawrence Guyot

Inside Agitator

He was born in Pass Christian, Mississippi. In 1957 he entered Tougaloo, a black college near Jackson, which, to the chagrin of Mississippi officials, had white faculty members and welcomed any white students bold enough to attend. The spirit of the Movement was strong there.

Then one weekend I went home with a young lady from Greenwood, Mississippi, who was attending Tougaloo, and I was immediately struck by the county.[1] Here's a county eighty percent black at that time that had one registered voter, and no one could find him. I went back to Tougaloo and became more and more involved with SNCC. Now my involvement with SNCC was at its earliest in Mississippi. I became involved late in '61. Late '61, early '62, I began becoming more and more involved in traveling with them around the state. Now the people . . . there was Charles McLaurin, Colia Ladelle, James Jones, Lafayette Surney, Hollis Watkins, Curtis Hayes, myself, Luvaughn Brown, Diane Bevel, Rev. Bevel, Chuck McDew, Marion Barry, who is now a city councilman in Washington, and Bob Moses, who was later to become a legend in Mississippi. While it was clear that Moses was the leader of this group, his style of leadership was by example and directional discussion.

We met in Jackson at 714 Rose Street, and from there we had begun to conduct small workshops, speak in small meetings, attempt to get people to register to vote. And then the decision was made that what we needed was to go to the Delta where there were harsher conditions, where there was a large black population, where there were some counties with no black registration. We needed a person to provide contacts on a local basis, to provide an entree for us into the counties, and that person was Amzie Moore.

We met at his house, we stayed at his house. He had a hell of a network of individuals throughout the state and had had it for years. . . . Whenever anyone was threatened, Amzie Moore was sort of an individual protection agency. He had successfully fought against the Klan, both politically and physically, [was] a noted Bible scholar, a very good stump speaker.

With Moore's home in Cleveland as its base, SNCC opened offices in the two key cities of the northern Delta—Greenwood in the interior and the river town of Greenville. He was assigned to Greenwood, the tougher of the two.

On August the fifteenth, myself and Luvaughn Brown and another guy left Jackson on the bus to go to Greenwood. We were instructed at the time—and we, of course, didn't need to be instructed, but we agreed with the instructions—that there would be no sit-ins on the way. Just go to Greenwood and start working on voter registration. . . . And it was very interesting, because as we were riding on the bus from Jackson, . . . the bus stopped in Yazoo City, and there was a member of the Bahai faith who taught at Jackson who was beaten on the bus because he attempted to use the waiting room. And we, of course, stayed uninvolved in that; we just wrote down what happened.

Now, Greenwood at the time we entered . . . there was a war going on, and the war was a very simple one—surviving and just walkin' around talkin' to [black] people about what *they're* interested in. And it didn't make any difference. If it was fishing, how do you turn that conversation into when are you gonna register to vote? If it was religion,

[1]As one approaches from the east, Greenwood is the gateway to the fertile flatlands of the Delta. Both the city of Greenwood and surrounding Leflore County take their names from the same curious historical figure, Greenwood Leflore, a wealthy slave owner who modeled his plantation home after the Empress Josephine's palace, Malmaison. Because of the United States' generosity in granting him title to certain Indian lands, Leflore supported the Union throughout the Civil War. He died on the front porch of his mansion with four grandchildren holding Union flags above him.

that was an easier one to turn into registering. If it was cotton acreage—our basic verbal mien was that there's nothin' that's not involved with polities.

How about getting doors slammed in your face?

You learned. You learned very quickly that if you got that door slammed in your face, it just takes a day or two of talking to people to find out whose face the door won't be slammed in. . . . I mean, there are some towns you go into, and you find a man who has none of the characteristics of leadership as we identify them. He is the leader [of the black community] and has been and is unquestioned, and mess with him wrong—forgit it. Don't speed him up too much, dialogue with him, find out what his tempo is, what his objectives are. Then you might alter them a little bit, but don't, don't, don't—be careful. We learned over and over and over again how to find potential leadership, how to groom it, and the most painful lesson for some of us was how to let it go once you've set it into motion. See, I *loved* it, because it was dealing with people, what they could do against large tasks.

What were the no-noes at the grassroots level . . . ?

Well, there's one no-no that you just never walked into a house and you see some kids sittin' around and you say, "Is this your child?" You just don't do it. . . . In a couple of months, it'll all be explained to you once the people know you. So why ask it? Because immediately by the question having to be answered, you're gonna immediately set up a defensive thing, even if it's her child. "Yeah, it's my child. Why? Why would you ask me that?" So we don't do that.

You don't alter the basic format that you walk into. Let's say you're riding past a picnic, and people are cuttin' watermelons. You don't immediately go and say, "Stop the watermelon cuttin', and let's talk about voter registration." You cut some watermelons, or you help somebody else serve 'em.

There were a lot of 'em. The SNCC organizers were no saints. We asked discretion. We were never able to enforce it. And there was a weird kinda thing about, in a town with no heroes, a SNCC organizer who publicly voiced opposition to the status quo and who physically carried that [opposition] out before the police was sought after as a sexual partner. And that varied with individuals. Now there were some clear no-noes. Hartman Turnbow[2] had a daughter, and it was clearly understood that if there ever was a no-no, that was *the* no-no. [Laughs]

It's no secret that young people and women led organizationally. When you talked about community mobilization, we not only did community mobilization in Greenwood, but the sociologists, when they were talking about community mobilization, would talk about "like what SNCC is doing in Greenwood." Okay . . . the organizationally hoped-for situation arose. Dewey Green's, a responsible black moderate, home was shot into. We had gathered a couple of hundred people together, so the thirteen of us [SNCC workers] and the couple of hundred people walked down to Chief Curtis Lowery's police force and asked for police protection. No one was arrested but the thirteen of us. The dogs were sent out and an interesting combination of things happened, because some of the highway patrolmen passed and saw me leading the line and the dogs coming at me and Mary Lane, a brave, courageous young lady from Greenwood. We didn't run from the dogs. They didn't bite us, but nevertheless we were arrested and taken to jail. . . .

The jailing of the SNCC workers was calculated to break up the voter registration activity in Greenwood, but it had the opposite effect. SNCC dispatched its entire field staff to the city. The U.S. Justice Department intervened on behalf of the jailed workers, creating the impression of "an alignment between us and the federal government." SNCC had a toehold in the Mississippi Delta.

---

[2]A black farmer who joined the voter-registration drive.

I guess the reason we got away with what we did in Greenwood was for a couple of reasons. One, we were soundly based in the churches. Two, our objectives were very clear. It was not to desegregate the two or three good local white restaurants. It was simply to register people to vote. One time we led a demonstration down to the courthouse, and we were met by the local Citizens Council and Hardy Locke, a big businessman, really one of the political leaders of that political-social complex, who said, "Look, y'all shouldn't be too worried. Y'all bring in more applicants now than anybody else." And our retort was, "But they're not getting registered." He said, "W-e-e-ll, that's another thing." [Laughs]

See, you have to understand the climate that we were dealing with. When people received a welfare check, there was a letter—a classic letter I'll never forget—stating that people should be very concerned about registering to vote at the request of "radicals" because this may terminate the . . . check.

Those who did attempt to register faced a battery of personal questions.

And then question seventeen, the classic one: "Read and interpret to the satisfaction of the registrar this section of the Constitution." At that time, there were two hundred eighty-two sections of the Mississippi Constitution. . . . Needless to say, we had some Phi Beta Kappas, some Ph.D.'s, and some college and high-school principals failing the literacy test. . . . It got to an extent where we started really marching people down simply to *attempt* to register, fighting for the right to take the damn unconstitutional literacy test.

The county decided that what it would do was it would cut off all welfare supplies. So it did just that. All food was cut off.

Then what we did was, with the assistance of Dick Gregory . . . he provided the money and the food, we set up our alternative service, which caused more people to register to vote. . . .

Where did you get the food?

You name it. Gregory spearheaded it and actually physically flew some of the food down. It came in truckloads . . . and we made it very clear, while we were concerned about feeding everyone, we were primarily concerned about feeding those who attempted to register to vote.

We did this in Greenwood, then we moved into other counties, picking up the beginning of a fledgling state apparatus: an individual here, someone who stood up to white folks here. But we were very, very conscious about one thing. Our objective was *simply* voter registration and political mobilization. We were *not* concerned about sit-ins. We were *not* concerned about desegregation.

→ DOCUMENT 22.4b ←

Enclosure in letter from SNCC: "SNCC Does Not Wish to Become A New Version of the White Man's Burden," *I. F. Stone's Weekly*, June 6, 1966. Personal collection of Peter Frederick.

I. F. Stone's Weekly, June 6, 1966

Behind the Hostile Press Campaign Unleashed by the Election of Stokely Carmichael

SNCC Does Not Wish to Become A New Version of the White Man's Burden

We hope white liberals will not be taken in by the press campaign against the Student Non-Violent Coordinating Committee since Stokely Carmichael succeeded John Lewis as national chairman. White sympathizers with the Negro have to keep several things in mind. One is that in any movement the leverage exerted by the moderates depends on the existence of an extremist fringe. The second is that a certain amount of black nationalism is inevitable among Negroes; they cannot reach equality without the restoration of pride in themselves as Negroes. The third is that this cannot be achieved unless they learn to fight for themselves, not just as wards of white men, no matter how sympathetic. SNCC is reacting against a new version of the White Man's Burden.

Fresh Approach to Southern Politics

No white man really knows what it is like to be shut into the ghetto. "The Negro," as Martin Luther King said in a vivid phrase on CBS *Face The Nation* May 29, "is still smothering in an air-tight cage of poverty in the midst of this very affluent society." For the white sympathizer, the struggle against the ghetto is an act of philanthropy; for the Negro, it is a battle to save himself, not just from poverty but from a corrosive self-contempt. The ghetto dweller distrusts the white SNCC worker. Mr. Carmichael's idea of recruiting black SNCC workers from Northern ghettoes is psychologically sound. His idea of using white SNCC workers to organize the Southern poor white to the point where joint action between white and black becomes possible opens fresh perspectives in Southern politics.

The wonderful white boys and girls who went South in the past few years helped to thaw out the Negro from political deep freeze. But now that the battle has shifted from the simpler symbolic acts of sitting at a segregated lunch counter or in a segregated waiting room to the harder and more complicated tasks of winning a real economic and social equality, the job will have to be done by Negroes themselves. These are not tasks for a summer adventure in between classes. They can only be accomplished if Negroes are mobilized to carry on for themselves. In such areas as the Black Belt, where the Negro is a majority, this means seeking majority rule and that means Negro majorities. Otherwise the Negro is at the mercy of a white minority. In Lowndes county, Alabama, for example, where the Negro third party, Black Panther movement, originated, the white Sheriff has deputized every white man over 21. To be a deputy is to have the right to carry a gun, and to have a kind of hunting license to shoot Negroes.

This is the background against which one must read Carmichael's statement, "We feel that integration is irrelevant; it is just a substitute for white supremacy. We have got to go after political power." He asked an audience in Washington last week-end, "How are you going to integrate a sharecropper making $3 a day with a plantation-owner making $20,000 a year?"

Some people were shocked by Mr. Carmichael's angry remark, "We want quality education, not integrated education." But here I believe he expresses the reaction of Southern Negroes to the bitter experience of integration. The *Wall St. Journal* (May 26) carried a story, "The Invisible Wall" on the ostracism and the humiliation visited on those few Negroes who have often literally risked their lives to get into white schools. Many are leaving. This frightened handful in white schools only distracts attention from the need for first rate education in the Negro schools. This is just as true in the North where the Negro schools are segregated by the flight to the suburbs. Only by improved schooling can the Negro be fitted to compete as an equal in a hostile white world. To dismiss this as Negro nationalism is neither fair nor perceptive.

Of course the main reason for the campaign against SNCC is the statement it issued refusing to take part in the White House Conference on Civil Rights which convened as we were going to press. "Our organization," it said, "is opposed to war in Vietnam and we cannot in good conscience meet with the chief policy maker of the Vietnam war to discuss human rights when he violates the human rights of colored people in Vietnam."

High Ratio of Negro Combat Troops

This speaks the unspoken thoughts of many Negroes. The war is an affront to them. The proportion of Negroes in combat troops Joseph Alsop reported May 25 was "running above 20 percent in the average infantry company" because Negro recruits, with a lower average of technical skills, are less likely to be assigned to one of the technical specialties." The ratio in combat units is thus almost twice the Negro's ratio to population. The same discrimination that deprived Negroes of education puts them into the front ranks of battle in a struggle supposedly to preserve abroad a democracy denied them at home. How can they be blamed if they, like so many Vietnamese, see this as another white man's war?

But the main point, as Dr. King expressed it on TV, is that the war is wasting the money and the energy which can alone rehabilitate the Negro and bring him fully into the American community. Dr. King sounded very radical when he said this would cost $10 billion a year for ten years. The Vietnamese war already costs more than that, and the price will rise as it escalates. Is it any wonder SNCC feels bitter?

→ DOCUMENT 22.4c ←

Black Panther Flyer, "If You're Not Part of the Solution You're Part of the Problem," 1968. Social Movements Collection, University of Virginia. With permission of the Black Panther Party Foundation.

IF YOU'RE NOT PART OF THE SOLUTION

YOU'RE PART OF THE PROBLEM

REVOLUTIONARY PEOPLE'S CONSTITUTIONAL CONVENTION - NOV. 27 - 29

Things in America are fucked up. The system doesn't work, it doesn't serve human needs; it serves capitalist greed which is ravaging the earth's air, land, and water in addition to killing people.

The Black Panther Party is calling for all people dedicated to changing the reality of Amerikkka to come to a Revolutionary Peoples Constitutional Convention. In Philadelphia, 10,000 to 15,000 people, mostly Black people and young people from all parts of the Movement, came together at the Convention Plenary Session to talk about their grievances and goals.

Huey Newton, just sprung from prison, spoke of the need for a socialist revolution -- and the right of people to rebel and build their own new world. Thousands gathered outside the packed hall to hear him repeat the Black Panther Party Platform demanding freedom, political power, an end to unemployment and exploitation, decent housing, exemption from the imperialist draft, an end to police brutality, fair trials by juries of peers, freedom for all political prisoners, a United Nations plebiscite to determine the will of Black people as to their national destiny.

Lots of people got high.off the fact that Huey was free and with them. But it wasn't just a bunch of speeches from a podium.

The Conference divided up into a dozen workshops on self-determination for Third World people, women, street people, workers, gay people, rights of children, control and use of the land and natural resources, reorganization of political, economic, legal, and military systems.

These workshops shattered the notion that people are just out to smash things mindlessly, without a program, unable to get together on goals. Each workshop delivered a report which will be used in drawing up the new Constitution at the next session of the Convention in D.C., Nov. 27,28,29.

➔ DOCUMENT 22.4d ⬅

Black Panther Flyer, "Racist Dog Policemen," 1968. Social Movements Collection, University of Virginia. With permission of the Black Panther Party Foundation.

"THE RACIST DOG POLICEMEN MUST WITHDRAW IMMEDIATELY FROM OUR COMMUNITIES. CEASE THEIR WANTON MURDER AND BRUTALITY AND TORTURE OF BLACK PEOPLE, OR FACE THE WRATH OF THE ARMED PEOPLE."

HUEY P. NEWTON, *Minister of Defense*

BLACK PANTHER PARTY
P.O. Box 8641, Emeryville, Calif.

DOCUMENT 22.4e

Black Panther Flyer, "We Will Not Sit Back and Let the Fascists Murder Chairman Bobby in the Electric Chair," no date. Social Movements Collection, University of Virginia. With permission of the Black Panther Party Foundation.

WE WILL NOT SIT BACK AND LET THE FASCISTS MURDER CHAIRMAN BCBBY IN THE ELECTRIC CHAIR!

BOBBY SEALE, CHAIRMAN, B.P.P. POLITICAL PRISONER

**BLACK PANTHER PARTY
BALTIMORE CHAPTER
1248 N. GAY ST.
342-8536**

Our Minister of Defense, Huey P. Newton, teaches us that in order to have security from the unceasing aggressions of the enemy, we must always be in a position to inflict a political consequence upon the aggressor for each act of aggression.

Bobby Seale Coldbloodly in the Electric Chair is an open provocation and the ultimate aggression against Black people. It is a well planned step in these goons blueprint that they plan to unfold on Black people if forced to go it alone must be prepared to unleash the ultimate political consequence upon this racist nation. The ultimate political consequencewhich Black people have in their power to unleash is Race War.

We have been and at this very moment still are victims of systematic racist repression.

The Black Panther Party as every one knows has taken a leading role in trying to avoid this disasterous Race War which these low life Coons have been working night and day to bring about.

But we cannot and will not carry this policy to the point of racial suicide. We will not sacrifice Chairman Bobby Seale on the hope of interracial harmony if white people, continue to sit back and allow this ghastly plot go forward. So if the so-called freedom loving white people of America do not stand up now while there is still a few moments of time left and put an end to the planned murder of Chairman Bobby Seale then Black People will have to go it alone and step forward alone. This will mean an end to the dreams of Class war which America needs and the being of a Race war which America cannot endure. This is the political Consequence which America faces because of this unspeakably evil attempt to Murder Chairman Bobby Seale in the Electric Chair.

Power to the People!

✧ DOCUMENT 22.5a ✧

Oral history of a student activist, James Seff, in Peter Joseph, *Good Times: An Oral History of America in the Nineteen Sixties* (New York: Charterhouse, 1973). By permission of Wendy Joseph.

James Seff

Jim Seff is in his late twenties. A graduate of Bolt Hall, the law school at the University of California's Berkeley campus, he now specializes in the legal problems of wine producers. He and his wife, who works in public relations, live in San Francisco.

I remember some of my classmates putting themselves on the line with the Free Speech Movement people. At that point they were putting themselves on the line because nobody knew what the State Bar Examiners were going to do with people who were arrested for these kinds of political expression. Ultimately, they did nothing, which was probably the right thing, but at that time there was a strong feeling that those people who participated in this and who did get arrested might very well not be admitted to the practice of law in California. And if, after all, you're going to be an attorney or a lawyer, it's very important that you be able to practice.

I remember the day of the Sproul Hall sit-in when all those kids were arrested and carted off to jail. Joan Baez was there, along with a number of other luminaries. There were a number of speeches on the steps of Sproul Hall and then Joan Baez said, "We're going to go in there now and we're going to sit down and we're not going to move until they return to us our rights. But when you go in there, go with love in your hearts." Or words to that effect. Then she started singing, "Blowing in the Wind," the Dylan song. It was like the Pied Piper of Hamelin. Everybody wanted to go. It was really an inspiring moment. Unfortunately, as I recall, Joan Baez left before the police said that the doors would be locked and that anyone who remained in the building would be subject to arrest. But I don't know how important that is. She certainly has taken her stand in other areas, the payment of taxes, for example, to support the war in Vietnam.

The police came that night, and the kids went limp and they dragged them down the marble steps, bouncing their heads on the steps, which was uncomfortable at the very least. Throughout the Free Speech Movement I can't remember a time when there was violence on the Berkeley campus. It was really passive resistance, kind of a noble thing.

One of the bad things that happened, one of the off-shoots of the Free Speech Movement was what came to be called the "foul speech movement," where some students were carrying around signs with the word "fuck" on them and walking up and down the streets. Other students were reading passages from *Lady Chatterley's Lover* to the Berkeley campus police. All under the guise of First Amendment rights. But the First Amendment rights are not absolute: for example, I believe Justice Holmes said, "You can't shout 'Fire' in a crowded theater under the First Amendment." Whether they were legitimately trying to test the First Amendment and to press it to its ultimate extreme, or whether in fact they were just having a lark, is something about which I know nothing. My guess is that they were probably just having a good time.

→ DOCUMENT 22.5b ←

Photograph of students and professors in a brawl at Columbia University, April 28, 1968, New York, New York. © Bettmann/CORBIS.

→ DOCUMENT 22.6a ←

Antiwar appeal from teachers, "Help Stop the War in Vietnam," 1967. Personal collection of Peter Frederick.

PAID ADVERTISEMENT **PAID ADVERTISEMENT** **PAID ADVERTISEMENT**

Educators Appeal To The American People...

HELP STOP THE WAR IN VIETNAM

HELP STOP

the killing of American youth . . . more than 5,500 already dead protecting a corrupt military dictatorship against the wishes of the Vietnamese people.

HELP STOP

the death and destruction in Vietnam . . . help stop the merciless bombing of men, women, and children; help stop the use of burning napalm, noxious gases, and chemicals that destroy the crops of this already impoverished country.

HELP STOP

the squandering of billions upon billions of our dollars in Vietnam . . . for which we foot the bill through inflation, cuts in essential government services, and inevitable tax increases.

HELP

bring our boys home.

The war continues because vital facts about its origin and development have been deliberately glossed over, distorted, and withheld from the American people. Only an informed public opinion can stop this barbaric conflict before it escalates into nuclear war. HELP destroy the myths about the war in Vietnam. HELP get the truth into your community.

WHAT YOU CAN DO

People all over the country are heartsick over the war and want to do something about it. Take the lead . . . get in touch with a like-minded colleague, a friend, a clergyman, or a neighbor. Decide TOGETHER what you can best do to get the facts into YOUR community. Maybe you should distribute fact sheets, have discussion groups in homes, or have a debate. Perhaps your community is ideal for a teach-in or an ad in a neighborhood newspaper. Make certain that your community's growing opposition to the war is made known repeatedly to Congress and the President by letter, telegram, or personal visit.

A wealth of factual material presenting a clear and forthright case for ending the war is now available. Do you want a reading list? Film strips? Would you like to know what other communities have done, how they got started?

Then please get in touch with us. We will help in every way we can. But the important thing is to get started, for every increase in casualties, every bombing of a bridge, every escalation of the war, makes peace that much harder to achieve, nuclear war that much closer.

Join Us In Urging That Our Government

1. End all bombings both in North and in South Vietnam.
2. Declare a cease-fire.
3. Adopt the realistic position that the National Liberation Front is the representative of a substantial portion of the South Vietnam people and is thereby destined to play a role in any future Vietnam government.
4. Arrange to implement the 1954 Geneva Accords which call for the removal of all foreign troops from Vietnam.

As American citizens we are responsible for the actions of our government. And as teachers we feel a particular responsibility to the youth and children of our nation—and of all nations—to guarantee their future. No teacher, no American citizen, can, in good conscience, sit idly by in the face of this illegal, immoral, and senseless war.

MORE THAN 6,750 TEACHERS (nursery school through university) *SIGNED THIS STATEMENT!*

(The text and complete list of nationwide signatories appeared originally in the March 12, 1967, NEW YORK TIMES.)

If you share our views—as a first step—write, wire, or visit your elected representatives. Impress upon them the need for ending the bombing NOW.

AFFILIATIONS FOR identification purposes only.

Co-Sponsored By:
TEACHERS COMMITTEE FOR PEACE IN VIETNAM
Rebecca Berman, Chairman;
Mona Monroe, Treas.
INTER-UNIVERSITY COMM. FOR DEBATE ON FOREIGN POLICY
(Organizers of the Teach-in)
Douglas F. Dowd, Pres. (Cornell Univ.—on leave);
Robert Greenblatt, Exec. Vice-Pres. (Cornell Univ.)

Teachers Committee for Peace in Vietnam
5 Beekman St., Rm. 1028, N.Y., N.Y. 10038

- ☐ Please put me in touch with interested faculty members in my community.
- ☐ Please place me on your mailing list.
- ☐ Please send me further information.
- ☐ Enclosed is $——— to support your effort to bring peace in Vietnam

NAME .... TEL. ....

ADDRESS .... CITY ....

STATE .... ZIP .... SCHOOL ....

⇾ DOCUMENT 22.6b ⇽

Photograph of Vietnam War Protestors outside the White House, November 30, 1965, Washington, DC

⇝ DOCUMENT 22.6c ⇜

Photograph, "Stop the Vietnam War rally, Central Park, NYC, 1968. Photograph by Elliott Landy, 1968.

→ DOCUMENT 22.6d ←

Photograph, "Along the March Route," Washington, DC, 1967. Photograph by Elliott Landy, 1967.

→ DOCUMENT 22.6e ←

Photograph, "Pentagon Peace Demonstration," Washington, DC, 1967. Photograph by Elliott Landy, 1967.

→ DOCUMENT 22.6f ←

Photograph, "Pro-war Demonstrator," New York City, 1968. Photograph by Elliott Landy, 1968.

→ DOCUMENT 22.7a ←

Oral History of cultural rebellion of Erika Taylor, in Peter Joseph, *Good Times: An Oral History of America in the Nineteen Sixties* (New York: Charterhouse, 1973).

Erika Taylor

At nineteen Erika Taylor left home to travel with the Hog Farm commune. Now twenty-three, she lives on a seventy-acre farm in Oregon with her husband, Bobby Flash. A dozen more people round out the semi-commune. Erika spends much of her time in the garden—hoeing the soil and harvesting vegetables.

I went to California in 1966 after I graduated from high school. My parents moved out there, and I went too. It was just when all that good stuff was happening. There was just the most incredible energy. I'd come from the Main Line in Philadelphia, really posh, egotistical, money-oriented scene, where our social stuff was based around drinking. I started trying to get in with the kids who looked like and acted like my friends back East, but for some reason nothing was happening. I just didn't like those people. I started noticing all the people with long hair, and these guys were the nice people. I had said, "Oh, marijuana, what's that all about? I'll never smoke grass." And then my younger sister turned me on. I went out with her and her friends and we started getting stoned, and then the next week we took acid. A month later I moved away from home and lived up on this mountain, which was just about a half hour away from where my parents lived. It was up in the redwoods. There was a little log cabin up there. It was the first commune that I ever lived in. A bunch of really nice people. We used to just take walks in the woods. It was a really natural, friendly scene. I went through a lot of changes in California just through the stuff that happened there. The beginning of that whole scene was really good. You'd go into a park and people would turn you on and smile, and you could just hold a stranger's hand and walk along and talk, and just feel really at ease. Then a lot of hard drugs started showing up, a lot of speed, and that naturally changed a lot.

We were working for Earth People's Park, turning people onto an idea of buying some land. Putting money together, putting your money where your heart is, buying some free land where everybody could come and live. It involved a lot of other stuff. We had a real beautiful scene there before we went to Woodstock. We just acquired this land and we were working on buildings. We didn't have hardly any money but it didn't seem to matter because we were working together. There were a lot of Chicano neighbors and we were having Spanish class every day, where we'd get together in our barn and pass whatever dope there was and this one girl who spoke Spanish real well was teaching us, just so that we could communicate with our neighbors the way we should be able to. That was real good.

But then, after Woodstock, the address got published and folks started coming out with everything they owned tied to their cars. And this was like fifteen acres of land, most of it with a road running right through it. This was in New Mexico. We traveled from back East, Pennsylvania, to New Mexico. It was just such a scene! So many new faces. There became very little past history with people. People came and went so often. So much confused energy without any center at all that I just got to a point where I didn't want to say hello to anyone. I almost couldn't acknowledge any new faces because I wasn't getting any feedback. There were a lot of young kids, and that had a lot to do with it. Most of the older guys left.

We were doing shows, that's what we were doing. A light show. Talking to people and collecting money. It wasn't a self-supporting scene at all, the people donated stuff. I got to feel like a scavenger after a while, and I didn't like that at all. You have to put as much into it as you're getting out of it and a lot of times that wasn't so. The balance wasn't there.

After I made the decision to leave, a lot of things became really clear to me about my own ideas. There was supposedly this group consciousness; we were as one as a group, to a point where I lost my individuality. I got to the point where I didn't know what my own beliefs were. I knew what we were supposed to be doing, but somehow I wasn't getting high doing it at all. I wasn't feeling it, and therefore I shouldn't be there. I was awakened at this point, because I could see that there were a lot of folks who were tagging along and hanging around and not doing anything. They were just a weight, a burden, for the people who were putting out energy.

Were your parents very upset when you first left home?

Yes, but I didn't realize it then. I had completely turned myself off to them. That's something I realized later: "How could I do that to my parents? How could I have not written them for a month at a time?" This was all during that Charlie Manson thing, too, which was really freaking them out. But after Woodstock they saw all the good stuff written about it and that pulled them out a little bit.

Many people are often turned off by the supposed free sex on the communes. Was it really all that free?

It was an individual thing. There were some people . . . some guys who slept with a lot of girls because that was their thing to do, but actually there was very little of it. There were very few couples. Most of the couples who were there in the very beginning of the Hog Farm got to where they were not financially able to take care of their families the way they wanted to. So they left and got jobs and a lot of them are living in San Francisco and having babies now, having a family. They all do different stuff: some of them are mechanics, one guy works for the railroad, one guy works for the telephone company, Hal Foster works for IBM.

They're living their lives the way they want to. Otherwise they wouldn't be doing it. They just want to live a certain way, and it becomes obvious after you reach a certain age that if you don't have money, you've got to work for it.

⟡ DOCUMENT 22.7b ⟡

Flyer, "Love: A Psychedelic Celebration, Tompkins Square Park," October 6, 1966. Social Movements Collection, University of Virginia.

A Prophecy of A Declaration of Independence

*When in the flow of human events it becomes necessary for the people to cease to recognize the obsolete social patterns which have isolated man from his consciousness and to create with the youthful energies of the world revolutionary communities of harmonious relations to which the two-billion-year-old life process entitles them, a decent respect to the opinions of mankind should declare the causes which impell them to this creation * We hold these experiences to be self-evident, that all is equal, that the creation endows us with certain inalienable rights, that among these are: the freedom of body, the pursuit of joy, and the expansion of consciousness • and that to secure these rights, we the citizens of the earth declare our love and compassion for all conflicting hate-carrying men and women of the world.*

• We declare the identity of flesh and consciousness; all reason and law must respect and protect this holy identity.

LOVE
A Psychedelic Celebration
Tompkins Square Park
Thursday October 6, 1966 5:00 P.M.

ON OCTOBER, 1966, THE CALIFORNIA LAW PROHIBITING THE POSSESSION OF LSD COMES INTO EFFECT. AT 2:00 P.M. IN THE PANHANDLE (5:00 P.M. IN NEW YORK) A LOVE-PAGEANT RALLY WILL TAKE PLACE. COPIES OF THE PROPHESY OF OUR DECLARATION OF INDEPENDENCE, LIVING MORNING GLORY PLANTS AND MUSHROOMS WILL BE PRESENTED TO SAN FRANCISCO MAYOR SHELLEY, CECIL POOLE, U.S. ATTORNEY GENERAL FOR NORTHERN CALIFORNIA, AND CAPT. KELLY OF GOLDEN GATE PARK DISTRICT STATION.

Bring

BRING THE COLOR GOLD ... BRING PHOTOS OF PERSONAL SAINTS AND GURUS AND HEROES OF THE UNDERGROUND ... BRING CHILDREN... FLOWERS ... FLUTES ... DRUMS ... FEATHERS ... BANDS ... BEADS... BANNERS FLAGS INCENSE CHIMES · GONGS CYMBALS... SYMBOLS

COSTUMES COSTUMES

Joy

→ DOCUMENT 22.8 ←

Book covers, *Our Bodies Our Selves: A Book by and for Women,* 1971 and 1998, by the Boston Women's Health Book Collective, Inc.

OUR BODIES OUR SELVES

A COURSE BY AND FOR WOMEN

NEW PRINTING OF

40¢

WOMEN & THEIR BODIES

NEWLY REVISED AND UPDATED

A Book by and for Women

Our Bodies, Ourselves

FOR THE NEW CENTURY

THE BOSTON WOMEN'S HEALTH BOOK COLLECTIVE

→ARCHIVE 23←

The Return of Conservatism to America

Archive Overview

AS you watch the news on TV, surf the Net, listen to talk radio, and read newspapers and magazines, you probably see, hear, and read quite a bit about the power of conservatism in American life today. What many refer to as a resurgence of conservatism, however, is not so much a resurgence as a synthesis of two forces: traditional conservative values (states' rights, individualism, free markets, anti-communism, anti-welfare, anti-big government) and the moral-issues focus of the new, primarily fundamentalist, Christian right. The sources presented here describe the hallmarks of this neoconservative synthesis.

In this archive you will explore these two political and social factions as a single coalition within the Republican Party and then assess this neoconservatism. Conservatism triumphed with the election of Ronald Reagan as president in 1980 and in 1984 and revealed its considerable power with the Republican "revolution" of 1994, which returned the first GOP-controlled Congress in several decades. Consider these central questions: What aspects of neoconservatism have made it appealing to so many Americans, and what vision of the nation does it present? To what extent has it transformed American politics and society? What role in the nation's life would you like to see conservatism play? In what ways has the Bush presidency promoted conservative values?

Placing the Sources in Context

NEOCONSERVATISM is unprecedented in the American cultural and political landscape for two reasons. First, it has had a huge impact on a major political party, the Republicans, and caused a rightward realignment of the Democrats as well. Second, neoconservatism includes a politicized religious, Christian right movement with an explicitly moral message (pro-life, pro-school prayer, pro-school choice). Neoconservatives, despite their lack of "pure" legislative and constitutional victories, have effectively redefined the language and focus of the nation's social-moral debates. Ironically, however, neoconservatives are non-conservative because they call for an energetic state and federal role in promoting a moral order, whereas traditional

TIMELINE

1960s	Decade of civil rights activism, liberalism, "god is dead" movement, student demonstrations and protests, increased sexual freedom
1960	Barry Goldwater's *The Conscience of a Conservative*
1964	Goldwater nominated as the Republican candidate for president
1964–1968	Lyndon Johnson's Great Society era of liberalism
1965–1969	Student protests against the war in Vietnam
1968	Year of assassinations, protests, violence; Richard Nixon elected president in "law and order" campaign
1970s	Equal Rights Amendment fails ratification by the states; rise of Christian right organizations and televangelism
1973	*Roe v. Wade* Supreme Court decision on abortion
1980	Ronald Reagan elected president
1981–1993	Republican control of the presidency
1994	Republicans win control of Congress; "Contract with America"
1998–1999	Clinton impeachment and trial
1999	Shootings at Columbine High School, other schools, and community centers
2000	George W. Bush "wins" the presidency in controversial election

conservatives are generally secular and opposed to an activist government.

Neoconservatism emerged from the political and social climate of the Sixties, the era portrayed in Archives 21 and 22, in several ways. First, Americans were badly divided on support for the war in Vietnam, and antiwar demonstrations sparked calls for patriotism. Second, the assassinations of Malcolm X, Martin Luther King, Jr., and Robert Kennedy devastated the political left, fractured the civil rights movement, and encouraged the growth of the more militant Black Panthers and black nationalist movements of the late sixties. Third, the Democratic Party convention in Chicago in 1968, where police attacked bystanders, news reporters, and delegates, damaged leftist idealism. These actions opened the way for even more violent expressions of discontent in the bombings of ROTC buildings and the "days of rage" attack on the Chicago police by the radical fringe group the Weathermen in 1969. Finally, Richard Nixon's law and order campaign in 1968 rallied "hard hat" workers tired of radical youth and hippies, ethnic Americans tired of the focus on blacks, and patriotic Americans tired of the antiwar movement.

Political and cultural radicalism and polarization, and the fragmentation of the New Deal liberal consensus of blacks, Jews, and organized labor, led inevitably to a right-wing reaction. So did several other developments in the 1970s. The fall of Saigon and South Vietnam to communism, the decline of *détente* with the Soviet Union, and the humiliation of U.S. power during the Iranian Revolution of 1979, when militants stormed the American embassy in Tehran and took scores of hostages, threatened America's vaunted international superiority. At home, an economic slowdown, combined with inflation and the oil embargo, the pro-abortion *Roe v. Wade* Supreme Court decision, the campaign for an Equal Rights Amendment for women, and the emergence of a more visible and politically active gay and lesbian community all disturbed conservative (mostly white, male) Americans.

The roots of conservatism go deep into American political history. The underpinnings of the neoconservative political movement were developed in the 1960s and 1970s, beginning with Arizona Republican Senator Barry Goldwater's little book, *The Conscience of a Conservative*, published in 1960, and his speech, "A Choice Not an Echo," accepting the Republican presidential nomination in 1964. As the 1960s archives show, college conservatives were organizing as were other conservatives outside of the college world. They enthusiastically embraced Goldwater. Although Goldwater lost the election, conservatism became a healthy grass roots movement.

Despite Watergate and his resignation in 1974, President Nixon's election and administration in the early 1970s continued the conservative impetus. It was in the late 1970s and early 1980s that the Christian right joined arms with secular neoconservatives (anti-Great Society at home and anti-Soviet abroad) by effectively injecting a religious-moral mission into a major political party for the first time in history. Ronald Reagan's nearly successful 1976 Republican presidential bid, his triumphant 1980 election, his "war on the poor," and his aggressive rhetoric against the Soviet Union's "evil empire" during the 1980s established a high-water mark for neoconservatism. George W. Bush's two electoral triumphs in 2000 and 2004 infused conservatism with new energy and an ambitious agenda. One of Bush's initiatives picked up on Goldwater's idea of eliminating Social Security. Bush did not propose ending the popular program, but allowing younger workers to invest some of what would have been paid into Social Security in a private investment account. At retirement, workers' income would depend on how well their investment accounts had performed. Despite a vigorous effort to sell his proposal, Bush did not pick up the necessary support to go ahead with his ideas.

Culturally, neoconservatism continues into the 21st century. Much of the neoconservative agenda was a reaction to the emergence of the counterculture in the 1960s, and it remains at war with the left to define "whose country it is." The religious wing of the movement has waged an all-out effort to establish the United States as a unified "Christian nation." Conservative intellectuals defend traditional American values like pride in the American and western intellectual tradition. In what has been called the "culture war," they assail what they see as leftist professors ("tenured radicals") and university programs in black, women's, and gay and lesbian studies and other manifestations of what they call "political correctness." These contentious cultural conflicts have been waged to determine the meaning of such central questions and symbols as family, education, sexuality, immigration, race, the arts, the fetus, and the flag. In many respects, the cultural and political right has proven itself much more adept than the left at capturing and framing ideas, as well as at motivating and deploying its supporters.

About the Sources

YOU will have no trouble working with these sources. The growth of neoconservatism within the Republican Party signifies a rightward shift in critical debates and decisions concerning welfare, affirmative action, abortion, education, church-state separation, family values, the rights of gays and lesbians, and foreign policy. The sources below focus on the evolution of neoconservatism in its approach to these political, religious, and moral issues. In particular, the documents demonstrate the cultural and political rallying of Christians around these moral imperatives: (1) to reverse abortion rights following the *Roe v. Wade* Supreme Court decision, (2) to restore God and family to their central place in society, and (3) to oppose gay marriage and (4) to use the political system to achieve these goals. Look for these three aspects in the source documents.

List of Sources

23.1a **Foreword to *The Conscience of a Conservative* by Barry Goldwater** (New York, 1960), pp. 3–6.

23.1b **Conclusion to speech, "A Choice Not an Echo," by Barry Goldwater,** 1964, accepting the Republican nomination for president, *New York Times*, July 17, 1964.

23.1c **Speech by Ronald Reagan to the National Association of Evangelicals,** March 8, 1983. Printed in the *New York Times*, March 9, 1983.

23.2 **Catalog cover and introduction, "Restoring America,"** 2007–2008, Peter Marshall Ministries, Orleans, Massachusetts. Courtesy Peter Marshall Ministries.

23.3a **Presidential election flyer, "Where Do the Candidates Stand on Abortion?"** 1992, Courtesy National Right to Life Committee, Inc.

23.3b **Planned Parenthood flyer, "A Closer Look at The Violent Opposition,"** undated.

23.3c **"Statement of Concerned Women for America on the Passing of Ruth Bell Graham,"** June 15, 2007, Concerned Women for America, Washington, D.C. Courtesy Concerned Women for America.

23.4a **"Mission Statement, Promise Keepers,"** 2001–2005, Promise Keepers Website. Courtesy Promise Keepers.

23.4b **Newspaper article, "Hundreds of Thousands Gather On the Mall in a Day of Prayers,"** *New York Times*, October 5, 1997. Story by Laurie Goodstein, photos by Stephen Crowley. *The New York Times*, 5 October 1997, 1, 24. Copyright © 1997 by The New York Times Company. Reprinted by permission.

23.4c "**Seven Questions Women Ask About Promise Keepers,"** 2001–2005, Promise Keepers Website. Courtesy Promise Keepers.

23.5 **Alliance Defense Fund pamphlet, "The Truth About Student Rights,"** Alliance Defense Fund, Scottsdale, AZ.

23.6 **Alliance Defense Fund pamphlet, "The Truth About Faith in the Workplace,"** Alliance Defense Fund, Scottsdale, AZ.

23.7 **Transcript of Bush statement on Constitutional ban on same sex marriage,** February 24, 2004, CNN.

23.8a **Photograph of gay couple,** 2003. *San Francisco Chronicle*, June 30, 2003. © Chronicle/Elizabeth Mangelsdorf.

23.8b **Photograph of man protesting gay marriage,** 2004. *USA Today*, July 1, 2004. Cindy Blanchard/AP/Wide World Photos.

23.9a **Excerpts from George W. Bush's discussion on Social Security,** 2005. White House news release, April 29, 2005.

23.9b Cartoon, "Fixing This Should Be Easy." © Bob Krohmer, Cartoon Stock.

Questions to Consider

By this time in *American History Firsthand*, you should be skillful at anticipating and answering the questions about sources such as these in this archive. You have learned how to "think historically" in interpreting primary sources, the basic building blocks of historical research and writing. For this archive, as you know from the Overview, the essential questions are: What aspects of neoconservatism have made it appealing to so many Americans, and what vision of the nation does it present? To what extent has it transformed American politics and society? What role in the nation's life would you like to see it play? In addition:

1. Considering the Goldwater, Reagan, and Bush sources (23.1a, b, and c and 23.9a), what consistency of values do you see in American conservatism over the past 35–40 years? What are the core beliefs?
2. What values from the American past are reflected in these sources? What values do neoconservatives oppose? What role does religion play in neoconservatism (23.2 through 23.7)?
3. What do these sources suggest about secular politics? What do they say about religious politics? What motivated nonpolitical Christians to enter politics? What core beliefs do you think brought secular conservatives and religious neoconservatives together? Which group made the greatest accommodations in creating a politically dynamic movement? What signs of opposition do you see?
4. What has happened to the abortion issue since the *Roe v. Wade* decision of 1973? How does this debate affect not only abortion but also other issues as well?
5. What gave rise to the Christian organizations aimed specifically at men or women—Promise Keepers and Concerned Women for America (23.3c, 23.4a, b, and c)? How do they differ? How are they similar? To what extent do you agree with one or both groups?
6. What issues beyond abortion have conservatives pursued in recent years? How have they pursued their agenda?
7. In what ways has the Bush presidency promoted conservative values?

→ DOCUMENT 23.1a ←

Foreword to *The Conscience of a Conservative* by Barry Goldwater (New York, 1960), pp. 3–6. By permission of the Arizona Historical Foundation.

Foreword

This book is not written with the idea of adding to or improving on the Conservative philosophy. Or of "bringing it up to date." The ancient and tested truths that guided our Republic through its early days will do equally well for us. The challenge to Conservatives today is quite simply to demonstrate the bearing of a proven philosophy on the problems of our own time.

I should explain the considerations that led me to join in this effort. I am a politician, a United States Senator. As such, I have had an opportunity to learn something about the political instincts of the American people, I have crossed the length and breadth of this great land hundreds of times and talked with tens of thousands of people, with Democrats and Republicans, with farmers and laborers and businessmen. I find that America is fundamentally a Conservative nation. The preponderant judgment of the American people, especially of the young people, is that the radical, or Liberal, approach has not worked and is not working. They yearn for a return to Conservative principles.

At the same time, I have been in a position to observe first hand how Conservatism is faring in Washington And it is all too clear that in spite of a Conservative revival among the people the radical ideas that were promoted by the New and Fair Deals under the guise of Liberalism still dominate the councils of our national government.

In a country where it is now generally understood and proclaimed that the people's welfare depends on individual self reliance rather than on state paternalism, Congress annually deliberates over whether the *increase* in government welfarism should be small or large.

In a country where it is now generally understood and proclaimed that the federal government spends too much, Congress annually deliberates over whether to raise the federal budget by a few billion dollars or by many billion.

In a country where it is now generally understood and proclaimed that individual liberty depends on decentralized government, Congress annually deliberates over whether vigorous or halting steps should be taken to bring state government into line with federal policy.

In a country where it is now generally understood and proclaimed that Communism is an enemy bound to destroy us, Congress annually deliberates over means of "co-existing" with the Soviet Union.

And so the question arises: Why have American people been unable to translate their views into appropriate political action? Why should the nation's underlying allegiance to Conservative principles have failed to produce corresponding deeds in Washington?

I do not blame my brethren in government, all of whom work hard and conscientiously at their jobs. I blame Conservatives—ourselves—myself. Our failure, as one Conservative writer has put it, is the failure of the Conservative demonstration. Though we Conservatives are deeply persuaded that our society is ailing, and know that Conservatism holds the key to national salvation—and feel sure the country agrees with us—we seem unable to demonstrate the practical relevance of Conservative principles to the needs of the day. We sit by impotently while Congress seeks to improvise solutions to problems that are not the real problems facing the country, while the government attempts to assuage imagined concerns and ignores the real concerns and real needs of the people.

Perhaps we suffer from an over-sensitivity to the judgments of those who rule the mass communications media. We are daily consigned by "enlightened" commentators to political oblivion: Conservatism, we are told, is out-of-date. The charge is preposterous and we ought boldly to say so. The laws of God, and of nature, have no date-line. The principles on which the Conservative political position is based have been established by a process that has nothing to do with the social, economic and political landscape that changes from decade to decade and from century to century. These principles are derived from the nature of man, and from the truths that God has revealed about His creation. Circumstances do change. So do the problems that are shaped by circumstances. But the principles that govern the solution of the problems do not. To suggest that the Conservative philosophy is out of date is akin to saying that the Golden Rule, or the Ten Commandments or Aristotle's *Politics* are out of date. The Conservative approach is nothing more or less than an attempt to apply the wisdom and experience and the revealed truths of the past to the problems of today. The challenge is not to find new or different truths, but to learn how to apply established truths to the problems of the contemporary world. My hope is that one more Conservative voice will be helpful in meeting this challenge.

This book is an attempt to bridge the gap between theory and practice. I shall draw upon my speeches, the radio and television broadcasts and the notes I have made over the years in the hope of doing what one is often unable to do in the course of a harried day's work on the Senate floor: to show the connection between Conservative principles so widely espoused, and Conservative action, so generally neglected.

→ DOCUMENT 23.1b ←

Conclusion to speech, "A Choice Not an Echo," by Barry Goldwater, 1964, accepting the Republican nomination for President, *New York Times*, July 17, 1964. By permission of the Arizona Historical Foundation.

My fellow Republicans, we do no man a service by hiding freedom's light under a bushel of mistaken humility. I seek an American proud of its past, proud of its ways, proud of its dreams, and determined actively to proclaim them. But our examples to the world must, like charity, begin at home.

In our vision of a good and decent future, free and peaceful, there must be room, room for the liberation of the energy and the talent of the individual, otherwise our vision is blind at the outset.

We must assure a society here which while never abandoning the needy, or forsaking the helpless, nurtures incentives and opportunity for the creative and the productive.

We must know the whole good is the product of many single contributions.

And I cherish the day when our children once again will restore as heroes the sort of men and women who, unafraid and undaunted, pursue the truth, strive to cure disease, subdue and make fruitful our natural environment, and produce the inventive engines of production-science and technology.

This nation, whose creative people have enhanced this entire span of history, should again thrive upon the greatness of all those things which we—we as individual citizens—can and should do.

During Republican years, this again will be a nation of men and women, of families proud of their role, jealous of their responsibilities, unlimited in their aspirations nation where all who can will be self-reliant.

We Republicans see in our constitutional form of government the great framework which assures the orderly but dynamic fulfillment of the whole man as the great reason for instituting orderly government in the first place.

We see in private property and in economy based upon and fostering private property the one way to make government a durable ally of the whole man rather than his determined enemy. We see in the sanctity of private property the only durable foundation for constitutional government in a free society.

And beyond all that we see and cherish diversity of ways, diversity of thoughts, of motives, and accomplishments. We don't seek to live anyone's life for him. We only seek to secure his rights, guarantee him opportunity, guarantee him opportunity to strive, with government performing only those needed and constitutionally sanctioned tasks which cannot otherwise be performed.

We Republicans seek a government that attends to its inherent responsibilities of maintaining a stable monetary and fiscal climate, encouraging a free and a competitive economy, and enforcing law and order.

Thus do we seek inventiveness, diversity, and creative difference within a stable order, for we Republicans define government's role where needed at many, many levels—preferably, though, the one closest to the people involved: our towns and our cities, then our counties, then our states, then our regional contacts, and only then the national government.

That, let me remind you, is the land of liberty built by decentralized power. On it also we must have balance between the branches of government at every level.

Balance, diversity, creative difference—these are the elements of Republican equation. Republicans agree, Republicans agree heartily to disagree on many, many of their applications. But we have never disagreed on the basic fundamental issues of why you and I are Republicans.

This is a party—this Republican party is a party for free men. Not for blind followers and not for conformists. Back in 1858 Abraham Lincoln said this of the Republican party—and I quote him because he probably could have said it during the last week or so—it was composed of strained, discordant, and even hostile elements. End of the quote, in 1958 [sic].

Yet all of these elements agreed on paramount objective: to arrest the progress of slavery, and place it in the course of ultimate extinction.

Today, as then, but more urgently and more broadly than then, the task of preserving and enlarging freedom at home and safeguarding it from the forces of tyranny abroad is great, enough to challenge all our resources and to require all our strength.

Anyone who joins us in all sincerity, we welcome. Those, those who do not care for our cause, we don't expect to enter our ranks, in any case. And let our Republicanism so focused and so dedicated not be made fuzzy and futile by unthinking and stupid labels.

I would remind you that extremism in the defense of liberty is no vice! And let me remind you also that moderation in the pursuit of justice is no virtue!

The beauty of the very system we Republicans are pledged to restore and revitalize, the beauty of this federal system of ours, is in its reconciliation of diversity with unity. We must not see malice in honest differences of opinion, and no matter how great, so long as they are not inconsistent with the pledges we have given to each other in and through our Constitution.

Our Republican cause is not to level out the world or make its people conform in computer-regimented sameness. Our Republican cause is to free our people and light the way for liberty throughout the world. Ours is a very human cause for very humane goals. This party, its good people, and its unquestionable devotion to freedom will not fulfill the purposes of this campaign which we launch here now until our cause has won the day, inspired the world, and shown the way to a tomorrow worthy of all our yesteryears.

I repeat, I accept your nomination with humbleness, with pride, and you and I are going to fight for the goodness of our land. Thank you.

✧ DOCUMENT 23.1c ✧

Speech by Ronald Reagan to the National Association of Evangelicals, Printed in the *New York Times,* March 8, 1983.

. . . [T]his administration is motivated by a political philosophy that sees the greatness of America in you, her people, and in your families, churches, neighborhoods, communities—the institutions that foster and nourish values like concern for others and respect for the rule of law under God.

Now, I don't have to tell you that this puts us in opposition to, or at least out of step with, a prevailing attitude of many who have turned to a modern-day secularism, discarding the tried and time-tested values upon which our very civilization is based. No matter how well intentioned, their value system is radically different from that of most Americans. And while they proclaim that they're freeing us from superstitions of the past, they've taken upon themselves the job of superintending us by government rule and regulation. Sometimes their voices are louder than ours, but they are not yet a majority.

An example of that vocal superiority is evident in a controversy now going on in Washington. And since I'm involved, I've been waiting to hear from the parents of young America. How far are they willing to go in giving to government their prerogatives as parents?

Let me state the case as briefly and simply as I can. An organization of citizens, sincerely motivated and deeply concerned about the increase in illegitimate births and abortions involving girls well below the age of consent, sometime ago established a nationwide network of clinics to offer help to these girls and, hopefully, alleviate the situation. Now, again, let me say, I do not fault their intent. However, in their well-intentioned effort, these clinics have decided to provide advice and birth control drugs and devices to underage girls without the knowledge or their parents.

For some years now, the Federal Government has helped with funds to subsidize these clinics. In providing for this, the Congress decreed that every effort would be made to maximize parental participation. Nevertheless, the drugs and devices are prescribed without getting parental consent or giving notification after they've done so. Girls termed "sexually active"—and that has replaced the word "promiscuous"—are given this help in order to prevent illegitimate birth or abortion.

Well, we have ordered clinics receiving Federal funds to notify the parents such help has been given. One of the Nation's leading newspapers has created the term "squeal rule" in editorializing against us for doing this, and we're being criticized for violating the privacy of young people. A judge has recently granted an injunction against an enforcement of our rule. I've watched TV panel shows discuss this issue, seen columnists pontificating on our error, but no one seems to mention morality as playing a part in the subject of sex.

Is all of Judeo-Christian tradition wrong? Are we to believe that something so sacred can be looked upon as a purely physical thing with no potential for emotional and psychological harm? And isn't it the parents' right to give counsel and advice to keep their children from making mistakes that may affect their entire lives? . . .

More than a decade ago, a Supreme Court decision literally wiped off the books of fifty States statutes protecting the rights of unborn children. Abortion on demand now takes the lives of up to 1.5 million unborn children a year. Human life legislation ending this tragedy will some day pass the Congress, and you and I must never rest until it does. Unless and until it can be proven that the unborn child is not a living entity, then its right to life, liberty, and the pursuit of happiness must be protected.

You may remember that when abortion on demand began, many, and, indeed I'm sure many of you, warned that the practice would lead to a decline in respect for human life, that the philosophical premises used to justify abortion on demand would ultimately be used to justify other attacks on the sacredness of human life—infanticide or mercy killing. Tragically enough, those warnings proved all too true. Only last year a court permitted the death by starvation of a handicapped infant. . . .

Now I'm sure that you must get discouraged at times, but you've done better than you know, perhaps. There's a great spiritual awakening in America, a renewal of the traditional values that have been the bedrock of America's goodness and greatness.

One recent survey by a Washington-based research council concluded that Americans were far more religious than the people of other nations; 95 percent of those surveyed expressed a belief in God and a huge majority believed the Ten Commandments had real meaning in their lives. And another study has found that an overwhelming majority of Americans disapprove of adultery, teenage sex, pornography, abortion, and hard drugs. And this same study showed a deep reverence for the importance of family ties and religious belief. . . .

And this brings me to my final point today. During my first press conference as President, in answer to a direct question, I pointed out that, as good Marxist-Leninists, the Soviet leaders have openly and publicly declared that the only morality they recognize is that which will further their cause, which is world revolution. I think I should point out I was only quoting Lenin, their guiding spirit, who said in 1920 that they repudiate all morality that proceeds from supernatural ideas—that's their name for religion. . . . Morality is entirely subordinate to the interests of class war. . . .

[T]hey must be made to understand we will never compromise our principles and standards. We will never give away our freedom. We will never abandon our belief in God. And we will never stop searching for a genuine peace. . . .

Yes, let us pray for the salvation of all of those who live in that totalitarian darkness—pray they will discover the joy of knowing God. But until they do, let us be aware that while they preach the supremacy of the state, declare its omnipotence over individual man, and predict its eventual domination of all peoples on the Earth, they are the focus of evil in the modern world. . . .

So, I urge you to speak out against those who would place the United States in a position of military and moral inferiority. You know, I've always believed that old Screwtape reserved his best efforts for those of you in the church. So, in your discussions of the nuclear freeze proposals, I urge you to beware the temptation of pride—the temptation of blithely declaring yourselves above it all and label both sides equally at fault, to ignore the facts of history and the aggressive impulses of an evil empire, to simply call the arms race a giant misunderstanding and thereby remove yourself from the struggle between right and wrong and good and evil. . . .

→ DOCUMENT 23.2 ←

Catalog cover and introduction, "Restoring America," 2007–2008, Peter Marshall Ministries, Orleans, Massachusetts. Courtesy Peter Marshall Ministries.

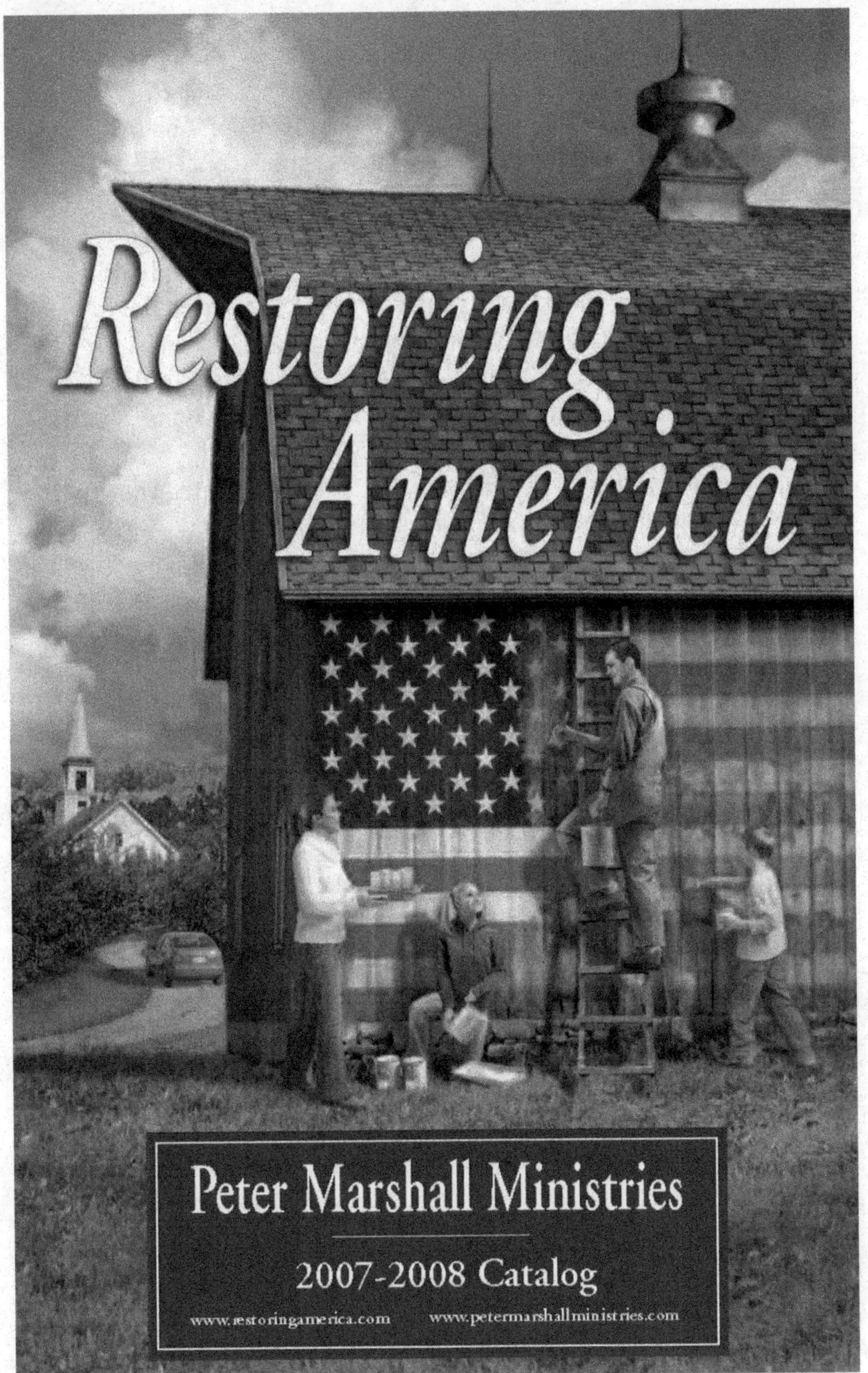

★ ★ ★ ★ ★ ★ ★ ★ ★ ★ ★ ★ ★ ★ ★ ★ ★ ★

How it all began. . .

In 1975, on the eve of the first National Day of Repentance in modern memory, the Reverend Peter Marshall was addressing a Cape Cod chapel full of committed Christians. As it had been for his father, the former Senate Chaplain, his concern was for America: "This nation was founded by God with a special calling. The people who first came here knew that they were being led here by the Lord Jesus Christ, to found a nation where men, women, and children were to live in obedience to Him. . . This was truly to be *one nation under God*." To make his point, he quoted from Columbus' then-unpublished spiritual journal and from the sermons and diaries of the Pilgrims and Puritans.

In the audience that evening was writer David Manuel who was galvanized by what he was hearing. Previously he had thought of one day tracing the faith and spiritual legacy of the Founding Fathers; now an idea was forming in his mind. . . .

He suggested a collaboration: a book on the founding of America, from the perspective just outlined. If God *did* have a plan for America, and if many of the First Comers *were* aware that they were part of His plan—then it would be a book that had never been done before, and one that was badly needed. For a great many Americans were not even aware that they *had* a Christian heritage.

The more they prayed about it, the more convinced they became that God was calling them to this joint mission. And the rest, as they say, is history.

David Manuel & Peter Marshall

★ ★ ★ ★ ★ ★ ★ ★ ★ ★ ★ ★ ★ ★ ★ ★ ★ ★

The best-seller that started it all. . .

The LIGHT and the GLORY

Peter Marshall
David Manuel

Did God have a plan for America?

The celebration of our nation's bicentennial awakened a great yearning for a Christian perspective on the birth of America. Three weeks after its publication, word of mouth had made ***The Light and the Glory*** a national best-seller.

Now, some twenty-four printings later, it has become a classic, read by more than a million Americans.

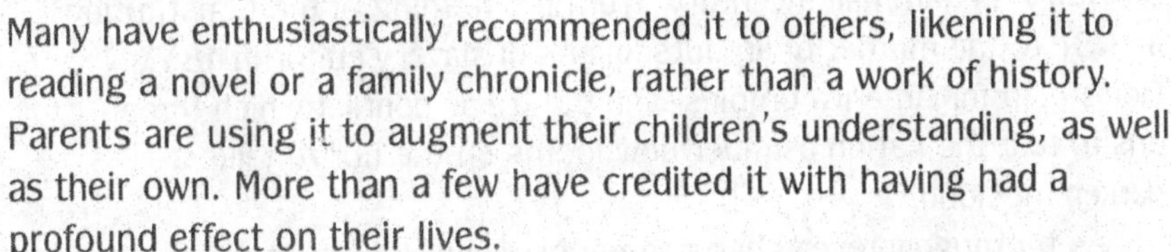

Many have enthusiastically recommended it to others, likening it to reading a novel or a family chronicle, rather than a work of history. Parents are using it to augment their children's understanding, as well as their own. More than a few have credited it with having had a profound effect on their lives.

Did God have a plan for America? The authors offer countless examples of His hand in the discovery and settling of this land, in its spiritual awakening, in its struggle for independence, and in its first years as a republic. As they document the Christian faith of key figures from Columbus to Washington, their often startling insights and inspiring stories have made this book "must reading" for all who would regain their national spiritual heritage.

Hardcover: $19.00
Paperback: $12.00
Study Guide (for group, personal, or home school use): $8.00

New! Audio Book (2 cassettes, 3 hours total): $15.00

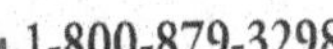

1-800-879-3298

★ ★ ★ ★ ★ ★ ★ ★ ★ ★ ★ ★ ★ ★ ★ ★ ★ ★

The sequel that carries the story forward half a century. . .

What happened next? How did God tame the western frontier? Why was slavery condoned by the Constitution? How could Christians remain slaveholders? It soon became obvious that Marshall & Manuel's mission, far from being accomplished, had only just begun.

They embarked upon a sequel to *The Light and the Glory*, carrying the story forward half a century. From the framing of the Constitution in 1787 to the murder of an outspoken antislavery editor in 1837, God's plan for America unfolds—and the tragic conflict which threatens to tear the nation asunder now looms on the horizon like a darkening cloud.

As thoroughly researched and popularly written as its predecessor, ***From Sea to Shining Sea*** traces the God's hand in the Great Revival of the West, in the fearless, sacrificial dedication of the Methodist circuit-riders, and in the brave and sometimes tragic saga of the pioneer families whose faith and courage opened the West. The incredible exploits of the Mountain Men, the brilliant generalship of Andrew Jackson, the quiet valor of the defenders of the Alamo—all are here in God's unfolding plan for America.

Hardcover: $19.00
Paperback: $12.00
Study Guide: $8.00

New! Audio Book (2 cassettes, 3 hours total): $15.00

The Restoring America DVD, CD, and Print

Restoring America DVD: 5 discs, 4 segments per disc. $99.00.
Running time: approx. 9 hours, 45 minutes.
Restoring America CD: 5 discs, 4 segments per disc. $50.00.
Running time: same as the DVD.

Filmed before a live audience, and formatted in twenty 28:30 segments for TV broadcasting, this exciting and inspiring DVD and CD seminar features Peter Marshall teaching on America's Christian heritage, and how we can get nation-wide revival! Displayed on the screen are quotes in an attractive and readable graphic, pictures of the persons or incidents he is speaking about, and crowd reaction shots. The segments are entitled:

- Introduction
- Christopher Columbus: The Missionary Explorer
- The Pilgrims: The True Founders of America (Parts I-II)
- The Puritans and the American Covenant (Parts I-III)
- The Christian Faith of the Founding Fathers (Parts I-V)
- The Christian Principles of the Constitution
- The False Issue of the Separation of Church and State (Parts I-II)
- Restoring America: How Can We Begin? (Parts I-II)
- How Can Revival and Restoration Come? (Parts I-III)

DOCUMENT 23.3a

Presidential election flyer, "Where Do The Candidates Stand On Abortion?" 1992, Courtesy National Right to Life Committee, Inc.

Where Do The Candidates Stand On Abortion?

George Bush   Bill Clinton

Roe vs. Wade

GEORGE BUSH has steadfastly called for the reversal of Roe v. Wade. As he told a rally of pro-lifers in Washington, D.C., **"The Supreme Court's decision in Roe v. Wade was wrong and should be overturned."** Bush appointee Attorney General William Barr said the Justice Department would continue to urge the Court to reverse Roe in future cases.

BILL CLINTON says he has "always been pro-choice" and has "never wavered" in his "support of Roe v. Wade." **"I have believed in the rule of Roe v. Wade for 20 years** since I used to teach it in law school." **(Roe v. Wade allows abortion for any reason, even as a method of birth control, even in the late stages of pregnancy.)**

Appointment of Judges

GEORGE BUSH has sought to appoint judicial conservatives, such as Clarence Thomas, to the courts. Thomas joined three other justices in dissenting from the Court's Casey decision upholding Roe. During the Bush/Reagan years, the pro-abortion majority on the Court has shrunk from 7-2 to 5-4.

BILL CLINTON says that support for Roe v. Wade would be a litmus test for his nominees to the Supreme Court. Referring to the one-vote margin by which the Court recently upheld Roe v. Wade, Clinton said, "As president, I won't make you worry about the 'one justice away' on the Supreme Court."

Unlimited Abortion

GEORGE BUSH has vowed he will veto the "Freedom of Choice Act" (FOCA). **FOCA goes well beyond even Roe versus Wade and forbids any significant limits on abortion.** The President pledged, **"it will not become law as long as I am President of the United States."**

BILL CLINTON has made support for FOCA a key part of his campaign. **"I would support a federal Freedom of Choice Act to protect a woman's right to choose."**

Abortion Without Parental Consent

GEORGE BUSH will fight proposals to allow minor girls to obtain abortions without parental consent. The President said, "This idea is crazy."

BILL CLINTON boasts that he has "fought against" parental consent laws in Arkansas, and says, "I'm opposed to parental consent, by the way, and I oppose a bill that would do that."

Harvesting Tissues of Babies Killed by Abortion

GEORGE BUSH has consistently refused to use tax dollars to pay for research that involves transplanting tissue taken from aborted unborn babies into other persons.

BILL CLINTON sharply criticizes the President for defending this pro-life policy, which Clinton called "an ugly bow to the far right."

Abortion as Birth Control

GEORGE BUSH has banned promotion of abortion as a method of birth control in federally funded clinics.

BILL CLINTON has said he would issue an Executive Order repealing this pro-life policy on his first day in office.

Government Funding of Abortion

GEORGE BUSH has strongly defended the Hyde Amendment, which prohibits the use of federal dollars to pay for abortions, except to save the mother's life.

BILL CLINTON would repeal the Hyde Amendment. Moreover, **abortion on demand would be paid for under his national health program.**

Ross Perot

has said he would sign the same radical legislation Clinton supports which would guarantee abortion for any reason...even as a method of birth control or for sex selection. He supports tax funding of abortion.

→ DOCUMENT 23.3b ←

Planned Parenthood flyer, "A Closer Look at The Violent Opposition," undated.

A Closer Look at The Violent Opposition

"Abortionists should be put to death. They are murderers."
Jeff Baker, 10th Amendment Militia

"We should be forming militias." "This Christmas, I want you to do the most loving thing . . . buy each of your children an SKS rifle and 500 rounds of ammunition."
Rev. Matt Trewhella, U.S. Taxpayer Party

"There aren't enough flak jackets ... to stop the spirit of murder that has been unleashed in this nation. I'm sorry, it doesn't work."
Rev. Flip Benham, Operation Rescue, on CNN, talking about the killing of Dr. Barnett Slepian

Willie Ray and Cecilia Lampley, J.D. Baird
Oklahoma Constitutional Militia
Arrested and convicted of conspiracy to bomb abortion clinics and other sites

Planned Parenthood needs your assistance to help protect health centers from these fanatics.

DOCUMENT 23.3c

"Statement of Concerned Women for America on the Passing of Ruth Bell Graham," June 15, 2007, Concerned Women for America, Washington, D.C. Courtesy Concerned Women for America.

Washington, D.C.—Concerned Women for America (CWA) offers its condolences to Ruth Bell Graham's family and loved ones. Mrs. Graham has gone home to be with the Lord.

Ruth was born to parents who were medical missionaries in China. At an early age Ruth decided she wanted to remain single and pursue missions in Tibet, but the Lord had a different plan for her life. In 1941 Ruth met Billy Graham and they married two years later. Mrs. Graham was a dedicated wife, mother of five children, and friend to so many people. She had a heart for people in need and spent her life sharing the Truth. She shared her faith in Christ with many and will be remembered by her faithfulness to her family, friends and God.

Beverly LaHaye, founder and chairman of CWA, remarked on Ruth's legacy: "What a wonderful example Ruth Graham has been for Christian women. Even though I did not have the pleasure of being a close friend, we met on a couple of occasions and were involved working on a book together with other women. She stood by Billy through the great days and through the difficult ones as well. I have never heard her give one word of negative criticism about her husband. I have met and known several of her children and they all have spoken so highly of their mother and her devotion to God and her husband."

Wendy Wright, president of CWA, said "Ruth Graham's gentle spirit and deep devotion to God fashioned her into a lovely model of Christian womanhood. She lived humbly in the glow of Billy's spotlight, her life quietly yet profoundly showing 'This is the way, walk in it.' Ruth was a rare person for whom fame did not distract her from what is True, right and best. Heaven must be rejoicing as the One she loved most welcomes her home."

→ DOCUMENT 23.4a ←

"Mission Statement, Promise Keepers," 2001–2005, Promise Keepers Website. Courtesy Promise Keepers.

Promise Keepers is dedicated to igniting and uniting men to be passionate followers of Jesus Christ through the effective communication of the 7 Promises.

A sovereign move of God's Spirit is stirring the hearts of men. In a world of negotiable values, confused identities, and distorted priorities, men are encountering God's Word, embracing their identities as His sons, and investing in meaningful relationships with God, their families and each other.

Clearly, Christian men have an unprecedented opportunity to seize this moment and make a difference for Jesus Christ. We believe that God wants to use Promise Keepers as a spark in His hand to ignite a nationwide movement calling men from all denominational, ethnic, and cultural backgrounds to reconciliation, discipleship, and godliness.

⇾ DOCUMENT 23.4b ⇽

Newspaper article on Promise Keepers rally in Washington, D.C., 4 October 1997, "Hundreds of Thousands Gather on the Mall in a Day of Prayers," story by Laurie Goodstein, photos by Stephen Crowley, *The New York Times*, 5 October 1997, 1, 24.

October 5, 1997

Hundreds of Thousands Gather On the Mall in a Day of Prayers

By LAURIE GOODSTEIN

WASHINGTON, Oct. 4 In a religious revival rally that stretched a mile from the Capitol past the Washington Monument, hundreds of thousands of Christian men hugged, sang and sank to their knees today, repenting for their own sins and what they see as a secular and socially troubled America.

The crowd, summoned here by Promise Keepers, a relatively new all-male evangelical movement, appeared to rank in numbers with the largest events ever held on the National Mall, including the civil rights marches and anti-Vietnam protests of the 60's and the Million Man March in 1995, said Samuel H. Jordan, director of the District of Columbia Office of Emergency Preparedness.

"It seems to far exceed the crowd at the Million Man March," Terry Adams, a photographer for the public affairs office of the National Parks Service, said as he surveyed the crowd from the Speaker's balcony of the Capitol building.

The crowd veered from ebullient, chanting "Je-sus" over and over like the "defense" cheer at football games, to solemn, as a multiracial cast of preachers exhorted the men to acknowledge their own racism.

"I want to see our nation restored, see us get back to God," said Wayne Hussong, 53, a shipping clerk from Rockford, Ill., who was sitting on a camp stool in the crowd. "If everybody got back to God, I'm sure crime would fall, racial prejudice would cease, the conflict between the sexes would cease, abortion would be done away with, just name it. I just feel these things can happen."

They fasted and confessed to one another inside canvas "prayer tee-pees" set up on the Mall. On 18 giant video screens, they watched a prerecorded message from a man asking forgiveness for allowing his wife to have an abortion. And the throng fell almost silent as one speaker directed the men to prostrate themselves while holding photographs of family members they had mistreated. Some men wept openly.

"It's kind of like an awakening for me," said Toney Burke, of Chester, Va. "I'm a recovering alcoholic and a recovering drug addict and I'm just trying to find something to replace drinking and taking drugs."

The first of many prayers from the stage came from a Messianic Jew, who blew a traditional ram's horn, or shofar, and said that the final, long blast represented victory for those who believe Jesus is the Messiah. He was followed by gospel choirs and Indian, African-American, Asian and Hispanic preachers.

Listening to them were lunch-bucket men and expense-account men, grandfathers using canes and teen-agers throwing footballs, men in ten-gallon hats and men with ponytails. The crowd was largely white men, but there were busloads of people from black churches and Hispanic churches and a sprinkling of Asian men and American Indians and Messianic Jews.

Bill McCartney, a former University of Colorado football coach who founded Promise Keepers, announced to the crowd that the organization's next goal was to convene Christian men on the steps of every state capitol at noon on Jan. 1, 2000. Mr. McCartney said that his vision was for every Christian man to work at forming relationships across racial lines so they could proclaim by that date that "the giant of racism is dead within the church."

In a speech intended to set the tone and respond to some of the group's critics, Randy Phillips, president of Promise Keepers, told the crowd: "We have not come to impose our religious beliefs on others. We celebrate a land of religious freedom for all. We gather not to denigrate other faiths, but to affirm our belief in the message that salvation comes through faith in the death and resurrection of Jesus Christ alone."

Neither Promise Keepers organizers nor police officials would provide a precise crowd count because of controversies over the size of the Million Man March in 1995. The United States Park Police estimated that crowd at 400,000, but the Nation of Islam claimed the march drew more than 800,000.

Six years ago, Promise Keepers drew a mere 4,200 men for its first event in a basketball arena in Boulder, Colo. Since then, the group has drawn, by its estimate, about 2.6 million men to 61 stadium rallies in cities around the country. Historians call it one of the fastest-growing religious revivals in American history.

President Clinton, in his weekly radio address today, said: "No one can question the sincerity of the hundreds of thousands of men who have filled football stadiums across our country and who are willing to reassume their responsibilities to the families and to their children and therefore to our future."

Misfortune early in the day cast a small shadow over the rally. A rented plane carrying six men from Pennsylvania crashed and caught fire hours before the event was to begin, near a commuter rail station in suburban Maryland. All six were taken to hospitals, but their injuries were not life-threatening.

With thousands standing to hear speeches for hour after hour, the Mall was hot and crowded. Senator Strom Thurmond, the 94-year-old Republican of South Carolina, was taken to a hospital for observation after becoming dehydrated and dizzy while on stage.

The idea for a nationwide men-only Christian movement originated with Mr. McCartney, a former football coach for the University of Colorado Buffalos. Mr. McCartney said he envisioned filling sports stadiums with men dedicating their lives to Jesus. The movement has made an effort to draw members from many Christian denominations, but its preaching style and theological orientation lean toward the charismatic and Pentecostal.

Under Mr. McCartney's guidance, Promise Keepers has managed to merge the spiritual abandon of a tent revival with the raucous enthusiasm of a sporting spectacle and the efficiency of a military mobilization. Today's event was a fast-paced production of energetic preaching, Christian music and emotional calls for confessions of sins.

Promise Keepers organizers said their goal was to reverse the moral and social deterioration caused by men abandoning their family responsibilities.

"We gather not to point fingers at society," the Rev. Dale D. Schlafer, the director of today's event, said at a news conference on Friday. "We're not here to say that the government has failed. We're here to say that the problem is with us, with us men who are in the church. We are coming to confess our sins."

Promise Keepers called today's event a sacred assembly, a reference to church gatherings called throughout history in times of perceived spiritual crisis. The event's title, "Stand in the Gap," is a reference to an apocalyptic passage in the biblical book Ezekiel (22:30) in which God declares, "I looked for a man among them who would build up the wall and stand before Me in the gap on behalf of the land so I would not have to destroy it, but I found none."

Hundreds of thousands of men chanted and sang prayers yesterday on the National Mall at a gathering organized by the Promise Keepers.

This Scripture reflects Promise Keepers' assessment that there is a moral deterioration in modern America. Mr. Schlafer said the group hoped God would "use this event to ignite a revival in his church" that would spread like a chain reaction. "Those who are non-Christian," Mr. Schlafer continued, will be so "drawn to this church that suddenly is alive, it's on fire, that they give their lives to Christ as well, and the church of Christ begins to swell and to pulsate with the life that is what the Scriptures say it ought to be."

The Rev. Billy Graham, the dean of evangelical preachers, sent a video-taped message from San Francisco. He encouraged men to evangelize and said: "God is not calling us to a playground. He is calling us to a battleground. This is warfare, and we are in the center of the battle."

The event has its critics. The National Organization for Women called it nothing more than a male backlash. Critics also say Promise Keepers teaches that the role of women in the family should be subordinate to men. More than 60 religious leaders who formed an anti-Promise Keepers coalition, called Equal Partners in Faith, signed a letter in May saying that by excluding women and female clergy from Promise Keepers events, "the message is that women belong behind men, not in equal partnerships, and that this is God's will for men and women."

Suzie Hill, 29, watching over her daughter in a stroller on the Mall, said that the criticism by the National Organization for Women was off-base. She said that Promise Keepers had helped her husband, Jeff, a 30-year-old engineer, "realize that work is not as important as family."

Today's event was initially planned for 1996, but the board members of Promise Keepers said they postponed it to avoid the political tone of an election year. But the group is still fending off critics who insist that no movement without political designs would call for such a show of force in the nation's capital.

"We are not a political organization," said Mr. Phillips. "We do not have any political goals."

Washington politicians, nevertheless, made an effort to be seen mingling with the Promise Keepers attendees from their home states.

Promise Keepers usually charges $60 a person for stadium rallies. Today's event was free, but barrels were placed around the grounds to collect money. The organizers said they expected to eventually recoup most of the approximately $9 million they said it cost to stage the event.

The average age of the men who attended Promise Keepers events in 1995 was 37, according to a survey then by the National Center for Fathering, in Kansas City, Mo., and more than half of 1,083 men who have attended Promise Keepers events said they had at least a bachelor's degree. The poll found that about 88 percent said they were married, and of those, more than 57 percent had wives who worked.

Steve Brown of the Cycle Disciples handed out some of the one million Bibles the group was distributing.

The survey also found that most of these men said they were already active in their churches.

A poll by Promise Keepers found that the men said their biggest problem was "sexual sin."

Mr. McCartney has said that he founded Promise Keepers because he "failed so miserably" in taking care of his own family. His only daughter, Kristyn, twice became pregnant out of wedlock. Mr. McCartney kept up a grueling travel schedule as his wife, Lyndi, grew more depressed. "I watched my own family suffer as I poured myself into my career," Mr. McCartney wrote in a recent essay.

→ DOCUMENT 23.4c ←

"Seven Questions Women Ask About Promise Keepers," 2001–2005, Promise Keepers Website. Courtesy Promise Keepers.

1. What is Promise Keepers?

Established in 1990, Promise Keepers (PK) is a ministry designed to ignite and unite men to become passionate followers of Jesus Christ through the effective communication of seven promises to God, other men, their family, their church and their community.

The men gather on Friday evening and Saturday morning to hear excellent Christian speakers on a variety of topics related to the seven promises. Along with praise and worship, the interaction has proven to be dynamic!

Promise Keepers has directly reached more than five million men in 16 years of over 200 stadium and arena events for men, youth, and clergy, through weekly radio and television broadcasts, the Internet, 16 CDs, more than two dozen books, Bible studies, multimedia resources, plus outreach programs to local churches.

Promise Keepers' vision is simple: Men Transformed Worldwide! You will find the Seven Promises in full text along with other PK related information by taking time to browse our website. Our Frequently Asked Questions section is a good place to start.

2. Are women allowed to attend PK meetings?

Yes, they are and they have! However, we have found that men are more apt to receive the content of the message in the company of other men as opposed to a mixed gender setting. Promise Keepers' program is aimed at the hearts of men, using language, illustrations, and experiences that are commonly understood by men.

Over the years, we have found that men tend to feel much freer and more open in expressing celebration and other emotions in the company of other men. At Promise Keepers, this predominately male setting is referred to as "the masculine context."

Many women have graciously volunteered at all our events to help in the various areas of production and support. They are highly appreciated and gratefully received. It is important to note that thousands of women pray each year for every one of our event cities.

3. Is Promise Keepers only for married men, or will it benefit men who are not married, i.e. fiancé or boyfriend?

While most men who attend Promise Keepers are married, according to a recent survey, 86% of single men (including widowed and divorced men) report that many of the insights gained at a PK event gave them a greater understanding in relating to God and in other significant relationships. Promise Keepers is all about relationships—transformed relationships.

Promise Keepers addresses such issues as anger and conflict management, the power of positive words, and the "why" and "how-to" of "servant leadership."

4. How old should a young man be to attend a Promise Keepers event?

Because of the length of the program, Promise Keepers suggests that boys no younger than 13 attend. However, many younger boys have attended and benefited from the "bonding" time with their dads and other men.

5. How can I encourage the man in my life to attend a Promise Keepers event?

Be sensitive that any suggestion or recommendation might be received as an accusation by a man who is defensive. Nevertheless, encourage him to spend time with other Christian men in the setting of a PK event. Suggest he use the weekend as a "father-son" event, or a good opportunity to spend time with his own father or father-in-law. Don't overlook the fact that he may wish to go alone, join a church or employee group, or just join another friend.

6. What should I expect from my man after he has attended a PK event?

It takes most men some time to process many of the things they experience at a Promise Keepers event (including worship, personal and relaxed prayer, confession, repentance, forgiveness, spiritual reflection, etc.). Change and growth often take time.

While a Promise Keepers event can jump-start a man's spiritual life, it takes more than a weekend with the guys to transform his heart and life. A large meal won't feed you for a lifetime.

Men are encouraged to personally pray for wisdom and strength as they begin their journey in following the seven promises. You can expect that you will need to continue to pray for him, as well.

7. What steps can I take to be an enthusiastic and effective "Promise Reaper?"

Be grateful for the spiritual hunger your man is showing. Acknowledge the little steps he is making to lead you and your family well. Be affirming in public. Practice patience. Paul wrote in Ephesians chapter five that respect is one of the important things we can give our husbands. It has been said that the wife is the spiritual barometer in the home. Protect your own time with the Lord so that you will be able to discern the spiritual cues in your home and with your man.

➜ DOCUMENT 23.5 ➜

Alliance Defense Fund pamphlet, "The Truth About Student Rights," Alliance Defense Fund, Scottsdale, AZ.

Truth in Our Schools

Although students have long had the right to engage in religious expression in public schools, districts across the country often prohibit them from exercising these rights based on a false view of the law.

As a legal alliance defending the right to hear and speak the Truth, ADF has been established, in part, to help protect these cherished freedoms and to restore rights guaranteed by the Constitution. This pamphlet briefly addresses some of these important rights.

★

1. Students have the right to pray, evangelize, read Scripture, distribute literature, and invite fellow students to participate so long as it is voluntary; it is not disruptive or coercive; and it occurs during noninstructional time.

   a. Schools may only prohibit student expression if there is specific evidence that the expression materially and substantially interferes with the requirements of appropriate discipline in the operation of the school or interferes with the rights of others.

   b. All student expression is subject to reasonable time, place, and manner restrictions imposed by the school. These restrictions must be content neutral, narrowly tailored to serve a significant government interest, and leave open ample alternative channels of communication.

2. Students have the right to express their religious views during class discussions or as a part of an assignment so long as the expression is relevant to the subject under consideration and otherwise meets the requirements of the assignment.

3. Students may lawfully study the Bible as a part of a secular program of education if the school should choose to use or allow use of the Bible as a part of its curriculum.

4. Students may lawfully study and perform religious songs as a part of advancing the students' objective knowledge of society's cultural and religious heritage, or furthering the study of music, if the school should choose to use religious songs as a part of the curriculum.

5. Secondary school students may form religious clubs if the school receives federal funds and allows non-curriculum related clubs to meet during noninstructional time.

    a. Religious clubs must be student-led—a nonstudent cannot lead the club. Regular attendance by an outside adult may be prohibited in order to avoid the appearance of the club being initiated or directed by a nonstudent.

    b. Teachers may be present at religious club meetings as monitors, but they may not participate in club activities.

    c. While the Federal Equal Access Act only applies to secondary school students (which is defined by the law of each state), a junior high and high school student's right to initiate and attend religious clubs, and to receive equal access to all club benefits has also been recognized as being protected by the First Amendment.

6. Religious clubs must be given full access to all school facilities, resources, and equipment that are used by secular student clubs, including, but not limited to, announcements on bulletin boards and the school's public address system, access to club funding and yearbook.

7. Students may wear religious attire required by their religion to the extent that other like articles of dress are permitted.

8. Students may wear clothing or jewelry displaying religious messages to the same extent that other messages are permitted.

9. Subject to applicable state laws, students may be able to attend off-campus religious instruction provided that schools do not encourage or discourage participation or penalize those who do not attend.

10. Subject to applicable state laws, students may be able to be excused from lessons that are objectionable to the student or the student's parents on religious or other conscientious grounds. Students also have a right not to be required to say or do something that violates their religious beliefs.

11. Subject to applicable state laws, students may be able to obtain an excused absence for the observance of religious holidays.

Students across the country are increasingly facing hostility and censorship while attempting to exercise their constitutionally protected religious beliefs—all in the name of "tolerance." If you experience a violation of your rights while in school, please call 1-800-TELL-ADF. You never know, it could help ensure that the avenues to proclaim the Truth remain open.

ADF, a legal alliance defending the right to hear and speak the Truth through strategy, training, funding, and litigation.

★

1-800-TELL-ADF

* *This pamphlet is for informational use only. For more in-depth information on this topic, and for required legal notification, go to www.telladf.org/issues.*

- ☐ I would like to receive the **ADF** monthly prayer, action, and information letter.
- ☐ I would like to receive a weekly e-mail or fax alert on **ADF**-backed legal cases, related issues, and prayer requests.
- ☐ I want to stand with **ADF** to defend the right to hear and speak the Truth. Here is my gift of

$____________________.

Thank you! The Alliance Defense Fund is recognized by the IRS as an organization exempt from taxation under Section 501(c)(3) of the Internal Revenue Code and gifts are tax-deductible to the extent allowed by law.

Please mail to: Alliance Defense Fund
15333 N. Pima Road, Suite 165
Scottsdale, Arizona 85260

ADF
ALLIANCE DEFENSE FUND
Defending Our First Liberty

www.telladf.org

TAB07

Name

Organization

Address

City | State | ZIP

Home Phone | Office Phone

E-Mail | Fax

☐ I would like to make my gift by credit card.
☐ Visa ☐ Mastercard ☐ Discover ☐ AMEX

Card Number | Expiration Date

Cardholder's Signature

☐ Check Enclosed

ECFA
A higher standard. A higher purpose.

Protecting what we have.
Reclaiming what we've lost.
Shaping who we become.

ALLIANCE DEFENSE FUND
Defending Our First Liberty

15333 N. Pima Road, Suite 165
Scottsdale, AZ 85260
1-800-TELL-ADF

→ DOCUMENT 23.6 ←

Alliance Defense Fund pamphlet, "The Truth About Faith in the Workplace," Alliance Defense Fund, Scottsdale, AZ.

PROTECTING WHAT WE HAVE.

RECLAIMING WHAT WE'VE LOST.

SHAPING WHO WE BECOME.

ALLIANCE DEFENSE FUND 15333 N. PIMA ROAD, SUITE 165
SCOTTSDALE, ARIZONA 85260 1-800-TELL-ADF

www.telladf.org

Do employers unlawfully discriminate if they base business objectives and goals upon Biblical principles?

No. An employer does not engage in discrimination if he/she is affirming the faith of its owners in business objectives. However, employers must be careful not to give prospective or current employees the perception that their employment or career advancement depends upon their compliance with the religious beliefs of the employer. If you are a secular employer, you can protect yourself by making sure that all employment applications specifically state that applicants are considered for all positions without regard to religious belief.

As an employer, can I witness to my employees?

Yes. An employer can generally talk about their religious beliefs as long as the employee knows that their continued employment or advancement is not contingent on compliance with the employer's religious beliefs. One court has held that an employer did not discriminate against an employee for sharing the Gospel with him and inviting him to church. However, if the employer made church attendance mandatory for continued employment, the employer could be held liable.

As an employer, can I give employees religious literature or post such literature in the workplace?

Yes. Like verbal religious speech, employers can share their religious beliefs with their employees in printed form such as pamphlets, books, and newsletters. Employers must be careful, however, not to give employees the impression that they have to agree with the employer's religious beliefs in order to keep their job or to be promoted. If an employer shares their religious convictions with the employee, no adverse action should be taken against the employee if they disagree or protest the sharing of those convictions.

As an employer, what is my obligation toward religious employees who have certain work requirements?

The religious freedom of most employees is protected by federal law under Title VII, which prohibits employment discrimination based on race, color, religion, sex, or national origin. In order to be protected by Title VII, an employee must meet the following three criteria: that a sincere religious belief conflicts with an employment requirement; that the employer was informed of the conflict; and that termination or discipline resulted from the employer failing to make accommodations regarding the conflicting employment requirement.

Religion under Title VII is broadly defined as including all aspects of religious observance and practice, as well as belief. The Equal Employment Opportunity Commission (EEOC) defines religious practices to include moral ethical beliefs about right and wrong that are held because of sincere religious views.

As an employer, can I regulate employee speech and the literature displayed on an employee's desk or in their office?

Yes. Employers have the right to control the image their business presents to the public. There is no right to free speech for employees of private companies because the First Amendment of the U.S. Constitution only applies to government entities.

Therefore, an employer can determine what literature can be displayed at desks and offices that are in the view of the general public. Employers can also prohibit employees from saying things to customers that they perceive would hurt business.

An employer must attempt to allow an employee's request to display items in their work area that reflect their personal religious beliefs, as long as it does not cause disruption in the workplace.

Are religious organizations treated any differently from secular businesses for employment law purposes?

Yes. The federal government does allow religious groups to have faith-based employment standards. To qualify for this exemption, the employer must establish that the primary or exclusive purpose of the organization is to engage in religious activities.

CONCLUSION

In an era of rampant litigation and constant demands for new and expanded "rights," it is essential that religious employers and employees know what they can and cannot do in the workplace.

ADF, a legal alliance defending the right to hear and speak the Truth.

☐ I would like to receive ADF's monthly prayer and information letter.

☐ I would like to receive a weekly e-mail or fax update on ADF-backed legal cases.

☐ I want to help ADF defend the right to hear and speak the Truth. Here is my gift of $__________.

Name: __________

Organization: __________

Address: __________

City: __________

State: ______ ZIP: ______

Home Phone: __________

Office Phone: __________

E-mail: __________

Fax: __________

I would like to make my gift by credit card.

☐ VISA ☐ Mastercard

Card Number: __________

Expiration Date: __________

Cardholder's Signature: __________

Thank you! The Alliance Defense Fund is recognized by the IRS as a 501(c)(3) organization, and gifts are tax-deductible to the extent allowed by law.

Please mail to:

ADF™
ALLIANCE DEFENSE FUND
Defending Our First Liberty

ALLIANCE DEFENSE FUND 15333 N. PIMA ROAD, SUITE 165
SCOTTSDALE, ARIZONA 85260 1-800-TELL-ADF

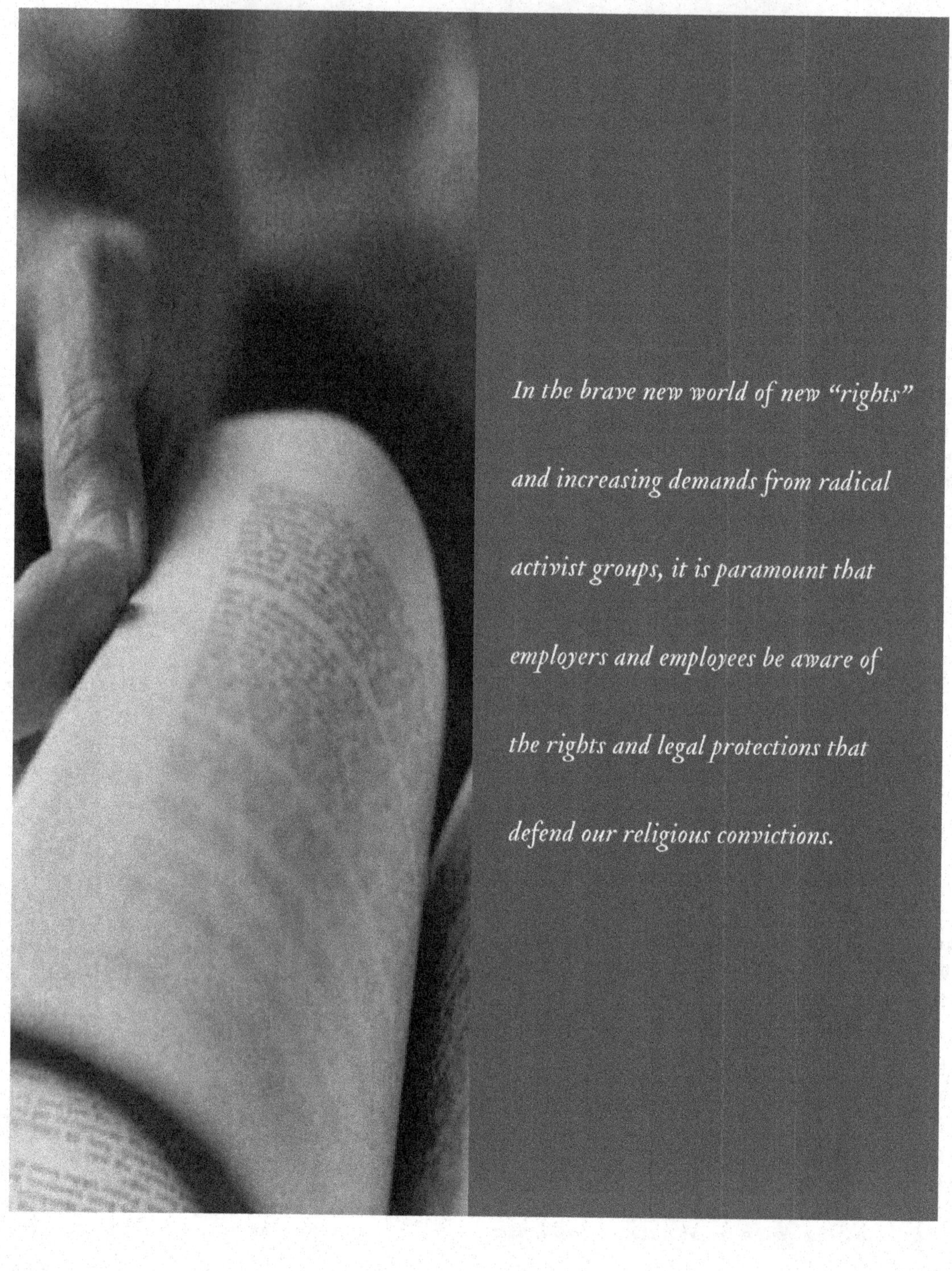
In the brave new world of new "rights" and increasing demands from radical activist groups, it is paramount that employers and employees be aware of the rights and legal protections that defend our religious convictions.

→ DOCUMENT 23.7 ←

Transcript of Bush statement on Constitutional ban on same sex marriage, February 24, 2004, CNN.

Good morning.

Eight years ago, Congress passed, and President Clinton signed, the Defense of Marriage Act, which defined marriage for purposes of federal law as the legal union between one man and one woman as husband and wife.

The act passed the House of Representatives by a vote of 342–67 and the Senate by a vote of 85–14.

Those congressional votes, and the passage of similar defense of marriage laws in 38 states, express an overwhelming consensus in our country for protecting the institution of marriage.

In recent months, however, some activist judges and local officials have made an aggressive attempt to redefine marriage. In Massachusetts, four judges on the highest court have indicated they will order the issuance of marriage licenses to applicants of the same gender in May of this year.

In San Francisco, city officials have issued thousands of marriage licenses to people of the same gender, contrary to the California Family Code. That code, which clearly defines marriage as the union of a man and a woman, was approved overwhelmingly by the voters of California.

A county in New Mexico has also issued marriage licenses to applicants of the same gender.

And unless action is taken, we can expect more arbitrary court decisions, more litigation, more defiance of the law by local officials, all of which adds to uncertainty.

After more than two centuries of American jurisprudence and millennia of human experience, a few judges and local authorities are presuming to change the most fundamental institution of civilization.

Their actions have created confusion on an issue that requires clarity. On a matter of such importance, the voice of the people must be heard. Activist courts have left the people with one recourse.

If we're to prevent the meaning of marriage from being changed forever, our nation must enact a constitutional amendment to protect marriage in America. Decisive and democratic action is needed because attempts to redefine marriage in a single state or city could have serious consequences throughout the country.

The Constitution says that "full faith and credit shall be given in each state to the public acts and records and judicial proceedings of every other state."

Those who want to change the meaning of marriage will claim that this provision requires all states and cities to recognize same-sex marriages performed anywhere in America.

Congress attempted to address this problem in the Defense of Marriage Act by declaring that no state must accept another state's definition of marriage. My administration will vigorously defend this act of Congress.

Yet there is no assurance that the Defense of Marriage Act will not itself be struck down by activist courts. In that event, every state would be forced to recognize any relationship that judges in Boston or officials in San Francisco choose to call a marriage.

Furthermore, even if the Defense of Marriage Act is upheld, the law does not protect marriage within any state or city.

For all these reasons, the defense of marriage requires a constitutional amendment.

An amendment to the Constitution is never to be undertaken lightly. The amendment process has addressed many serious matters of national concern, and the preservation of marriage rises to this level of national importance.

The union of a man and woman is the most enduring human institution, honored and encouraged in all cultures and by every religious faith. Ages of experience have taught humanity that the commitment of a husband and wife to love and to serve one another promotes the welfare of children and the stability of society.

Marriage cannot be severed from its cultural, religious and natural roots without weakening the good influence of society.

Government, by recognizing and protecting marriage, serves the interests of all.

Today, I call upon the Congress to promptly pass and to send to the states for ratification an amendment to our Constitution defining and protecting marriage as a union of a man and woman as husband and wife.

The amendment should fully protect marriage, while leaving the state legislatures free to make their own choices in defining legal arrangements other than marriage.

America's a free society which limits the role of government in the lives of our citizens. This commitment of freedom, however, does not require the redefinition of one of our most basic social institutions.

Our government should respect every person and protect the institution of marriage. There is no contradiction between these responsibilities.

We should also conduct this difficult debate in a matter worthy of our country, without bitterness or anger.

In all that lies ahead, let us match strong convictions with kindness and good will and decency.

Thank you very much.

⇢ DOCUMENT 23.8a ⇠

Photograph of gay couple, 2003. *San Francisco Chronicle,* June 30, 2003.

❖ DOCUMENT 23.8b ❖

Photograph of man protesting gay marriage, 2004. *USA Today,* July 1, 2004. Cindy Blanchard/AP/Wide World Photos.

→DOCUMENT 23.9a←

Excerpts from George W. Bush's discussion on Social Security, 2005. White House news release, April 29, 2005.

... But our seniors have got to understand the system is solvent for them. Nothing changes for people who were born prior to 1950. It's those born after 1950 that need to ask our elected representatives, there is a problem, and what you going to do about it?

I want to tell you what I think we ought to do about it. I think we ought to come together in good faith and discuss good ideas. I laid out some ideas—I have been laying out ideas about what I think we ought to do. First, I know that we ought to be able to say in a new system, as we fix the safety net for future generations, that you must receive benefits equal to or greater than the benefits enjoyed by today's seniors. In other words, any reform has got to say that to those who are paying into the system.

Secondly, I think the country needs to set this goal for future generations: that if you've worked all your life and paid in the Social Security system, you will not retire into poverty. And there's a way to make that happen, and that is to have the benefits for low-income workers in a future system grow faster than benefits for those who are better off.

If Congress were to enact that, that would go a long way toward making the system solvent for a younger generation of Americans. I have a duty to put ideas on the table—I'm putting them on the table. And I expect Republicans and Democrats to do the same kind of thing, and so do the American people.

The American people expect us in Washington, D.C. to do our duty and not play politics as usual with an issue as important as Social Security. When Congress comes together to discuss this issue, it's important for us to permanently fix Social Security. The reason I say that is because some of us were around in 1983 when Ronald Reagan called Tip O'Neill and said, we got a problem, and they came together and put together a 75-year fix. That's what they said. We got us a 75-year fix.

The problem is 25 years—or 22 years after 1983, we're still talking about it. The 75-year fix lasted about 22 years. And so now is the time to permanently fix Social Security. Any solution that comes forth out of Congress must permanently fix it.

As we permanently fix it, we have a great opportunity to make the system a better deal for younger workers. And here's how: Younger workers should be allowed to take some of their own money, some of their own payroll taxes they pay into the system, and set it aside in a personal savings account. Now, this isn't the government telling you what to do, the government saying you must set aside a personal savings account. This is the government saying, you should have the option, if you so choose, to take some of your own money, some of the money that you've earned, and put it aside in a personal savings account.

And here's the benefit from such an idea. One, the government does not—doesn't get a very good return on your money when we take it from you. If you were to put your money in a conservative mix of stocks and bonds, you would get a better rate of return. And that rate of return over time will make an enormous difference to somebody who wants to build a nest egg. Do you realize that stock investments have returned about 9 percent more than inflation per year since 1983, while the Social Security real return is only about 2 percent. That means if you were to invest a dollar in the market in '83, it would be worth $11 today, while your dollar in Social Security is worth $3. Think about what that means if you put a fair amount of money aside over time. It means your own money would grow better than that which the government can make it grow. And that's important.

It's an important part of being a part of a vibrant—a retirement system. You're going to get a check from the government. The question is how big. If you're allowed to take some of your own money and watch it grow faster than the rate at which government can grow it, it means you've got a bigger nest egg.

Secondly, I like the idea of people owning something. We want more people owning their assets in America. There's kind of a concept around that says maybe only a certain kind of people should own assets, an investor class, maybe only the rich. I firmly reject that idea. That's not how I view America. I want more people owning things, owning their own home, owning their own business, owning their own retirement account, owning assets that they can pass one from one generation to the next. The more people that are able to do that, the better off America is.

Thirdly, the system today is patently unfair for families if a spouse is to die earlier than expected. Think about this kind of system we have today. You work all your life, your husband or wife works all their life, and one of you dies before 62 years old, or after 62—if they die before 62, you get no survivor benefits, you get a little stipend to help bury your spouse, period. All the money goes in, waits until you reach retirement age. When you reach retirement age, if you have worked, as well, you get either your spouse's benefits or your benefits, which are ever higher, but not both.

So if one of the two of you have worked all your life, or worked your life and put money in, you don't get anything as result of your labor. I think it will make sense to allow people to set aside some of their own money in a personal account so they have their own assets, and if they happen to die early, they can pass it on to their wife or husband. In other words, your assets just don't disappear like the current system encourages.

But you've got something you call your own, finally. I like an idea—remember, this is a pay-as-you-go system. People are going to be counting on future Congresses to make decisions what to do with your money. I like the idea of you being able to have an asset base that the Congress can't take away. The Congress doesn't get to spend on your behalf, because it's your asset. You own it. It is your nest egg.

Personal—personal savings accounts make a lot of sense to me. They also make a lot of sense to a generation of Americans that are used to investing. I was telling the folks up here that when I was in the 20s, I don't remember spending a lot of time thinking about my 401(k). It's because they didn't exist. Think about what's happened in our society. A lot of people are becoming accustomed to watching their money grow. There's a new and—a group of investors from all walks of life that are comfortable with watching their assets grow and expect to be able to manage their own assets. The culture has changed when it comes to investing.

Now, people often ask me, you know, can I—are there going to be wise ways to set up these savings accounts? Of course there will be. I'm not going to say, you can—we want you to have a retirement fund; you can take your money and put it in the lottery. In other words, there's a conservative mix of bonds and stocks that will be available. If you're risk adverse, you can buy Treasury bonds, as far as I'm concerned.

You know, people say, well, you know, what happens if I'm getting close to retirement and there's a market swing? Well, when you get close to retirement, there are ways to diversify out of a mix of bonds and stocks and get into—get into strictly bonds—government-backed bonds. People can manage your money in smart ways. And the role of—it seems like to me a proper role for the government is to say, here are the guidelines in which you can—should be allowed to invest, but there's a lot of flexibility so you can choose how best to manage your own assets.

So this makes sense, and Congress needs to hear the voices of people who believe it is right and fair to give them the option to watch their own money grow. And we've got some people up here today that have got a pretty good idea about what they want to do with their own money.

Oh, by the way, just as an aside, I think it'll interest you to know that this isn't a new idea I'm discussing. As a matter of fact, Congress has given themselves the same opportunity that I think ought to be available for younger workers. There's what they call a thrift savings plan in Washington, D.C. It's available for federal workers. It says if you're unhappy with the government's rate of return, you ought to be able to set aside some of your own money—manage your own money in a retirement account. Seems like to me that if a member of the United States Congress thinks it's okay to manage his or her money, that same privilege and opportunity ought to be extended to workers all across America. What's good for the Congress ought to be good for the working people in the United States.

DOCUMENT 23.9b

Cartoon, "Fixing This Should Be Easy." © Bob Krohmer, Cartoon Stock.